The Construction of an Urban Past

The Construction of an Urban Past

Narrative and System in Urban History

Harry Jansen

**Translated by
Feike de Jong**

BERG

Oxford • New York

First published in 2001 by
Berg
Editorial offices:
150 Cowley Road, Oxford OX4 1JJ, UK
838 Broadway, Third Floor, New York, NY 10003-4812, USA

Berg is the imprint of Oxford International Publishers Ltd.

Library of Congress Cataloging-in-Publication Data

A catalogue record for this book is available from the Library of Congress.

British Library Cataloguing-in-Publication Data

A catalogue record for this book is available from the British Library.

ISBN 1 85973 437 5 (Cloth)

Typeset by JS Typesetting, Wellingborough, Northants.
Printed in the United Kingdom by Biddles Ltd, Guildford and King's Lynn.

Contents

Contents

Acknowledgements

First, I must acknowledge a debt to NWO, the Dutch Organisation of Scientific Research and the Research Institute of the Faculty of Arts of the University of Nijmegen for funding this book. Second, I am pleased to express my thanks to Prof. Jan de Vries of Berkeley University of California for his help in getting the book published. Third, I owe a particular debt to David Phelps, for scrutinizing the book and to the two translators Robert Bland (second chapter) and Feike de Jong. Especial thanks go to Seke Drost for correcting the bibliography, to Noortje and Mark van 't Nedereind for their help with the indexes and to Maartje Wolff and Angelique Janssens for their mental and practical support. Last but not least I want to express my appreciation to Berg publishers for their patience and help.

Nijmegen, July, 2001
Harry Jansen

Acknowledgment

Part I
Systems Theory and
Urban Historiography

'One wonders sometimes if science will grind to a stop in an assemblage of walled-in-hermits, each mumbling to himself words in a private language that only he can understand.' K. L. Boulding, 'General Systems Theory – The Skeleton of Science', in: Management Science 2 (1956) 198.

Introduction

Postmodernism: Rhyme and Reason

Towards the end of the seventies of the twentieth century, the philosophy of history had taken a deep plunge into the well of postmodernism. In order for this to happen, three little pushes were necessary. The first was scepticism with regard to epic narratives, especially those of Marxism; the second consisted of a renewed attention to cultural history; and the third concerns the linguistic or even rhetorical turn in the theory of history. In themselves, these developments were not negative. What is lamentable, however, is the one-sided manner in which many philosophers of history currently strive to support their arguments. It is *bon ton* amongst them to equate the discipline of history with that of cultural history and only to consider it in the light of narrativism.[1] Contemporary thought about history is scarcely occupied with political and social-economic history, and expositions outside narrativism, aside from the odd exception, are deemed irrelevant for discussions on the philosophy of history.

The cause of the dominance of cultural history and the philosophy of language should be sought in the popularity of postmodern philosophers such as Jacques Derrida and Michel Foucault, who developed concepts appropriated by philosophers of history such as Hayden White and Frank Ankersmit.[2] The affinity between Derrida and Foucault on the one hand and White and Ankersmit on the other can, despite their diversity, be reduced to three important claims.

The first of these has to do with an aversion to the tradition of the Enlightenment. It is noteworthy not only that modes of thought modelled on the natural sciences are rejected, but also that every form of modernistic rationality is abandoned. This implies a philosophical revolution,[3] which is primarily marked by anti-essentialism and anti-reductionism. In Foucault both these characteristics are expressed in his exclusory histories of crime and madness. In these studies Foucault shows how modernist rationality defines criminals and madmen, and then marginalizes them.[4] Derrida seeks anti-reductionism and anti-essentialism in the denial that a text can be reduced to the meaning given it by the author or the context behind it discovered by the researcher.[5] The meaning of texts is undetermined; and, what is more, every text generates its own decon-struction. White also refuses to admit that texts can be reduced to the reality behind them. Historical reality in particular takes shape, according to White, only when it has been absorbed in a story.[6] For the understanding of texts, their political thrust, argumentational structure, plot, style, and vocabulary are more important than their topic and how that topic relates to reality.[7] This, however, does not convince White – as it does Derrida – that the meaning of a text is undetermined. Ankersmit lends the same importance to anti-reductionism as Derrida, and therefore also holds to the non-referential nature of narratives. He expresses this in his Ph.D. thesis, in which he claims that the historical narrative concerning the Renaissance, for example, by author A pertains to a completely different phenomenon than the Renaissance of authors B or C.[8] Ankersmit in the 1990s goes even further. Together with the incommensurability of historical narratives, even if they have a similar topic (for example the Renaissance or the Industrial Revolution), the whole Western epistemo-logical tradition can be discarded. This tradition runs from the Stoa, with its *logoi spermatikoi,* by way of the epistemological theory of Descartes, to the categories of Kant. Between the knowing subject and the object to be known, this tradition has assumed a third factor – called the *tertium comparationis* by Ankersmit – that enables knowledge of reality and hence communication about it. Our contemporary epistemologies and concep-tions of truth are based on such a *tertium.* These epistemologies can, with Ankersmit's blessing, follow the *tertium* to the rubbish heap.[9]

From the above the second claim of postmodernism can be deduced: the meaning of language and discourse, for all varieties of cultural expression, should weigh far more heavily than any element of reality whatsoever. With his 'Il n'y pas dehors texte' [There is nothing outside the text], Derrida is quite radical in this claim. In the eyes of Derrida, not only can the truthfulness of a text be examined by comparing it to an extra-textual reality, but that reality *itself* is textualized. Foucault goes even further. He not only separates the text from reality: he reifies it. By using a certain form of definition, anonymous 'powers' try to manipulate reality.[10] Power is therefore the key term in Foucault's postmodern philosophy. By defining madness and delinquency in a certain manner, madmen and delinquents are created. Knowledge hence becomes an instrument of power. White also considers text to be non-referential, but unlike Derrida, in White's case the number of possible meanings is not undetermined. White has examined nineteenth-century histories with regard to their plots, their style and their use of language. He subsequently came to the conclusion that historians such as Michelet, de Tocqueville,

Ranke, and Burckhardt should be interpreted by attending to their romantic, tragic, comic or satirical emplotments and their uses of metaphor, metonymy, synecdoche and/or irony. Such an interpretation, in White's opinion, teaches us more concerning history than we could learn from comparing their representations of reality to reality itself.[11] Ankersmit considers historical writing metaphorical. Metaphors do not reflect reality, nor do they correspond to it: they are, at best, a representation of it.[12] Historical concepts such as the Middle Ages or the Industrial Revolution are such metaphors. They therefore cannot be examined with regard to their veracity. Ankersmit calls these 'narrative substances' or 'language things'. Narrative substances, like metaphors, are only real within the historical narrative. Beyond the narrative they do not exist and, in this sense, they therefore cannot be true or false.[13]

Finally, postmodernism minimizes or denies the value of science. Science concerns itself with discovering truths concerning reality. This implies that a distinction is made between fact and fiction, and that two-way traffic is possible between truth and reality. To paraphrase Hegel: a *wahre Wirklichkeit* and a *wirkliche Wahrheit* are possible. Derrida does not accept the distinction between fact and fiction, and only considers how truth can influence reality, not how truth can be obtained through confrontation with reality. Continuing deconstruction must ultimately undermine even textual 'truths'. Foucault considers reality and truth to be mere constructions of knowledge and therefore of power. Furthermore, science does not have a methodological basis from which truth can be found. Hence Foucault does not make any real distinction between a scientific and a political design of reality. Hayden White is the least radical a-scientist. Although he thinks that texts should mainly be examined on their literary and aesthetic qualities with regard to their plots and use of language, he also recognizes styles of argumentation. He distinguishes formalistic, mechanistic, organic, and contextual methods of reasoning.[14] This implies mitigation but not denial of, epistemological precepts. Albeit somewhat thinly, in this manner White accepts the existence of an argumentative infrastructure in addition to a linguistic superstructure.[15] In his studies in the 1990s, Ankersmit has revealed himself to be a fervent proponent of rediscovering reality – not, however, as we saw above, through man's epistemological capacities, but exclusively through historical aesthetic experience. Representation of that reality is positioned in a 'picture view of knowledge'. By rejecting the *tertium*, Ankersmit also rejects historical-scientific methodology.[16]

With regard to all three post-modern dogmas – textualism, anti-reductionism and anti-scientism – postmodernism contradicts itself. As to anti-essentialism and anti-reductionism, one can raise the question of whether a statement such as Derrida's – that nothing exists beyond the text – is not in itself strongly reductionistic. Something similar can be said of Foucault's theoretics of power or Ankersmit's rejection of the *tertium*. Is it not true that a much stronger form of pluralistic thought is present when one gives reality its due and if, in addition to aesthetics, another epistemology is available for gaining access to reality? Textualist reductionism becomes even more curious if one realizes that the conceivers of the proposition that texts are not referential consist mainly of those philosophers who are constantly involved with texts. The great importance given by Foucault to power and language, which is based on the concept of a world that can be shaped by man – an idea for which positivists have been sharply attacked – excludes any other influence of reality on thought. Foucault, for example, views the modern manner in which criminals are punished – no longer stocks but jail – as being determined by a discourse regarding crime and criminals in which the leading role is played by the power of language and its definitive function. One could, however, also view the modernization of punishment as being derived from the compassion for the private space of criminals, which precedes language. Foucault, as a vehement opponent of modern exclusionism, thus lapses into a new form of exclusion, namely the exclusion of influences on reality other than language.

The (natural) philosopher Mary Hesse has made a noteworthy remark on textualism. She claims that just as the use of theories in the natural sciences does not have to be antagonistic to the empirical search for truth, the use of metaphors does not have to be separated from the criteria for truth. Metaphors can be more or less valid in relation to other metaphors, in which case empirically tested propositions on which metaphors are based can be used as measuring rods.[17]

Finally, the smudging of the line between fact and fiction due to postmodern anti-scientism is especially antagonistic to the historian who wishes to distinguish his or her work from that of a historical novelist.[18] This distinction rests not so much in the fact that the work of the historian refers to a historic reality and that of the novelist doesn't, but in the idea that the narrative elements in a historical work are alternated with argumentations that strive to support the truthfulness of the narrative elements. A historical novel does not need these argumentations.[19] Chris Lorenz and Bart Verschaffel have justly pointed out that postmodernism finds little support among historians because the work of the latter has an argumentative context. In addition to the context of persuasion, to which the postmodernists lend such importance, historians as scientists attach much importance to the context of discovery and the context of justification. This implies that theory and methodology are of eminent importance for the historical discipline.[20]

Seeking a logical infrastructure

In itself, there is nothing wrong with subjecting historical texts to analysis from the perspective of the philosophy of language.[21] After all, historians use language, and their use of language in historical writing might have specific characteristics. It is, however, curious that in the critical philosophy of history, textual exposition has become so predominant that extensive discussions of 'normal' logic, which were common among philosophers of history and historians in the past, suddenly seem irrelevant. The question of whether the historical sciences concerned the discovery of general causes or specific intentional explanations seems to have gone up in smoke. So-called narrative logic made the previous debate over which kind of logic should prevail apparently superfluous. Derrida's statement that nothing exists beyond the text became a mandate for occupying oneself solely with the linguistic superstructure of historical writing. With the notion that narratives are in themselves explanatory, a long tradition of infrastructural logic was discarded. As a result, the inventive and lively debate that had been ongoing since the end of the nineteenth century on the question of whether history is a science like all the others or a (special) discipline of the humanities fell silent at the start of the 1980s.

The reader should not conclude from this that I wish to dredge up old discussions. It is by no means the intention of this book to revive the old opposition between positivism and hermeneutics. I do, however, wish to show that in addition to attention to the linguistic superstructure, we must retain an interest in the logical infrastructure of the historical sciences. Such a non-linguistic but (culture-oriented) field logic becomes superfluous if one ignores the relation between thought and reality.[22] Postmodern philosophers negate reality.[23] In doing so, science may get thrown overboard, leaving nothing but the aesthetic experience.[24] It is lamentable that in the last two decades the philosophy of history has given so much attention to problems concerning narrativism, but has neglected infrastructural logic. This forces the adherent of culture-oriented field logic to turn to concepts and historiographic examples from the 1960s and 1970s.

A field- and problem-related logic

Historiographic examples are of special importance. After all, I am not concerned with resurrecting the opposition between positivism and hermeneutics, but with showing that positivism and hermeneutics have had a great influence on the products of historiography and that this influence has advanced the scientific nature of history rather than damaged it.

That is also the main impetus for my desire to examine what lies beyond style and language usage in history. I want to find not a textual logic, but a historical or cultural-scientific logic, like that which can be found in historical writing itself. What I have in mind is a *field-related logic*, as it is called by David Hackett Fischer.[25] To this end, the manner in which historians define, explain, conceive time and classify periods are analysed with the objective of optimizing the historical synthesis.[26]

Synthesis is a recurrent problem in historical writing. Kocka states the following concerning this: 'An der Fülle der Kenntnisse mangelt es nicht, an ihrer Zusammenfassung schon eher'. [The difficulty lies not so much in the completeness of what is known, but in its integration].[27] Zunz, Huizinga and others have also occupied themselves with the problem of the integration of historical knowledge. It should be noted here that the purpose of Ankersmit's quest for the implications of metaphors for historical writing is an emphasis on the synthesizing characteristics of historical writing.[28] It is unfortunate that in pursuing this quest he chooses the philosophy of language as an instrument and does not opt for a 'historical' logic. I wish here to advocate the latter. In doing this I am concerned not only with a 'historical' logic, but also with a logic that concentrates on the problem of synthesis. In other words, this study is centred not only on a field-related logic but also on a problem-related logic.[29]

Historical research and historical writing

Postmodern philosophers of history make a sharp distinction between historical research and historical writing.[30] Historical *research* concerns – in this I follow Ankersmit – tracking down historical facts[31] and making individual statements about these facts in a historical narrative. Such statements can be calibrated with regard to their truthfulness. Historical *writing* is more than the sum of the individual statements. The historical narrative as a whole cannot be subjected to truth criteria. Only norms from narrativism and in particular aesthetic-literary norms apply to it.

Because of the rhetorical nature of these norms, the postmoderns exchange the context of justification for the context of persuasion.

Although I consider historical research an important element of historical practice, this study is primarily concerned with historical writing. Not that I think that historical research and historical writing are completely distinct compartments of historical practice, but precisely because I wish to remove the border posts that contemporary philosophers of history all too eagerly erect between the two. Historical writing cannot be separated from historical research for it has to show that it contains not only a literary-aesthetic element, but also an evident scientific and craft element. If one sought to distinguish between historical research and historical writing, then, in my opinion, that distinction would have to lie in the fact that historical research is mainly analytical and historical writing mainly synthetic.[33] But analysis and synthesis both have craft aspects that must simultaneously be exercised in historical practice and regularly overflow and impinge on each other's territories.

The treatment of historical writing implies that I shall mainly occupy myself with historical texts, not because there is nothing beyond the text, but precisely to show that there is an argumentative infrastructure behind the linguistic superstructure of a text. This infrastructure calls for just as much or perhaps even more historical-theoretical analysis than the style or the linguistic usage of the writer. This infrastructure does not replace the narrative, but carries and supports it. Aesthetics and persuasive power are not only dependent on figures of speech and a pretty turn of phrase, but also on the elegance of the argument.[34] Just as a beautiful building in part derives its beauty from physical laws and mathematical logic, a beautiful historical narrative should also rest upon sensible arguments and a historical logic.[35]

The reconciliation of monists and dualists in systems thought

There is a long tradition involving the quest for a historical logic: a quest that thankfully has not yet completely disappeared.[36] The philosophers of history in that tradition can basically be divided into two groups: monists and dualists. Monists claim that there is, in the end, only one scientific model, that this model is more or less positivistic, and that it holds for all sciences. Dualists advocate a separate scientific model for cultural studies. Both narrativists and hermeneuticians can be found among the dualists. Narrativists and hermeneuticians seek a logic specific to historical studies. Positivists wish to show that the logic of the historical sciences is not different from that of other empirical sciences.

The opposition between the monists and the dualists stems from the nineteenth-century debate on the subject of science in general and history in particular. Historians and philosophers such as Droysen, Dilthey, Rickert and Windelband assumed that notions of regularity and causality that were inappropriate for the cultural sciences dominated the physical sciences. Although these philosophers of history produced extremely interesting expositions on the nature of the historical sciences, they devoted too little attention to developments in the physical sciences themselves. If they had peered more beyond the humanities, they would have seen that since Mach the notion of regularity in the physical sciences had also been called into question.[37]

In the twentieth century the significance of notions of regularity and exclusive causal relations to the scientific ideal of the physical sciences has continually been decreasing. These relations have gradually been replaced by the much more restricted concept of the *system*, in which, in addition to causal relations, non-causal relations also play a role, and in which there is much more room for matters such as chance, contingency and probability. Further on in this book I shall try to show that the contemporary predilection for chaos theories is the latest offshoot of systems thought. Intentional relations, which are of crucial importance to the historian, can also be given a place within systems theory (see Chapter 3).

The universality of systems theoretical logic is therefore the main reason why I have chosen it and not a form of textual logic. Systems thought is certainly not popular among philosophers of history and cultural scientists. If anything, systems thought seems to carry with it an aura of modernism. Yet I think that systems thought is less reductionistic and therefore less modernistic than it appears at first sight.[38] Systems theory is not aprioristic, and offers a great deal of freedom for the examination of the infrastructural logic of a text.

It is notable in the discussion between monists and dualists that philosophers of history of modernist (positivist), anti-modernist (hermeneutic or historist) and postmodernist (narrativist) bents have never done anything but to choose someone among the three viewpoints mentioned. The reason for this should be sought in the fact that they work from a context of justification (positivists and hermeneuticians) or a context of persuasion (postmodernists), and neglect the context of discovery.

Van den Braembussche has noted that all three categories of philosophers of history can be brought under one common denominator. They all seek an *a priori*, a-historical and static logic. They seek a logical foundation for the historical sciences that can reach from Thucydides to

Braudel and from Vancouver to Vladivostok. Searching for such a logic covering the historical sciences as a whole has led to the task of justification gaining a central position in the minds of most critical philosophers of history. Defence, claims, the emphasis on differences: these are all probably matters that (very likely with due cause) belong to the philosophy of history. However, if one seeks a logical infrastructure for historical writing, then one must be more pragmatic, and supplement the context of justification with the context of discovery. What Toulmin, Kuhn[39] and more recently McAllister[40] have done for the physical sciences will also have to be done for the historical sciences.[41]

Theory of history instead of philosophy of history

Rarely have philosophers of history asked themselves the question of how the influence of positivism and hermeneutics can be made evident in historiography itself. Perhaps taking a position is intrinsic to being a philosopher of history, but examination of the manner in which historians are engaged in science and how this is expressed in their works remains interesting nevertheless. I would like to call this the occupation of theoreticians of history and to encapsulate this idea in the term 'paradigm study', without going into all the minutiae involved in such a term. Paradigm study involves tracking down the complex of presuppositions, methods, metaphors and/or examples upon which a science is based.[42]

For an examination of the workings of historiography, I advocate a resurrection of Romein's theory of history. The Dutch historian Jan Romein advocated a theory of history as an intermediary between history as a science and the philosophy of history.[43] This theory of history resembles what Van den Braembussche calls a pragmatic philosophy of history.[44] This pertains to a meta-theoretical examination of history – more on this later – in order to find instruments for its improvement. To Romein, this improvement mainly signified historical synthesis. Integral historical writing was the chief goal of Romein's theory of history. In the Netherlands, an extensive discussion took place regarding the value of Romein's ideas. Many opposed Romein's theory of history;[45] only Ankersmit and Jansen defended it.[46] The great service of Romein's theory of history lies in its advancement of the idea that the conception of the problem of synthesis should not be solved by philosophical claims, but through examination of historiography.

Metatheoretical examination and the fallacy of the declarative question

As a no-man's-land between the philosophy of history on the one hand and the empirical historical sciences on the other, the theory of history can examine the results of empirical historical science as to their problems and arrive at solutions. The apriorism that is so essential to the philosophy of science can be replaced by an attitude of inquiry. Such an attitude of inquiry is directed towards demythologization, removal of ideological bias, and the solution of problems, such as that of synthesis. Historical inquiry demands attitudes such as openness with reference to the information, ideas and methods of others (including non-historians). Precepts and prohibitions are not easily accepted under these circumstances. In the case of an assertion that something is A, the researcher will not exclude the possibility of not-A; and he will exchange A, or not-A, for B, if the examination of empirical data so demands. While doing this he will make sure to leave space for the possibility of differentiation within A and B in the form of A1, A2, B1, B2 etc. . . . . Justification leads to the denial that A can be not-A. After all, it is impossible for a philosopher of history to claim that the logic of the historical sciences is both deductive-nomological and its contradiction. The *a priori* nature of a certain discipline's identity can almost never be questioned through the context of justification.[47]

From the perspective of a pragmatically-conceived theory of history, debating every *a priori* claim is a necessity. For research the axiom that A might be not-A is a *conditio sine qua non*. Executing an inquiry solely on the basis of the context of justification has led many a researcher into the trap referred to by D. H. Fischer as *the fallacy of the declarative question*. This error occurs, according to Fischer, when the question of whether A is the case is not formulated as a heuristic hypothesis. When such a heuristic hypothesis is missing, we have merely a proposal to consider A as a fact. Such a proposal is not subsequently accompanied by the question of whether not-A might not also be the case. This implies a study of events not based on the exchange of arguments, but conducted by the juxtaposition of proposals concerning that state of affairs. Anker-smit advocates the advance of such a form of historical study, and therefore advises historians – and here the philosopher of history raises his head – as follows: 'Only metaphors falsify metaphors.' As a result, he seems to reduce the goals of historical study to the explicitation of (philosophical) *a priori* statements. Through a dialogue between Hamlet and Polonius in Shakespeare's play, Fischer illustrates what kind of results and scientific discussions the fallacy of the declarative question can lead to.

> Hamlet: Do you see yonder cloud that's almost in the shape of a camel?
> Polonius: By the mass, and 'tis like a camel indeed.
> Hamlet: Mehinks it is like a weasel.
> Polonius: It is backed like a weasel.
> Hamlet: Or like a whale?
> Polonius: Very like a whale.

Are the philosophers of history not in danger of referring exclusively to nomological camels, hermeneutic weasels or narrative whales when they venture into historiographical research founded on a context of justification concerning the whole of historical science? In the most favourable case the beasts are unmasked as vapour, as with Lorenz;[48] but even he cannot resist blowing his own little cloud of comparative explanation into space. This cloud which we might, in opposition to hermeneutics, narrativism, and positivism, call comparativism, is 'examined' by Lorenz on the basis of a non-open question. His analysis of the historical writings of Paul Bois and Barrington Moore boils down to a declaration that these authors are good examples of the comparative method he propagates.[49]

This does not mean that I hold anything against the work of philosophers of history, so long as they leave space for a *theory* of history with a real attitude of inquiry. My tolerance towards the philosophy of history even extends to the point that I consider the *fallacy of the declarative question* inapplicable to the philosophy of history. It is good that there is a quality-control service with regard to scientific products and values. The justification of certain theoretical premises of science and scientific method is an important issue that should not be neglected. The opposition broached here between historical theory and the philosophy of history concerns itself with the sharp delimitation of each's respective domains. The study of 'how the historical discipline should be', with which the philosophy of history concerns itself, should not be confused with the objects of the theory of history, for example: the examination of the question of how historical 'science' works in practice, which goals it has, and how these goals can be achieved in the most efficient manner. An approach towards the empirical practice of history based purely on the philosophy of history carries with it the danger of confusion.

Problem-solving

While philosophers of history generally work from a context of justification, theoretical historians generally work from a context of discovery.[50] This means that they do not view the historiography as a source of reflection but as 'empirical' evidence. If, in the case of the historian, the past itself (or preferably the archives) yields the historical data, the theoretician of history receives his data from historiography. The mentality with which the theoretical historian approaches his empirical data is the same as the historian's mentality. The theoretical historian is not positioned behind the historian in helping him to subdue his historiographical problems, but next to him. Theory of history does, however, have a more abstract approach towards historiography. It uses meta-theories to place certain historiographical phenomena in the limelight and to elucidate them. In this manner, it draws closer to the philosophy of history. These meta-theories stand to the writing of history as 'normal' theories stand to the empirical practice of history.

In the theory of history, one is concerned with the examination of historical literature rather than archival materials. The theory of history hence differentiates itself from the ways in which the philosopher of history, as well as the 'ordinary' historian, regards historiography. The philosopher of history extracts from historiography the examples with which certain problems of the philosophy of history can be illuminated. He contemplates historical writing from the outside. The 'ordinary' historian seeks out matters in historiography that can be of service to him in his own study, such as further definition of the object of his studies, clarification of their theses, expansion of the data and sources available, etc. . . . Historiography is used as a self-service counter. What is needed for one's own study is what is taken from the shelves.

The domain of competence of the theoretician of history lies between that of the philosophy of history and empirical historical scholarship in his approach to as well as in his 'use' of historiography. The theoretical historian does not view historiography as an illustration of a problem in the philosophy of history, nor does he view it as a place for finding supplementary historical evidence. The theoretical historian views historiography as empirical material as well as a reservoir of assignments.

In their approach to historiographical questions, philosophers of history function as ambassadors and theoretical historians as problem-solvers. Philosophers of history generally do not concern themselves with solving historiographical problems, or at least not those problems that emerge from historiography itself. In the most favourable case, they make suggestions concerning the methods through which a solution may be found. Such methodological tips are made on the basis of that particular movement or trend in the philosophy of history one adheres to. In this sense, philosophers of history can favour positivistic, hermeneutic or narrative methodologies. The theoretical historian is concerned with the solution itself. In order to attain his solution he may use the methodologies developed in philosophy of history without having to identify himself with the movement that accompanies them. Hence the theory of history is particularly pragmatic.

Here the question arises of the extent to which there is a difference between the theory of history constituted here and the pragmatic philosophy of history that has evolved since the 'science of science' movement in the thirties, developing more specifically after the publication of Thomas Kuhn's *The Structure of Scientific Revolutions*. The pragmatic philosophy of history attempts the empirical reconstruction of historical knowledge, just as the theory of history does. Both consider the paradigm category a practical instrument for a reconstruction of this type. Even in their approach to the context of justification both disciplines show similarities. They advocate a pluralistic historical science in which the border posts between history and the social studies have been uprooted. Yet it is exactly in the context of justification that their differences lie. The pragmatic philosophy of history does not give up the idea of the optimization of science.[51] A task of the philosophy of history, even if it calls itself pragmatic, is the promotion of this growth. Though the theory of history does strive toward an optimal solution of problems that historiography offers it, it does not ask itself whether the historical sciences as a whole 'grow' or 'advance' or not. The theoretician even rejects the analysis of historiography in terms of growth. First of all historical interests continually shift – according to D. H. Fischer pyramids are 'out' and obelisks are 'in' – which makes it difficult to measure progress. Furthermore, the tendency is present in the physical sciences to view the convergence of rival paradigms in one viewpoint as a sign of progress. Interpretational divergence renders it difficult to observe such a criterion of progress in historical writing. Finally, the theoretical historian does not consider it impossible that the ability of contemporary historiography to solve the problem of integration is diminished in comparison with that of the historiography of previous centuries.

This does not mean, however, that there are no forms of justification present in theoretical history. The theory of history does not intend to throw every form of logic overboard. On the contrary: it seeks a historical pattern of inference, as I noted above. This logic, however, is closely linked to historiography and the problems that arise from it. In his capacity as a theoretical historian, for example, Van den Braembussche used this method to develop an empirical typology of comparative historical writing, while also taking the first steps towards a comparative logic by taking inventory of the pros and cons involved in the diverse types of comparisons and by elucidating the complementary character of these types.[52] Although it is difficult to speak of progress or growth in the historical sciences, partial improvements in the form of more accurate, more comprehensive, better balanced and better justified interpretations can be observed.[53]

In this study the main issue is to show the complementarity of positivistic (behaviouristic) and interpretative (hermeneutical) explanations. In order to do so, both explanatory forms are placed in a systems-theoretical framework.

A systems-theoretical logic

In both the physical sciences and the humanities, systems theories or at least systems-theoretical notions are used. Systems theory is therefore a fairly neutral logical *tertium* that can serve as research theory for the paradigm problem mentioned above. Systems theory also has the great advantage that it commands a great deal of respect scientifically. Theories in various fields can be fitted into a systems-theoretical mould. Beyond that, systems theory is very flexible. Various kinds of problems, both analytical and synthetic by nature, can be addressed. This is highly important for the study to come. Historical writing has, after all, both a synthetic and an analytic aspect. Because I focus on urban historical writing in this study, I shall appeal mainly to the synthesizing capacities of systems theory.

Systems, their meaning, heuristic function and epistemological status

Studies concerning the possibilities of integration in historiography hinge upon the question of how detailed studies can be fitted into larger contexts in a methodologically-justifiable manner. As a result, such a study should target the discovery of part–whole relations. Because systems theory is explicitly occupied with such relations, here historiography will be subjected to systems-theoretical analysis.

What systems are and how they are applied in this study will be discussed extensively in Chapters 3 and 4. For the benefit of the reader, I will give here in advance a somewhat impressionistic account of a system, as given by the cybernetician Jordan. 'Whenever one person can point to or explain a set of elements and the nature of the connectivity between these elements to another person, then the other person will perceive/ conceive of the set as an entity, a thing. The word system will then spontaneously emerge as the adequate expression, as the proper name for this thing. A system is therefore an interaction between the objective world and how it is looked at or thought about it; it denotes a mode of perceptuo/cognitive organisation.'[54] A system is therefore, according to Jordan, a rational model for the organization of perceived reality that shows a high degree of isomorphy with that which is perceived.

Important problems in the philosophy of history regarding a realistic or an idealistic approach to reality can be coupled to this concept. Realists assume that reality is structured, which makes systematic isomorphy possible. Idealists view reality as ineffable or chaotic, which entails that systems are solely the product of the structuring activities of the researcher. I make no principled claims in this debate in the philosophy of history. After all, I am not examining the past itself, but historiography.[55]

Because this study deals with the results of scientific activity, it is evident that systems have an onto/epistemological status within historiography. After all, historiographical reality is structured, even if the name 'system' is not always given to that reality. That is why Jordan's description of systems is also applicable to the conception of system that I use.

Systems theory in urban historiography

Examinations of the paradigms and argumentational conventions in all of historiography would be a tremendous undertaking. I must therefore restrict myself to a particular domain of historiography: urban historiography and the conventions used by *urban* historians to order the past are the reality with which this study is concerned. This immediately has the advantage that the instrument used to order these conventions – systems theory as meta-theory – closely resembles the conventions used by most urban historians themselves. I call a coherent description of a city a 'system'. These systems do not bear a direct relation to real cities, such as New York or London, but to the descriptions urban historians give of them.

Furthermore, urban historians are not always occupied with the examination of actual towns. In many cases, urban historical writing concerns itself with aggregations of urban phenomena such as urban networks and the relation between towns and the countryside, or geographical or historical aggregations such as the *European* or the *medieval* city. Such aggregated phenomena are also counted as urban historiography and examined as to their systems-theoretical merit. Because urban historians themselves also use many theoretical – sometimes even systems-theoretical – notions and models for the analysis of such urban aggregations, systems theory as I apply it in this study must be dubbed meta-theoretical. With this in mind, I differentiate between three levels of examination:

a. Examination of urban phenomena in reality itself, in which case it is concerned with concrete towns (i.e. New York, London) or their geographical and historical aggregations, town–countryside relationships, or urban networks. (These last are sometimes also called *systems of cities.*)
b. The forming of theories within urban historiography itself, in which urban phenomena are assailed with theoretical models that are sometimes systems-theoretical and sometimes not.
c. The systems-theoretical analysis of urban historiography.

The writer of history organizes the past itself with his or her systems: I organize urban historiography with my systems. Hence my analysis lies at level *c.* and concerns itself with level *b.* The systems I construct may be related to the systems used for empirical study, but they are not identical to them. Therefore the reader must take care not to identify the systems applied by many urban historians to empirical inquiry with the system models I use for the analysis of urban historiography. Meta-theories in the following study are intended to show how theories and models used by urban historians have an integrating effect.

The differentiation between the theoretical and the meta-theoretical use of systems is also important for another reason. Not all 'normal' urban historians rely on systems-theoretical models. To involve this 'non-systematic' urban history too in this meta-theoretical study, a very specific *part* of systems theory is exploited: the theory of relatively-closed systems. I will not elaborate on this, as these systems will be treated extensively later on.

A relationship does exist between the formulation of theories in urban history and the systems-theoretical analysis of historiography I propound. Because I take inventory of the implicit or explicit use of systems by urban historians and place them in a certain order, and especially because I show their effect, I hope to enable urban historians to organize urban history in a manner that is systems-theoretically stronger, hereby making it easier to integrate data regarding cities.

Method of study

In the above I continually speak of urban historiography in general. This suggests that the results of this study are valid for the whole of urban historiography. Indeed I do consider these results applicable to urban historiographical study in general. On what do I base this presumption? Not on a quantitative study of the material examined. Such an examination would be impossible – given the complex process involved in discovering systems-theoretical depth structures. Here another approach has been taken, which nevertheless guarantees satisfactory representativity. The research method applied works as follows. Following the example of Checkland and the Social Science Study Council, three sets are formed:

a. Long-term studies that depict the history of several towns or of one town over a long term span (generally more than two centuries). These studies can be considered macro-historical.
b. Comparative studies of towns or urban phenomena.
c. Studies of specific cities in isolation. These studies can be considered micro-historical.[56]

These three sets contain studies whose provenance lies mainly in American, English, and German urban historiography. Hence there is a reasonably large areal spread of authors. The borders of the different categories, especially between the comparative studies of towns and long-term studies, may not be sharp; but any overlap between the sets is restricted.

The selection criteria for these three sets show no relation at all to the systems-theoretical classification as representative for all Anglo-Saxon and Western European urban historiography is justifiable.

Finally I would like to make a remark regarding the urban historians whose works have been examined here. The term 'urban historian' should be understood in a broad sense. This study deals with authors who have occupied themselves with examinations of the past of towns, without asking themselves whether these authors have enjoyed a specifically historical training to this end. Sociologists, economists and other researchers from social sciences are also called urban historians if their work encompasses the history of towns.

Does this not inherently lead to a simple paradigmatic dichotomy, with the historians in one camp and social scientists in the other? The outcome of this study is completely different. 'Urban historians' from both disciplines are encountered in the two approaches pointed out in this study: relatively-closed and half-open systems theories. The sociologists

Mumford and Bahrdt, for example, are active in the paradigm of the relatively-closed system; the sociologists Rozman and Sjoberg in the other. Some urban historians hold a disciplinary point of view that is scientifically amphibious. This is especially true for Weber and Lampard. In addition to being a historian, Lampard is an economist, and Weber is both a historian and a sociologist. They also happen to hold to different systems-theoretical approaches.

Overview of the book

I start my analysis with a description of urban historiography in the last 150 years (Chapter 2). The central question here is: how have urban historians conceptualized cities? Despite the many variations in the answer to this question, I have found it possible to differentiate between two major types of conceptions: a dichotomous type and a complementary type. Those using the dichotomous conception of a town try to delimit the phenomenon town in opposition to other phenomena, such as the countryside. This in contrast to those using a complementary conception of a town, considering it as part of a larger whole. Several theoretically-minded urban historians are displeased by this ambivalence, which they generally try to resolve by dismissing the dichotomous conception. In my approach to the problem, no type of conception is excluded. I only try to understand the consequences of the two conceptions for the integrated writing of the history of towns and urban phenomena.

In Part 2 the first principles of systems theory are explained. This part is mainly concerned with the explication of relatively-closed (Chapter 3) and half-open systems (Chapter 4). In this part I also discuss the relativity of Von Wright's intentional, or perhaps even teleological explanation, by showing the causal elements in it. The same is done with causal explanation in Chapter 4 by showing its chaotic aspects. Causal and intentional explanations can be reconciled in systems-theoretical structures.

Parts 3 and 4 (Chapters 5 to 8) deal with the integrational properties of explanatory methods in urban historiography. These integrational properties differ conspicuously depending on whether one is concerned with a relatively-closed or a half-open system. The explanatory methods of relatively-closed systems are discussed in Chapters 5 and 6 (Part 3); those of half-open systems in Chapters 7 and 8 (Part 4).

In Part 5 (Chapters 9, 10 and 11), the conception of time is examined as an instrument of integration. The urban histories with a relatively-closed systematic structure integrate by means of a undulant, homogenizing conception of time, while half-open systems integrate by means of a discontinuous and/or compounded conception of time. In contrast to the preceding chapters (chapters 5 to 8, in which each chapter is devoted to either relatively-closed systems or half-open systems), both the homogeneous temporality derived from the closed system construction and the compounded temporality derived from the half-open system are discussed collectively in Chapter 9. Both types of time have consequences for temporal arrangement. The fluid, homogeneous conception of time leads to a temporal arrangement that is derived from the better-known periodizations of countries and cultures. Here, an important role is played by the traditional periodization *Ancient, Medieval, Modern,* etc. In urban histories with a discontinuous and compounded conception of time, it is divided into phases. A well-known example of such a phased time conception is Marx's division of history into: *proto*-communism, the Asiatic mode of production, the ancient slave economy, the Germanic mode of production, feudalism, capitalism, and communism. The compounded conception of time is an elaboration of the principle of 'the simultaneity of that which is non-simultaneous'. Both forms of temporal arrangement are discussed in Chapter 10. Part 5 also contains the concluding chapter of this book.

In short, it can be said that this book attempts to discover various patterns of inference that play a role in historical writing and that constitute the infrastructure of the historical narrative. I thereby also wish to emphasize those patterns of inference supporting the synthesizing properties of historical writing. I am therefore concerned with a field-(history) and problem-related logic, where the problem is constituted by the desire of historians to write studies about more comprehensive patterns in the past.

Notes

1. It is curious that many expositions have dealt with the language of historians, but little analysis has been performed on historical texts from the viewpoint of the philosophy of language. See also Note 21.
2. White and Ankersmit, however, were also influenced by more people than the two mentioned above. In particular, the influence of Rorty on Ankersmit cannot be discounted.
3. I am here concerned with an internal evolution in philosophy or, rather, with a view of postmodern philosophy on developments in philosophy

itself. Like Zagorin, I would like to express my doubts as to the external validity of this evolution, especially with regard to its influence on historical writing. See P. Zagorin, 'History, the referent, and narrative: reflections on postmodernism now', *History and Theory* 38 (1999): 1–24.

4. M. Foucault, *Histoire de la folie à l'âge classique* (Paris 1972, 1st edition 1961); idem, *Naissance de clinique. Une archéologie du regard médical* (Paris 1963); idem, *Surveiller et punir. Naissance de la prison* (Paris 1975). See for the defining and exclusory nature of, for example, punishment: M. Karskens, *Waarheid als macht. Een onderzoek naar de filosofische ontwikkeling van Michel Foucault* [Truth as power. An examination of the philosophical development of Michel Foucault] (Nijmegen 1986), pp. 114–15, 130–1 and elsewhere.

5. J. Derrida, *Margins of philosophy* (Chicago 1982). For this see also Chr. Lorenz, *De constructie van het verleden. Een inleiding in de theorie van de geschiedenis* [The construction of the past. An introduction to the theory of history] (Amsterdam, Meppel, 4th edition 1998), pp. 124–7, especially p. 125.

6. H. White, *The content of the form. Narrative discourse and historical representation* (Baltimore, MD and London 1987), esp. pp. 3–4.

7. H. White, *Metahistory. The historical imagination in nineteenth-century Europe* (Baltimore, MD 1973). Chr. Lorenz opposes the anti-empiricism of White and Ankersmit, as presented in the form of a picture view of knowledge, with the argument that this 'picture view' brings with it all the problems of picture theory without solving them. See Chr. Lorenz, 'Can histories be true? Narrativism, positivism and the "metaphorical turn"', *History and Theory* 37 (1998): 309–30.

8. F. R. Ankersmit, *Narrative logic. A semantic analysis of the historian's language* (Groningen 1981, The Hague, Boston, London 1983). See p. 96 and elsewhere (1981 edition).

9. F. R. Ankersmit, *De macht van de representatie. Exploraties II: Cultuurfilosofie en esthetica* [The power of representation. Exploration II: philosophy of culture and aesthetics] (Kampen 1996), pp. 179–201. By taking this position, Ankersmit seems to contradict his exposition of Wolfgang Welsch's 'transversal reason' in *Exploraties I*.

10. Ibid., p. 198.

11. Ankersmit also thinks that Hayden White sometimes exaggerates the non-referential nature of historical writing, even though he expresses this subtly. According to Ankersmit, historians are restricted in their views by historical facts. See F. Ankersmit, 'Hayden White's appeal to historians', *History and Theory* 37 (1998): 182–93.

12. Ankersmit uses the term representation here differently from, for example, Rorty. The latter sees a form of correspondence with reality in representation, which Ankersmit rejects. Ankersmit also rejects correspondence theory, but, in contrast to Rorty, does not consider representation to be a form of correspondence, but an autonomous representation of reality. See F. R. Ankersmit, *De macht van de representatie*, p. 191.

13. See also: J. H. Zammito, 'Ankersmit's postmodernist historiography: the hyperbole of "opacity"', *History and Theory* 37 (1998): 330–46. In his later work, Ankersmit does involve reality in his philosophy, but then he does not see the access to it in a *tertium* or language, but in the aesthetic-historical experience. The non-referential character of metaphors, however, remains a foundation of his philosophical endeavours.

14. For this also see: Chr. Lorenz, 'Can histories be true? Narrativism and the "metaphorical turn"', *History and Theory* 37 (1998): 309–30.

15. Hereinafter I shall use the terms 'infrastructure' and 'superstructure' of historical narratives more often. In particular with reference to the term 'infrastructure', I believe that it is not considered an equivalent of the same term as used by Goldstein. Goldstein is more concerned with techniques for taking inventory of sources and much less with argumentative logic than is the connotation of the term as I use it. It is, however, the case that issues such as the criticism of sources, auxiliary sciences and so on are not excluded in the least from the infrastructural domain as I see it; but 'cultural scientific' patterns of inference are far more important for me than for Goldstein. See, for example, L. J. Goldstein, *Historical knowing* (Austin, TX 1976), p. 140.

16. F. R. Ankersmit, *De macht van de representatie*, pp. 171–5 and elsewhere.

17. M. Hesse, 'Models, metaphors and truth', in F. Ankersmit and J. A. Mooij (eds), *Knowledge and language 3. Metaphor and knowledge* (Dordrecht, Boston, London 1993), pp. 50–67.

18. See also: P. Zagorin, 'History, the referent, and narrative' (mentioned above in Note 3).

19. P. Ricoeur, *Time and narrative* I (Chicago, London 1984), pp. 175–80. It is incomprehensible that Ankersmit labels Ricoeur an anti-scientist (see Ankersmit, *De macht van de representatie*, pp. 203–4). Although Ricoeur is no positivist, he rejects the proposition that historical narratives are self-explanatory. Arguments are of essential importance to Ricoeur's (historical) scientific conception.

20. I share the opinions of Lorenz and Verschaffel with regard to these issues. See Chr. Lorenz, *De constructie van het verleden* (Amsterdam, Meppel 1998, 5th edition), pp. 135–6 and B. Verschaffel, 'Geschied-schrijving – een waar verhaal of de waarheid over verhalen?' [Historical writing – a true story or the truth about stories], in F. R. Ankersmit *et al.* (eds), *Op verhaal komen: over narrativiteit in de mens- en cultuurwetenschappen* [A narrative pause: narrativity in the humanities] (Kampen 1990), pp. 83-107. I especially agree with Verschaffel's statement that the historian not only narrates but also argues and that his colleagues must have access to the manner in which he develops his conception of the past. When I discuss the infrastructure of historical writing, I am concerned with what Verschaffel calls the argumentative context of a historical text. I do have serious objections to the manner in which Verschaffel criticizes narrativism and the incomprehension he shows towards Ricoeur in particular.

21. Philosophers of history devote many expositions to the language of historians, but there are few linguistic analyses of historiography. Exceptions to this rule, in addition to H. White, are: D. Capra, *History and criticism* (Ithaca, NY 1985); H. Kellner, *Language and historical representation* (Madison, WI 1989); Ph. Carrard, *Poetics of the new history: French historical discourses from Braudel to Chartier* (Baltimore, MD 1992); S. Bann, *The clothing of Clio: a study of representation in nineteenth-century Britain and France* (Cambridge 1984); L. Orr, *Jules Michelet: nature, history and language* (Ithaca, NY 1976); A. Rigney, *The rhetoric of historical representation: three narrative theories of the French revolution* (Cambridge 1990).

22. Of note here is the fact that many studies are devoted to nineteenth-century historiography, but few to that of the twentieth century.

23. Ankersmit's claim that he wishes to do justice to both the subject and reality and does not wish to elevate the one above the other is based on his notion that it is not epistemological theory but the historical-aesthetic experience that links the subject and reality. This may be true for a great deal of our non-scientific knowledge, but certainly not for most scientific knowledge. Ankersmit's return to Aristotle in order to defend his theory of experience and his integral condemnation of, especially, Cartesian epistemology and that which followed upon it can be called both atavistic and revolutionary: F. R. Ankersmit, *De macht van de representatie*, pp. 171–82.

23. See, for an excellent analysis of these issues: J. Rüsen, 'Rhetoric and aesthetics of history: Leopold von Ranke', *History and Theory* 29 (1990): 190–204; and A. Megill and D. McCloskey, 'The rhetoric

of history', in J. Nelson, A. Megill and D. McCloskey (eds), *The rhetoric of the human sciences. Language and argument in scholarship and public affairs* (Madison, WI 1987). It should be noted here that McCloskey has tended more to an aesthetic–narrative approach in the 1990s (see also Chapter 4, paragraph 5 'Systems theories and chaos theories' of this monograph); also B. Verschaffel, 'Geschiedschrijving – een waar verhaal of de waarheid over verhalen?', in F. R. Ankersmit *et al.* (eds), *Op verhaal komen: over narrativiteit in de mens- en cultuurwetenschappen*, pp. 83–107.

24. See for example: F. R. Ankersmit, *De macht van de representatie. Exploraties II: cultuurfilosofie en esthetica* (Kampen 1996), pp. 179–82 and 190–201.

25. D. H. Fischer, *Historians' fallacies. Towards a logic of historical thought* (New York, Evanston, IL 1970) p. IX.

26. One could add to this the historical logic of comparison. The role of comparison is this study is negligible. For those who have command of the Dutch language, I refer to: H. S. J. Jansen, 'De voorwerpen van vergelijking. Op zoek naar een nieuwe vergelijkingstypologie' [The objects of comparison. Towards a new typology of comparison], *Tijdschrift voor Geschiedenis* 110 (1997): 329–56 and idem, 'Het vergelijken vergeleken. Skocpol and Goldstone' [Comparison compared. Skocpol and Goldstone], *Theoretische Geschiedenis* 24 (3) (1997): 289–304.

27. J. Kocka, *Sozialgeschichte* (2nd edition, Göttingen 1986), p. 160.

28. In his article concerning Romein's theory of history, Ankersmit explicitly defends synthesizing historical writing. I will return to this issue later on. See F. R. Ankersmit, 'Een rehabilitatie van Romeins conceptie van de theoretische geschiedenis' [A rehabilitation of Romein's conception of theoretical history], in idem, *De navel van de geschiedenis* [The navel of history]. On the other hand, there are also tendencies in Ankersmit's work that seem defeatist with regard to the possibility of writing historical syntheses. See F. R. Ankersmit, 'Tegen de verwetenschappelijking van de geschiedwetenschap' [Against the scientification of the historical sciences], in F. Van Bersouw *et al.*, *Balans en perspectief. Visies op de geschiedwetenschap in Nederland* (Groningen 1987), pp. 55–72, esp. p. 56.

29. O. Zunz, *Reliving the past. The worlds of social history* (Chapel Hill, NC and London 1985). See also D. Cannadine, 'British history, past, present and future', *Past and Present* 116 (1987): 169–91, esp. 188–91. Furthermore: E. H. Kossmann, 'Jaarrede voorzitter Nederlands Historisch genootschap. Utrecht, 26 oktober 1979'

[Annual speech of the Chairman of the Dutch Historical Society, Utrecht, 26 October 1979] *Bijdragen en mededelingen betreffende de geschiedenis der Nederlanden* 95 (1980): 242–7, esp. 244. See also the contributions of R. T. Griffiths, B. H. Slicher van Bath, H. Soly, Th. Van Tijn and G. Trienekens in F. Van Besouw *et al.*, *Balans en perspectief.*

30. See F. R. Ankersmit, 'Een rehabilitatie van Romeins conceptie van de theoretische geschiedenis', pp. 233–5. See also Chr. Lorenz's criticism of it in 'Can histories be true?'.

31. With his statement that the theoretical dimension of facts has little importance in historical practice, Ankersmit tries to justify his separation of historical research and historical writing. Especially in social economic history, however that dimension is of eminent importance. This confirms, as I have observed earlier, that social-economic history falls outside the consideration of many philosophers of history. Furthermore, it remains to be seen whether the 'anti-foundationalism' that Ankersmit adheres to and the importance of the 'thick-crust' of historiographic discourse for historical practice observed by Ankersmit do not imply a theoretical bias of facts. See F. R. Ankersmit, 'Een rehabilitatie van Romeins conceptie van theoretische geschiedenis' pp. 234 and 235.

32. See also: P. Ricoeur, *Temps et récit* (Paris 1983), pp. 162–4.

33. In this respect, I completely agree with Ankersmit: the theory of history has only started to occupy itself with the historical text as a whole since Hayden White, which was much too late. See F. R. Ankersmit, *De spiegel van het verleden. Exploraties I. De geschied-theorie* [The mirror of the past. Explorations. The theory of history] (Kampen 1996), pp. 62–3.

34. Or, as Kant explained: '(. . .) historical narratives without analyses are empty (. . .)'. Peter Gay parrots Kant: 'Historical narration without analysis is trivial; historical analysis without narration is incomplete' (quoted from: H. White, *The content of the form*, p. 5).

35. Logic and aesthetics form the duality on which historical synthesis is based. See also: J. Topolski, 'The role of logic and aesthetics in constructing narrative wholes in historiography', *History and Theory* 38 (1999): 198–210.

36. See for example: P. H. H. Vries, *Verhaal en betoog: geschiedbeoefening tussen postmoderne vertelling en sociaalwetenschappelijk analyse* [Story and exposition: historical practice between postmodern narration and social scientific analysis] (Leiden 1995).

37. E. Mach, *Die Mechanik in ihrer Entwicklung historisch-kritisch dargestellt* [The development of mechanics represented in a critical historical manner] (1883). See also: C. Van den Berg, 'Chaostheorie als regressietherapie. Een natuurwetenschappelijke reflectie op de geschiedtheorie' [Chaos theory as regression therapy. A reflection on the theory of history from the perspective of the physical sciences] (Master's thesis, Nijmegen 1998), p. 24.

38. The opposition between modernist systems thought and postmodern anti-systems thought is not completely justified. Foucault, presented here as a postmodernist, was also a systematic thinker, even a very rigid one. Foucault, for example, leaves little room for intentions, while intentional relations can play an important role in my conception of systems. Furthermore, it should be remembered that the philosophy of language has been strongly influenced by the systems thought of De Saussure. Systems thought also has anti-positivist and therefore anti-modernist elements, as we shall see; it is therefore curious that so little research has been done in postmodernism with regard to systems thought itself. It seems as if they reject yet, at the same time, make use of it.

39. See T. Kuhn, *The structure of scientific revolutions* (Chicago 1962). See also Hoyningen-Huene, *Reconstructing scientific revolutions. Thomas S. Kuhn's Philosophy of science* (Chicago 1993).

40. J. W. McAllister, *Beauty and revolution in science* (Ithaca, NY, London 1996).

41. Only Van den Braembussche has attempted this in Dutch. See A. A. Van den Braembussche, *Theorie van de maatschapijgeschiedenis* (Baarn 1985). Also see Note 36.

42. T. Kuhn, *De structuur van wetenschappelijke revoluties,* pp. 199, 202–3, 263–4; Hoyningen-Huene, *Reconstructing scientific revolutions. Thomas S. Kuhn's Philosophy of science*, p. 135; and J. W. McAllister, *Beauty and revolution in science*, pp. 54 ff.

43. J. Romein, 'Theoretische geschiedenis', in *Historische lijnen en patronen* (Amsterdam 1971). This form of the theory of history should not be confused with that proposed by L. Hölscher in *History and Theory*. See L. Hölscher, 'The new annalistic: a sketch of a theory of history', *History and Theory* 36 (1997): 317–35. It does show some resemblance to the apology for a theoretical history by Nikolai Rozov. I, too, am mainly concerned with (among other things) the moderation of the rigid logic of Popper without completely discarding theorizing in terms of regularity and causality (N. S. Rozov, 'An apologia for theoretical history', *History and Theory* 36 (1997): 336–52).

44. A. A. Van den Braembussche, 'Historical explanation and comparative method: towards a theory of the history of society', *History and Theory* 28 (Feb. 1989): 1–24.
45. See especially: W. J. Van der Dussen, 'Geschiedenis en filosofie' and 'Geschiedfilosofie, theorie en historiografie', in F. R. Ankersmit *et al.* (eds), *Groniek* 89/90 (1984, *Taal en Geschiedenis*): 103–17 and 118–28, respectively; see also: W. J. Van der Dussen, 'Geschiedfilosofie als geschiedtheorie', *Groniek* 93 (1985): 191–6.
46. F. R. Ankersmit, 'Een rehabilitatie van Romeins conceptie van de theoretische geschiedenis' and H. S. J. Jansen, 'Geschiedfilosofie en geschiedtheorie', *Groniek* 93 1985): 180–90. The difference between Ankersmit and Jansen is that Ankersmit mainly defends the synthesizing intention behind Romein's theory of history, while Jansen also accentuates pragmatism and thereby the attention Romein's conception implicitly demands for the context of discovery.
47. The only way out of this is the solution given by Feyerabend. This philosopher of science wishes to throw out the axiom that scientific practice is bound by certain ground rules. With this *anything goes* Feyerabend wishes to undermine the desire for logical and methodological justification. Yet this anarchistic position with regard to the philosophy of science is still bound to the ground rule that A cannot be not-A. Even Feyerabend cannot simultaneously claim that scientific practice needs ground rules anyway.
48. Chr. Lorenz, *De constructie van het verleden*, pp. 163–7.
49. The big problem here is that there is not one but several methods of comparison. See: Van den Braembussche. 'De funderingscrisis van de historische kennis. Lorenz' revindicatie van een historische sociale wetenschap' [The justification crisis of historical knowledge. Lorenz's vindication of a historical social science], in Chr. Lorenz *et al.*, *Het historische atelier. Controversen over causaliteit en contingentie in de geschiedenis* [The historical workshop. Controversies about causality and contingency in history] (Meppel, Amsterdam 1990), pp. 49–50. See also: H. S. J. Jansen, 'De voorwerpen van vergelijking'.
50. The terms 'context of discovery' and 'context of justification' hail from the history of science. Here they have been applied to historiography. See also H. S. J. Jansen, 'Waarheid en schoonheid in de wetenschapsgeschiedenis' [Truth and beauty in the history of science], *Theoretische Geschiedenis* 26 (1) (1999).
51. See: J. W. McAllister, *Beauty and revolution in science* (Ithaca, NY 1996).

52. A. A. Van den Braembussche, 'Historical explanation and comparative method, towards a theory of the history of society', *History and Theory* 28 (1989): 1–24.
53. R. Martin, 'Progress in historical studies', *History and Theory* 37 (1998): 14–39.
54. N. Jordan, 'Some thinking about "system"', in S. L. Optner (ed.), *Systems analysis* (Harmondsworth 1973), p. 61.
55. Nevertheless, and this follows from my post-postmodern approach, I assume that there is 'a' reality that is accessible to our cognitive capacities.
56. In the original study Marxist studies were also treated. Comparative studies also are only scantly represented in this examination. This is for reasons of brevity.

–2–

Wrestling with the Angle: On Problems of Definition in Urban Historiography

To date no satisfactory answer has yet been found to the question of how urban historians should define the town as an object of historical study. In the English-American edition of Weber's *The City*, one of the translators, Don Martindale, complains: 'One may find anything or everything in the city texts except the informing principle that creates the city itself. One is reminded of Pirandello's "Six characters in search of an author". Everything is present except the one precise essential that gives life to the whole. When all is said and done, the question remains: What is the city?'[1]

Another question, closely linked to this, is of course: Does urban history constitute an autonomous historical (sub)discipline? The respected British urban historian Dyos thinks it does not:

> Urban history is not a discipline. It is not even a clear-cut field. It has to be regarded as a kind of strategy, an operational strategy. It is a preoccupation with certain kinds of issues, certain sorts of material, certain elements in contemporary history. . . . It can't be said to be more than that. It would be a gross conceit to pretend than it did somehow have a distinctive discipline.[2]

Therefore, Dyos understanding of the term 'discipline' seems to imply a certain methodology. In the Netherlands the discussion about urban history as a subdiscipline of social and economic history is more about definition than about methodology. Messing and Stokvis think urban history does constitute an autonomous subdiscipline.[3] However, they are not very clear as to the identity of the object of research.[4] Kooij is more forthcoming. He sees the city as a 'multi-functional central place which functions as a centre for a surrounding agrarian area and which, within the framework of a network of towns, has links with other central places'.[5] Notwithstanding the fact that definition problems have methodological implications, urban history is viewed here as a separate subdiscipline, since 'urban' can be given a specific meaning.

Despite this observation, the definition of 'urban history' can be viewed from various perspectives. Kooij's definition is clear, but rather restricted. He allies himself to an American tradition of 'urban historians', whose research themes have been largely orchestrated by Lampard. This appraisal sees cities primarily as subsystems of more comprehensive systems, which themselves involve both urban networks and patterns of town–country relations.[6] In allying to this 'Lampardian' approach of urban history Kooij rules out what he calls the 'biographical' method of urban-historical research, that is the research tradition 'in which cities and towns are depicted as rounded units each with its own character and even its own will.[7] Although he concedes that a number of excellent urban histories have been written within it, he considers this tradition to be outdated, and still, regrettably, retained by many amateur historians and local re-searchers.

Kooij's objections to the biographical genre remain a little vague. Besides the complaint that such a conception of the town derives from legal history and is unfashionable, his only other negative argument is that many commemorative books have been written in this form, which tends to portray towns in isolation from their surroundings.[8] These criticisms can hardly be called fundamental. Before whole traditions of research are designated old-fashioned and promptly banned, we should first pose the question: 'What are the requirements that an object of historical research must fulfil?' Without getting involved in a prematurely extensive theoretical discussion here, such an object must be so conceived as to allow subsidiary aspects to receive specialist study – for example, the demographic, the economic, the social, the political and the cultural – without the whole's being reduced to any one of these aspects.

The implication for urban history is that the town should be more than the sum of the parts from which it is constructed. This might be called the synthesizing factor of urban historical research. At the same time, whilst not everything that has happened in the urban past can be consi-dered urban history, the boundaries of the object must not be so sharply drawn that a large measure of pluriformity in research is lost. Thorough analysis of various component fields remains necessary, precisely for the sake of writing of new syntheses.[9]

An important question, therefore, is whether the urban historian is presenting a consistent conception of the town, one that can allow the clarity necessary for analysis together with the imaginative power required for synthesis. It is these conceptions of the town, and the changes that they have undergone, that can be traced by examining the historiography. Two conceptual cores can be found in urban historical research, both of which comply with the requirements outlined above. In the first we find the more traditional, biographical, somewhat closed and actionistic view, in which the city is conceived as an independent variable. In the other more modern, open and behavioural conception the town is interpreted as a dependent variable.[10] These two core conceptions can be considered as the pillars of the subdiscipline 'urban history'. However, the two approaches need to be carefully differentiated. If they are not, confusion, as we shall soon see, will run riot.

This investigation into historiography is restricted to Anglo-Saxon and German urban history. The French dimension is present too, since that part of Braudel's work that deals with urban history is the starting-point of the analysis. The extent of the investigation is also limited in another way. It is not the intention here to produce a total review of paradigms; the aim is purely to look at the ways in which urban historians themselves define the object of their research. The purpose is not to pronounce upon the quality of the research carried out within either the 'biographical' or the more modern tradition, but rather to question whether the old tradition should be entirely replaced by another. In approaching this issue, we perhaps should bear in mind that within the old tradition there still exists enormous expertise, as well as widespread enthusiasm, amongst a large number of historians, both professional and amateur.

Braudel's confusion

Braudel's contribution to urban history has to be looked for in the impressive three-volume *Civilisation matérielle, économie et capitalisme*.[11] In Part 3 (*Le temps du monde*), in which he describes the development of a number of integrated economic systems, each with a central dominant city at its heart: Bruges, the Hanseatic towns, Venice, Antwerp, Genoa, Amsterdam and London are presented one after the other. It is true that the subject here is urban subsystems, but these subsystems play an active role in the system of which they form the centre. To find the basis for this urban interpretation of world history we have to turn to the last chapter of Part 1. This chapter, entitled '*Les villes*' deals not only with dominant cities, but also in a more general sense with the entity 'the town' in the period 1400–1800.

At the start of the chapter Braudel states that throughout the world towns are the same kind of creature, distinct from the country and from each other. 'Towns embody intelligence, risk, progress and modernity, as opposed to the sluggish country. The opening of the chapter is revealing: 'Towns are so many electrical transformers. They increase tension, accelerate the rhythm of exchange and ceaselessly stir up men's lives.' No great understanding of electricity is needed, and still less of transformers, to understand two things from this pronouncement:

(a) The town is a historical entity that can be clearly defined in respect of other social entities: '*Every town is, and wants to be, a world apart*', is how Braudel puts it.[12]

(b) As a separate entity, the town can exert an influence on other social entities.

Braudel ascribes such great influence to the town that he designates it the generator of progress and the motor of civilization. That sounds promising. With such an opening, people are going to take this very seriously. Braudel is not just anybody. When the chapter is over, various examples have been paraded, though these are in general descriptions of Naples, St Petersburg, Peking and London, which are largely unconnected to each other. Common features have not emerged. Seventy pages after his remark that towns constitute a world apart, Braudel even announces that towns '. . . *are all products of their civilizations*'.[13] It seems that Wesseling's verdict on the whole of *Civilisation matérielle et capitalisme* also applies to its treatment of urban history. 'The subject too was inexhaustible, since there were actually no clear questions formulated and thus no real answers given.[14]

Braudel anticipated this sort of criticism. At the end of the first part he writes: 'Books, even history books, run away with their authors. This one has run on ahead of me. But what can one say about its waywardness, its whims, even its own logic, that would be serious and valid?'[15] Braudel's vision of urban development from 1400 to 1800 does indeed display some strange whims. Here the town is described as an autonomous phenomenon, there it is conceived as a dependent variable of the society of which it forms a part. The aim of introducing this harsh criticism is not to drag Braudel down from his deserved pedestal, but to show how even an eminent historian can become entangled in the hooks and snares of urban historical synthesis and its methodological and theoretical implications.[16] A historiographical analysis of the conceptual problems surrounding the idea of 'the town' might clarify the matter. Thus, first of all, we will go in search of the roots of Braudel's confusion.

The Marxist roots of Braudel's confusion (c. 1850)

In the introduction to his chapter on *Les Villes*, Braudel refers to the well-known passage in Marx's critique of Feuerbach in which he links the transition from barbarism to civilization to the emergence of a distinction between town and country.[17] Marx appears to present a dichotomous definition of the town, based on a contrast with the country, which is expressed in two ways:

1 The town is a concentration of people, means of production, capital, needs and enjoyment. This concentrating functioning of the town stands in direct contrast to the deconcentrating functioning of the country. The country disperses, breaks up and isolates.
2. The town is the result of community-forming. Marx calls towns *Vereine* (unions), a term that, in the Young Hegelian jargon of the time, stood for a voluntary association of individuals.[18] As a *Gemeinwesen* (community) the town functions as a centre of government, policing and tax collecting, a function not present in the country.[19]

The contrast between town and country is based on division of labour, where the manual forms of labour largely fall to the country, and the non-manual forms to the town. In this light the pronouncement that the town–country divide arises with the transition from barbarism to civilization becomes understandable. The notion of 'civilization' itself has a strong urban/bourgeois connotation. The struggle of town against country is in other words a struggle of the bourgeoisie against the feudal powers, of movable bourgeois private property against immovable feudal estates and common-ownership.[20]

At first sight Marx's definition of the town seems to be wholly positive. He regards it, after all, as the origin of civilization. Marx hereby implies that an important role in the history of mankind is reserved for the town. Indeed, it would seem to be a dynamic role, in which the town features as the pioneer of civilization and modernity, and as the originator of new means of production.

The French philosopher and sociologist Henri Lefebvre concludes from this that Marx ascribes to the town the role that Hegel gave to the state. For Hegel, the state is the incarnation of the Absolute Idea, 'the subject' of history. Its development is *der Gang Gottes in der Welt* (God's motion in the world).[21] Lefebvre considers that, in the *Deutsche Ideologie*, Marx imputes a similar role to the town. 'Here [i.e. in the *Deutsche Ideologie* – HJ] the Subject of history is incontestably the Town', according to Lefebvre.[22]

That the town is, for Marx, an important social agent is beyond question; but whether it takes on the guise of a subject, almost of a quasi-personage, is quite another question. In fact there is a very different possible view: that for Marx the town is a dependent variable of the division of labour or of the separation of capital from landownership.[23] Lefebvre does not deny that there is such a view of the town to be found in Marx, but he sees these ideas only emerging in the later Marx. In the 'Introduction' to the *Grundrise der Kritik der politischen Oekonomie* of 1857, Marx and Engels still see the town as a separate social entity, as a distinct *Gemeinwesen*, that stands in contrast to the entity of the country.[24] A year later, in Lefebvre's opinion, this dichotomous definition is gone. In Marx's *Grundrisse der Kritik der politische Oekonomie* (1857/9) the town is no longer a distinct community, but the place, the space, the laboratory from which new means of production originate. The town is no longer the coachman, but the coach of social and economic change. According to Lefebvre, the town has moved from being the *agens* to being the *locus* of developments in the production process. He describes this transition in the Marxist conception of the town as the transformation of the town from the *sujet* to the town as the *lieu et milieu* of history.[25] The epistemological break construed by Althusser – a controversial construction, be it said – between the younger and the older Marx, between a humanistic and a structuralist Marxism, is thus also perceived by Lefebvre in the conception of the town.[26]

Lefèbvre's remarks make the question of Marx's conception of the town very interesting. Is Marx already at this early stage contemplating the idea, so original for his time, that the town is the dependent variable of the process of the division of labour? Or is he still employing the conventional view, of the town as an entity *sui generis*, as an independent variable?

In *The Condition of the Working Class in England*[27] Engels explores the negative aspects of nineteenth-century English industrial towns.[28] The gap between rich and poor widens to an unprecedented degree; the groups in the middle disappear.[29] The value-based approach favoured by Marx and Engels would seem to argue in favour of the independent entity view. After all, it makes little sense to apportion praise and blame to an agent that is not responsible for its actions (as is naturally the case with a dependent variable). To do so would be to produce a more subjective approach. Marx and Engels do indeed produce a balanced evaluation of the town. Although Marx considers it as the motor of progress, he is also aware of its negative and alienating characteristics.

If we put Marx's and Engels' visions of the town next to each other, we see different accents. For Marx the town is the origin of civilization, while for Engels the town creates a new barbarism. Is Marx then an urbanist and Engels an anti-urbanist? It looks rather like it. All the more reason to bear in mind the fact that Marx is dealing with the medieval and Engels with the nineteenth-century town. Moreover, Marx does indeed point out that the medieval town already bore within itself the germ of alienation. Thus the discrepancies between them do not necessarily mean that there are contradictions.

Marx and Engels do certainly agree in their evaluation of the entity 'town', and in this they belong with the discussion that occupied nineteenth-century urban historians. If we extend our view to include Braudel, it has to be said that Marx's and Engels' conception of the town has the tendency, like his, to waver between the town as a dependent and as an independent variable.[30]

Urbanism and anti-urbanism (1850–1900)

Nineteenth-century, usually liberal, optimists see the town, or rather the growing industrial city, as a centre of industry and technology, and thus of progress. Conservatives see it as the place where old values and social ties are being lost. For the English dissenter and liberal Robert Vaughan, towns are bulwarks of the commercial class against the conservative landed aristocracy, making the point that it is the trading class who represent the spirit of the age.[31] In his novel *Coningsby* (1844), the young Disraeli reveals himself to be still a believer in urban progress, in spite of all his criticism of the misery of industrialization. When Coningsby enthusiastically lets it be known that he is mad keen to see Athens, his companion destroys his illusions with the reply: 'The age of ruins is past.' Whereupon Coningsby visits Manchester and comes to the conclusion that, 'Certainly Manchester is the most wonderful city of modern times'.[32]

In Germany, the optimistic view of towns is represented by Karl Bücher, a professor at the University of Leipzig in the 1890s, who stressed that nineteenth-century urban growth was so positive because it was not the result of any sovereign decree but of the spontaneous social activity of ordinary people. The banner of modern civilization was not carried on a bit of parchment but by the selective operation of intellectual and economic forces. Towns were important building-blocks in the liberal tradition because they promoted the division of labour and individual opportunities for all. The highest possible individual reward involved also promoting the general good of the whole community. Bücher also noted that community spirit and sense of solidarity were missing in towns, and that towns promoted the rich–poor divide, through which community spirit was further eroded and the pursuit of self-interest encouraged.[33]

Within these remarks there resounds a weak echo of the powerful anti-urban cry that had issued from the Bavarian professor and journalist

Wilhelm Heinrich Riehl a generation or so before. In his four-volume *Die Naturgeschichte des Volkes als Grundlage einer deutschen Social-Politik*, which appeared between 1854 and 1869, it was claimed that Europe was sick as a consequence of her monstrous towns. Through urbanization there had arisen a cosmopolitan mentality that, especially in Germany, was undermining the national character. Stable social classes and dependable family life were being undermined by urbanization. Urbanization drew people from the country to the town, creating a rootless proletariat that respected neither God nor Man. Thus had the town become the cradle of immorality and a rebellious political mentality. In addition towns were unaesthetic. The broad straight streets of proletarian warehouses had robbed the town of her old picturesque aspect. Riehl was particularly upset about the Ludwigsstrasse in Munich.[34]

While Bücher was beginning, subtly, to take issue with Riehl's anti-urbanism, a new anti-urban wave broke loose in England. J. A. Hobson viewed towns, or rather cities, as the cause of uncontrolled economic growth, with all the misery that that entailed.[35] The most radical anti-urbanism came from the United States, where among others the Reverend Josiah Strong saw cities as a grave threat to civilization: '. . . here roughs, gamblers, thieves, robbers, lawless and desperate men of all sorts congregate . . . here gather foreigners and wage-workers; here scepticism and irreligion abound, here inequality is the greatest and most obvious and the contrast between opulence and penury the most striking; here is suffering the sorest . . .'.[36] Strong sought to lay the blame for this misery on the new technology and the building of railways, the solution to which could only be found in Christianity.[37] Wilcox and Steffens were other outspoken examples of American anti-urbanism.[38]

However great the gulf between the optimistic and pessimistic verdicts on the town, there are also striking similarities of approach. The sources of admiration and horror are identical, namely the stupendous growth of cities and urban regions, such as the Ruhr, Lancashire, New York and Chicago. One of Disraeli's characters says, full of wonder: '. . . Have you seen Manchester?' Rudyard Kipling says of Chicago, 'Having seen it, I urgently desire never to see it again.' These concrete references make it absolutely clear that the writers are taking their stand in relation to contemporary examples. It was urban development itself that demanded that a position be taken. This affective polemical approach led again to a dichotomous definition of the phenomenon 'town'. The good dynamic town as opposed to the sluggish and conservative country (Vaughan and Bücher), or the horrendous city as opposed to the stable country, which still harboured moral solidarity within its small towns and villages (Riehl).

Because of this dichotomous definition, the town was usually seen as an *autonomous social entity*. As many sharp distinctions as possible were drawn between 'the town' and other social entities such as 'the country' or 'the village'. The autonomous town influenced the rest of society, either for good (the town as the motor of progress) or for ill (the town as the stimulator of decline and decay). The town is thus not exclusively an entity *sui generis*, but is also a discernible explanatory factor in other phenomena. It is an independent variable.

The town as an 'organic, yet man-made community' (1900–1940)

The abhorrence of Riehl and others for the urban development of the second half of the nineteenth century had its roots in organological ideas. Such thinking stemmed from the first half of their century and had found fertile ground, particularly in Germany. Here both Hegel and the romantic conservatives are encountered.

Three characteristics are of interest for the current enquiry.

1. Gradualism, tradition and history are revered and discontinuity and rapid change opposed.
2. Concern for the parts in relation to the whole. The relationship of the parts to the whole finds its spatial expression in the notion of the concentric development of the whole.
3. As in every organism, the whole is a physical–spiritual unity, which the optimists saw as a combination of material progress and spatial-morphological expansion on the one hand, and of intellectual dynamism, creativity and renewal on the other; pessimists saw it as an organism with problems, where dereliction and dilapidation represented the physical illness and loneliness and violence the mental equivalent.

Largely as a result of the work of Tönnies, Durkheim and Spencer, around the turn of the century the old organological tradition was modernized and transformed into a usable theory for sociologists.[39] As a consequence, American urban sociologists perceived the city as an 'organic, yet man-made community'.[40]

The Chicago school, the first scholarly community to be engaged in the scientific – that is to say, non-moralistic – definition of the phenomenon 'town', was strongly influenced by organological thinking. R. D. McKenzie emphasized the town's character as a community; Park saw the town not only as a whole consisting of people, streets and buildings, but also as a 'state of mind', built up of traditions and customs, attitudes and feelings, which were kept alive by these traditions. They defined the town as 'a moral as well as a physical organisation and these two mutually interact in characteristic ways to mould and modify one another'.[41]

In 1925 McKenzie and Park, together with Burgess, published *The City*, in which their organological ideas – which they referred to as ecological – were clearly laid out. Cities display a form of concentric expansion, zonal growth, which is much like the development of annual rings in a tree. However, in contrast to annual rings, spatial expansion did not lead to coherence in the urban community.[42]

They observed a continual crumbling of old traditional structures and primary ties (such as family and kinship), and the emergence of new values and secondary ties (such as work and club contacts). The Chicago school in fact stressed the disintegrative character of spatial expansion.

Later Louis Wirth saw the city as a new cultural form, as a 'way of life', understandable in the light of this organological 'Chicago' thinking. For Wirth, the tremendous expansion and population density of the city

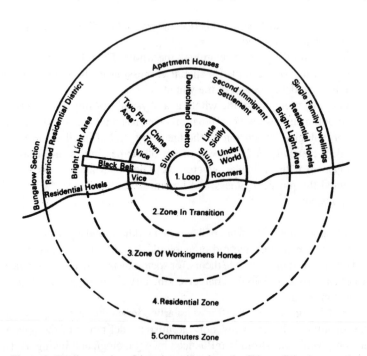

Figure 1. Zonal expansion of American cities from the Chicago School perspective

brought with it an increasing heterogeneity of the urban milieu, with drastic consequences for social life and human awareness. In contrast to traditional country life, cities engendered a decline in family and kinship ties, the replacement of territorial community bonds by the solidarity of interest groups, and a shift from primary to secondary group formation. Ethnic minorities gradually assimilated, but neighbourhood life lost much of its meaning. Wirth thus picked out all the elements by which urban life differed from other forms of society. On this basis, he argued for a new way of building communities no longer based on apparently self-evident truths but on political consensus and planning.[43]

As well as the influence of the Chicago school, the views of Tönnies, Durkheim and Maine are also discernible here. The last pair observed the world-wide shift from communities based on kinship, natural social control, status and religion to communities based on work and social life, consensus, calculation, science and planning.[44] Tönnies sees these developments as taking place particularly in towns and cities, and captures them in the twin poles of the terms *Gemeinschaft* (a sense of community) and *Gesellschaft* (social organization).

Wirth's conception of the town owed much to nineteenth-century anti-urbanists such as Engels and Riehl. It should be said immediately that there is a greater sense of intellectual responsibility, and a clearer effort to find solutions. For Wirth, the city becomes a problem that demands a solution.[45] However, this means that the city is still regarded as an autonomous social given, an entity *sui generis*. The explicit comparisons he draws with the non-urban part of society ensure that, with Wirth, the dichotomous view of the town reaches a culminating point.

The dichotomous conception of the town also plays a role in Arthur M. Schlesinger's influential article, 'The city in American history', published in 1940.[46] Schlesinger saw the city as an important factor in American history. It was the cities that awoke the spirit of revolution in colonial America. It was urban interest groups that determined the federal nature of the constitution. It was the cities of the North that began the Civil War against the rural South. In short, 'the urban dynamic . . . was the governing force'.[47] In an earlier study, *The rise of the city 1878–1898*, Schlesinger claimed: 'Underlying all the varied developments that made up American life was the momentous shift of the centre of national equilibrium from the countryside to the city.[48]

In the same year R. E. Turner's *The industrial city and cultural change* appeared. Turner saw in the industrial city the emergence of a new culture – we should now say a new mentality – that was the result of three factors: economic competition, technology and modern urban social life. There is no denying the resemblance to the description offered by the young Marx.[49] In this article, Turner proceeds from the same assumptions as Schlesinger and the prevailing conception in 1930s American urban history could almost be described as a Schlesinger–Turner thesis. This conception was governed by the notion that the city functions as the motor of civilization and thus as an independent variable.

A paradigm shift (1940–1960)

A counter-movement appeared. William Diamond raised objections to Schlesinger's use of the terms 'city', 'urban' and 'urbanization'. According to Diamond, when Schlesinger introduces the city as a causal factor, he meant several different things. Sometimes the city was identified with a particular economic activity, sometimes with a closed aggregation of people (for example in the case of housing shortage), and sometimes with a putative 'nerve-centre' of creative cultural activities. Besides, Diamond wondered, was the city really such a separate entity? Research into the political behaviour of citizens revealed that analyses based on class differences displayed a higher degree of correlation than those based on the town–country polarity.[50] What is alleged for political behaviour, also holds for reproductive behaviour. Although country women seem more fertile than women in the town, Diamond noted even greater differences between various urban groups of women than between urban and rural groups. These differences are linked, amongst other things, to differences in profession and social status.[51] Diamond claimed that: 'The differences between various groups within the urban and rural environment may be much greater and therefore more important than the differences between the total urban and total rural environments'.[52] All kinds of developments that Schlesinger ascribed to urbanization could equally well be attributed to other social processes, such as technology or industrialization.[53] Miller, Griffen and Stelter consider Diamond's protest against Schlesinger as a protest against the whole organological view of the town. According to them, Diamond was protesting against 'the familiar notion that urban society constituted an organic yet man-made community, a distinctive society different from that of the countryside or the frontier'.[54]

Diamond's protest also won applause from another corner. In 1942 the demographer Hope Eldridge Tisdale published her article, 'The process of urbanization'.[55] She regarded urbanization as a process of population concentration, and pointed out two ways in which this takes place: firstly, through the multiplication of concentration points, and secondly, through population increase at these concentration points. She thus rejected two rival views: first, that of urbanization as a process of radiation under which urban conditions and ideas coming from the city are transferred to the surrounding area (Tisdale thus takes a position opposed to that of Schlesinger and R. E. Turner, who did indeed take towns to be just such radiating centres of innovative ideas and achievement); and second, that of urbanization as the increase in the number and intensity of urban problems (a judgement aimed primarily at the work of Wirth).

Tisdale's objection to these two approaches was that both regarded the city itself as the origin of the urbanization process, while in fact it was the urbanization process that gave rise to the individual cities. Her views meant that individual cities functioned as *explananda* of the urbanization process, which was played out on a macro level. This split into a micro and a macro level is such a total revolution in urban historiography, that we can speak here of a paradigm shift. The new paradigm distinguished itself from the old by providing a definition of the city that was no longer dichotomous but complementary.[56]

Tisdale's approach was not wholly new – not even in America. N. S. G. Gras was one of the first to spot this development and to give it some academic shape. In an article in the 1922 *American Historical Review*, he describes the big American cities as economic nerve-centres of enormous regions. Instead of being autonomous units, these cities are the nuclei of much more comprehensive territories. City and region are thus complementary, particularly in terms of industry, transport and communications.[57]

It is interesting to see a complementary conception of the city turning up as early as 1922, and even more surprising to find it in a historical periodical. After all, it is usually attributed to geographers, more precisely to Christaller and Lösch, who published their ideas on urban research in the next decade. Christaller followed a train of thought in which cities were regional service centres. Indeed, the functionality of a city was only understandable in the context of regional needs. Lösch filled in Christaller's theory by pointing out that cities could be regional production centres as well as regional service centres.[58] The functionality of the city varied according to its size. Larger cities served a larger region, smaller cities a smaller one. Smaller cities usually formed a sub-part of a region that 'belonged' to a larger city. Every large city had such a hierarchy of smaller cities and towns around it, grouped in a hexagon.

Although this rigid mathematical symmetry only seldom corresponds with reality,[59] the concept of the 'central place' continues to play an important role in both contemporary urban geography and current urban

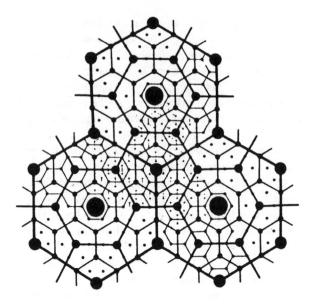

Figure 2. Christaller's central place model

history. Lampard, Rozman, and, in Holland, Pim Kooij and Clé Lesger, in their definitions of the city, presented her as a nodal point at the heart of an urban–rural region. Lampard in particular tried, in a theory of urbanization that began to take form in the 1950s, to combine the demographic ideas of Tisdale and the idea of the city as a central place. To Lampard urbanization meant growth in the scale of population and territorial expansion (cf. Tisdale).[60] The study of individual cities served only to contribute to the macroscopic urbanization process: every urban situation, though different, conformed if to a different degree.[61]

The initial urbanizing impulse, Lampard argued, was associated with areas where groups were segregated. When these areas are not too far away from each other and the cultures of the peoples are not too divergent, an interaction between the different areas is possible. On the basis of this interaction, nodal points develop where goods, ideas and services are exchanged. This is nothing more than adapting the theory of multi-functional central places to the origins of towns. Tisdale limited herself almost exclusively to demography, Christaller primarily to the spatial factor. Lampard offers his complementary definition of the city on the basis of a cocktail of demographic and spatial-economic factors.

The pendulum swings back towards a dichotomous definition (1960–1970)

With the appearance of Mumford's *The city in history* in the early 1960s we witness the return of the dichotomous approach to the entity 'city'. For Mumford the city is no longer the dependent variable of technology, as he had explained in an earlier study,[62] but has become an organism that attracts people from outside to maintain itself and that in its turn can influence external circumstances. In this connection Mumford uses the metaphor of the city as magnet, '. . . and that term is all the more useful in description because with the magnet we associate the existence of a field and the possibility of *action at distance*, visible in the lines of social force which draw to the centre particles of different nature'.[63]

In a theoretical sense, Mumford thus turns back to a view of the city as an autonomous social given. The dichotomous approach to the phenomenon 'city' is clearly not yet dead, and following in Mumford's footsteps, Briggs and Jane Jacobs breathed new life into it during the sixties and seventies. Jacobs sees towns throughout history as the *causa prima* of economic development. Briggs, who compared the 'Victorian cities' in England (and Australia), claimed that each city autonomously developed its own community spirit, its own 'civic pride'.[64]

Contrary to what might be expected, we find Dyos opting for the middle course. He was 'anxious to chart a course between the Scylla of old-fashioned city biographies, and the Charybdis of galactic surveys of the urbanisation process', as Cannadine eloquently formulated it. Moreover, in contrast to many other researchers, Dyos did indeed 'practise what he preached'. In his study about Camberwell, according to Cannadine, he succeeded in describing the London suburb as a subsystem of a great urbanization process on the one hand and as a whole system on the other.[65] Others were less enthusiastic about Dyos's attempts to reconcile the two urban conceptions. Aiming at the impressive array of essays, published in *The Victorian City*, E. P. Thompson could see no clarity about the 'Victorian-ness' nor about the 'urban-ness' of the Victorian city.[66] Despite this criticism I think it is justified to place Dyos in the vicinity of Jacobs and Briggs. Three arguments may support this statement. First, what mattered to Dyos was the city as a total phenomenon. The urban historian should commit himself to the city as a whole. This implies that for Dyos the city was an entity in itsself.[67] Second, Dyos obviously employed an action point of view. The urbanization process could in most cases only have an impact on the city when it worked through the mind and spirit of city dwellers.[68] Third, Dyos made a stand against the

American so-called 'New Urban History' of Stephen Thernstrom.[69] In the next paragraph we shall look at this third argument in more detail.

New urban history (1970 and after)

To Mumford, Briggs, and Jacobs, and probably also to Dyos, the great challenge was to assess the impact of the city as an independent variable.[70] Therefore they found themselves in direct opposition to a group of young American urban historians who gathered round Stephen Thernstrom in 1967, and who have since been known as the 'new urban historians'. These new urban historians were not so preoccupied with the phenomenon of 'the city' as were Dyos, Briggs, Mumford and Jacobs. They were busy, apparently, with the history of individual cities, and they concentrated their attention on American and Canadian cities in the nineteenth century.

Thus Thernstrom himself studied Newburyport and Boston; Philadelphia was investigated by both Blumin and Warner; Katz made a study of Hamilton, Ontario, and Chudakoff of Omaha. The study of individual cities was nothing new in the United States. A whole generation of urban biographers had preceded the new urban history. But the very term 'urban biography' leaves no doubt that this older generation of urban historians saw each city as a unique phenomenon, of which the political-institutional, cultural, architectural and morphological developments could (and perhaps should) be portrayed separately from similar processes in other cities.

There are similarities to be found between this 'old' American school of urban history and Dyos's Leicester school. Cannadine placed both schools against the New Urban History. The two schools developed primarily a subject and a *field of study,* whereas the New Urban historians worked out 'a *methodology* and a *way of doing things'*.[71] It was not the particularities of individual cities that interested the new urban historians, but precisely their general social features. They scoured city archives with social-historical questions in mind, about social stratification, geographical mobility and the social, religious and ethnic composition of the urban population. This meant that they were not in fact interested in the city as a city, in the way Dyos, Briggs and others were, but in all sorts of phenomena that, more or less by chance, could best be researched in cities. Because of their strong orientation towards the social sciences, and their enthusiastic adaptation of all kinds of quantitative research techniques, the new urban historians received considerable attention.[72]

Surveying the history of the problems of definition in urban historiography, it becomes clear why there is so much confusion amongst urban historians, and why urban historiography presents so chaotic an appearance.

Some attempts at a solution

Considering the way urban historical research swings between a conception of the town, first as an independent, then as a dependent variable, it is understandable that Braudel was caught up in the confusion. A number of scholars, impelled by a sense of responsibility, have devoted themselves explicitly to the conceptual problem, and especially to the issue of the two contrasting definitions, that has been outlined here. Oscar Handlin analyses the problem as follows. A distinction must be made between the preindustrial town and the modern industrial city. From the Middle Ages up to and including the eighteenth century, towns were 'self-contained entities walled off from their surroundings with which they had only precisely defined contacts'.[73] The preindustrial town was still a place within which 'the movement of goods came to a halt, started and stopped . . . and that discontinuity gave the entrepot a high degree of autonomy'.[74] The modern industrial city became more a nodal point in a web of relationships. It did not obstruct or block the flow of money or goods, but specifically promoted a quicker flow through from producer to consumer. Handlin is particularly thinking here of transshipping, transport systems and banking and credit facilities. The city was bound in with a thousand and one ties to a greater social-economic whole, and thus lost its autonomy.

According to Handlin this development from a rather closed to a more open city was due to the rise of the centralized, national state, the transformation of the economy from a traditional–household to a rational–capital basis; and the technological development that had removed the problem of distance.[75]

Handlin's recipe against ambiguous definitions of the town is simple: the medieval town can be quietly studied as an autonomous organism; the modern city should be seen as an organ of a greater whole. In short: the modern city must be studied on the basis of a complementary definition. Arguably this is a practical–empirical analysis of an epistemological problem. As such it offers an illusory solution, and is simple to refute. On the one hand, a great number of authors have studied nineteenth- and twentieth-century cities with a dichotomous definition in mind. The nineteenth-century English industrial city in particular was defined and researched as an autonomous entity by such leading urban historians as Briggs and Fraser. Some modern American historians have worked in the same way, as for example Frisch and Blumin in their respective studies of nineteenth-century Springfield and Kingston.[76] On the other hand, since the beginning of the 1960s there has been, notably in Germany, an about-face in research into the medieval town. The *auctor intellectualis* of this shift is Carl Haase. He abandoned the accepted institutional definition of the town (derived from legal history), which presented the town as a juridical–political immunity *vis-à-vis* the surrounding feudal countryside, and replaced it by a broad, more social-scientific analysis on the basis of multiple criteria.[77] In 1968 the medievalist Edith Ennen went yet a step further and constructed a definition of the town based on (a) the town as material form, further specified as a concentration point for people and activities; (b) the town as structure, which heading is to include the economic specialization and the social differentiation of the population; and (c) the town as central place.[78] In the light of such examples as these, Handlin's solution to the problem must be rejected.

In another analysis Abrams asks whether the town, in the process of economic growth, should be seen as a dependent or an independent variable.[79] He considers that in the past the town was conceived of too much as an independent variable, without that conception's being supported by solid research. He encounters this conceptual ambiguity in Braudel, Lampard, and others.[80] His advice is as follows: let us stop using the idea of the town as an independent variable in our research.[81]

Abrams has two arguments to support this advice. First, the relationship between urbanization on the one hand, and the division of labour, technological development and the dispersal of consumer goods on the other, is often opaque. Second, even where relatively convincing statistical relationships are found between particular forms of urbanism on the one hand and stages of economic growth on the other, these relations can neither be explained in themselves nor by means of any exclusively 'urban factor'.[82]

There are, however, rather more reasons not to follow Abrams' advice. The fact that links between urban development and economic growth are often vague is still no reason to throw the baby – in this case the town – out with the bathwater. Even if there are only a few studies in which these links are clear, then that is reason enough to uphold the town as 'an agent in its own right'. If there is an 'urban factor' to be postulated, it is not enough simply to deny it, as does Abrams. Every object of study, the town included, is in large part a construction of the scholar, a consequence of his or her conceptualizing activity; it is not a purely empirical fact, which can be said to exist or not exist. In any question of historiography it is the persuasiveness of the scholar's arguments that determines whether an 'urban factor' exists or not. In the collection of essays in which Abrams article appears, and to which he himself has written the introduction, there appear a number of contributions that treat the town as an autonomous entity; and they are certainly no less convincing to me than the other studies.[83]

There is thus a worthy tradition amongst urban historians that can get along very well with a conception of the town as an entity *sui generis*, as an independent variable. Why should this tradition be demolished? Because some other urban historians do not accept the existence of the 'urban factor'? As an alternative to an autonomous view of the town, Abrams decrees that it be studied as a dependent variable of 'the complex of domination' (Weber). He is of the opinion that Weber himself employed a similar complementary definition. His reasoning is in direct contradiction to that of Song-U Chon, Abramowski, Tromp and other Weber authorities. They point out that for Weber the town, especially the ancient and medieval town, must precisely be considered as one of the *explanantia* for the rise of modern Western civilization.[84] As such, for Weber, the city is an independent variable. This is not the place to go into Abrams' exegesis of Weber. But it should be stated clearly that Abrams' advice is based on unusually shaky arguments.[85]

The pragmatic and methodological character of this sally into the historiography means that the important question here is of the epistemological origins of our two rivals, the dichotomous and the complementary conception of the city.

Two ways of arriving at definitions

In his book *Analyzing concepts in social sciences*, Abraham Edel draws attention to a number of traditions within theory formulation that concern definition.[86] Two of these are important for my purposes. The first stems from Aristotle (the *Topics*), and states that definitions must be unambiguous. Concepts that have two different opposites are especially dangerous for such a simple view. Thus 'right' can just as well be the opposite of 'left' as of 'wrong'. In this tradition special skills are developed to avoid ambiguities of definition. The underlying assumption, that definition rests on dichotomies, is allowed to go unchallenged. The reader will have no difficulty in fitting the historiography of the dichotomous conception of the town into this tradition.[87]

To make clear how such a definition can be constructed, he proposes the metaphor of the wheel. The spokes constitute the different aspects of the phenomenon 'city'. Here must be included such matters as large concentrations of population, diversity of ethnic and social groups, large-scale division of labour and diversity of social role patterns, major qualitative and quantitative distinctions of occupation, fewer social bonds based on blood-ties and kinship and many forms of social organization based on territory and secondary groups, a more or less high degree of personal anonymity, many segmented social relationships, great tolerance of different value systems, the reinforcement of 'deviant' behaviour, and little physical but great social distance between citizens. This wide range of aspects can indeed be found, evenly distributed and equally substantiated, throughout the empirical material. But whereas in the model, a nice regular line runs round through the spokes more or less equidistant from the centre, linking all these aspects into a coherent and balanced whole (we are of course dealing with an ideal city here – in the theoretical, not in the normative sense), in any empirically encountered version there may well appear great distortions in this line. Perhaps the city has not developed all these aspects to an equal degree, or has failed to ensure they are represented by equally full documentation. There is then no question of a closed circle, but rather of an irregular star form. Thus early-antique Rome, with her tribally-based population, does not completely satisfy the criterion of territorially-based social bonds, according to Edel. This is not necessarily the end of a dichotomous definition, because greater weight can be given to some aspects than to others.[88] Such adjustment means, however, that the definition itself is dependent on some other (implicit) theoretical model. Thus Weber, with his *'verstehende'* (interpretative) historical sociology, laid the accent on economic and political-organizational aspects, while Mumford, with his organological views, laid it on demographic-spatial, social and cultural dimensions.[89] Such definitions of the town, formulated on an 'ideal type' basis, erect a sharp boundary, through their dichotomous character, between the phenomenon 'town' and other phenomena.

The second, more modern, tradition repudiates a method of defining that attempts to draw clear boundaries between a phenomenon and its apparent opposite. It dismisses the 'dichotomy school', with its striving for the purest possible definition. Its fundamental idea is: 'Don't ask for the meaning, ask for the use.' Such a functional method of reaching a definition comes down to the view that a given phenomenon is defined by explaining what significance it has for a greater whole. Such a definition is more adequate, claim the representatives of this tradition, because it is more complete and more realistic. Edel: 'After all, why define "definition" by an ideal which is rarely attained?'[90] In the case of urban historiography Kooij points to studies in which town and country are not each other's opposites, but each other's complements. This is one of the streams in urban historiography, which flow from a functional, or as Kooij would say, a complementary definition of the town.[91]

What do we win by knowing this? There may well be a link between the way an urban historian defines his object of research and the explanations he gives for urban phenomena. The definition will then support all sorts of implicit or explicit theoretical presuppositions. Thus the dichotomous definition might indeed have a greater affinity with more phenomenological and hermeneutic approaches to history, and the complementary definition with positivist and structural approaches. It is unnecessary to come down on the side of either one of these two traditions. The subdiscipline of urban history would be greatly impoverished if it were to be limited to one approach. It would almost certainly lose its pluriformity. Each tradition provides valuable descriptions of towns and urban phenomena, and the two together form two points of focus in that multicoloured field of research known as urban history.

To avoid confusion it is preferable that the two approaches should remain discrete – that is to say, on a certain level. Only some basic features that distinguish the two conceptions of urban history have been addressed here. Other important elements will be described hereafter.

Notes

1. Max Weber, *The City*, ed. Don Martindale and G. Neuwirth (New York, 1958), p. 11.
2. B. M. Stave, 'A conversation with H. J. Dyos: Urban history in Great Britain', *Journal of Urban History* 5 (August 1979): 491. See also: idem, 'A view from the United States', in D. Fraser and A. Sutcliffe (eds), *The pursuit of urban history* (London 1983) 421.
3. The difference between Dyos and the Dutch urban historians mentioned here, may therefore not be so great as it seems. According to Dyos urban history not only differs from local history, or from social, municipal, or economic history, but also from any other form of history. See H. J. Dyos, 'Urbanity and suburbanity', in D. Cannadine and D. Reeder (eds), *Exploring the urban past. Essays in urban history by H. J. Dyos* (Cambridge 1982), p. 36. See also: R. Rodger, 'Theory, practice and European urban history', in R. Rodger (ed.), *European urban history. Prospect and retrospect* (Leicester, London 1993), p. 3.

4. P. R. D. Stokvis, 'Moderne stadsgeschiedenis, een nieuwe sub-discipline', *Spiegel Historiael* (1986): 333–8 and F. A. M. Messing, 'Stand van Zaken: een inleidend overzicht', in P. A. M. Geurts and F. A. M. Messing (eds), *Theoretische en methodologische aspecten van de economische en sociale geschiedenis I. Geschiedenis in veelvoud* 7 (The Hague 1979) pp. 1–53; see especially pp. 30–3.

5. P. Kooij, *Stadsgeschiedenis* (Zutphen 1989), p. 8. See also: P. Kooij, 'Stad en platteland', in F. L. van Holthoon (ed.), *De Nederlandse samenleving sinds 1815* (Assen 1985), pp. 93–119.

6. E. E. Lampard, 'The history of cities in the economic advanced areas', in idem, *Economic development and cultural change* III (1955), pp. 81–136; idem, 'American historians and the study of urbanization', *American Historical Review* LXVII (Oct. 1961): 49–91; idem, 'Urbanization and social change; on broadening the scope and relevance of urban history', in O. Handlin and J. Burchard (eds), *The historian and the city* (Cambridge, MA 1963); idem, 'Historical aspects of urbanization' in P. M. Hauser and L. F. Schnore (eds), *The study of urbanization* (New York 1965), pp. 519–54; idem, 'The evolving system of cities in the United States, urbanization and economic development', in H. S. Perloff and L. Wingo jr. (eds), *Issues in urban economics* (Baltimore, MD 1968), pp. 81–140; idem, 'The dimensions of urban history, a footnote to the "urban crisis"', *Pacific Historical Review* (1970): 261–78; idem, 'The urbanizing world' in H. J. Dyos and M. Wolff (eds), *The Victorian city. Images and realities* (London, Boston 1973); idem, 'The nature of urbanization', in D. Fraser and A. Sutcliffe (eds), *The pursuit of urban history* (London 1983), pp. 3–53.

7. P. Kooij, *Stadsgeschiedenis*, p. 8.

8. Ibid. p. 9.

9. See volumes like D. Fraser and A. Sutcliffe, *The pursuit of urban history* (London, 1983) and R. J. Morris and R. Rodger, *The Victorian city. A reader in British urban history 1820–1914* (London, New York 1993).

10. The somewhat closed, actionistic 'independent' approach to urban history sees the town as an entity in itself. It is the form of urban history Zane Miller called the 'cultural approach'. Lubove saw it as the history of the city-building process. See Bruce M. Stave, 'A view from the United States', in Fraser and Sutcliffe (eds), *The pursuit of urban history*, p. 419. By 'biographical' I mean a conception of the city as a cohesive and active social body. I do not ascribe it the 'descriptive' and 'non-interactional' connotation Dyos and Rodger

assign to it. See: R. Rodger, 'Theory, practice and European urban history', pp. 2–3.

The more open, behavioral approach has already been outlined above, where I referred to Kooij and Lampard. It is a kind of urban history in which the city is a subsystem of a more comprehensive system. In England Abrams and Pahl advocated this approach (as we shall see Abrams interpretation of Weber as an advocate of such an approach is, to say the least, not very fortunate'): R. Pahl, *Whose city?* (London 1970); P. Abrams, 'Towns and economic growth: some theories and problems', in P. Abrams and E. A. Wrigley (eds), *Towns in societies. Essays in economic history and historical sociology* (Cambridge 1978). See also R. J. Morris and R. Rodger, *The Victorian city. A reader in British urban history 1820–1914*, pp. 11-12.

11. F. Braudel, *Civilisation matérielle, économie et capitalisme. XVe–XVIIIe siècle* (Paris 1979): Part 1: *Les structures du quotidien: le possible et l'impossible*; Part 2: *Les jeux de l'échange*; Part 3: *Le temps du monde*. The translated passages are from the English edition: *Capitalism and material life 1400–1800*, trans. Miriam Kochan (London 1973).

12. 'Toute ville est, se veut un monde à part': F. Braudel, *Civilisation matérielle, économie et capitalisme*. Part 1: *Les structures du quotidien: le possible et l'impossible*, p. 376 (Kochan trans., p. 382).

13. Ibid., p. 446: 'Les villes . . . sont toutes les produits de leur civilisations.' Abrams and Pahl also see logical inconsistencies between Braudel's initial assertion 'a town is a town wherever it is' and his later comment 'the town in the end is what society, economy and politics allow it to be'. They are astonished that Braudel himself has overlooked this problem: R. E. Pahl, 'Pursuing the urban of "urban" sociology', in Fraser and Sutcliffe (eds) *The pursuit of urban history*, p. 379 and P. Abrams, 'Introduction', in P. Abrams and E. A. Wrigley, *Towns in societies*.

14. H. L. Wesseling, 'Fernand Braudel', in A. H. Huussen jr., E. H. Kossmann and H. Renner (eds), *Historici van de twintigste eeuw* (Utrecht, Antwerp, Amsterdam 1981), p. 240.

15. Kochan trans., p. 441.

16. Braudel was not the only one. Dyos also got caught in the pitfalls of the urban conception. I shall comment on that in sections 6 and 7 of this chapter.

17. K. Marx and F. Engels, 'Die deutsche Ideologie. Kritik der neuesten deutschen Philosophie in ihren Repräsentanten Feuerbach, B. Bauer und Stirner, und des deutschen Sozialismus in seinen verschiedenen

Propheten', in *Marx–Engels Werke 3*, ed. Institut für Marxismus-Leninismus beim ZK der SED (Berlin 1969), p. 50. Referred to henceforth as *MEW*.

18. Ibid., p. 51. While he was writing his critique of Feuerbach, Marx was embroiled in a fierce dispute with the *Freien*, a Berlin group of Young Hegelian thinkers of whom the brothers Bauer and Max Stirner were the leading lights. He was not yet, however, wholly free of their terminology.

19. Shlomo Avineri, *The social and political thought of Karl Marx* (Cambridge 1970), p. 157: 'Thus the structure of the late medieval town cannot be reduced to its material components.'

20. H. Lefebvre, *La pensée marxiste et la ville* (Paris 1972), p. 41.

21. G. W. F. Hegel, *Grundlinien der Philosophie des Rechts*, ed. H. Reichelt (Frankfurt 1972), p. 218 (para. 259).

22. 'Ici le Sujet de l'histoire, c'est incontestablement la ville': H. Lefebvre, *La pensée marxiste et la ville*, p. 45.

23. K. Marx, 'Die Deutsche Ideologie', *MEW* 3, p. 50.

24. H. Lefebvre, *La pensée marxiste et la ville*, pp. 72–4

25. Ibid., p. 81.

26. Lefebvre and another French urban Marxist, Manuel Castell [*The urban question* (London 1977)] greatly influenced urban sociologists in England and the USA in the seventies and early eighties of the twentieth century. See e.g. D. Harvey, *Social justice and the city* (London 1973). They all advocated a concept in which the town figured as a dependent variable of capitalism and urbanism. See A. Sutcliffe, 'In search of the urban variable: Britain in the later nineteenth century', in Fraser and Sutcliffe (eds), *The pursuit of urban history* pp. 236 and 243.

27. F. Engels, 'Die Lage der Arbeitende Klasse in England. Nach eigner Anschauung und authentischen Quellen', in *MEW* 2, pp. 225–650, esp. pp. 254–5.

28. 'It is a struggle of all against all, a Hobbesian world [. . .] people regard each other only as useful objects; each exploits the other, and the end of it all is, that the stronger treads the weaker under foot, and that the powerful few, the capitalists, seize everything for themselves, while to the weak many, the poor, scarcely a bare existence remains': *MEW* 2, p. 257 (McClennan edition, p. 37).

29. *MEW* 2, p. 255. Central to Engels's analysis of the nineteenth-century town is the dialectical unity of bourgeoisie and proletariat. The misery of the proletariat is necessary to provide the bourgeoisie with luxury. According to Engels, this dialectical connection is also expressed in

the morphology of the industrial town. The office and shopping streets of the bourgeoisie function as screens to camouflage the wretched workers' neighbourhoods. The shops and workplaces of the *petite bourgeoisie* in particular are intended 'to conceal from the eyes of the wealthy men and women of strong stomachs and weak nerves the misery and grime which form the complement of their wealth'. *MEW 2*, p. 279. The translation is by Florence Kelley-Wischnewetsky (1887), *The condition of the working class in England*, ed. David McClennan (Oxford 1993) p. 58.

30. Most contemporary English Marxist urban historians conceive the (nineteenth-century) city as a dependent variable of capitalist society. See e.g.: G. Stedman Jones, *Outcast London. A study of the relationships between classes in Victorian society* (Oxford 1971), J. Foster, *Class struggle and the industrial revolution. Early industrial capitalism in three English towns* (London 1974) and T. Koditschek, *Class formation and urban-industrial society. Bradford 1750–1850* (Cambridge 1990).

31. R. Vaughan, *The age of great cities . . . or modern society viewed in its relation to intelligence, morals and religion* (London 1843). See P. Clark, P. Burke, and P. Slack, *The urban setting* (Walton Hall 1977), pp. 20 and G. Davison, 'The city as a natural system', in Fraser and Sutcliffe (eds), *The pursuit of urban history*, pp. 355–7. Vaughan here takes a similar position to that of Marx in 1844.

32. B. Disraeli, *Coningsby*. ed. A. Briggs (New York 1962 [1st edn. 1844]) p. 133. See also: A. Briggs, *Victorian cities* (2nd edn, Harmondsworth 1968) p. 92, and P. Clarke et al., *The urban setting*, p. 22.

33. A. Lees, 'Critics of urban society in Germany, 1854–1914', *Journal of the History of Ideas* XL (1979): 61–83, esp. 78 and idem, 'Perceptions of cities in Britain and Germany 1820–1914', in Fraser and Sutcliffe (eds), *The pursuit of urban history*, pp. 151–66.

34. A. Lees, 'Critics of urban society in Germany', pp. 63–4.

35. A similar approach in: E. Howard, *Tomorrow: a peaceful path to real reform* (London 1898). See also: Clark, *The urban setting*, p. 24 and A. Sutcliffe, 'In search of the urban variable', in Fraser and Sutcliffe (eds), *The pursuit of urban history* p. 241.

36. Clark, *The urban setting*, p. 24.

37. W. Diamond, 'On the dangers of an urban interpretation of history', in F. Goldman (ed.), *Historiography and urbanization. Essays in American history in honour of W. Stult Holt*, (Port Washington NY 1968 [1941]) pp. 67–108, esp. p. 71.

38. Ibid., p. 72.

39. R. P. Appelbaum, *Theories of social change* (Boston, Dallas, London 1970), and J. A. Banks, 'The contagion of numbers', in H. J. Dyos and M. Wolff, *The Victorian city* I (London 1973), pp. 105–22, esp. 110–13.

40. P. Burke, 'Urban history and urban anthropology of early modern Europe', in Fraser and Sutcliffe (eds), *The pursuit of urban history*, p. 80.

41. R. E. Park, E. W. Burgess, R. D. McKenzie, *The city*, ed. M. Janowitz (Chicago 1967 [1926]), p. 4. Critical remarks on the urban concept of the Chicago school can be found in R. E. Pahl, 'Pursuing the urban of "urban" sociology', pp. 372–73.

42. The centre (the CBD = Central Business District) was ringed by four zones, the first of which contained the very poorest neighbourhoods. This was the world of immigrants, criminals, and coloured population groups. The second zone was inhabited by the lower-middle and working class. The third and fourth zones were the residential areas for the middle and higher layers of the population, with their neat single-family homes. Every zone stood on its own and maintained virtually no links with other parts of the city.

43. M. P. Smith, *The city and social theory* (Oxford 1980), p. 44.

44. R. P. Appelbaum, *Theories of social change*, pp. 28–9.

45. Having said this I realize that there is a strong similarity between Wirth and the urbanist Vaughan. The latter assumed that the improvement of communication facilities (roads, railways, newspapers) made urban evils better known and in doing so helped to combat them. According to Vaughan, the history of great cities is pre-eminently the history of social experiment. Wirth perceived the urban problems in the same way, and saw planning as the solution: R. Vaughan, *Age of great cities*, p. 61. See also: G. Davison, 'The city as a "natural system"', p. 356.

46. A. M. Schlesinger, 'The city in American history', *Mississippi Valley Historical Review* XXVII (1940): 43.

47. Ibid., *passim*, esp. p. 57. See also: W. Diamond, 'On the dangers of an urban interpretation of history', p. 96.

48. A. M. Schlesinger, *The rise of the city 1878–1898* (New York 1933), p. 435. See also: W. Diamond, 'On the dangers of an urban interpretation of history', p. 93.

49. W. Diamond, 'On the dangers of an urban interpretation of history', p. 89.

50. Ibid., p. 101.

51. Ibid., p. 105.

52. Ibid., p. 104.

53. Ibid., p. 107, and R. A. Mohl, 'The history of the American city', in *The reinterpretation of American history and culture*, ed. W. H. Cartwright and R. L. Watson jr. (Washington, DC 1973), p. 166.

54. Z. L. Miller, C. Griffen and G. Stelter, 'Urban history in North America', *Urban History Yearbook* (1977): 8–9.

55. H. E. Tisdale, 'The process of urbanization', *Social Forces* 10 (1942): 311–16. See also J. de Vries, *European urbanization 1500–1800* (London 1984), pp. 10–11, 32.

56. P. Kooij, 'Het gewest uitgetest I. Theorieën en modellen voor de regionale geschiedenis', *Groniek* 16 (s.a. no.76): 14.

57. N. S. B. Gras, 'The development of metropolitan economy in Europe and America', *American Historical Review* XXVII (1922): 695–708. See also: W. Diamond, 'On the dangers of an urban interpretation of history', pp. 85–6.

58. P. Kooij, 'Het gewest uitgetest', p. 138.

59. C. Lesger, 'Hiërarchie en spreiding van regionale verzorgingscentra. Het centrale plaatsensysteem in Holland benoorden het Y omstreeks 1800', *Tijdschrift van Sociale Geschiedenis* 16 (2) (1990): 128–53. Thus Lesger finds a wide divergence between Christaller's model and the actual spread of central places in Holland north of the Y around 1800: ibid., p. 142.

60. E. E. Lampard, 'Urbanization and social change: on broadening the scope and relevance of urban history', in O. Handlin and J. Burchard (eds), *The historian and the city* (Cambridge, MA 1963), p. 233.

61. Ibid., p. 237.

62. L. Mumford, *The culture of cities* (New York 1938).

63. L. Mumford, *The city in history. (Origins, its transformation and its prospects*. Harmondsworth 1979 [1961]), p. 101; see also p. 117.

64. A. Briggs, *Victorian cities* (2nd edn, Harmondsworth 1968), pp. 33–4 and elsewhere. That Briggs here takes a position opposed to Mumford's depiction of nineteenth-century English cities as 'Coketowns' does not detract from the theoretical similarity of their views of the city.

65. D. Cannadine, 'Conclusion. The "Dyos phenomenon" and after', in D. Cannadine and D. Reeder (eds), *Exploring the urban past. Essays in urban history by H. J. Dyos* (Cambridge 1982), pp. 211–12.

66. E. P. Thompson, 'Responses to reality', *New Society*, 4 October 1973. See also Cannadine, 'Conclusion', p. 209.

67. Ibid., p. 208. See also: H. J. Dyos, 'Editorial', *Urban History Yearbook* (1974): 5–6 and R. Rodger, 'Theory, practice and European urban history', p. 2.

68. Dyos preferred to write about 'speculative builders' and 'urban developers' rather than about 'fluctuations in house rents' or 'building cycles'. See e.g. H. J. Dyos, 'The speculative builders and developers of Victorian London' and 'A Victorian speculative builder: Edward Yates', in D. Cannadine and D. Reeder (eds), *Exploring the urban past*, pp. 179–202 and see also: D. Reeder, 'Introduction', in *Exploring the urban past*, p. xiii.

69. See e.g. H. J. Dyos, 'Urbanity and suburbanity', p. 33.

70. Ibid.

71. D. Cannadine, 'Conclusion', p. 219. Incidently, not all of the above-mentioned 'new urban historians' approached their work in the way described here. Warner, Katz and Blumin were more `urban' than Thernstrom and his followers.

72. Z. L. Miller *et al.*, 'Urban history in North America', p. 15.

73. O. Handlin, 'The modern city as a field of historical study', in O. Handlin and J. Burchard (eds), *The historian and the city* (Cambridge, MA 1963), p. 2.

74. Ibid., p. 8.

75. Ibid., pp. 2–5.

76. A. Briggs, *Victorian cities*; S. M. Blumin, *The urban threshold. Growth and change in a nineteenth-century American community* (Chicago 1976); D. Fraser, *Power and authority in the Victorian city* (Oxford 1979) and idem, *Urban politics in Victorian England. The structure of politics in Victorian cities* (2nd edn, London 1979); M. Frisch, *Town into city. Springfield Massachusetts and the meaning of community 1840–1880* (Cambridge, MA 1972) and idem, 'The community elite and the emergence of urban politics', in: S. Thernstrom and R. Sennet (eds), *Nineteenth-century cities: essays in the new urban history* (New Haven, CT 1976 [1969]), pp. 277–96.

77. C. Haase, *Die Enstehung der Westfälischen Städte* 3rd edn (Munster 1965).

78. E. Ennen, 'Die Stadt zwischen Mittelalter und Gegenwart', *Rheinische Vierteljahrsblätter* 30 (1968): 118–31.

79. P. Abrams, 'Towns and economic growth: Some theories and problems', in Abrams and Wrigley (eds), *Towns in societies*, pp. 9–33.

80. Ibid., p. 17.

81. Ibid., p. 19.

82. Ibid., p. 20.

83. See e.g. E. A. Wrigley, 'The town in a pre-industrial economy', in Abrams and Wrigley (eds), *Towns in societies*, p. 304 and M. J.

Daunton, 'Towns and economic growth in eighteenth century England', ibid., p. 276.

84. G. Abramowski, *Das Geschichtsbild Max Webers. Universalgeschichte am Leitfaden des okzidentalen Rationalisierungsprozesses* (Stuttgart 1966), p. 83; B. A. G. M. Tromp, 'De sociologie van de stad bij Max Weber', in *Max Weber. Zijn leven, werk en betekenis*, ed. H. P. H. Goddijn (Baarn 1980), pp. 113–33, esp. pp. 121 and 130.

85. It is unfortunate that Abrams's misinterpretation of Weber has had a great impact on many English urban historians and urban sociologists. See e.g. A. Sutcliffe, 'In search of the urban variable. Britain in the later nineteenth century', in Fraser and Sutcliffe (eds), *The pursuit of urban history*, p. 235: R. E. Pahl, 'Pursuing the urban of "urban" sociology', ibid., p. 379 and R. J. Morris and R. Rodger (eds), *The Victorian city*, pp. 2 and 16.

86. A. Edel, *Analyzing concepts in social science. Part 1, Science, Ideology and Value* (New Brunswick, NJ 1979).

87. Kooij speaks of the antithetical approach within urban history and observes that the cultural–mental and some of the 'older sociologically tinted' urban studies proceed from such a definition of the town. In these works, Kooij says accusingly, the town functions 'as a centre of wickedness and decay, creator of unrest and individual problems, which threatens the happy life of the countryside': P. Kooij, 'Het gewest uitgetest', p. 14.

88. Edel: 'Of course, we can trim it by removing some of the disturbing dimensions – if we do not have to remove too many – or else by pulling back some of the jagged points and accepting the consequences': A. Edel, *Analyzing concepts in social science*, p. 97.

89. Ibid., pp. 101–3.

90. Ibid., esp. pp. 32–3.

91. For a comprehensive inventory of complementary studies covering the history of town–country relations see: G. A. Hoekveld, 'Theoretische aanzetten ten behoeve van het samenstellen van maatschappijhistorische modellen van de verhouding van stad en platteland in de nieuwe geschiedenis van Noord west-Europa', *Economisch en Sociaal-historisch Jaarboek* 38 (1975): 1–47.

Part II
Relatively-Closed and Half-Open Systems

'It is one of the main objectives of General Systems Theory to enable one specialist to catch relevant communications from the others.'

K. L. Boulding, 'General Systems Theory – The Skeleton of Science', p. 199.

-3-

Relatively-Closed Systems and a World Full of Black Boxes

In the preceding chapter we discovered how the manner of definition determines to a great extent how cities are both analysed, and, especially, synthesized in urban historiography. In addition to analysis, synthesis is, after all, an important aspect of historical writing. This is certainly true for urban historiography, because cities are complex phenomena that cannot be reduced to one singular characteristic. A city is, after all, not merely a number of inhabitants or an agglomeration of non-agrarian activities. Cities are wholes in which demographic, economic, social, political and cultural aspects are closely interwoven. These parts of urban life should be differentiated, but not separated. This maxim makes research concerning cities in general, and urban historiographical research in particular, very demanding.

Another important aspect of the synthesizing work of the urban historian is the manner of explanation. In order to make a deeper exploration of this aspect we shall call upon systems theory. Systems theory has an eye for the synthesis of the whole, as well as for the analysis of the parts. Boulding does not call systems theory the 'skeleton of science' without reason.[1] This study on urban historical synthesis will therefore use systems theory as the methodological warehouse from which it will proceed. This warehouse has an extensive arsenal of shelves and trays where various coagulants for synthetical use can be stored. For example: it is noteworthy that theoretical historians as dissimilar as Berkhofer, Topolski and Von Wright regularly draw from systems theory to defend their respective positivistic and (moderately) hermeneutic positions. Even narrativists such as Ankersmit and Mink at times cannot resist the temptation. Nevertheless, for most historians systems theory is somewhat awkward material, owing to its modernistic, or rather positivistic, origin. Hopefully philosophers and historians will once again become better acquainted with this manner of thought, now that we have passed postmodernism.[2]

The central question in this chapter is: Which types of systems can a historian use if he proceeds from a dichotomous method of definition? Before getting into the answer to that question, I shall make some general remarks concerning the use of systems theory in the historical and social sciences.

Systems-theoretical interpretations

Berkhofer uses categories of systems theory in his plea for a social scientific approach, which he calls behaviouristic, towards historical practice.[3] Von Wright defends a hermeneutic approach towards the humanities by way of systems-theoretical analysis.[4] Systems theory apparently offers a spacious structure for the analysis of historiography in general and, in particular, urban historiography in all its diversity. It therefore seems natural to use the work of these authors as the starting-point of an exposition of the systems-theoretical approach I use.

Berkhofer sums up several questions with which systems theoreticians occupy themselves. Among his inventory the following can be found: What is a system? What are its boundaries? Of which elements is it composed? Do sub-systems exist? How can a system take a constant shape?[5] He considers several definitions and ultimately decides to differentiate between two major categories of systems theories, which he calls mechanical and organic. The mechanical conception of a system proceeds from the thought that the whole is equal to the sum of its parts and that a certain balance between the whole and the parts is evident. Organic systems theory is based on the idea that the whole is more than the sum of the parts, and that the parts and the whole are involved in a constant process of transformation. The mechanical conception of systems is mainly oriented towards classical physics; the organic conception of systems towards biology.[6] Berkhofer may be an advocate of a systems-theoretical approach towards history, but he himself does not choose between the two model types.

In addition to the ideas of Berkhofer, those of Henrik von Wright are also important to my topic. Von Wright argues against the positivistic explanatory model (explanation) and proposes an actionistic or, in other words, a moderately-hermeneutic explanatory model (understanding). In his defence he chooses to proceed from a systems-theoretical premise, which is also of import to my analysis. Von Wright describes a system as a state/space, an initial state, several stages of development and several alternatives for every stage. He considers this definition to deviate from the customary one, yet states that they are related.[7]

Conspicuous in Von Wright's definition is his recognition of both a static (the state/space) and a dynamic (development stages) element in systems. Although he does not use the terms 'mechanical' and 'organic', the similarities with Berkhofer are striking.

Proceeding from the above I arrive at the following definition of systems. Systems are efficacious wholes that consist of elements. There are either actual or potential relationships between these elements, and they can therefore interact. Change within and of the system is therefore possible.[8]

This definition is mainly directed towards the internal characteristics of systems. The relationship between the system and its environment is not considered. Talcott Parsons points towards a way of eluding this problem. He has noted that systems can influence their environment and can be influenced by their environment. That systems can influence their environment means that systems can function as independent (i.e. explanatory) variables for phenomena occurring outside them. The influence a system is subjected to from its environment can reduce it to a dependent variable; but this does not always have to be the case. One of the characteristics of systems is, after all, the maintenance of their boundaries. Through this characteristic they incline towards maintaining their status as an independent variable. Systems with weaker boundary maintenance capacities have the status of a dependent variable, or may even disintegrate. In these cases we are concerned with half-open and open systems.

The fact that coherent systems in particular have a strong tendency to maintain the integrity of their boundaries is self-evident. Coherent systems maintain a sharp dichotomy between themselves and their environment. With this characterization the question arises of whether the dichotomously-conceived cities encountered in the preceding chapter possess strong integration properties. Urban historians who work with a dichotomous conception of cities seldom use the term 'closed system'. That cities nevertheless can be fitted into a construction of this type will be shown in this chapter and in Chapters 5 and 6.

Systems wholly incapable of boundary maintenance stand in opposition to coherent systems. We are then dealing with complete influence of the environment on the system – in other words, the system is totally open. According to the economically-oriented cybernetician Hagan, all systems as they occur in reality are open. He adds, however, that with regard to research a system is an intellectual construct. What is or isn't a system is up to the researcher.[9] Because I am at present discussing a type of system developed by researchers, I shall consider those systems incapable of any boundary maintenance, and changing as the environment changes, to be open. In the next chapter I shall examine these 'open systems' and their importance for urban historiography at greater length.

Systems exist for which the activities are determined by given conditions in the environment. This does not necessarily mean that the system completely lacks boundary maintenance, and therefore lacks identity. It only means that in order to understand some of the activities of such a system, systematic knowledge of the environment is necessary.[10] As a result, relationships between the environment and the system could become the subject of systematic research. In that case the environment becomes a system of which the original system is a sub-system. In the following I shall call such system/sub-system constructions 'half-open' systems. As the influence of the environment becomes more specific, or rather, as the need of the researcher to specify further the influence of the environment increases, the terminology also changes. Mitchel and Hall respectively speak of a central system and a centralized sub-system. Mitchel notes that the central system guides the sub-systems and supplies them with possibilities for future behaviour.[11]

Not only is the concept of a half-open system often encountered in urban historiography, but it is also often explicated in terms of system and sub-system. Schmal clearly expresses this in the following quotation: 'The most important property that can be attributed to this kind of complex urban system as a totality is that *the system is the dominant factor* in the location and growth of every economic or social activity within it.'[12] The theories of Christaller and Lampard mentioned in the preceding chapter can be counted among those applying a half-open systems approach. In Chapters 7 and 8 the meaning of the construct 'half-open system' for urban historiography is explicated in more detail.

In the rest of this chapter, the examination of closed systems is the main topic.

A world full of black boxes

Because of their structure, closed systems are relatively unsusceptible to outside influences, indicating strong boundary maintenance and a large measure of coherence. With regard to transformation properties, this means that the function of goal attainment, also mentioned by Talcott Parsons, is strongly present in closed systems. The property 'goal attainment' and its role in procedures of explanation will be demonstrated by analysing the elements of which a closed system consists.

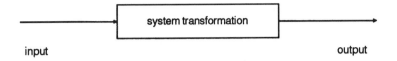

Figure 3. Hare's black box

The smallest element of a closed system is a black box. A black box is a closed system in its most elementary form. This means that any explanation of the transformation in such a system using more than one external factor and any internal factors at all is inadequate. The systems theoretician Hare depicts the operation of a black box in the following manner.[13]

A black box is supposed to embody either an invariable or a law-like relationship. Law-like relationships differ from invariable relationships by their probabilistic nature. In the case of invariable relationships, there is a connection between two phenomena, p and q, in which p, which acts as input, always results in the output q. The predictive nature lies in the fact that all p's are always accompanied by q. In the case of law-like relationships, *always* should be replaced by *in many cases*.

If I note that my car radiator is damaged, that its temperature is x degrees below zero and that there is not enough anti-freeze in it, I use, in order to explain this phenomenon, either a black box comprising a law that states that car radiators without anti-freeze *always* burst if the temperature is x degrees below zero, or a black box comprising a law-like relationship that states that car radiators are *usually* damaged at a temperature of x degrees below zero. This case of a broken car radiator concerns itself with a given condition, namely a certain temperature below zero (x) and a car radiator with insufficient or no anti-freeze (p) that is broken (q). The process from p to q happens (*a.*) empirically, that is to say it can be experienced in reality (especially if it is a cold winter's day and one's presence is desired twenty kilometres further down the road); (*b.*) mechanically, that is to say without human interference; and (*c.*) in a forward direction as far as time is concerned.

This last aspect is of importance because black boxes play an eminent role in thinking and writing[14] about, as well as in explaining, acts. Acts are marked by significant intentional, teleological and finalistic aspects. The Finnish-English philosopher of science Henrik von Wright in particular has drawn attention to the fact that acts can only be understood and explained if one knows their associated intentions and goals (*telos* is the Greek word for goal).[15] Acts, however, also have unintended consequences. That is the reason that, in addition to the goals, one must consider the consequences and endings of acts. Here the finalistic aspect becomes important. Teleology and finalism have their forward direction in common.[16] That is why the observation that black boxes are marked by a forward directionality may be considered significant. I shall return to the problems regarding teleology and finalism later. Because the *functionality* of black boxes is pre-eminent in the description above, and because the transformation in black boxes takes place *without human intervention*, we call these black boxes *mechanical*.

Law-like relationships are concerned with probabilistic predictions, which can be empirical as well as conceptual in nature. As we have seen above, empirical probabilistic black boxes differ from black boxes with an invariable relationship between input and output in the fact that the predictive capacity of the former is weaker than that of the latter. Conceptual probabilistic relations belong to the domain of knowledge. These in particular require consideration at greater length. Conceptual probabilistic predictions are what Rex Martin has called 'generic assertions of intelligible connection',[17] that is to say: experiential knowledge of regularities in reality (hence *mechanical* black boxes) on the basis of which these conceptual, probabilistic relationships become *comprehensible*. Without such knowledge we could not act. In systems-theoretical terms, we call such nomological knowledge an *intentional* black box. Von Wright, as we know, used a logic of acts based on systems theory. In the following I wish to follow his lead, although I shall be making a significant amendment to his systems-theoretical ideas. Von Wright applied the notions of systems theory only to the exterior aspects of human action, not to the internal intentional aspects.[18] With intentional black boxes, I shall expand systems-theoretical thought regarding acts to cover the *internal* aspects of those acts as well. In order to clarify the combination of Von Wright's systems-theoretical approach towards acts and the amendments developed by myself, in the footsteps of the American Rex Martin and the Dutchman Chiel Van den Akker, I give the example of opening a window. This act can be dissected into several elements to which units of time can be coupled. This is because acts are, after all, marked by a certain temporal course.[19]

Time	Example	Action terminology
T1	An actor finds himself in a stuffy room and concludes	Observation of state of affairs and finding or

	that an open window would alleviate this condition.	establishing the goal of the act
T2	The actor carries out the act of opening the window.	The act
T3	The result of the act is an open window.	Result of the act + temporary new state of affairs–object of intention
T4	Musty air flows outside, fresh flows inside	Effect + mechanical function
T5	The actor finds himself in a refreshed room	Consequence of the act + envisaged final situation

It is assumed to be clear that a mechanical black box is operating in T4. In T3, the open window is the input of a black box that comprises the physical law that the musty air, which is lighter due to its warmth, will rise (outside) and the heavier cold air will fall (inside). The output of this black box is a consequence of this act: fresh air in the room. This black box shows a great resemblance to the one concerning the car radiator. The intentional black box is more difficult to find. It is hidden in T1. T1 can be subdivided into four units of time:

T1.1	The actor notes that he/she is in a stuffy room.	Observation of state of affairs and judgement of affairs as undesirable
T1.2	He/she wishes to end this stuffiness.	Intention to act in order to remedy the undesirable state of affairs.
T1.3	He/she knows a law-like relation: open window, hence fresh air, or: warm air, hence rising, and cold air, hence falling	a. Contemplation of possible means to remedy state of affairs b. Contemplation of nomological knowledge about these possible means (this involves reasoning as to the relative ease or difficulty and the relative efficaciousness of particular available alternative means)

T1.4	The actor knows what he/she must do: open the window	Intention to perform goal-oriented act

If we interpret this in terms of the logic of systems theory, we see in T1.2 the input of an *intentional* black box; the nomological knowledge of T1.3 is concerned with the black box itself, and T1.4, comprising the intention of goal oriented behaviour, is the output of the black box.[20] Here the importance of goal attainment, which was noted at the beginning of this chapter, becomes evident. Van den Akker notes that steps T1.1 through to T1.4 form the four premises of a practical syllogism, while T2, the act itself, can be seen as the conclusion of such a syllogism.[21]

Several matters are important when dealing with intentional black boxes. They have things in common with mechanical black boxes; for they are both black boxes, but there are also differences. The most important difference is that a mechanical black box is empirically efficacious, while an intentional black box concerns itself not with efficacy but with knowledge: to be precise with knowledge of the regularities working in a mechanical black box. In the example of opening the window, a regularity is enclosed in the mechanical black box comprising the rising warm air and the falling of the cold air; in the intentional black box the knowledge of this regularity or even of the natural law itself is enclosed. The example also suggests that the intentional black box is dependent on the mechanical one. One can only possess knowledge of nature if one already has experienced or discovered these regularities. This dependence should not be overestimated. We shall see that mechanical black boxes can to a certain extent also be dependent on intentional ones. Nevertheless, it should be noted that in the act itself intentional black boxes are always coupled to mechanical ones.[22]

We must shift from the level of actor to that of researcher in order to note another important difference between mechanical and intentional black boxes. A researcher attempts to explain phenomena, among which there are also acts. Explanation can proceed by seeking out the intentions and goals of acts, or by searching for causes of phenomena. We could now say that intentional black boxes contain (goal-oriented) intentions and mechanical black boxes causal relationships. These are *prima facie* two clearly-differentiated forms of explanation. Because both mechanical and intentional black boxes are involved in the explanation of acts, this could cause some confusion. Can acts only be teleologically explained, or are they also causal? Here we have arrived at an important point of contention among theoreticians of science. In the following, I wish to show that by indicating teleological as well as causal elements in the explanation of acts, we can discover that in the explanation of acts not only are teleological and causal elements simultaneously present, but also hybrid forms, which we may call quasi-causal and quasi-teleological.

Because intentions are inalienably linked to acts, it is said that intentions cannot be viewed as the causes of acts.[23] Although this proposition comes from Von Wright, he himself immediately moderates it. Even though intentions cannot be viewed as the causes of acts, they can be placed in a practical syllogism, which does seem to indicate a certain type of causal relationship.[24] In this context Von Wright speaks of a quasi-causal relationship, which he ultimately qualifies as conceptual.[25]

Rex Martin has tried to specify further the causal aspect of teleological explanations. He did this by linking Collingwood's well-known procedure of re-enactment of past thought for ascertaining the intentions of acts to Von Wright's teleological explanatory procedure. Characteristic of the re-enactment procedure is the datum that the historian asks himself which problem and/or which situation with which the actor was confronted caused him to act as he did. The historian can find the intention – not through empathy, as the traditional nineteenth-century, mainly German, hermeneuticians would have it, but through his ability to solve problems – and thereby the meaning of an act. Martin labelled this empathic procedure with the letter R for re-enactment.[26] It is a concrete procedure that does not relate in any way to a Humean law. This procedure offers no justification for an explanation, and is therefore far removed from any form of positivism. By way of this procedure, the researcher places himself in the situation of the actor as best he can.[27] Here the researcher maintains an actor's point of view. The following syllogism taken from Martin (who in turn appropriated it from Collingwood) can clarify this.[28]

Premise 1   After conquering Gaul, Caesar was confronted with raids from Britain.

Premise 2   Caesar wanted to change this situation, in other words solve this problem.

Premise 3   Caesar thought that an invasion of Britain would be a solution.

Conclusion Caesar invaded Britain

In addition to R, Martin also used R′, which was derived from Von Wright. R′ is a reasoning backward from the conclusion or *consequens* to the premises or *antecedentia*. In doing this, the researcher leaves the actor's point of view and returns to an observer's point of view. R′ thus becomes a paradigm or model of conceiving actions.[29] As such it is part of a pattern of inferences I have called a relatively-closed system.

Law-like reasoning plays an important role in such a system. In this respect it is of concern to see how the step is made from the undirected will to act in premise 2 to the goal-oriented act of premise 3. This actually lies in the following hypothetical generalization: if rulers are confronted with foreign plunderers, an armed invasion of that foreign country is probably the most adequate measure for ending these raids. This generalization can be added to R as a fourth premise.[30] With this, the four premises almost necessarily lead to the conclusion that it is now, in essence, a case of an *if* (the four premises) – *then* (conclusion) relationship. The fourth premise seems to be a law-like construction and is actually nothing less than an intentional black box.[31]

The relation between intention and act is still the subject of an extensive scientific debate. It would take too long to explicate this *in extenso*. I should like to observe that in the above-mentioned example concerning the opening of a window, a distinction is made between the input of the intention to act (T1.2) – the intentional black box with nomological knowledge regarding the mechanics of cold and warm air (T1.3) – and its output, namely the intention of acting in an effective manner (T1.4). One could say that there is no causal relationship between the intention to act effectively and the act itself (i.e. between T1.4 and T2), because there is no external relationship, and it can therefore be neither verified nor falsified. After all, only the act is external. The intention is so inalienably linked to the act that it cannot be conceived without it, because the intention only manifests itself in the act. The relationship between the intention to act (T1.2) and the intention to act effectively (T1.4) is another matter. Between these two there is a link constituted by the fourth premise of R noted above. To return to systems-theoretical terminology, this is a case of an intentional black box (T1.3). The intentional black box carries the rule justifying the relationship. Although this may be an internal and therefore unfalsifiable relationship,[32] it remains a case of two elements of action that can be clearly differentiated and that are even linked by a law-like relationship, which gives this relationship at least the appearance of being causal. This solves the problem that Von Wright, Collingwood, and Martin wrestled with, namely that explanations of acts on the one hand are intentional and therefore a-causal and, on the other hand, can be captured in a syllogism, which presupposes a causal relationship.[33]

The example of opening a window suggests another difference between intentional and mechanical black boxes. Intentional black boxes seem dependent on mechanical black boxes for their existence. I have already remarked upon this above. The intentional black box, which contains experiential knowledge of the behaviour of warm and cold air, is dependent for this knowledge on the mechanical black box embodying this behaviour. There are, however, other intentional black boxes in addition to those containing nomological knowledge of physics. The example of Caesar and the plunderers from Britain already pointed in that direction. In his aforementioned article 'Determinism and the study of man', Von Wright answers the question as to the possibility of what I should like to refer to as 'cultural–mechanical black boxes'. By people's participation in various social-cultural relationships, they are bound to various rules and prescriptions that work in the same manner as the aforementioned 'natural' mechanical black boxes. Through the internalization of values, norms and obligations in various socialization processes (and especially in education), these social rules can exert a coercive force almost equal to that of physical laws.

Von Wright, however, amends this statement by noting a difference between mechanisms (in my terminology, mechanical black boxes) in nature and those in culture. Physical black boxes hold *semper et ubique*. Cultural mechanisms do not hold everywhere and always and, therefore, they can change under the influence of human action. This differentiation lies, I believe, in an eighteenth-century notion of physical laws. Einstein's relativity theory and Heisenberg's indeterminacy theorem[34] show that the *semper et ubique* of natural laws can also be questioned. In a sense, natural laws, as laws – that is to say as forms of knowledge – are a consequence of human design, are thereby linked to culture, and are therefore mutable. In addition, mechanical black boxes usually contain not invariable but probabilistic law-like relationships, making the *semper et ubique* even more questionable.

The difference lies not so much between nature and culture as between action in nature and action in culture. This difference is based on a different relationship between intentional and mechanical black boxes within culture on the one hand and nature on the other. In nature, there is usually a singular relationship between mechanical and intentional black boxes. There the intentional black boxes are solely dependent on mechanical black boxes. The intentional black boxes only contain knowledge regarding the workings of the mechanical ones. They can amend these workings or interpret them in a totally different manner; they can even manipulate the workings of the mechanical black boxes, but they usually cannot change anything about them. When Einstein amends the theory of gravitation by noting that gravity in the universe works in a completely different manner at the speed of light than here on earth, this does not automatically change the manner in which roof tiles will fall here on Earth. It is therefore wise during storms and avalanches to think not of the relativity theory but of the simple laws of gravity, or, even better, to seek safe shelter.

Within culture, a reciprocal relationship is possible between mechanical and intentional black boxes. Despite the coercive force that values, norms, social obligations and role patterns can exert on a participant in culture, and despite the fact that these can be fixed in mechanical black boxes, a reversal can occur in the relationship between these two forms of black boxes. Intentional black boxes can assign new forms of regularity to mechanical black boxes. Patterns of marriage and reproduction, the workings of the market, and political and diplomatic strategies may exist for centuries as regularly-functioning mechanisms, but the manner in which they function can change, either abruptly or gradually, as a result of the creation of new intentional black boxes (for example: processes of secularization). Intentional black boxes change from entities deriving their meaning from mechanical black boxes to entities giving meaning to mechanical black boxes. Other examples of the genesis of cultural mechanisms through intentional processes are concentration and accumulation processes in the economy, which may have originated with the introduction of an *Erwerbwirtschaft* (aiming for a maximization of profit) as a replacement for a *Bedarfdeckungswirtschaft* (seeking to cover basic needs), or a shift from *ausserweltliche* to *innerweltliche Askese* (ascetism outside of the world [as in the case of a monk] and that within the world) (Weber). Traffic jams and environmental pollution are examples of cultural mechanisms in traffic. Because the car was viewed not only as a means of transportation but also as a status symbol, these intractable cultural mechanisms came into existence.

These types of 'mechanization processes' in culture are a consequence of the collective human desire for money, power, status, security, health, and safety. Social obligations (discipline) can also lead to such cultural mechanisms.[35] The fact that these mechanisms have usually not originated in individual intentions but in collective ones justifies their being placed in intentional black boxes. In this manner it becomes clear how intentional black boxes can generate new mechanical ones. Interference between intentional and mechanical black boxes is possible. Teleological relationships can 'deteriorate' to quasi-teleological ones.[36] By examining this process we can get a better perspective on the unintended consequences of acts.

In addition to teleological and quasi-teleological relationships, acts, as we know, also have causal and quasi-causal elements. This indicates that the differentiation between intentional and mechanical black boxes, albeit important, should be considered only relatively important.

The collective and possibly active character of intentional black boxes is also relevant for other reasons. These black boxes supply the infrastructure of what Ricoeur calls the *appartenance participative* within the domain of culture and the acts that play a role in it.[37] People live in various cultural communities, which are sometimes more and sometimes less institutionalized. They are part of what Ricoeur has called *entités de premier ordre*.[38] He counts states, nations, associations, and cultures as well as cities among such entities. By participating in these entities, people act – to use Von Wright's words – 'in conformity with rules such as the laws of a state or the codes of morality and good manners or customs and traditions'.[39] Despite Ricoeur's not referring to this passage by Von Wright, the infrastructure of the *appartenance participative* lies enclosed within the meaning of this sentence, and with it the interference between intentional and mechanical black boxes with regard to culture. This problem will also be dealt with later.

By means of the systems theory of acts presented here, Von Wright's systems-theoretical analysis of the *external* dimension of action is augmented by a systems-theoretical analysis of its *internal* dimension.

During all this, it should not be forgotten that, in addition to intentional and mechanical black boxes, a third factor is important, namely the actor himself. The role of the actor will be dealt with extensively in the remainder of this study. I refer here to the actor in order to complete the picture of a closed system – the topic of this chapter. The term 'closed system' should not be taken too literally. The initial point of a closed system is open. Various external influences can activate a closed system. Furthermore, actors can make appraisals of their situations and can design new intentions, ideas, or the like. By doing this, they remove direct linearity from the black boxes.[40] Because actors can get their ideas from anywhere and everywhere, the insularity of these (closed) systems should be taken with a grain of salt. The insularity merely indicates that the actors exercise their influence in a certain context, which is relatively closed for research purposes.[41] On grounds of the possibly unpredictable intentions of the actors, rigid forms of determinism and evolutionism have justifiably been combated within the historical sciences.

However, it cannot be claimed that actors are always complete masters of their own fate. They are bound by the circumstances in which they find themselves when generating new intentions. Their actions can be determined by the practical inferences that they *could* draw under the circumstances. 'Could' here has a determinative as well as a self-determining connotation: determinative because the circumstances do not allow any practical inference whatsoever, and self-determining because there is usually no mechanical, coercive relationship between circumstances and the actor. This means that explaining human action is always linked to the explication of the system within which this action occurred.[42]

Links between actors and black boxes have not only an explanatory but also a synthesizing value.[43] After all, they string events together. That is also the reason why so much attention is paid here to the bonding properties of black boxes.

The level of synthesis

With the above, I hope to have made clear that the role of (quasi-)causal relationships *within* teleological explanations is not unimportant. Nevertheless, it should be observed that when viewing these explanations the explanatory effect lies mainly in the intention. In the aforementioned example of opening the window, 'getting fresh air' is a case in point. Here it is the motive that ultimately determines why the window is opened, and not laws regarding warm and cold air, nor the knowledge of these laws. In the case of teleological explanations, just as among intentional explanations, a subsequent phenomenon is not explained by its antecedent, but the subsequent phenomenon explains its antecedent.[44] This gives teleological explanations a finalistic character. Closed systems are constructions with forward-directed dynamics, used by historians to describe the past in a finalistic manner. Such constructions are inspired in the historian by the more or less favourable position he has with regard to the events in the past he wishes to describe.

Danto has drawn attention to the three temporal positions with which the historian is concerned when describing the past. These are:

1. the position in time of the event described;
2. the position in time of another event that is described in relation to the event described in (1); and
3. the position in time of the person who describes.

The sentence 'In 1717 the writer of the *Neveu de Rameau* was born', for example, clarifies these three positions. In 1717 (1) nobody could have written such a sentence, because nobody at that time knew that Diderot would later write a book with that title (2). A historian can write such a sentence because he can survey Diderot's life until his death (3). In the previous sentence, two elements of that life are important:

The book that Diderot wrote, which was titled *Neveu de Rameau* (2), and
Diderot's date of birth (1).

These two data mean that the book *Neveu de Rameau* is a necessary condition for the significance of the year 1717 in the context of writing. It should also be noted that the book appeared after Diderot's date of birth.[45]

I call the closed-system construction, of which the aforementioned statement regarding Diderot is a manifestation, finalistic. The term 'finalistic' in this context concerns itself with the nature of historical writing and not with an actionist method of explanation. This implies that the synthesizing historical writer concerns himself not only with the intentions of acts, but also with those results unforeseen by the actors. This marks an important difference between teleology and finalism.[46]

The American philosopher of history Mandelbaum and, following in his footsteps, the French philosopher Ricoeur distinguish between analytical and synthetic historical writing. Using their distinction we could say that the four explanatory methods, labelled as I have observed them in the closed-system construction as 'teleological', 'quasi-teleological', 'causal', and 'quasi-causal', belong to the domain of analytical historical writing. The strong dominance of teleology in such closed-system constructions leads to a mildly hermeneutic explanatory pattern. This pattern is mainly concerned with the actor's point of view. On this level it can be important that the historian, in so far as possible, takes the perspective of the historical actors themselves, though we have seen that explanation sometimes also demands an observer's point of view.

Something else must be done at the level of synthesis. Without completely distancing himself from the analysis, the historian should decide which black boxes will completely disappear from his synthesis, which deserve to be mentioned but should remain unopened, and which must be opened. These decisions are dependent on the construction of the closed system. For the historian, the end-point of the historical process he wishes to describe will be the lodestone for his decisions. In most cases the end-point of the process will have been unknown to the actors themselves. Still, they will have realized that they played a part in it. In many cases the *faits et gestes* of the actors will be given a new meaning by the historian in the light of later events. That is why the historian with his finalism shows some resemblance to Hegel's *List der Vernunft* [Cunning of Reason]. Hegel was of the opinion that the rationality of the acts of historical individuals only becomes visible when the historical processes are completed and philosophy has described and analysed them.

What seemed without reason and meaning to the actors turns out to have been a 'trick' of the *Weltgeist* [World Spirit] in order to effectuate progress in rationality.[47] Without directly making an appeal for a new form of speculative philosophy of history, the philosopher of history Fain posits that, on the basis of the finalistic character of synthesizing historical writing, it is natural that historians should let themselves be inspired by philosophers of history.[48]

Closed systems have a teleological stamp on the analysis level. They form an even more expansive closed system on the level of synthesis, and at that point acquire a more or less finalistic character. Although finality concerns itself with the consequences of intentions which, to the actors, are unknown and unintended, the historian can construct 'actors' that can, as it were, pursue a certain development. We are concerned here with social entities, which the American philosopher of history Mandelbaum called 'continuing entities' and which Ricoeur called 'entités de premier ordre'. The 'acts' of these actors are marked by a teleology, or rather finality, that cannot always be understood by the individual actors. They are not directed towards a concrete goal, but are the result of a process or, to put it in systems-theoretical terminology, the achievement of an output. This means that the output determines to a great extent which (quasi-)teleological and (quasi-)causal relationships at the level of analysis should be given particular attention during synthesis.

Knowledge of 'acts' of supra-personal actors or, even better, their finality can lead to a better understanding of the acts and intentions of the individual participants in a collective actor of this type. The intentions cannot always be directly distilled from the motivations the actors themselves give for their actions. When the American journalist Joseph Kraft travelled in the entourage of President Nixon on his visit to China, he visited an automobile factory in Beijing. While doing this he tried to ascertain the motivation of one of the managers of the factory for increasing the production of the factory. Throughout the factory slogans by Mao were hung. Kraft describes his attempts as follows:

> The manager, Mister Ching, observed that the production of jeeps had recently doubled from five to ten thousand. I made several attempts to find out how Mao's ideas had helped him do this. The first time I asked this question, I was shown how front grills were dipped into a paint bath by means of a conveyor belt. In the past, I was told, they were spray-painted one by one. When I asked my question again, I was shown a machine from western Germany with which wires could be pulled. After that I gave up my efforts and asked Mister Ching what influence the Cultural Revolution had had on the factory.'[49]

Kraft saw no relationship between the ideas of Mao as a motive for action and procuring a new machine as a result of the motive. He did not realize that the actions of the manager were directed towards the achievement of a national production programme with a socialist stamp. Mao's ideas made the socialist production programme acceptable to China and, in doing this, presented the manager with the motivation for his action. In this case, knowledge of the finality of the collective actor China offers a clarification in a simple way of the motives of the individual actor Ching.[50] In this manner, teleology and finality have close mutual ties.

This is also the case for other reasons. It is not only the historian who views events with hindsight, as Danto and Carr remarked: every acting individual in daily life does so. An actor tries, through the formulation of goals, to anticipate the future. He even attempts, while anticipating the consequences of his actions, to develop a kind of hindsight. Thus there is also a reasonably strong analogy between the positions of the actor and the historian, between teleology and finality.[51] Of course it should immediately be noted here that this 'as if' retrospection is vastly different from the real hindsight of the historian. That is why we speak of teleology with regard to the former and finality with regard to the latter.[52]

Weber's ideal types

In order to ensure that the reader is not withheld an urban-historical illustration of this theoretical exposition for too long, I shall use Weber's ideal type of the classical city to show how such a finalistic construction is achieved. Certain precautionary measures should be taken to prevent describing oversimplified and directly linear processes. Input and output should carefully be constructed, and the finality should not infringe upon the (quasi-)causal and (quasi-)teleological relationships on the level of analysis.

Weber distinguishes between three urban ideal types: the Asiatic, the classical, and the medieval city. These are mental constructs reducing the pluriformity of historical reality in the light of a particular line of inquiry to those elements that are most efficacious for the examination.[53] Because during this selection one may speak of 'a unilateral accentuation of one or more points of view'[54] to form a coherent image, the ideal type is a dichotomous concept. This dichotomous concept has a heuristic function because it separates possible and impossible relationships. Ideal types 'are fabrications in which we construct correlations under the guise of *objective possibility*'.[55] As such, ideal types can act excellently as input.

The answer to the question of how something is possible forms the premise of an ideal type and the input of a closed system.

In order to understand the history of cities in ancient times, Weber begins with market-places with a mainly agrarian-feudal form of society, based on the power of knights with large landholdings, who also have important income from trade.[56] The organization of such a 'city' is based on the presence of tribal or clan organizations. The heads of houses and their families are free; the inhabitants of the cities, themselves, are not. The feudal polis forms the ideal type of the input. The output is formed by the ideal type of the classical polis. In contrast to the members of the feudal polis, the members of the classical polis were in the first place 'citizens' (*Demos*) and only secondarily members of a family, tribe, gens, class and so on. They formed a community on the basis of inhabiting a common territory, in which they created rational law and self-government by means of communal institutions. To do this the citizens appointed administrators from their midst (*Autonomie* and *Autokephalie*). The difference between an aristocratic polis and the classical city determines the finality of the closed system connecting the aristocratic polis of the eighth century BC and the civil polis of the fifth century BC. This finality functions as a searchlight on the events occurring between the eighth and fifth centuries. The aristocratic polis may still have been based on clan relationships (*Personal-gentilische Gliederung*), but in this period local cult communities had already come into existence in which the *Synoikismos*, in other words the community of those who lived together, was celebrated. Although non-necessary, such communities, which were not bound to persons, clans or tribes, were non-redundant prerequisites for forming territorially-bound urban communities. The demolition of the power of the aristocracy, the rise of the hoplite polis and after that of a plebeian class, which was tied to neither clans nor tribes (*sippenlos Plebs*) engendered a further disintegration of the pre-urban communal ties and a consolidation of individual urban citizenship.[57]

Weber brings the finality of the ideal type of the classical city into even sharper relief by comparing it to an ideal type which lies even closer to the period of the historian: the medieval city. As with the classical city, the medieval city is characterized by free and (administratively) independent citizens. However, the status of the citizens is mainly determined by their economic position. For the classical citizen, his status is differently determined. He is more of a *zoön politikon*, while the medieval citizen should be considered more of a *homo economicus*.

Because the ideal type of the classical city acts as output of the process of development of the aristocratic polis, its finality is sought in the actions of the civilians of the polis, which have a military-civilian character. To show this Weber remarks that various events and actions in the history of the classical *poleis* (for Weber this mainly means Athens and Rome[58]) assume a political-military guise. This development is especially distinguished by the expansion of the military authority to non-aristocrats. Thus hoplites, soldiers descended from the bourgeoisie or farmers, came into existence. Because of the many wars with neighbouring peoples, more and more troops were needed for the army and the fleet, making expansion of citizenship to socially lower groups (for example the 'thetes') necessary. All these developments ensured, according to Weber, that the polis of the fifth century BC developed into 'the most perfect military organization that antiquity brought forth'.[59]

The political-military aspect occupied such a prominent place among all the characteristics of the classical city that economic life was also permeated by it. To the extent that one may speak of capitalism in the classical period, it was a profiteer's and booty capitalism. Capitalists earned their capital by the provision of military equipment to the state or by selling slaves, which had been captured in the many wars. Trade could barely be distinguished from piracy, nor land seizure from just plain robbery. Political-military building projects and taxes were easy pickings for respectively wealthy lenders and tax collectors. Capitalism was military and political: ' it (the capitalism) was, as it were, only indirectly economic: the political ebb and flow of the polis with its various opportunities for renting governmental office, snatching people and (especially in Rome) seizing land, was its element'.[60]

In all areas of this society Weber directs his actors and black boxes towards the fulfilment of the military-civilian ideal type of the classical polis. This finality gives coherence to actions as well as black boxes, which play a role in the synthesis of the polis. Thus Weber lets such diverse and dispersed historical data as cult communities, the granting of a political voice to hoplites and thetes, the phenomenon of leasing tax collection, government contracts, capturing slaves and so on converge in a closed-system construction having the explicitly-formulated ideal type of the warrior-citizen and his community, the polis, as output.

In particular Weber's *zweckrationales Handeln* [goal-oriented action] forms the teleological basis for the finalistic manner of consideration evident in his urban ideal types. Here finalism ensues from the ideal types, which are after-the-fact conceptual constructions of the historical researcher. They should not be seen as the concrete ideals, ethical norms or ideologies of the actors operating in the past.[61] The ideal type is a model of social-cultural relationships, with its own logic, in the light of which acts of individuals or groups from the past can be interpreted. This interpretation ensues from acts being placed within a larger whole and, hence, receiving a certain directionality. The finalistic level of synthesis is explicitly present in Weber's works. Smelser has observed that actors are given intentions and goals in Weber's work by means of ideal types.[62] Whether they really maintained these intentions and goals can only be partially determined. And even if this is possible, it must still be double-checked by 'normal' procedures of explanation.[63] That is why the ideal type can, in most cases, be conceived of as a 'neutral analytical concept'.[64] In Chapter 5, I shall return to the finalistic character of closed systems and to the often non-teleological explanatory moments in Weber's city types.

Partial systems or aspect systems[65]

Systems theoretically, Weber's ideal types can be interpreted as an instrument for relating the different domains in which human actions figure. Partial systems divide the system in layers, where every layer contains states of affairs related by their nature and the category to which they belong. Examples of such layers are population, technical development, economy, social life, politics, mentality, culture and so on.[66] In the example of the classical polis, phenomena from the cultural–mental, social- and political-aspect systems, represented respectively by the cult communities, the hoplites and the leasing of tax collection, have been synthesized in the ideal type of the military–civil polis. I have not yet exhaustively treated the problem of sub-systems. When discussing half-open systems in the next chapter, I shall expand on this subject. The same holds more or less for closed-system construction as a whole. This also will be given much attention in the following chapters.

   In summary, we can say that closed systems are built up of actors and black boxes, and that the working of a closed system is directed towards the internal achievement of an output. This tendency towards output gives closed systems a finalistic manner of working sustained by the (quasi-) teleological and (quasi-)causal explanatory patterns used in the analysis. This, however, does not mean that teleology and finalism may be confused with one another. In the case of teleology, emphasis lies on the intentional element in the explanation. Von Wright does not remark without reason that a teleological explanation brings with it an intentional form of understanding.[67] In the case of finalism, less attention is paid to the intentions and more attention is paid to the unknown and unintended consequences and end-points of the acts. Teleology partially originates from an actor's point of view; finalism does not completely leave an actionist view of the past behind, but because the historian is not an actor himself, the viewpoint of the observer is not alien to him. Because observers tend to analyse events by seeking their antecedents, (quasi-) causal explanations are often used during the synthesis. The historian who wishes to write syntheses places forward-directed (forward-directed because of their finalistic nature) dynamics in his synthesis without completely letting go of the backtracking element of the (quasi-)causal explanation. Speaking for all synthesizing historians, Mink says: 'We retrace forward what we have already traced backward.'[68] I shall use Weber's singular causal imputations as a guide to explain this at first sight somewhat cryptic statement in Chapter 5.

Closed systems suggest an internal working. The internal character of closed systems has not been dealt with in this chapter. This, too, will be treated in Chapter 5.

In opposition to closed systems stand open and half-open systems. The basic principles of these two types of systems will first be dealt with now, before we return at greater length to the closed system construction in Part 3.

Notes

1. K. Boulding, 'General systems theory: the skeleton of science', *Management Science* 2 (3) (1956): 197–208, esp. p. 197. See also: B. J. L. Berry, 'Cities as systems within systems of cities', *Papers of the Regional Science Association* 13 (1964): 147–63, esp. p. 158.
2. A. A. Van den Braembussche, *Voorbij het postmodernisme. Bedenkingen aan gene zijde van het fin de siècle* [Past postmodernism. Considerations on the opposite side of the *fin de siècle*] (Best 1996).
3. R. F. Berkhofer, *A behavioral approach to historical analysis* (New York, London 1969), esp. pp. 169–210.
4. G. H. Von Wright, *Explanation and understanding* (New York 1971).
5. Berkhofer, *A behavioral approach to historical analysis*, p. 174.
6. Ibid., pp. 173–83.
7. Von Wright, *Explanation and understanding*, pp. 49–50 and 185 note 2. He considers the definition formulated by Hall and Fagen in 1956 to be such a traditional definition that it reads as follows: 'a system is a class of elements with a coordinated set of relations': A. D. Hall

and R. E. Fagen, 'Definitions of systems', in W. Buckley (ed.), *Modern systems research for the behavioral scientist: a sourcebook* (Chicago 1968), p. 81.

8. The 'potential relationships' in this definition are the equivalent of Von Wright's alternative stages.

9. E. E. Hagan, *On the theory of social change: how economic growth begins* (Cambridge, MA 1962), p. 507. See also: Berkhofer, *A behavioral approach*, p. 81.

10. R. F. Berkhofer, *A behavioral approach*, p. 181.

11. W. H. Mitchel, 'Relevant neoscientifc management notions', in S. Optner (ed.), *Systems analysis* (Harmondsworth 1973), pp. 305–24.

12. H. Schmal, 'Epilogue: one subject, many views', in H. Schmal (ed.), *Patterns of European urbanization since 1500* (London 1981), pp. 288–307, esp. p. 295.

13. V. C. Hare, *Systems analysis: a diagnostic approach* (New York 1967), p. 20.

14. In order to understand the intentions of acts, these acts must be described. 'To understand behaviour as intentional, I shall say, is to fit it into a "story" about an agent': G. H. Von Wright 'Determinism and the study of man', in I. Manninen and R. Tuomela (eds), *Essays on explanation and understanding. Foundations of humanities and social sciences* (Dordrecht 1976), p. 423.

15. The extent to which intentions and goals of acts are interwoven is evinced by Von Wright's statement: 'in order to become teleologically explicable, one could say behaviour must first be intentionally understood': G. H. Von Wright, *Explanation and understanding*, p. 121.

16. Teleology and finalism are often used as synonyms. An example of this usage is the fact that both Christian and Marxist historical writing has been called teleological or finalistic. It will soon become apparent that the terms 'teleological' and 'finalistic' are not used this way in the above, and therefore are not synonyms as I use them.

17. R. Martin, *Historical explanation. Re-enactment and practical inference* (Ithaca, NY and London 1977), pp. 100–2, 110–12, 120–22, 147–48, 150, 221 and 247. Martin at times also speaks of 'generic assertions of appropriateness'.

18. Von Wright, *Explanation and understanding* pp. 55 and 68–74. In Von Wright's case the relationship has been restricted to an action that interferes with the system. Von Wright does not make the action itself (partly) systematic. See also: G. H. Von Wright, *Causality and determinism* (London 1994), pp. 339–42 and 50–1.

19. The idea of the division of acts into temporal elements is derived from Ch. Van den Akker, 'De idee van de mens in het verleden. Een geschiedtheoretische analyse van de mogelijkheid handelingen van actoren te verklaren' [The idea of man in the past. A historical-theoretical analysis of the possibility of explaining the actions of actors] (Nijmegen 1996, unpublished Master's thesis), esp. pp. 44, 52, and 91.

20. The distinction between the intention to act and the intention to act purposively is derived from Ch. Van den Akker, 'De idee van de mens in het verleden', pp. 47–8 and 87–8.

21. In addition to his systems-theoretical approach, Von Wright uses the practical syllogism. See, for example, H. Von Wright, *Explanation and understanding*, pp. 96–107 and Von Wright, 'Determinism and the study of man', pp. 415–35, esp. p. 417. Although he only uses two premises, the third and fourth premises leave the principle of the syllogism intact. It is, however, the case that the fourth premise plays an important role in making the practical syllogism more or less causal. I shall discuss this point further elsewhere. The fourth premise is derived from Van den Akker, 'De idee van de mens in het verleden', pp. 87–94.

22. It will be clear to the reader that I support those authors who claim that causal and teleological explanations do not exclude but rather supplement one another. I mention without any presumption to exhaustiveness: Stegmüller, Hausman, Nagel, Hempel, and Braithwaite. See also: M. Karskens, 'Leven als anti-teleologisch begrip' [Life as anti-teleological concept], in G. Debrock (ed.), *Rationaliteit kan ook redelijk zijn. Bijdragen over het probleem van de teleologie* [Rationality can also be reasonable. Contributions on the problem of teleology] (Assen, Maastricht 1991), p. 54.

23. G. H. Von Wright *Explanation and understanding* (London 1971), pp. 103–8 and 117.

24. Ibid., pp. 121–4.

25. Von Wright, 'Determinism and the study of man', p. 422.

26. R. Martin, *Historical explanation*, p. 79.

27. Ibid., pp. 67, 77–81 and 185.

28. Ibid., p. 67.

29. Ibid., p. 198.

30. Ibid., pp. 80–81, 100 and 186.

31. Ibid., p. 99. The intentional black box also solves the problems posed by Stoutland's criticism of Davidson's causal theory of acts. Davidson posits that the reasons for action are composed of (a) an internal

preview or *pro attitude* (T1.2) before the intention to act purposively (T 1.4), and (b) knowledge of the nature of a certain action (T 1.3). According to Davidson (a) and (b) together form the *primary reason* or cause of the act. Stoutland's criticism is that (a) and (b) are not necessary and sufficient conditions for an act. After all, (a) and (b) should lead almost coercively to a certain act. This is not brought about by (a) and (b) because they do not select from the many possible conditions for an act the causally-dominant ones. The above-mentioned shift from causality between the intention to act effectively and the act itself to causality between the intention to act and the intention to act effectively (a causality that is justified by an intentional black box) ensures, precisely through this justification, that the dominant link is sought out, even though this link is not a mechanical and coercive, but a quasi-causal one. In history conditions are seldom both necessary and sufficient. Compare: D. Davidson, 'Actions, reasons and causes', *The Journal of Philosophy* 23 (1963): 685–700, and F. Stoutland, 'The causal theory of action', in J. Manninen and R. Tuomela (eds), *Essays on explanation and understanding*, pp. 271–304.

32. R. Martin, *Historical explanation*, pp. 118–19, 186 and 191.
33. R. Martin, *Historical explanation*, pp. 83 and 186.
34. J. W. McAllister, *Beauty and revolution in science* (Ithaca, NY and London 1996), p. 190.
35. G. H. Von Wright, 'Determinism and the study of man', pp. 427–32.
36. I use the term quasi-teleological somewhat differently than Von Wright, even though a more or less causal element can be discerned in both. See Von Wright, *Explanation and understanding*, pp. 139–43.
37. In the English translation of this work, called *Time and narrative,* this term is translated as 'participatory belonging'; I prefer the term 'collective participation': P. Ricoeur, *Temps et récit* (Paris 1983), pp. 275–76.
38. Ibid., pp. 273–5.
39. Von Wright, 'Determinism and the study of man', p. 419.
40. Behaviour of actors, according to Stegmüller, constitutes the difference between teleological and non-teleological explanations: W. Stegmüller, *Wissenschaftliche Erklärung und Begründung. Probleme und Resultate der Wissenschaftstheorie und analytischen Philosophie I* (Berlin, Heidelberg, New York 1969), p. 587.
41. The limits of this context are determined by the dichotomous definition of the research subject. As we shall see, Weber's ideal types are the best candidates for such definitions.

42. Compare with Topolski: 'This mean[t]s explanation of human actions as linked with an adequately-treated system within which that action took place. The concept of motivation may be interpreted so as to imply an analysis of the substratum of the external stimuli which help to shape the goals of human actions: J. Topolski, *The methodology of history* (Dordrecht 1976), p. 547.

43. As a matter of course, in this study I shall discuss only those explanations of which the synthesizing effect in urban historiography is manifest.

44. G. H. Von Wright, *Explanation and understanding*, pp. 86–9.

45. A. C. Danto, *Analytical philosophy of history* (Cambridge, London 1965), p. 183; Danto himself gives as an example 1618 as the beginning of the Thirty Years War. The example used here is derived from P. Ricoeur, *Temps et récit*, pp. 206–208 (*Time and narrative* p. 146).

46. P. Ricoeur, *Temps et récit*, p. 265. Ricoeur does not use the term 'finalism'. He does use the term *mise en intrigue* (emplotment). In addition to finalism, this term also encompasses the continued effect of the origin. Because continuing effects of the origin are accepted methodological insights, I shall not devote much attention to them in this context. Finalism is much less accepted, and hence deserves further explication. See also Chapter 9, 'Time and entity'.

47. 'die Eule der Minerva beginnt erst bei der einbrechende Dämmerung ihren Flug' [The owl of Minerva starts its flight at the fall of dusk]: G. W. F. Hegel, *Grundlinien der Philosophie des Rechts* (Suhrkamp edn, Frankfurt am Mainz 1972), pp. 28. See also Chapter 9, 'Time and entity'.

48. Fain gives a psychoanalytical explanation of this finalism. A brilliant student repeatedly failed his exam because he resisted the authority of his teachers owing to an anarchistic attitude towards life. According to the psychoanalyst the student wanted to fail subconsciously, although he himself would resist such an interpretation. Fain: 'He was quite unaware of what he was really doing, but what he was really doing could not be assessed until after the consequences of his actions figured in the redescription of them': H. Fain, *Between philosophy and history. The resurrection of speculative philosophy of history within analytic tradition* (Princeton, NJ 1970), p. 275.

49. Joseph Kraft, 'China diary', *The New Yorker* (11 March 1972): 100–13, esp. 105. Cited in R. Martin, 'G. H. Von Wright on explanation and understanding: an appraisal', *History and Theory* 19 (2) (1990): pp. 205–33, 216–17.

50. That is why Von Wright reappraised his 'Logical connection argument' after *Explanation and understanding* appeared. Understanding the intentions of the actors and their description does not nearly always directly result in a satisfactory explanation. The description of the intentions must possess some coherence. R. Martin, 'G. H. von Wright on explanation and understanding: an appraisal', pp. 205–33, esp. 216–20. In my opinion, Weber's ideal types and the finality of suprapersonal actors can be feasible instruments for creating such coherence.

51. D. Carr, 'Narrative and the real world: an argument for continuity' *History and Theory* 25 (1986): 117–31, esp. 125. Carr is too eager to identify teleological and finalistic constructions; see also Chapter 9 'Time and entity'.

52. See also Chapter 9 'Time and entities'.

53. M. Weber, *Gesammelte Aufsätze zur Wissenschaftslehre*, (4th edn; (Tübingen 1973) (abbr. *WL*), pp. 190–7 and 559–63. See also A. Giddens, *Capitalism and modern social theory. An analysis of the writings of Marx, Durkheim and Max Weber*, 3rd edn (Cambridge, London, New York, Melbourne 1975), p. 142.

54. M. Weber, *WL*, p. 191.

55. Ideal types 'sind Gebilde in welchen wir Zusammenhänge unter Verwendung der *objektiven Möglichkeit* konstruieren [italics mine]', Ibid., p. 194.

56. Besides Max Weber, *Wirtschaft und Gesellschaft*, (5th edn (Tübingen 1972) (abbr. *WuG* 1973), pp. 727–815, esp. 742 and 766–75 this sketch of the classical polis also uses M. Weber, *Wirtschaftsgeschichte. Abriss der universalen Sozial- und Wirtschaftsgeschichte*, ed. S. Hellmann and M. Palyi (Munich, Leipzig 1923) (abbr. *WG* 1923), pp. 270–89. The aristocracy sometimes had their slaves work for them in the city as artisans or retailers: M. Weber, *WuG* (1972) pp. 742 and 772–5.

57. G. Abramowski, *Das Geschichtsbild Max Webers. Universalgeschichte am Leitfaden des okzidentalen Rationalisierungsprozesses* (Stuttgart 1966), p. 98.

58. Ibid.

59. 'die volkommenste Militärorganisation, die das Altertum hervorgebracht hat': M. Weber, *WuG* p. 752 and further Abramowski, *Das Geschichtsbild Max Webers*, p. 96.

60. 'Der [capitalism: HJ] war, sozusagen, nur indirekt ökonomisch: das politische Auf und Ab der Polis mit seinem variierenden Chancen von Staatspachten, Menschen- und (speziell in Rom) Bodenraub war sein Element.' M. Weber, *Gesammelte Aufsätze zur Sozial und*

Wirtshaftsgeschichte, ed. Marianne Weber (Tübingen 1924) (abbr. *SWG*), pp. 4–39 and 271; M. Weber, *WuG* pp. 808–11; Abramowski, *Das Geschichtbild Max Webers*, p. 99; J. Love, 'Max Weber and the theory of ancient capitalism', *History and Theory* 25 (1986): 152–72).

61. J. P. Verhoogt, 'De wetenschapsopvatting en methodologie van Max Weber' [Max Weber's conception of science and methodology], in H. P. M. Goddijn, *Max Weber. Zijn leven, werk en betekenis*, (Baarn 1980) pp. 56–81, esp. p. 66.

62. He posits that Weber sees historical situations as the result of goal-directed efforts by actors. 'Stated most generally, Weber's explanatory strategy unfolds in the following way. Involvement in a given ideal-typical social or cultural relationship (for example, being a member of a charismatic community or a rational-legal bureaucracy, or believing in a kind of religious faith) constitutes a kind of *'program' for individual and group action; it orients behaviour in certain directions* (italics his) rather than others and imbues this behaviour with meaning': N. Smelser, *Methods in the social sciences* (Englewood Cliffs, NJ 1976), pp. 129–30. Smelser's perspective is understandable but can be misleading with regard to Weber's method of working with ideal types. Weber emphatically warns against confusing the ideal types with possible ideals of the historical actors. Smelser here seems to identify Weber's finalism, which is present at the level of synthesis, with teleological explanations, which can be found at the level of analysis.

63. 'Immer muss vielmehr das "Verstehen" des Zusammenhangs noch mit den sonst gewöhnliche Methoden kausaler Zurechnung, soweit möglich, kontrolliert werden' [After all the 'understanding' of the coherence must still be tested as thoroughly as possible by the commonly used methods of causal imputation]: M. Weber, *WL*, p. 428.

64. These terms have been derived from: C. H. Botter, *Produktie-management* [Production management] (Deventer 1993) p. 46.

65. J. P. Verhoogt, 'De wetenschapsopvatting en methodologie van Max Weber', p. 66. There are, as we shall see, some important exceptions to this.

66. This depiction of affairs somewhat resembles that of Fain. He, too, sees the past as a kind of closed system. He speaks of a thick, massive pipe, which is also composed of different layers. For Fain, every layer corresponds to a certain speculative philosophy of history: the layer of the history of thought with Hegel's philosophy of history

and the layer of economy to Marx's dialectic of production forces and production relationships. Because of this stratification of the past, one cannot move randomly from one layer to another, according to Fain. The exposition or narration would then become incomprehensible. Ankersmit rightly remarks that historians in practice quite easily move from layer to layer. 'Apparently the separation between layers is not as clear cut as Fain wishes us to believe': F. Ankersmit, *Narrative Logic: A semantic* analysis *of the historian's language* (Meppel 1981), pp. 45–6. This is caused by the fact that the layers that Fain is discussing are not directly related to a speculative philosophy of history, but to another specialized form of historical practice, such as economical, social, and political history, et cetera.

67. Von Wright, *Explanation and understanding*, p. 121. See note 15.
68. L. O. Mink, 'Philosophical analysis and historical understanding', *Review of Metaphysics* 20 (1968): 667–698, esp. 687.

-4-

Half-Open and Open Systems, Order and Chaos

Just as relatively-closed systems are a result of a dichotomous definition, half-open systems are the result of a complementary method of definition. This seems simple, but much is tied to it. The American philosopher of history Maurice Mandelbaum makes a distinction between synchronic and diachronic laws of history. He calls synchronic laws 'laws of functional relation' and diachronic laws 'laws of directional change'. As an example of a synchronic law, he gives Marx's statement that the superstructure of ideas and institutions is determined by the substructure of economic organization. Marx's theory of the phases of succession of production relationships is, according to Mandelbaum, an example of a diachronic law.[1] Analogous to this differentiation we could call the closed systems mentioned in the previous chapter 'directive systems' and the half-open systems, which will be discussed in this chapter, 'functional systems'. This differentiation calls attention to the fact that the operation of half-open systems is different from that of closed systems. In contrast to the diachronic operation of closed systems, half-open systems operate synchronously. This has everything to do with the structure of the latter. This structure leads – as we have remarked – to the possibility of the environment of half-open systems developing into a macro-system and the half-open system itself being 'degraded' to a sub-system. This double level can also be found in their operation. Schmal therefore states that the behaviour of half-open systems can be explained by way of the elements of which they are constituted, or by the higher systems of which they are part.[2] I have already explained above that half-open systems can be considered sub-systems of a system.[3] To this Mitchel has added the notion that the system supplies the sub-system with possibilities for future behaviour. For this reason the macro- or system level plays a major role in a large number of half-open system explanations.

The functioning of half-open systems is central to this chapter. Just as the operation of the closed system was illustrated by Weber's ideal types of classical and medieval cities, the operation of half-open systems will be illustrated by Sjoberg's models of pre-industrial and industrial cities. Subsequently, open systems will be examined, as well as their paradigmatic meaning for urban historiography. Furthermore, the important question of 'what should be considered a *partial* system in urban historiography' arises. Briggs and Lampard have answered this question. Their ideas will therefore be discussed at the end of this chapter. Finally, the question of why systems theory and not chaos theory has been used here for the analysis of urban historiography will be posed in this chapter.

The properties of half-open systems

Coherence, association and distribution

In relatively-closed systems, black boxes or combinations of black boxes, in some cases in co-operation with actors, form sub-systems that are strongly integrated in the system as a whole. The removal or addition of such a sub-system soon results in a change in the character of the system. In half-open systems the relationship between the system and the sub-system is much less tight than in closed systems. Sub-systems in half-open systems maintain, to use Talcott Parsons' terminology, their boundaries much less forcefully, and the systems do not need to preserve their patterns as persistently. Sub-systems in half-open systems are therefore easier to replace than sub-systems in closed systems. In systems-theoretical jargon, one says that sub-systems in half-open systems are more *commutative* than the sub-systems in relatively-closed systems. The inverse also holds true: sub-systems can be fitted in with greater ease at the macro-level of half-open systems than at that of closed systems. Therefore sub-systems almost necessarily must have good associative properties. Thus macro-systems have strong integrational properties and sub-systems have strong associative properties.

   In order to clarify all this, an example: in an ecological system, fish have greater associative properties with regard to water than dogs, despite the fact that water without fish is not at all unimaginable. The greater associativity of fishes is a result of their organs, which are specifically adapted to water, such as gills and fins. Dogs lack these organs, and therefore have fewer associative properties with regard to the system water, although water without fish and with dogs is entirely possible. This possibility of accommodating sub-systems in systems can be used to explain phenomena.

Von Wright furnishes the following procedure for this explanation. An event, process or state is placed in a system and is thereby given the role of explanandum (the phenomenon to be explained). Certain conditional relationships in the systems serve as explanantia (the phenomena used to explain). Von Wright calls this explanatory procedure 'causal explanation' and distinguishes it from causal analysis, which corresponds to the operation of closed systems as indicated above.[4] Causal explanations answer the question of what enables a certain phenomenon.[5] Within systems theory, the relationship between a system and a sub-system can be characterized as a relationship between necessary conditions and the phenomena they explain. Hence the necessary conditions can be viewed as integrational properties of the system with regard to the sub-system. Explanantia in the form of enveloping systems only have predictive power in special cases. They usually are not predictive but retrodictive. This means that they explain by reasoning from the explanandum back to the explanans.[6]

The reverse also holds true. Systems have distributive properties, as a result of which certain sub-systems can be assimilated more easily in that system than others. Systems are permeable for certain sub-systems and impermeable to others. Water can permeate the body of fishes more easily and more functionally (by way of the gills) than it can the body of dogs (who can moreover barely use that water in their bodies). Parsons' goal-attainment function lies in the distribution properties of systems with regard to sub-systems. However, in this case, this function is not directed 'outward' towards an end-point, but 'inward', towards the sub-system.

Partial systems or aspect systems

To what do systems owe their distributive properties? In order to answer this question the aid of partial systems must be called in. Partial systems are present in relatively-closed systems (as we have seen in the previous chapter) as well as in half-open systems. Just like sub-systems in half-open systems, partial systems are parts of the system as a whole. In contrast to sub-systems, which, despite their associative tendencies and capacities, possess their own coherence, partial systems in half-open systems lack this property completely. On the contrary: they have the tendency to spread themselves over the whole system, including all its sub-systems. Their imperialism is only halted by other sub- and partial systems. Just as in closed systems, partial systems in half-open systems have an analytical function, for they split the system into layers. Sub-systems, however, are excisions from the system, which can contain

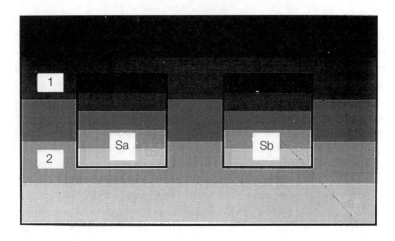

1 and 2 are partial systems
Sa = sub-system a
Sb = sub-system b

Figure 4. Partial systems and sub-systems

several such layers. In systems theory, the difference between partial systems and sub-systems is not made clear. Yet it is not unimportant. For the systems theoretical organization of the past, as composed by the historian, it is a differentiation between analytic and synthetic intentions. Partial systems split the system in layers, parts of which show an intrinsic relatedness. Sub-systems are parts of systems relating several partial systems to one another, for example in the context of certain objects of study such as the city. The following diagram (Figure 4) uses a half-open system construction to show the difference between sub-systems and partial systems.

Partial systems are parts of the system that try to integrate other system elements completely in the system. Sub-systems do endeavour to associate with the system, but also try to maintain a certain internal coherence (see Figure 4).

Sub-systems as dependent variables of systems

The dependency between systems and sub-systems is asymmetrical. Systems can lead an independent existence with regard to their sub-systems with greater ease than vice versa. Von Wright even goes so far as to claim that 'if a condition holds in the bigger system, then it also necessarily holds in the smaller system which is a fragment of it but not conversely'.[7] With this Von Wright wishes to say that conditional relationships in the system also form conditions for the sub-system. The reverse need not be the case. Schmal claims something similar with regard to (half-open) urban systems. According to him 'the system [is] the dominant factor in the location and growth of every economic or social activity within it'.[8] The origin of this asymmetrical dependency should probably be sought in the nineteenth-century sociology of Spencer and especially Durkheim. To them, that which was social was sociologically pre-existent to that which was individual. These nineteenth-century sociologists still formulated this asymmetry ontologically, while systems theoreticians actually formulate the problem in epistemological terms. This asymmetrical relationship implies that the distributive effects of the system prevail over the sub-system's tendency towards coherence.

This asymmetrical relationship also has consequences for the intentional aspects of systems. What this means is that intentional explanations take a causal form in half-open system constructions. Let us examine the following example taken from Von Wright. An archaeologist discovers a city and is impressed by the enormous stones of which the city wall is built. He wonders how the past inhabitants lifted these great blocks two metres high. In order to answer this question, he must discover the specific technology characterizing the urban culture of the city's inhabitants. The question 'how was building such a wall possible' makes the wall with colossal stones a sub-system of a system in which a certain urban culture and technology form the explanatory partial systems. This culture and this technology form the necessary conditions for building the wall and, as such, one may say there is a causal relationship, but the culture and technology are also the result of individual or collective actions and, as such, intentional or teleological.[9] The prerequisites for wall building can hence continually take another form. In the one culture the wall may be the result of techniques involving stacking, in another it may involve the use of levers. The distributive effect of systems on sub-systems is therefore marked by both causal and teleological elements.[10] In systems-theoretical explanations working with half-open system constructions, the causal explanations dominate because the intentions of the actors are derived from the properties (dispositions) of the system. The actors fulfil 'roles' imparted to them by the system in which they figure. The causal relationship thereby acquires a functionalistic character. Goals of actors become functions of systems or sub-systems. In half-open systems, such functionalistic explanations play an important role. Urban systems, which are only defined demographically or economically – or by a combination of both approaches – approximate most closely to this type.

As a consequence of the distributive functioning of the system, causal explanation occurs by reasoning backward from the sub-system to the system. It is not without reason that I have called this type of explanation 'retrodictive'.[11] One remark is pertinent here. We have observed that there are also active sub-systems. Although such sub-systems are dependent on the system for their initial operation, they may also implement changes in the system. In Chapter 8 these will be discussed.

Sjoberg's pre-industrial city

Weber, as we know, differentiated between Asiatic, classical, and medieval city types. Sjoberg differentiates between pre-industrial, transitional and industrial city types. Weber constructed his ideal types by deriving the characteristics of each type from the history of the cities themselves. Sjoberg first develops a functionalistic theory regarding the societies concerned as a whole before he examines the city itself. This theory signifies that he views society as a system determined by many partial systems, of which three play a special role, namely: technology, values and social structure.[12]

According to Sjoberg, technology is the most imperialistic of the three. If technology changes, so do forms of organization. The simple technology of pre-industrial society leads to little specialization and thereby to restricted forms of division of labour. This implies that only a small elite of non-producers can exist in the social partial system. They must therefore maintain their position of power by means of great political and religious force.[13]

The city, as a sub-system of the pre-industrial social system as described above, retains all its characteristics.[14] These characteristics are expressed in the organizational aspects of the pre-industrial city as well as in its spatial arrangement. What is noteworthy here is that the identity of the sub-system in itself is very restricted. Most of the cities concerned have between 3,000 and 100,000 inhabitants, and only in very exceptional cases does their number exceed 100,000. The functions of these cities are primarily of a religious-administrative nature, their roles in trade and crafts being secondary.

The important and powerful position of the wealthy combined with a low level of technological development, especially in the area of transport, leads to a use of space in which the elite commandeer the centre of the city and leave the periphery of the city to the lower classes. In this way the elite are close to the administrative, religious, commercial and industrial centres, and the lower classes miss this proximity.[15]

With regard to organization the pre-industrial cities are remarkable for the dominant position of guilds (which encourage harmony), the hierarchical political structure, in which an extensive system of patronage is present, and the dominant position of religion in social life, especially in education. The city as sub-system in most cases conforms itself to the encompassing social system. Here we are clearly dealing with a passive sub-system. This means that the effect of the system on the sub-system is significant. The sub-system is closely directed in its behaviour towards the determinants of the system. Although one can say there is an effect of the system on the sub-system, this does not lead to a finalistic conception of explanation, as is the case among Weber's ideal types. Here we do not observe a development from input to output, but rather an influence of the system on the sub-system. This leads to a retrodictive model of explanation. The phenomena in the sub-system 'city' are explained by reasoning backward from the sub-system to the system that underlies it. In Chapters 7 and 8 I shall discuss half-open systems more thoroughly than is possible here.

Open systems

Three grains of sand

Those systems that consist of relatively autonomous elements are open. The relationship between such elements is called 'a-serial' because there are no intermediate elements. The systems theoreticians Feibleman and Friend use three grains of sand as an example of such a system.[16] On the beach three grains of sand cannot be distinguished as a separate system. The relationship between the system elements is purely additive. In other words: the whole system is never more than the sum of its elements. A thousand grains of sand only differ from three grains of sand in that there are 997 more.[17] This example illustrates that these systems are not able to delimit and maintain their boundaries within the environment.

On the basis of their limited coherence, open systems do not show any internal process of change. Three grains of sand cannot transform themselves into twenty-five in a more or less autonomous manner. They can, however, change by way of their environment. Grains of sand can be transformed into a new 'system', for example from a heap of sand to a dune, by the wind. Owing to their lack of coherence and transformation mechanisms, Feibleman and Friend consider these types of systems borderline cases.

In chaos theory, which I shall discuss at greater length later on, we also encounter the phenomenon of an open system. There, too, the image of a heap of sand is used to illustrate the functioning of open systems.[18] Just as the last grain of sand in a heap of sand can cause an avalanche, a diminutive cause can make a system collapse to chaos, say many chaos theoreticians. That is also the reason why open systems now enjoy the attention of many researchers. In the following section I hope to show why open systems are of limited consequence for urban historiography, and in Section 5 I shall discuss the limits to the importance of open systems as they have been developed within chaos theory.

Application to urban historiography

Despite open systems' being rather uninteresting from the perspective of systems theory, they are not completely without import for urban historiography. In Chapter 2 the new urban historians were mentioned. They considered the city as merely a site or an archive, without according any specifically urban meaning to it. At that point I noted that the great helmsman of new urban history, Stephen Thernstrom, even explicitly distanced himself from the appellation 'urban historian' in 1972. All this indicates that here we are dealing with the city as an open-system construction.[19]

Such a conception of the city is diametrically opposed to that of the English historian Asa Briggs. To him the city is a supra-personal individuality with its own wholly individual characteristics. In *The other Bostonians* Thernstrom opposes Briggs's individualizing approach. Boston is not an independent identity but rather 'a fraction of the civilized world, just as its harbour was "part of the ocean"'.[20] This statement could still lead to the interpretation that Boston is considered a sub-system of a larger system. Thernstrom's own article 'Reflections on the new urban history' disabuses us of this illusion. In that article he mentions the five research themes with which new urban historians are concerned. These are: (1) migration as a purely demographic phenomenon; (2) geographic mobility, seen in the light of ethnic differences and differentiation between classes; (3) social mobility, with regard to size, gradation and trends; (4) immigration and the differences in opportunity for upward mobility; and (5) the difference in opportunities for black Americans and European immigrants.[21] These themes are all most accessible in cities, but in essence they are not typically urban phenomena.[22] They are, however, subjects that are highly amenable to quantification. That is perhaps the most important characteristic of what has come to be called 'new urban history'.[23] Cities as quantitative aggregations of the elements of which they are composed are systems-theoretically identical to a certain number of grains of sand on the beach. With regard to new urban history, Schnore even wonders whether 'new urban history' is possessed of enough unity with regard to subject-matter, hypotheses, and method to be called urban history at all. The Canadian urban historian Gilbert A. Stelter does not consider American urban historians worthy of the name. According to him, they are much too occupied with general social research: 'they don't really grapple with the question of what difference the adjective "urban" makes in the societies they are studying'.[24]

Partial systems in urban historiography

Closed and half-open systems have in common the fact that they are composed of partial systems. In urban historiography this is evident in the identical inventories of the different areas of urban-historiographical research performed by Asa Briggs, a representative of the closed-system-construction, and by Eric Lampard, a representative of the half-open systems approach. Both of these researchers distinguish between the following partial systems:[25]

1. *Population*. This comprises size, growth percentages, composition of the population with regard to age, gender and social position, and the physical distribution of the population.
2. *Topography and space*. This deals with topics such as permanent settlements and territorial expansion ('physical expansion') caused by a growing population and new means of transportation.
3. *Economy*. This covers subjects such as local job opportunities and the division of income and wealth. According to Lampard, this partial system yields the most comprehensive explanation for the concentration of people in a certain place.
4. *Social organization*. This concerns the full range of the relationships that come into existence through the daily intercourse of citizens organized in households, occupations and associations. Lampard posits that social organization is the institutional side of the economic, spatial and demographic partial systems of a city or urban agglomeration. He sees these four partial systems as a kind of substructure of urban life. The super-structure comprises:

5. *The political process.* This partial system is composed of two elements: (1) the distribution of favours and sanctions, rewards and punishments to individuals and special interest groups if called for; and (2) public services in the administrative or fiscal sense. To this the legal structure can be attributed the basis upon which the urban community as a whole – sometimes in opposition to individuals – confiscates or grants land, breaks or makes contracts, declares the rights of public institutions valid or invalid, and so on.[26]

6. *'Civic leadership'.* This partial system concerns politicians and other leaders in the urban community. They form the intermediaries between the political process on the one hand and the demographic, topographical, and economic elements on the other.

7. *'Civic culture'.* This concerns recurrent activities in the life and work of the city's inhabitants and public institutions of the government and/or private citizens concerned with upbringing, education and recreation. Politics (5) and political leadership (6), but also primary demographic issues such as birth, death and migration (1) and social organization (4) influence this system.

8. *External relations.* The relationships between a city and its environment can be economic and demographic as well as political and cultural in nature. They can be based on rivalry as well as on co-operation and be concerned with the exchange of administrative, informational and cultural services as well as material goods.

9. *The image of a city.* How do the inhabitants of a city, as well as outsiders, view the city, and what kind of 'personality' does it have?

10. *The process of city building.* With this Lampard in particular means the developments of a city with regard to buildings, streets and parks. These are developments linked mainly to technological changes with regard to transport, communication, zoning, sanitary conditions, government financing and taxation. Here physical artefacts and the fabric and form of the city are at stake. Briggs does not mention this partial system. Although Lampard has his reasons for mentioning the fabric and form of a city separately, it seems none the less quite reasonable to classify this process of city-building under the topographical or spatial partial system (2).

Noteworthy in Briggs's and Lampard's descriptions of partial systems is the fact that they do not limit themselves to delimitation, but also endeavour to indicate that there are sundry reciprocal relationships between the partial systems. Their description of partial systems is also aimed at indicating possibilities for synthesis. Despite the extensive similarities between the positions of Briggs and Lampard, there are also noteworthy differences. Lampard's attention goes mainly to the first four partial systems, to which we may also add the tenth. These four partial systems form the core of his 'human ecological framework', which he has expounded elsewhere and which I shall deal with extensively in Chapter 7.[27] Briggs considers partial systems 6 to 10 more important. He especially emphasizes the examination of the 'personality' of a city.[28] In contrast to the urban theoretician Lampard, Briggs is much more an *urban biographer*.

In this second Part of the book I have dealt with closed, half-open and open systems. Open systems will not reappear in what follows. Although they do play a role in urban historiography, they have no synthetic possibilities. For integral urban history the closed and half-open systems are of great import. They can demonstrate how a great deal of specialist urban historical research in many areas can be brought together in a synthesis. The closed-system construction achieves this by considering specialist research to be research of partial systems and by assembling these partial systems in a unitary construction; the 'city', striving towards identity. Half-open systems operate differently as constructions for synthesis. Systems of this type can achieve synthesis by indicating the relationships between the system on the one hand and the partial systems and sub-systems of which the system is composed on the other.

Systems theories and chaos theories

Terms such as 'open', 'half-open' and 'relatively-closed systems' provoke the question what the relationship is between the systems-theoretical approach offered here and an approach based on chaos theory.[29] Chaos theory, after all, also claims to work with non-closed systems.

Because many chaos theoreticians emphasize the complete openness of their systems, it would seem that there are major differences between the systems presented by myself and those systems stemming from chaos theory. Yet this is merely a superficial appearance. The openness of the systems originating from chaos theory is only concerned with two issues: the possibility of external influences and the possibility of non-linear development.[30] We shall see below that the openness of systems in chaos theory is only relative.

Because there is great deal of similarity between 'my' relatively-open systems and those of chaos theory, the question of why I prefer a systems-theoretical analysis to one that is chaos-theoretical becomes relevant. This question is all the more relevant because several authors have proposed the idea that the conflict among philosophers of history – which is over a century old – concerning the question of whether or not the historical disciplines should satisfy a positivistic model of science can be solved by chaos theory. Chaos theory, after all, modifies the conception of strict regularity and leaves much more room for contingency. Might this not offer a foundation for a convergence between the physical sciences and the humanities?

I am certainly not opposed to the convergence of the humanities and the physical sciences. Relatively-open systems even play a major part in my analysis of urban historiography. Nevertheless, chaos-theoretical aspects are of subordinate importance in my research. In this section I want to explain why I prefer a systems-theoretical analysis to a chaos-theoretical one.

With regard to the convergence of the humanities and the physical sciences, it should first be noted that many historians and philosophers of history have a one-sided view of the physical sciences. This view has a strong Newtonian bias. For many philosophers of history, the paradigm of the physical sciences is still dominated by a linear, regular conception of the world. As we saw in the Introduction, this has led to strife among philosophers of history. Some philosophers of history opined that if the historical sciences were to become a real science, they had to satisfy the causal regularity model. Hempel in particular, with his Covering Law Model (CLM), was an exponent of this position. Others did not wish to accept this model. Both those for and against CLM did not realize that even in the nineteenth century and early in the twentieth century much doubt had arisen among physical scientists with regard to the Newtonian conception of physics.[31] Among these may be counted Mach, Einstein, Niels Bohr, and Heisenberg.

This doubt led to the rise of systems theory in various disciplines, fed by the various branches of the (physical) sciences and engineering, after the Second World War.[32] Among those contributing to this development were Bateson (anthropologist, 1904–1980), Bertalanffy (biologist, 1907–1972), Ashby (cybernetician, 1903–1972) and Boulding (economist, 1909–1993). They had an eye for the dynamic, non-linear and creative character of systems. One could even say that one of the fundamentals of chaos theory, namely the fine sensitivity of the development of a system to the initial conditions upon which that development is dependent, was already formulated by Bateson when he stated: 'All creative systems necessarily exhibit sensitive dependence on initial conditions, and are therefore chaotic'.[33]

On the basis of both this and the fact that chaos-theoretical phenomena are constantly formulated in systems-theoretical terms, the statement that chaos theory is nothing other than the latest version of systems theory does not seem reckless to me.[34] It is true, however, that chaos theory observes several phenomena that have been given little or no attention in traditional systems theory. I mean, for example: *the butterfly effect, strange attractors, autopoiesis* and *fractals*. In what follows I shall discuss these chaos-theoretical peculiarities, and in the course of this discussion which I hope to elucidate several similarities with my systems analysis on the one hand and to give the reader an idea of why I consider chaos theory less apt for the study in hand on the other.

The sensitivity of dependence on initial conditions was formulated illustratively by the 'founder' of chaos theory, the meteorologist Edward Lorenz, at a conference in Washington in 1979. He used the image of a butterfly's wing in Brazil causing a tornado in Texas. Since then this has been called the 'butterfly effect'. In the historical sciences the butterfly effect has often been formulated in terms of small causes having large effects. In the relatively-closed system mentioned above concerned with the development of the Athenian polis as Weber conceived it, one could consider local cult societies from the eighth century BC to be the stroke of the butterfly's wing from which the Athenian democracy in the fifth century BC blossomed. The battle of Marathon, which I will discuss in what follows, was considered by Weber and others to be a small cause that had vast implications for Western societies and, in particular, for their democratic development.

In the above I have described open systems as those that do not have any boundary maintenance properties, as a result of which they are considered borderline cases in systems theory. From the viewpoint of chaos theoreticians, open systems seem to be crucially important. In fact, the 'open' systems of the chaos theoreticians are not as open as their name would suggest.

In particular, the Belgian Prigogine – in collaboration with Isabelle Stengers – has emphasized the importance of open systems. However, he is referring to something other than the systems mentioned above that do not have boundary maintenance properties. By 'open systems' Prigogine means systems that are constantly interacting with their environment, such as biological and social systems. Systems of this type consist of sub-systems that constantly influence one another. These are actually half-open systems. One might even think of them as relatively-closed systems, if one considers combinations of actors and black boxes such as those I observed in relatively-closed systems: sub-systems of those relatively-closed systems. The interaction of these sub-systems can, according to Prigogine, strengthen the coherence of the system, but also weaken it: 'Both deterministic and stochastic elements characterize the *history* of such a system [. . .] The mixture of necessity and chance constitute the history of the *system*' (italics HJ).[35] This is an excellent description of a relatively-closed system. If this system weakens, it can reach a point at which any form of predictability for the further development of the system is lost. At that moment one may actually no longer speak of a system, but one should speak of contingency. We shall see that relatively-closed systems are also subject to sequences of coherence and disintegration. Coherent systems have few and disintegrating systems many unintended consequences.

The point at which a system 'opts' for conserving the system or for contingency is referred to by Prigogine as the *bifurcation point* or the *singular moment*. In the singular-causal imputation, which will be discussed in the following, and its meaning for relatively-closed systems, it is fairly easy to recognize a chain of bifurcation points or singular moments pervading relatively-closed systems.

The Englishman Kaldor developed a model of restrained growth for macro-economic developments, which was later elaborated by H. W. Lorenz (not the same person as the Eduard Lorenz mentioned above) in his *Non-linear dynamical economics and chaotic motion*. This study concerns the development of capital goods (K) in combination with the development of the national income (Y), first taking K= 265 and Y= 65 as initial values and after that taking K = 266 and Y = 66 as initial values. After a relatively short period in which K and Y developed almost identically over both cases, a point arrived at which enormous divergences occurred in the further development of the initial values. (Figure 5).

The development from order to chaos as it can occur in a model of restrained growth can be depicted in the following manner. The stationary state depicts the period in which one may speak of order, of system conservation with a predictable linear development. After that a bifurcation point occurs at which the system as it develops further adopts two different values, which can increase to 4, and to 8, and ultimately end in chaos. Visualizations of doubling bifurcations take the form of the branching structures we see in nature, such as the veins of leaves, fern structures, or bronchi (Figure 6).

One of the most remarkable discoveries in chaos theory is that many chaotic developments do show a pattern when visualized. It appeared that points of bifurcation creep close to each other after some time; this is a phenomenon for which chaos theoreticians coined the term 'strange attractors'. Because of these strange attractors, cloud-like structures appeared in the visualizations of chaotic systems. Furthermore, parts of

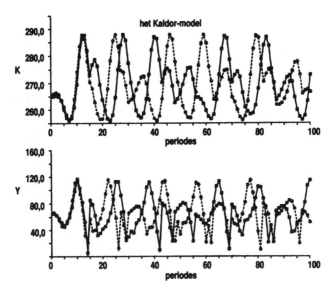

Figure 5. A chaotic development

such cloud-like structures turned out to have the same shape as the structure as a whole. These isomorphous parts of the whole are called 'fractals' in chaos theory (Julia and Mandelbrot fractals). Fractals are actually nothing other than sub-systems of apparently chaotic systems. Because chaos-theoretical terminology is not customary in urban historiography, I shall continue to use the systems-theoretical terminology of system/sub-system for half-open systems.[36] It should be noted here that these 'fractalized' sub-systems are not merely passively subjected to the operation of the system, but can also actively influence the system.

Bifurcation, strange attractors and order from chaos have all been subsumed by Prigogine under the term *autopoiesis,* or the self-organization of systems. The Englishman Zeeman and the Frenchman Thom discovered continually more order in the chaos, making the systems-theoretical character of chaos theory again noticeably evident. Thom formulated this as follows:

> Whatever is the ultimate nature of reality (assuming that this expression has meaning), it is indisputable that our universe is not chaos. We perceive beings, objects, things to which we give names. These beings or things are forms or structures endowed with a degree of stability, they take up some part of space and last for some period of time.[37]

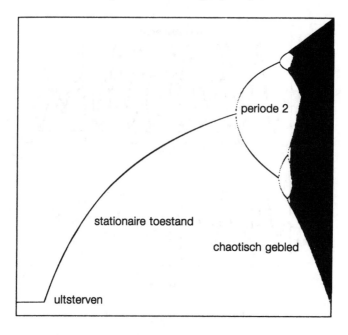

Figure 6. Order and chaos in a model of restrained growth

I consider this sufficient reason to use systems theory and not chaos theory for my analysis. But there is more.

Several historians and theoreticians of history who have occupied themselves with chaos theory still have a rather awkward attitude towards it. They appreciate that chaos theory pays special attention to contingency, but conclude from that fact that the physical sciences would do better to direct themselves towards historical narrativism rather than towards a 'chaos theory'. Thus McCloskey equates chaos theory to a non-explanatory, metaphorical ordering of statements regarding reality, thereby incorporating the physical sciences and the hard social sciences, such as economy, in the cultural sciences. Contingency and 'butterfly effects' also force the physical sciences to take a narrative approach. 'Chaos is merely the historian's way of thinking getting into science', according to McCloskey.[38] Just as historical narration depicts the chaotic reality of the past from a certain perspective, the metaphor does the same with reality in general. McCloskey leaves every form of causal thought behind and, in doing this, abandons the idea that in addition to a superstructure of images and metaphors, historical stories also have an infrastructure of arguments. He expresses a position also defended by Ankersmit.[39]

Reisch does not go as far as McCloskey. Although he also considers narrativism to be the only feasible alternative to chaos theory, he primarily identifies chaos theory with the principle of dependency on initial conditions. He sees in this a version of CLM and, according to him, CLM is unusable for the practice of history.[40] In the narrativistic alternative that Reisch designs for all this, in contrast to McCloskey he creates an infrastructure with alternatively-causal elements based on CLM on the one hand and narrativism (narrated scenes) on the other.[41] Reisch has thereby actually conceived a systems-theoretical alternative to chaos theory. Combinations of CLM-like constructions ('my' black boxes) with chaotic elements (coincidental individual decisions and circumstances) are exactly the three elements that play a role in relatively-closed systems. Relatively-closed systems are nothing more than combinations of linear and non-linear developments. Although Reisch abjures chaos theory as a model for convergence between the physical sciences and the humanities, he approaches such a model more closely than other researchers with his (unconscious) systems-theoretical approach.

Roth and Ryckman maintain the validity of causal thinking for chaos theory, but take issue with its validity for historical thought. They thereby reject the metaphorical convergence of humanities and physics envisaged by McCloskey. Chaos theory, after all, does not work with metaphors in order to master contingency. In historical practice, no covering laws, such as those proposed by Reisch, can be found: not even small ones. Convergence between the humanities and causal thought *à la* Reisch is therefore impossible in their opinion.

Michael Shermer has the greatest faith of all in the convergence of the humanities and the physical sciences on the basis of chaos-theoretical notions. He considers the alternation of contingency and necessity its most important premise. In accordance with this premise, he formulates six principles – which he calls corollaries – and seeks historical examples of them. I wish to discuss one of these. It concerns the fact that the alternation mentioned above between contingency and necessity cannot happen at just any moment. At the beginning of a development, the linearity of a certain process is less evident than at later moments. Initially, the fluttering of a butterfly can cause a typhoon; but when the tornado from Brazil strikes Texas, the fluttering of a million butterflies' wings will not stop it. As historical examples of such processes of development, Shermer gives a stock-market crash and the decline of a city, state, or empire (the Roman example).[42] Thus Shermer uses several principles from chaos theory that are wholly or partially applicable to historical practice.[43]

Shermer is right and Roth and Ryckman are wrong: chaos theory is a feasible paradigm for the convergence between the physical sciences and the humanities. This theory could be even more useful if, in contrast to McCloskey, one were to recognize that historical writing has not only a narrative superstructure, but also an explanatory infrastructure. I derive the idea of such an infrastructure from the French philosopher Paul Ricoeur, who differentiates between an argumentary infrastructure, for which he uses the term *mise en intrigue*, and the narrative superstructure, which he calls the 'plot'.[44] (I shall return to this issue later.) This infrastructure consists of orderly elements such as the small CLMs of Reisch (or the black boxes I propose) and more or less chaotic elements in the form of mini-narrations. That these two moments, respectively contingent and necessary, can be joined together in systems that satisfy the principles of order and chaos formulated by Shermer underscores the fact that systems theory is even better suited for the examination of the infrastructure of historical narratives than chaos theory.[45]

The (urban) historical methodology I seek concerns itself with how historians can examine phenomena from the past that have a 'holistic' character, and how they can give these phenomena shape as they write. This concerns itself with methodological questions such as how one should define, explain and temporally arrange.

Because of the 'holistic' character of the problem I am examining (how should an urban-historical synthesis be written), a systems-theoretical approach is more apt than a chaos-theoretical one. To that is added the fact that systems theory, with its open, half-open and relatively-closed systems, has a larger arsenal of different types of systems than chaos theory, for which a dichotomy between closed and open systems suffices. Nevertheless, as I proceed I shall direct the reader's attention where possible to the chaos-theoretical aspects in my systems-theoretical analysis of urban historiography.

Notes

1. M. Mandelbaum, 'Societal laws', in W. H. Dray (ed.), *Philosophical analysis and history* (New York 1960), pp. 330–46, esp. 333–4. Also see: Chr. Lloyd, 'Realism and structuralism in historical theory; a discussion of the thought of Maurice Mandelbaum', *History and Theory* 28 (1989): 296–325, esp. 303.

2. H. Schmal, 'Epilogue: one subject, many views', in H. Schmal (ed.), *Patterns of European urbanization since 1500* (London 1981), pp. 287–307, at p. 289.
3. A. D. Hall, 'Some fundamental concepts of systems engineering', in S. L. Optner, *Systems analysis* (Harmondsworth 1973), pp. 103–20, esp. 111.
4. 'Causal analysis should be distinguished from causal *explanation*. In the former we are given a system and try to discover conditionship relations within it. In the latter we are given an individual occurrence of some generic phenomenon (event, process, state) and look for a system within which this (generic) phenomenon, the *explanandum* may become correlated with another through some conditionship relation': G. M. von Wright, *Explanation and understanding* (New York 1971), p. 55.
5. W. Stegmüller, *Wissenschaftliche Erklärung und Begründung. Probleme und Resultate der Wissenschaftstheorie und analytischen Philosophie* (Berlin, Heidelberg, New York 1969), pp. 527–33.
6. H. Von Wright, *Explanation and understanding*, pp. 58–59.
7. H. Von Wright, *Explanation and understanding*, 53.
8. H. Schmal, 'Epilogue: one subject, many views', p. 295.
9. H. Von Wright, *Explanation and understanding,* p. 138.
10. Ibid.
11. Ibid., p. 58. Von Wright uses the term *retrodiction* in a sense somewhat different from the usual one. For example, Ankersmit and Stegmüller describe retrodiction as the mirror image of prediction; in other words: as a prediction from hindsight. Stegmüller uses the example of the discovery of a comet at a moment in time before the birth of Christ through the use of astronomical data collected after that moment (to R. Ankersmit, *Denken over geschiedenis, Een overzicht van de moderne geschiedfilosotische opvattingen* (Groningen 1984), p. 113; Stegmüller, *Wissenschaftliche Erklärung und Begründung*, p. 16). The congruence between prediction and retrodiction does not, according to Von Wright, lie in a historian's making a prediction after the fact, but in his reasoning backwards from effect to cause. This concerns itself with an explanation of necessary conditions, addressing the question of what makes a certain phenomenon possible.
12. G. Sjoberg, 'Cities in developing and in industrial societies: a cross-cultural analysis', in Ph. M. Hauser and L. F. Schnore (eds), *The study of urbanization* (New York, London, Sydney 1967), pp. 213–64, esp. 214–16.

13. Ibid., pp. 216–20.
14. 'And one of our primary assumptions is that the city cannot be understood except in its relationships to the broader society of which it is part': ibid., p. 215.
15. Ibid., p. 216.
16. J. Feibleman and J. W. Friend, 'The structure and the function of organization', in F. E. Emery, *Systems thinking*, 2nd edition (Harmondsworth 1978), pp. 30–55, esp. 32–3.
17. This example becomes contestable in the case of very large quantities: a dune with billions of grains of sand and its functioning as a defence against the sea is qualitatively something other than three grains of sand, and this holds even more true for a desert. Open systems probably merge into half-open systems in such cases.
18. M. Shermer, 'Exorcising Laplace's demon: chaos and anti-chaos, history and metahistory', *History and Theory* 34 (1995): 59–63, esp. p. 76.
19. In addition to his references to the city as a 'site' and an 'archive', the term 'dropping place' is also used to indicate that research only takes place in the city by 'coincidence'. The city itself is not the actual research subject.
20. S. Thernstrom, *The other Bostonians* (Boston 1976), pp. 220–21.
21. S. Thernstrom, 'Reflections on the new urban history', in P. A. M. Geurts and F. A. M. Messing (eds), *Theoretische en methodologische aspecten van de economische en sociale geschiedenis* II [Theoretical and methodological aspects of economic and social history] (The Hague 1979), pp. 75–90, esp. 83–9 (first published in *Daedalus* 100 (1971): 359–75).
22. Ibid., p. 78.
23. L. F. Schnore and E. E. Lampard, *The new urban history. Quantitative explorations by American historians* (Princeton, NJ 1975), pp. 4–5.
24. 'Editorial' *Urban History Yearbook* (UHY) (1980) p. 188. See also the remark by Clyde Griffin 'the "new" urban historians see themselves as having an important contribution to make to the history of cities, but *they do not presume to comprehend that subject nor to see it particularly as their domain*': Z. L. Miller, C. Griffin and G. Stelter (eds), 'Urban history in North America', *UHY* 1977, pp. 6–29, esp. 15.
25. A. Briggs, 'The study of cities' *Australian Journal of Adult Education* II (1962): 15–20; E. Lampard, 'The dimensions of urban history: a footnote to the "urban crisis"', *Pacific History Review* 39 (1970),

261–78, esp. 271–74. Briggs and Lampard don't use the term partial system'. They use expressions such as 'aspects of community life' or 'continuously interacting elements'.

26. E. Lampard, 'The dimensions of urban history', p. 274. Lampard presents this legal structure as a separate (eleventh) partial system. Briggs does not mention it. For reasons of logical economy, I have placed legal structure in the political partial system.

27. Ibid., pp. 268–9 and E. Lampard, 'Historical aspects of urbanization', in P. M. Hauser and L. F. Schnore (eds), *The study of urbanization* (New York 1965), pp. 522–4.

28. Lampard: 'Briggs stresses the importance of the "image" of a city', *The dimensions of urban history*, p. 273.

29. In the following I shall use the terms 'systems theory' and 'chaos theory'. This is not actually correct. One can only speak of systems and chaos theori*es*, but for reasons of linguistic convenience I use the singular.

30. In so far as these two aspects of openness have not yet been made clear in the systems discussed above, they will be dealt with in the following chapters.

31. It should be noted that the notion of strict regularity does not stem from Newton, but from the interpretation of his ideas given by eighteenth-century Enlightenment philosophers, including Voltaire, Lagrange and Laplace.

32. Thinking in terms of systems originated in the 1930s in the field of electronic engineering.

33. Quoted in: C. Dijkum and D. De Tombe, (eds), *Gamma chaos. Onzekerheid en orde in de menswetenschappen* [Gamma chaos. Uncertainty and order in the humanities] (Bloemendaal 1992), p. 22.

34. C. Van den Berg, 'Chaos theorie als regressietherapie. Een natuur-wetenschappelijke reflectie op de geschiedtheorie' (unpublished master thesis, Nijmegen 1998) [Chaos theory as regression therapy. A reflection on the theory of history from the perspective of the physical sciences] is inclined to a somewhat different opinion, but he bases his opinions on only a single aspect of systems theory, namely the black box. See pp. 66–71 and especially p. 70.

35. I. Prigogine and I. Stengers*, Order out of chaos. Men's new dialogues with nature* (Toronto 1984), pp. 169–70.

36. The only author who uses the term 'fractals' and indeed also uses it in the meaning of a sub-system of a half-open system is Goldstone in his *Revolution and rebellion in the early modern world* (Berkeley,

CA, Los Angeles and London 1991), pp. 46 and 346. See also H. S. J. Jansen, 'Het vergelijken vergeleken. Skocpol and Goldstone' [Comparison compared: Skocpol and Goldstone], *Theoretische Geschiedenis* 24 (3) (1997): 294/5.

37. R. Thom, *Structural stability and morphogenesis* (London 1975), p. I.

38. D. M. McCloskey, 'History, differential equations, narratio', *History and Theory* (1991): 21–36, esp. 36.

39. F. Ankersmit, *Denken over geschiedenis* [Thinking about history], p. 190. In his later work Ankersmit prefers the term 'representation' to metaphor, but the metaphorical knowing of reality does not lose importance because of this: F. Ankersmit, *De macht van de representatie. Exploraties II: Cultuurfilosofie en esthetica* [The power of representation. Explorations II: Philosophy of culture and aesthetics] (Kampen 1996), pp. 154–67.

40. Reisch's opposition to CLM is most curious. According to him CLM as Hempel originally intended it should give an explanation of historical events with a large time-span. A Hempelian historical explanation would, according to Reisch, look like this:

$$
\begin{array}{ll}
A \ E & = \text{larger-scale covering law} \\
\underline{A } & = \text{initial condition} \\
E & = \text{final state, explanandum}
\end{array}
$$

Reisch claims that a historical explanation is in reality very different:

$$
\begin{array}{llll}
A \ B & B \ C & C \ D & D \ E \qquad = \text{general principles} \\
\underline{A} \quad \ \ \underline{B} \quad \ \ \underline{C} \quad \ \ \underline{D} \qquad \ = \text{narrated scenes} \\
B \qquad C \qquad D \qquad E \qquad = \text{inferred, justified story}
\end{array}
$$

This second historical explanation uses small covering laws, which Reisch calls 'general principles', supplemented by non-lawlike information, 'narrated scenes', which do not move in one sweep from A to E but do so in smaller stages. What is remarkable is that a fervent adept of Hempel's CLM, Stegmüller, considers Reisch's second model of explanation a historic-genetic explanation, a variant of CLM that can be used in historical practice. In other words, by way of chaos theory and narrativism, Reisch nevertheless remains in positivist or, if one prefers, Newtonian waters: G. A. Reisch, 'Scientism without tears', in *History and Theory* 34 (1995): 45–58, esp. 46.

41. G. A. Reisch, 'Chaos, history and narrative', *History and Theory* 30 (1991): 1–20, esp. 18. See also Note 35 and M. Shermer, 'Exorcising Laplace's demon', p. 65.

42. M. Shermer, 'The chaos of history: on a chaotic model that represents the role of contingency and necessity in historical sequences', *Nonlinear Science Today* 2 (1993): 3–13, esp. 9.

43. M. Shermer, 'The crooked timber of history', *Complexity* 2 (1997): 23–30, esp. 24ff. See also Van den Berg, 'Chaostheorie als regressietherapie', pp. 88–9.

44. P. Ricoeur, *Time and narrative 1* (Chicago, London 1984), pp. 65–7. See also P. Ricoeur, *Temps et récit* tome 1 (Paris 1983), pp. 62 and 175–82.

45. With this I arrive at another conclusion, opposite to that of C. Van den Berg, who views chaos theory rather than systems theory as the theory that is able to achieve the convergence of the humanities and the physical sciences. See C. Van den Berg, 'Chaostheorie als regressietherapie', *passim*. Furthermore, it should be noted in this context that I am indebted for a large part of the content of this section to Van den Berg's work.

Part III
Relatively-Closed System Constructions in Urban Historiography

'. . . the explanations found in history books are a logically miscellaneous lot.' W. Dray, *Laws and explanation in history*, p. 85.

−5−

Cities as Quasi-personages:
The Long-Term Studies

In the preceding two chapters we have seen that systems theoretical interpretations of urban historiography are possible. As to the closed-system construction,[1] this implies a form of historical writing in which actors and black boxes play an important role and in which finalistically-interpreted developments are central. An important question at issue here is to what extent such a form of historiography conforms to the rules and traditions of extant historical writing. Might not, for example, the finalistic character that emerges in a closed system construction of urban historiography be contradictory to research rules? In other words: doesn't the closed system construction demand a historical-theoretical justification? These questions are legitimate, because we assume urban historiography to be, to a large extent, representative for history as a whole.

Therefore, I will first more closely examine the closed-system construction itself in this chapter. Of special importance here is the comparison between closed systems and the phenomenon 'continuing entities' introduced by Mandelbaum. Continuing entities and closed systems coincide with regard to their internal operation, but differ with regard to finality. Closed systems have finalistic dynamics, while continuing entities lack these. This raises the questions of to what extent and in what manner finalistic explanations are legitimate when seen in the light of the theory of history. These problems are dealt with in the first two sections of this chapter.

The internal, finalistic dynamics give closed systems the nature of an actor. The non-linear character of the dynamics and the possibility of growing coherence with regard to spatial organization not only gives these closed systems a great capacity for synthesis, but also identity. The question of why closed systems can act as collective subjects is hence answered in Section 3.

Because the closed-system construction is an unknown phenomenon for the empirical urban historian, uncovering these constructions in urban historiography is a rather complicated operation. For this reason the last two sections of this chapter will examine whether the characteristics, mentioned above, of closed systems are indeed present in long-term studies of cities and urban phenomena.

Internal explanations, continuing entities and 'performance systems'

It was observed in Chapter 3 that closed systems show a great deal of coherence and are built up of mechanical and intentional black boxes linked to actors. Black boxes and closed systems should not be equated to one another. Closed systems enclose several black boxes and, as such, embody a more complex type of explanation. Black boxes did not need an 'inside test' to ascertain their influence; for the operation of closed systems such an inside test *is* needed. This means that the internal links between actors and black boxes should be a topic of research when dealing with closed-system constructions.

Examination of internal developments also plays a major role with regard to the continuing entities proposed by Mandelbaum. Mandelbaum states that a general – in contrast to a specialized – historian occupies himself with individualities such as groups, organizations, communities and even cultures, which all are characterized by a certain unity, institutionality, continuity, and often locality. Here we are dealing with a unit 'possessing a degree of continuity and unity of its own'.[2] Communities such as a nation, culture, class, state, city, company and so on are all cases of continuing entities, which can often be localized on maps and which are capable of according certain roles to the individuals who are part of them (institutionalization).[3]

This all implies an internal development, which Mandelbaum tries to clarify for the reader in the following manner. If an external matter, for example an earthquake, is the cause of changes in the economic development of a country, then how these economic developments were changed by the earthquake is what is at issue in general history. No analysis is made of the earthquake itself and its destructive forces, but an attempt is made to penetrate deeper into what is happening in the continuing entity itself, in this case the economy of this particular country and nation.[4]

The systems theoretician Mitchel gives us a description of closed systems with many similarities to Mandelbaum's description of continuing entities. Mitchel makes the following statement: 'This view [that of the closed system conception, HJ] sees the organization as a dynamic entity with activities which interact, require co-ordination and control, are concerned with survival and change, and which form one element of the economic, technical and social system of the nation.'[5] Nations or their economical, technological and social components – amongst which of course are cities – are therefore organizations in which social forces showing co-ordinated interaction are at work. All this, according to Mitchel, occurs 'on a continuing basis and within some framework, which displays a greater performance than the specific interactive elements' (italics: HJ).[6] Mitchel calls these closed systems 'performance systems' and with this terms refers to the *internal* and *continuous* active nature of the process and the fact that the system as a whole shows more efficacy and potency than its elements individually.[7] This last property of Mitchel's system is comparable to the institutional character of Mandelbaum's continuing entities.

Mandelbaum and Mitchel are not completely original in constructing continuing entities and performance systems. Max Weber in *Wirtschaft und Gesellschaft*[8] and in *Gesammelte Aufsätze zur Wissenschaftslehre*[9] considers institutions and associations (*Anstalte und Verbände*) continuing entities. He calls them *perennierende Gebilde* [continuing entities, literally 'continuing forms'] and notes that individuals can participate in them on the basis of different talents, values and interests. Amongst these I mention participation on the basis of linguistic affiliation, political-governmental cohesiveness or associations grounded on common goals. Such *Perennierende Gebilde* form the infrastructure of what Weber calls 'dem historischen Individuum "höchsten" Ranges' [a historical individual of the highest rank].

As an example of such a 'first-order entity' Weber uses the German Empire. Various matters fall within the entity German Empire, such as paper documents, military terrain, ideas of diplomats and so on. We can 'conflate [these matters] to the individual concept "Deutsches Reich", because "we" give to it a definite, to "us" thoroughly unique, "interest" based on an unquantifiable "value" (which is not only political)'.[10] Here Weber emphasizes not only the role of those interested, a role that Mitchel also noted in his system construction, but also the synthetic character of his continuing entities. In this too Weber's and Mitchel's notions run parallel to those of Mandelbaum. The latter points out that in contrast to specialist history, general history must work with concepts based on continuing entities, which do not 'explain' correlations between different sub-domains (in the positivistic sense of explanation), but which should *describe* these sub-domains in relation to one another.[11] The French philosopher Paul Ricoeur appropriates Mandelbaum's concept and gives it the Weberian name *entité de premier ordre*.[12]

Finalistic, causal and teleological explanations

Finalism

The similarities between closed systems and continuing entities still lead to an important question. In Chapter 3 I called attention to the finalistic nature of closed systems. Mandelbaum's continuing entities seem to completely lack such a characteristic. Mandelbaum's recognition of an internal developmental nature in the subjects of general history is closely related to the notions on the same subject of the English philosopher of history Professor Oakeshott. He opposed a finalistic conception of historical processes.

The great importance of finalism for the closed-system approach unfolding here necessitates that we make a closer examination of Oakeshott's objections. The English professor voices objections to an organological, finalistic and evolutionistic conception of historical change. He calls a sequence of events finalistic if every event is conceived as an indispensable pre-condition for a result. Such an event is seen as the potential carrier of the result. A finalistic process is, according to Oakeshott, a process in which potentiality becomes actuality.

To illustrate this he uses the example of boiling water. The initial condition – the input – consists of the measurable data heat and water, with a known and limited capacity of water for absorbing heat. The output is the boiling water. The intermediate stages of change can be read from a thermometer. The output is, given the input, so predictable that there is barely any difference between input and output, and hence barely any real change. The same can be said of an organological change. The transformation of an acorn into an oak tree is just as predictable as the boiling of water at a certain temperature. Historical changes, according to Oakeshott, are very different by nature. 'They are an assemblage of multiform, unrelated historical events, gathered from here and there, the alleged antecedents of an outcome, itself a difference, whose unknown and unforeseeable character they circumstantially converge to compose.'[13] Historical changes consist of merging events that have no relation to one another (differences), and, if seen from the initial condition, their end result is unpredictable.

Two objections can be made to the above. The first is Oakeshott's view of historical events as between previous and consequent events, based on the notion that historical actors cannot predict the consequences of their actions. This is only partially true and certainly does not mean that they did not make plans for the future or that their actions were without purpose. Acts can converge or be attuned to one another, and actors can pursue common goals. In all these cases one can speak of a certain goal-directedness.

A second point is even more important. Though history may not be predictable from the viewpoint of the actor,[14] this is not the case for the writer of history. He knows the continuation of that history, and using that he can (re-)construct the 'output' of the whole process.[15] This output determines whether the circumstances (black boxes) that were considered useful for their purposes by the actors were also really present.[16] Again it is Weber who has eye for the finalistic role of such practical conclusions in historical writing: 'The historian is in a better position than his historical actor, in that he in any case knows *a posteriori* whether the evaluation of the conditions solely as they figured in the mind of the actor as knowledge and expectation corresponded to the actual conditions: [the historian] can determine this by the real consequences of the actions.'[17] Weber goes even further. He recognizes that some ideal types should not be considered ethical norms. Nevertheless, they could have functioned as goals of action (intentional black boxes) for the actors. That even occurs quite often according to Weber. 'An ideal type of a certain social state, which can be abstracted from certain characteristic phenomena of an era, may – and this is even often the case – have appeared to [historical] contemporaries as a practical ideal to be achieved or as a maxim for the regulation of certain social relationships.'[18] With regard to this Weber emphatically refers to the ideal type of a medieval urban economy.

One could argue against the finalistic character of ideal types, that ideal types only depict static relationships and not processes. It is, however, forgotten that for Weber even such static relations concern acts, acts usually having a *zweckrationales* [teleological] nature. Furthermore, Weber does not deny the possibility of making ideal types of processes. 'Also processes can be constructed as ideal types, and these constructions may have great heuristic value.'[19] Historical writing about continuing entities has, come high or low, finalistic characteristics. This is a legitimate issue, and historians need not be ashamed of it.

Weber's singular causal imputation

Oakeshott's objections to finalism are hence largely unjustified. On one point, however, he is in the right. To whatever extent historiography shows finalistic characteristics, in most cases one cannot speak of a linear process going from starting-point to terminus, as in the cases of cold water's being boiled or an acorn's becoming an oak tree. In the closed-system construction discussed above, there is usually no linear process from input to output. Although black boxes represent linear processes, they are not the only elements in a closed system. Such a system also encompasses actors, and they form a much less predictable factor in the whole. The actors determine which conclusions they draw from the conditions that they encounter, and which goals they choose on the basis of these conditions (see Chapter 3).

With a specific causal analysis derived from Weber, the objectionable linearity can be removed from the finalistic operation of closed systems. In order to understand the meaning of Weber's conception of causality better, we must return to the closed-system construction. We shall now take account of its possibilistic character, which I noted in Chapter 3 during the definition of systems (see pp. 64 and 65). This means that closed systems should be viewed not as actual but as possible chains of actors and black boxes. From such a viewpoint the input of the system offers nothing but a broad range of possibly-relevant black boxes and actors. The ideal type forms the selection criterion. It therefore determines the borders of the transformation processes that *could* take place in the system. In Weber's causal analysis, the main issue is first to find possibly relevant causal categories. '*Nota bene:* "possibility" is a "moulding" category, that is to say that it functions in such a way, that it makes a *selection* [italics: HJ] of certain possibly causal links in a historical representation.'[20]

An example can serve to clarify this. Someone who has not contracted the flu virus cannot get the flu. He falls outside the process of possible flu phenomena; he, for example, falls outside the biological closed system flu epidemic. By contrast, it is the case that someone who has contracted the flu virus does not necessarily have to get the flu. The virus is a necessary condition, yet it is not sufficient. Hunger, old age or a weakened constitution can be the non-necessary but also non-redundant conditions for getting the flu. Besides necessary conditions that are selected in the input (such as the abundant presence of flu virus), there should be specific mechanical and intentional black boxes indicated in order to explain the whole process from flu virus to epidemic. In this case famine and grain speculation could function specifically as such black boxes.[21]

For this reason, Weber is not content with merely treating the selection of possible causes. He wants to trace the *specific paths* within possible processes in order to find the most adequate explanation. In his eyes the historian does nothing more than indicate the individual passage of events. This means that he continually tries to select the most probable from a plurality of possible causes. Weber's method of selection shows great similarity to what Dray calls the selection procedure of a continuous series.[22] This is a procedure directed towards finding the most satisfactory candidate for the role of cause. Methodologically this means that the historian should 'think away' the suggested cause in order to judge what difference it would have made in that situation if that particular cause had not been present.[23]

Weber uses a similar causal selection procedure. To illustrate it he comments upon an argumentation given by the German historian of ancient history Eduard Meyer with regard to the battle of Marathon. According to Meyer the meaning of the battle lay in its causal function for rationalizing Western culture.[24] If we consider this culture as a gigantic closed system, then we realize that Hellenism has exerted great influence on this rationalization. The reason historians are interested in the battle of Marathon has to do with this later Hellenistic influence. (Note the finalistic nature of this argumentation.) The origin of Hellenism cannot be described by an exhaustive description of the historical facts preceding it. (Oakeshott does suggest something like this, but his position is rather nonsensical, and is opposed by Ankersmit and others, as well as by Weber, *avant la lettre*. Weber posits that he who uses everything to explain a phenomenon actually explains nothing.) In the broad track of the actors, black boxes and smaller closed systems preceding Hellenism, people and events must be pointed out as having a special 'finalistic force'. One of these forces is the outcome of the battle of Marathon.

The procedure with which Weber points out the battle of Marathon as relevant for later developments is essential for the explanatory function of the closed systems presented here. Within the closed system that results in (Western-)European culture, of which Hellenism forms an early stage, we can differentiate two possible tracks before the battle of Marathon. (Keep in mind that closed systems are mental constructions based on empirical data.) One path is formed by Greek culture, the other by Persian – more theocratically oriented – culture. Given that the Persians and not the Greeks had won the battle of Marathon, European history might have developed differently. By analogy with what happened in Persian dominions elsewhere, the Persians in Greece would have stimulated religious cults in such a form that not only their possibilities for political control would have been reinforced, but also that the Greek tendency towards rationalization would have been crushed. On the basis of this contrafactual deliberation one may conclude that the battle of Marathon plays a major causal role in the closed system 'Western European cultural development'.[25] Weber's procedure for imputing cause leads to the indication of singular causal links within the broad tracks of possibility in closed systems. From this perspective one can no longer speak of a directly linear finalistic process, because these tracks can make various detours. For example, the Athenian polis is supposed to have great explanatory power for Western-European culture, yet democracy foundered there, so that with regard to this aspect no directly-linear contribution can be pointed out.

Weber's explanatory procedure is, all in all, composed of three different types of explanation: finalistic, in the form of a rationalistic interpretation of Western-European culture, generalizing, and individualizing. This last type involves indicating a particular phenomenon – such as the victory at Marathon or the freedom and autonomy of the Athenian citizens – which respectively influenced and evinced demonstrable correspondence[26] to the result of the development examined, namely rationalistic and democratic Western culture. Ricoeur in this context speaks of a 'force de diffusion' in order to clarify that an important explanatory force exudes from such an uncovered fact.[27]

Of the three types of explanation mentioned, the generalizing type still needs some explanation. In order to clarify the special importance of the Greek victory at Marathon, Weber advised contemplating the possible consequences of a Persian victory. By generalizing from the consequences of a Persian victory elsewhere, for example in Palestine, it may be concluded that a Persian victory in Greece would not have done Hellenic rationalism much good.[28]

Denying directly linear finality does not necessarily mean that teleological, organological or evolutionistic metaphors are completely illegitimate in the domain of the historical narrative. In the case of the analysis of a process, knowledge of the process as a whole can only occur if the outcome is known. By knowing that an oak tree grows out of an acorn, we can discover the total process of growth from an acorn into an oak. The perspective advocated here of urban history as a closed-system construct even makes such metaphors quite plausible. Nevertheless, we see historical writers reacting ambivalently to the organological metaphor. Some use it, others repudiate it. The latter consider patterns of thought modelled on biology to be antagonistic to the description of historical processes. This ambivalent posture among historians with regard to organological thought has to do with the finalistic nature of (synthetic) historical writing on the one hand and to its non-linear character on the other.

This systems-theoretical construction also uncovers a highly curious fact. In diachronous, synthetic historical writing one does not work with one explanatory model, but with several explanatory models, which are used next to and intermixed with one another. Apparently historians consider more than one model to be explanatory. This insight undermines the work of philosophers of history and theoreticians of science who try to impose one specific explanatory model on historical practice, whether it be narrative, hermeneutic, or positivistic. A more pragmatic theory of history, more disposed to knowing how historiography functions than to how it should function, in this approach discovers a more multiform explanatory method.

Collective participation and quasi-subjects

Mitchel has examined the internal operation of closed systems more closely, and he observes that they can best be compared to acts of individuals. These performance systems are marked by the fact that they are subject to internal change and can initiate activities. Mitchel considers representing the interests of those concerned and producing different types and amounts of output to be the most important activities, in accordance with the possibilities and limitations of the system. These activities proceed according to certain codes of behaviour and notions of administrative rationality.[29] The correspondence noted above between performance systems and continuing entities raises the question of whether the latter can also be considered collective actors. Mandelbaum makes no comment in this direction with reference to his continuing entities. However, Ricoeur, who continues Mandelbaum's work, does. He considers his *entités de premier ordre* to be quasi-personages. This view is based on the fact that these entities are 'composed' of acting individuals, who through institutionalization and continuing participation partly determine its actions. Participation or, to use Ricoeur's term, *appartenance participative* forms the cultural-mental core of such a quasi-personage. As examples of such first-order entities he mentions nations or classes. These have patriotism and class-consciousness, respectively, as a basis for participatory belonging, called 'collective participation' hereinafter. For cities the civic culture posited by Briggs could, for example, function as a participation characteristic. Ricoeur also points out that this participation does not always mean harmonious cohabitation. Patriotism or class-consciousness can also be forgotten, denied, or combated. Even in the most negative form, however, one may speak of a mental bond between the participating individual and the continuing entity.[30] Bahrdt's conception of the city as a battle between the private and the public spheres, like Briggs' civic culture, therefore fits excellently into the concept 'participation' as described by Ricoeur.[31]

Ricoeur's ideas on this point are also closely related to those of Max Weber. Although Weber, even more so than Ricoeur, should be seen as a methodological individualist, this does not mean that he rejects collectives as historical actors. According to him the individual is continually absorbed in numerous forms of *Gemeinschaftshandeln, Einverständnishandeln* and *Gesellschaftshandeln*. These three types of social actions indicate different gradations of the engagement of individuals with the continuing entity. Thus markets and linguistic communities are continuing entities, participation in which is characterized by a thoroughly self-evident and unquestioned *Gemeinschaftshandeln*. The inevitable participation can also be mingled with expressions of agreement, such as participation in the political, social, or cultural life of a state or nation. This form of collective participation Weber calls 'Einverständnishandeln'. Finally there are institutions, of which a few people consciously become members because they want to contribute in some way to the realisation of their goals. These *Zweckvereine* [associations with a certain purpose] are marked by *Gesellschaftshandeln*.[32]

Social action, for Weber, yields a broad range of individualities. These may be states, bureaucracies, religions, or forms of authority, but also works of art and literature. Weber considers various ideal-typical phenomena to be *Historische Individuen* – for example Christianity and capitalism – that can have scientific value within certain systems of values and that can be understood [*verstehend*], but can also be analysed causally. It is precisely this collective individualism that makes Weber's procedure for imputing a single cause, explained above, so understandable. A causal effect (*force de diffusion*) can only be imputed to historical individualities (note that these are also taken to include collective 'individuals'). Therein lies the actionist basis of Weber's sociology. This sociology synthesizes and individualizes. First of all, the historical individualities, because of their unique process of development, give the *perennierende Gebilde* their own identity. Furthermore, they give this identity the power to be effective. That is why, in the analysis afterwards, these individualities can be pointed out in the historical process and can be brought forward as explanatory instances. In addition to these primary causal bodies, Weber also differentiates secondary causes. These concern 'Causes which are found in the "evaluated" uniqueness of an "individual" in causal back-tracking.'[33] These secondary causes are, in my terminology, the actors and black boxes forming the building-blocks of the relatively-closed system that functions as the skeleton of a historical quasi-subject.

Closed systems in urban historiography: questions for analysis

In order to ascertain whether the development of urban phenomena is viewed in a major part of urban historiography as a closed system with an internal, single and finalistic operation, in which collective participation occurs, owing to which such systems appear as quasi-subjects, the following questions must be answered:

1. Are the cities or urban phenomena conceived as continuing entities? In other words: are dichotomous definitions of cities and urban aggregations used? Or are the separation, coherence, continuity, institutionalization, localization or autonomy of urban phenomena clarified in another way?
2. Is it possible to speak of an internal, finalistic operation, and in which manner is it explained? Which partial systems are concerned in the finality? Are organic or biological metaphors used to clarify the separation of the system as well its finalistic operation? Or is such a metaphor explicitly rejected?
3. Can one speak of a collective finality? Can that finality be understood as participation in an urban continuing entity?
4. Is the city considered an independent variable, an explanans, and can the city be regarded a quasi-subject on the basis of all this?

If each of these four types of questions can be answered affirmatively, we are dealing with the integral writing of history of the closed-system type with subjectifying characteristics.

These questions are applied to two urban historians, who have occupied themselves in different ways with the history of urban phenomena. Weber and Mumford have written long-term studies with pretensions of writing world history. That is to say that their urban histories are concerned with cities and the phenomenon 'city' in general, and encompass more than two centuries and more than one period (for example the classical and medieval periods).[34]

Max Weber and the city

In the following I wish to show that Weber's conception of a city, as it is developed in his essay *Die nichtlegitieme Herrschaft. Typologie der Städte*, displays the infrastructure of a closed system.[35]

Continuing entities

Weber begins his historical urban typology, as we know, with an economic definition of cities. He considers these to be settlements of which the inhabitants satisfy an economically essential part of their everyday needs at the local market, these needs largely being met by goods the local populace and the populace of the environs have produced for the market or have acquired for supply to that market.[36]

Does this not imply that the city is a variable that is dependent on local market mechanisms? An affirmative answer to this question would imply that this is not a case of an autonomous, closed system. For explanations would then occur through reference to the encompassing market mechanism and not through developments in the urban system itself. Bahrdt has noted that the importance Weber attaches to the local market should be seen in the light of the economic system from which cities have had to struggle free in classical as well as in medieval times. That economic system is called Oikos, and has as its most important characteristic the lack of economic freedom.[37] It is the economy of the feudal domain, in which only one person enjoys economic liberty, namely the owner of the domain. His will is law, as it is also with regard to the economic actions of the inhabitants of the domain. In contrast to the inhabitant of the *oikos* the inhabitant of the city – see Weber's definition – has more economic freedom. He is an autonomous economic subject, whose economic freedom of action can form the basis for other autonomous social actions. The market can, in this case, be viewed as an economic condition for individual freedom. Weber's definition of the city hence emerges from the dichotomy with the *oikos*.[38] Furthermore, the local market is not completely an autonomous, anonymous economic mechanism that functions independently of the inhabitants of the city themselves. On the contrary: the market is subject to political-institutional actions for its existence and survival. Tromp states this as follows: '[Weber's] economic definition of cities actually presupposes certain political-institutional arrangements'.[39] Yet this still does not quite bring us into the clear. The city as economic unit has not yet been differentiated from villages as economic units, even if one takes into account that the economic unit 'city' exists by grace of institutional measures. After all, villages also have 'Flurzwang, Weideregelung, Verbot des Exports von Holz und Streu [. . .]'.[40] A city as a complete contrast to countryside, village and *oikos* must be the result of a consciously-desired formation of a community (*Vergesellschaftung*). These are finally sealed in the birth of 'comradly alliances'. These especially occurred in Europe in the

– 128 –

eleventh and twelfth centuries.[41] After their victory over the legitimate authorities (especially the feudal lords), they were institutionalised into municipalities and thereby made more permanent. Their members obtained the legal status of 'citizen', and on this basis can claim equal treatment by the law. With the term *Verbandcharacter der Stadt* [the associational character of a city] Weber clearly indicates that cities are distinguished by internal coherence; he also notes the dichotomous construction that corresponds to this coherence: 'Begriff des Stadtbürgers im Gegensatz zum Landmann' [the conceptualization of the urbanite in contrast to the villager].[42]

Weber distances himself from a purely objectifying description of the city based on, among other things, population size and area. He emphasizes an economic contrast between the city and the countryside, in which market behaviour and trade activities distinguish the inhabitant of the city from the inhabitant of the countryside. Finally, he stipulates political, legal, and cultural factors as a result of which the city can be considered a specifically non-agrarian community.[43] Thus the city becomes a dichotomously-defined entity *sui generis*, a closed system. (This, of course, does not mean an actual independence from the surrounding agricultural world.)

Neil Smelser notes an important difference between Weber and Durkheim with regard to explaining phenomena. According to Smelser, through the observation of similarities between phenomena, Durkheim tries to find their common causes ('concomitant variation'). For Weber, the examination of similarities is only intended to discover the comparability of phenomena and 'to facilitate the development of type concepts'. In the end, according to Smelser, Weber is concerned with the 'indirect method of difference'.[44] Weber's development of ideal types hence implies a dichotomous way of operating. Nelissen observes a kinship between an approach to cities as 'entities *sui generis*' and an ideal-typical approach. Ideal types are generalizations, he states, that originate through the reduction, in a rational way, of phenomena present in reality to a certain number of characteristics considered most important; this in such a manner that these characteristics show coherence. For the ideal type 'city', this means that the city is reduced to its non-agrarian characteristics.[45] Weber's urban ideal types are dichotomous conceptions. That is why the objects of study they indicate bear the characteristics of autonomous entities. Weber's ideal types of cities can therefore be considered relatively-closed systems.

Finalism

This holds even more true because his ideal types, just like closed systems, are characterized by an internal, finalistic operation. His three urban ideal types are actually *termini* in protracted processes of urban development. Eventually the medieval city will correspond most completely with Weber's urban ideal type. The closed system that Weber has designed with his urban ideal types proceeds from the *oikos*, by way of the contrasting market-place and classical polis, to the complete medieval city. The description of this city should therefore be examined for a closed structure layered in partial systems and a finalistic operation.

Weber's city as a closed system is the synthesis of the following;

a. a military partial system with fortified works such as a moat or a wall, as a result of which there is also a spatial separation of the city and the countryside;
b. an economic partial system consisting of a market;
c. a social–mental partial system marked by an associative nature: the inhabitants wish to form a unit (comradely alliances);
d. an institutional partial system , which deals with the city's laws and legal system (wholly or partially); and
e. a political–administrative partial system, which encompasses self-administration and the right of citizens to appoint their own governments (autonomy and *Autokefalie*).[46]

The consequences of this synthesis are expressed in the spatial and organizational aspect of urban development. A finality can be discerned here, marked by a development from little to great coherence. Thus Weber observes that before the Middle Ages in Europe cities still had autonomous quarters and neighbourhoods, which could institutionally and politically still act autonomously. Thus it was normal in Byzantium that administrators of the various quarters acted as representatives of the populace. In this instance the city as a whole is not autonomous: it is an agglomeration of more or less autonomous quarters. In systems-theoretical terms, such 'cities' should be considered 'incoherent'. The medieval European city shows coherence because it forms a spatial whole, visibly delimited by the city walls. Organizationally, this type of city is coherent because of great administrative autonomy.[47] Weber uses no organological or biological metaphors to stress this coherence. Those who work in his footsteps often expressly reject such metaphors. This especially has to do with Weber's non-rectilinear conception of history.

An example of the non-rectilinear character of the urban contribution to the process of European rationalization is the classical slave economy. Although the hoplite polis could not function without slaves, slavery creates an irrational form of capitalism, owing to which the classical city cannot make a direct contribution to the *Entzauberung* [disenchantment] of the European world.[48]

If we depict all this we get the following system construction (Figure 7):

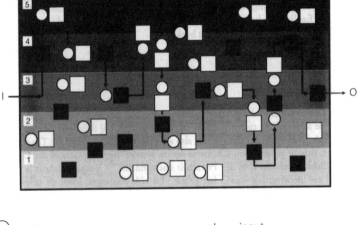

◯ actors	I input
◼ mechanical black boxes	O output
▢ intentional black boxes	1, 2, 3, 4 and 5 partial system
→ connecting line of singular causal imputation	

Figure 7. A relatively closed system

The closed system hence contains actors and black boxes. In the case of the classical polis, we can count among the actors the ordinary inhabitants of Athens, but also Cleisthenes and Pericles. Markets and the slaves may be considered mechanical black boxes of the classical city. Although the politics of most classical cities was directed towards preventing farmers from getting into debt, this was almost never successful.[49]

In the medieval city, the rise of mercantile capitalism was guided by the *intentions* of the merchant class, but the opposition between capital and labour to which it is linked was of an unintended nature. The latter are therefore mechanical black boxes.[50] The guilds generated intentional black boxes in medieval cities, for example by their measures against asking excessive interest rates for loans and competition. The guild measures directed towards control of the market, after first having had positive effects, were ultimately counter-productive for the process of city formation. Here we also can see mechanical black boxes at work. The finality thereby loses its *intentional* character, as can be seen by the solid connecting line. This connecting line represents the singular causal analysis expounded by Weber. This figure also clarifies its synthesizing effect. For this line is uninhibited by any potential boundaries between partial systems. This last fact is important, because imputing singular causes in this manner summarizes the partial systems in one finalistic sweep. Here the integral operation of the closed systems construction peeps around the corner.

Collective participation

That Weber's conception of city shows finalistic and teleological character-istics was already evident in the above from the term *Vergesellschaftung*. This concept, important for Weber's conception of the city, indicates a goal-directed participation of the citizens of the city. This goal-directed participation of the city's inhabitants is the result of a protracted historical process.

For a proper understanding of that process, one should first look at where it all began: the Asiatic city. That city cannot function as an independent variable because there is no complete participation of the inhabitants. The city inhabitant there, posits Weber, is first of all a member of a caste or 'gens'.[51] It is only in the European city (classical and medieval) that there are real city-dwellers. These are citizens of a city in the first place and only in the second place members of a church, clan, family or other form of social group.

Weber seeks the origin of the individual, participating citizenship of a city, in religion. In the *gentilische* aristocratic polis in ancient Greece, local communal festive meals, open to all those living in the same area, came into existence next to the extant cult meals linked to clans. The cult groups on a local basis, no longer bound to gens or *phratria*, evolving from these meals form the proto-participation of the later autonomous *poleis*.[52]

Weber credits the development of the medieval city dweller into an individual with a city consciousness to another meal ceremony, namely

the Eucharist.[53] Religious meal ceremonies, in which every individual –
without being a member of a class, caste, gens or cult group – can
participate, in Weber's opinion form the groundwork for or prologue to
individual membership of an urban community. A *Wahlverwandschaft*
[conceptual kinship] exists between participation in cult communities and
participation in urban communal life. In both communities, participation
is based on personal membership. One cannot be a member of an agrarian
community on one's own cognizance.

Precisely because Weber emphasizes the individual character of the
citizen of the Western city in this manner one may speak of a new form
of urban participation, which he describes as the 'solidarische Rechts-
Gemeinschaft von Einzelnen' [legal association of individuals]. When in
the eleventh century cities turned against the feudal lords by means of
coniurationes and formed a new community on the basis of rational
agreement, they performed a revolutionary act. They replaced the 'noble'
form of organization through patrimonial law, with its many forms of
dependence, by uniform, territorial law. They traded a society bound to
persons for one bound to institutions (*anstaltmässige Vergesellschaftung*).
What is revolutionary about this is that the citizen of the city dwelt under
a self-appointed government and a uniform, communal law, of which he
himself, sometimes fulfilling positions in the urban administrative and
judicial organs, was partially the creator.[54]

Quasi-subjects

In contrast to the polis, which often also had the above-mentioned
characteristics, a new political concept emerged in the medieval city,
namely the separation of public and private law. With this, in Weber's
opinion, the medieval city has given one of its most fundamental contributions to the conception of the modern state. It is a definitive step from the
feudal and patrimonial exercise of power to the modern rational state
with a business-like bureaucracy and systematized law.[55] Besides the
'capitalistic' contribution of the medieval city to Western civilization
already mentioned, this political innovation demonstrates that the medieval
city plays an important role as explanatory variable for European culture
(in so far as this diverges from the 'general human pattern').[56]

Weber therefore lays down explicit links between cities, in this case
the medieval city, and other historical developments essential to Europe.
The city serves as an explanatory ground, as an independent variable.
This holds true in particular for the genesis of rational capitalism,
bureaucracy and the modern state.

In addition to functioning here as an actor, one could ask to what extent the medieval city could act directly. To what extent could it engage in 'internal' and 'foreign' politics? To what extent does the city act as quasi-subject? Weber answers these questions as follows:

- The medieval city pursues its own 'foreign' politics, also in the context of alliances, on the basis of its own army and army command.
- It gains the right to taxation and is freed from taxation by authorities outside the city.
- The city formulates its own market law, creates autonomous political control over trade and artisanship, and lays the foundations for its own economic policy though the protection of its own trade markets.
- The medieval city creates its own law not only for markets and trade but also for landownership.
- Finally, as we have observed earlier, the city acquires not only the right to govern itself, but also the right to appoint administrators and officials of the lawcourts.[57]

On the basis of all these it may be said that Weber's ideal type of the Western, and in particular the medieval city can be considered a continuing entity, an independent variable, and an integrated quasi-subject.

Cities in history: Lewis Mumford

Continuing entities

In his *The city in history* Mumford posits that cities emerge from villages. This does not mean, however, that a city may be viewed as a village with more inhabitants.[58] For the transition from a pre-urban core, such as a village, a fortress, or a sanctuary, to a city, Mumford proposes the term urban implosion. He prefers this term to Childe's urban revolution, because Childe's term suggests that the pre-urban core completely disappears and is replaced by something completely different. Gordon Childe leaves the impression that a conceptual differentiation between, for example, city and village also necessitates the actual historical elimination of the village in the city.[59] It is precisely the continuous nature of villages and cities that convinces Mumford to use the term 'implosion' instead of 'revolution'. By the term 'urban implosion' Mumford means a process in which all kinds of partial systems, which satisfy a diverse range of social-economic and cultural needs, are brought together within the city walls. Consider, for example, a temple for the satisfaction of religious needs, a market for the satisfaction of economic needs and a citadel for defence. These institutions and their functions at first were spread out and badly organized in villages and hamlets. Through their bundling, new, qualitatively-different forms of communities arise, without the agrarian functions completely disappearing.[60] This is why Chapter 2 of *The city in history* is given the title 'The crystallization of the city'.[61] On the basis of this spatial and organizational coherence, Mumford considers a city more dynamic than a village. This dynamism lies in the conscious and purposeful use of a large number of agencies in the city.[62]

Furthermore, Mumford assumes a dichotomy between villages and cities. Opposite the passive agrarian community stand the active institutions of the city, supported by 'secondary' group forming (that is to say group formation on a voluntary basis, not on the basis of familial ties), with self-chosen goals, selective membership and goal-directed activities.

Finalism

According to Mumford the big difference between a city and a village is that a city does and a village does not have a finalistic tendency. For Mumford Tönnies's dichotomy between *Gemeinschaft* and *Gesellschaft* is important for the understanding of the finalistic tendency of cities. According to Tönnies the *Gemeinschaft* is distinguished by a will to conserve traditional community ties (*Wesenswille*), while the *Gesellschaft* is equipped with a dynamic will to create new communal ties in order to organize society better (*Kurwille*). In the latter case conflicts cannot be avoided. The *Kurwille*, after all, offers possibilities to choose from for the basically free and goal-directed individual. According to Mumford, the city is more *gesellschaftlich* than *gemeinschaftlich*. 'The mark of the city is its *purposive* [italics: HJ] social complexity', he states. Yet the traditional element is not completely driven out of the conception of the city. The finalistic tendency with which it is equipped is a mix of striving towards social harmony and a desire to develop more political and military power. Mumford seeks the origin of both efforts in the way cities originated. Cities, according to him, came into existence through a coup by a nomadic chieftain against a democratic–harmonious village community. The former gave the city its aggressiveness; the village community gave the city-dweller the ideal of harmony.[63]

In all this Mumford is a clear example of an author who views the city as a closed-system construction in which a finalistic force is at work, ranging mainly through the social, political, military and cultural partial systems. Mumford is barely interested in the demographic and economic domains.

In Mumford's view, there is a false opposition between a view of cities as a consciously-desired result of human actions and an organological conception of the city. Mumford uses an organological – and therefore finalistic – view of urban development, which in his case does not mean a complete exclusion of the idea that cities are man-made environments, but quite the opposite. Mumford thinks cities, just like living creatures, grow from a nucleus, the pre-urban core. A village, a fortress, a shrine, a market, a spring and so on can function as such a nucleus. Characteristic of this – and all – growth is that it proceeds from simple to more complex but nonetheless coherent structures.[64]

Collective participation

Writing about the emergence of cities from pre-urban cores – which are also all man-made objects – Mumford calls attention to the unavoidable role played by the hunter king in the emergence of cities.[65] With a king as the power in cities, a new phase dawns in the history of humanity: the development of the human personality. This personality is capable of developing new values, making decisions, and going in new directions. Gradually – and this is important in this context – these new human possibilities devolve from the king to the townsmen.[66] Mumford describes the collective participation that comes forth from this phenomenon, on page 113 of *The city in history*. There Mumford, with a reference to Rousseau, offers as a difference between village communal consciousness and urban participation the inability of the former and the capacity of the latter to develop its own dynamics, putting old structures to use for new goals. He concludes: 'Yet one must remember Rousseau's definition "houses make a town, but citizens make a city"'.[67] It is precisely the collective citizenry that makes the city a 'purposive complexity': an urban quasi-subject.

Quasi-subject

Mumford's organological terminology regarding the phenomenon 'city' offers the basis for such a subjectifying conception of cities. The city as a living organism can function independently like any other living creature, which naturally does not necessarily mean that such an organism could exist completely independent of its environment. According to Mumford the autonomous nature of cities lies in the realization of the corporate will. Such a will makes striving for self-knowledge, self-administration and self-actualization possible.[68]

Because of this it seems likely that one could find statements of Mumford's that would indicate that he bestows the role of independent variable on the city. For example, he points out the simultaneous emergence of cities and writing. In a discussion with Pirenne Mumford turns Pirenne's claim that cities originate because of long-distance trade around and says: the cities are the independent and the long-distance trade routes are the dependent variable.[69] In this manner Mumford clearly gives the city a function as actor. Because of its 'implosive character' the city is more than the sum of its parts. The city is more than a storage space, a warehouse, or even an accumulator: the city is a 'transformer'.[70] The city attracts people from outside to maintain itself. These strangers, outsiders, travellers, traders, refugees and slaves, and even enemies – attracted by the city – continually make a contribution to the further development of the city, and thereby to society as a whole. The city is a magnet '[. . .] and that term is all the more useful in description because with the magnet we associate the existence of a field and the possibility of action at a distance, visible in the "times of social force" which draw to the centre particles of different nature'.[71]

In this chapter it has been explained how cities in historiography take the form of closed systems. These closed-system constructions show a great deal of resemblance to Mandelbaum's continuing entities, but also show finality. This finality, however, is not of a deterministic nature but of a possibilistic nature, as a result of which rigid linearity in historical practice is avoided. This possibilism has been derived from Weber. He also launched many ideas concerning the issues discussed here that still play an important role in the modern critical philosophy of history. For example, one might think of Mandelbaum's concept 'continuing entities', which we find in Weber as *Perennierende Gebilde*, or of Ricoeur's *entités de premier ordre*, which we found in Weber as 'das historische Individuum "höchsten" Ranges'. The singular causal imputation is a multiple explanatory method showing much resemblance to what Dray has called the selection procedure of a continuous series. This procedure also makes clear that one cannot, in history, speak of the dominance of one method of explanation. We can say together with Dray that: '[. . .] the explanations found in history books are a logically miscellaneous lot'.[72]

Certain questions with regard to urban historiography with closed-system constructions must still be answered. What role does the input of the closed system play in urban historiography? Are there any other closed systems? Can the closed-system construction be found in comparative urban historiography and in studies of individual cities? I shall try to answer these questions in the next chapter.

Notes

1. In this chapter I shall speak mainly of closed systems or closed-system constructions. The reader is requested to append the term 'relatively' to these.

2. M. Mandelbaum, *The anatomy of historical knowledge* (Baltimore, MD, and London 1977), pp. 11 and 17–19. P. Ricoeur, *Temps et récit*, Vol. 1 (Paris 1983), pp. 272–3. See also: D.-H. Rubin, *The metaphysics of the social world* (London 1985) In the first chapter of this book, 'The existence of social entities' (pp. 1–45), Rubin discusses five types of social entities: 1) 'social substances' such as countries (for example, England) and national or international organizations (unions, United Nations, or the Red Cross); (2) 'social types' such as capitalism or bureaucracy; (3) 'events', such as the murder of Allende or the conversion of Constantine the Great; (4) processes such as the decline of the Roman empire or the emergence of the bourgeoisie; and (5) 'states of affairs', such as class oppositions or the division of labour between men and labour. The continuing entities as I – in Mandelbaum's footsteps – have described them pertain especially to categories 1 and 4.

3. Ibid., p. 10. See also P. Ricoeur, *Temps et récit*, pp. 273–5. The characteristics mentioned above, such as determinability of geographic location, institutionality, extension, etc. of continuing entities can be viewed nominalistically or realistically. This is a problem belonging to the debate in the philosophy of history concerning the question of whether 'social entities' really exist or are merely methodological constructions. See C. Lorenz, *Het historisch atelier. Controversen over causaliteit en contingentie in de geschiedenis* (Meppel, Amsterdam 1990), pp. 49, 63–80, 98–123. I do not wish to participate in this debate here. I do, however, wish to point out that the closed systems figuring here are nothing other than what Ankersmit, in the footsteps of Foucault, calls 'language things'. These 'language things' can be traced and analysed in (urban) historiography: F. R. Ankersmit, *De spiegel van het verleden. Exploraties I: De geschiedtheorie* (Kampen 1996), pp. 103–9 and F. R. Ankersmit, *De macht van de representatie. Exploraties II. Cultuurfilosofie en esthetica* (Kampen 1996), p. 198. In contrast to what Ankersmit claims, these 'language things' not only have a superstructure, they also have an infrastructure.

4. M. Mandelbaum, *The anatomy of historical knowledge*, p. 133. See also G. H. von Wright, *Explanation and understanding*, (New York 1971), pp. 136–7.

5. H. Mitchel, 'Relevant neoscientific management notions', in S. Optner (ed.), *Systems analysis* (Harmondsworth 1973), pp. 311/312.

6. Ibid.

7. Stegmüller in this context speaks of a 'Verhaltensplastische Systeme', even though he does not bestow an executive role on these systems in striving towards goals. This all has to do with the fact that Stegmüller does not accept teleological explanation, as I have described in Chapter 4. Stegmüller, *Wissenschaftliche Erklärung und Begründung*, pp. 586–94, especially 594.

8. Max Weber, *Wirtschaft und Gesellschaft. Grundriss der verstehende Soziologie* (Tübingen 1972) (abbr. *WuG* 1972), pp. 727–41.

9. M. Weber, 'Ueber einige Kategorien der verstehende Soziologie', in *WL* (1973) pp. 427–74, esp. 441–74.

10. *WL* (1973), p. 253. Weber also illustrates the concept 'historical individual' by Marx's *Das Kapital*: '[. . .] was es für uns zu einem "historischen" Individuum macht, ist aber doch nicht etwa jene Zugehörigkeit zur Gattung, sondern umgekehrt der durchaus einzigartige "geistige Gehalt", den "wir" in ihm "niedergelegt" finden' [(. . .) what makes it [capital] into a historical individual is not belonging to a certain category, but, on the contrary, a thoroughly-unique "mental content", which "we" have imputed to it'.

11. M. Mandelbaum, *The anatomy of historical knowledge*, pp. 134–5.

12. P. Ricoeur, *Temps et récit*, pp. 273–5.

13. M. Oakeshott, *On history and other essays* (Oxford 1983), p. 104.1.

14. Though not predictable, it is not as open as the advocates of contingent ontology maintain. See: T. Blom and T. Nijhuis, 'Ontology and methodology in sociology and history', in Chr. Lorenz et al., *Het historisch atelier. Controversen over causaliteit en contingentie in de geschiedenis* (Meppel, Amsterdam 1990), pp. 90–141, especially p. 122. See also: T. Nijhuis, *Structuur en contingentie. Over de grenzen van het sociaal-wetenschappelijk verklaringsideaal in de Duitse geschiedschrijving* [Structure and contingency. On the boundaries of a social scientific ideal of explanation in German historiography] (Assen 1996), esp. pp. 79–86.

15. Von Wright in this context makes a meaningful differentiation between 'predictability and "intelligibility"': *Explanation and understanding*, p. 161.

16. Historical events – 'the facts', as they are usually called – have two sides. On the one hand they are objective; on the other they become subjective by the position and meaning such an event receives in a narration. See H. Krings, H. M. Baumgartner and Ch. Wild (eds),

Handbuch philosophischer Grundbegriffe. Studienausgabe Bd. 2; Dialektik – Gesellschaft (Munich 1973). L. Eley posits on page 436 of this work: 'Zwei Bestimmungen sind vornehmlich gemeint, wenn in der Philosophie wie in den Wissenschaften vom Faktum (Tatsache) gesprochen wird: Faktum ist 1. Das, was objektiven Bestand hat, 2. Das, was seiner Bestimmung nach anders sein kann.' [Two meanings are generally intended, when in philosophy as well as in the sciences people speak of facts: 1. That which exists objectively; 2. That, which can have a different interpretation.] See also: D. H. Porter, *The emergence of the past. A theory of historical explanation* (Chicago 1981) p. 20.

17. 'Der Historiker nun ist seinem Helden zunächst darin überlegen, dass er jedenfalls a posteriori weiss, ob die Abschätzung der gegebenen, "ausserhalb" desselben vorhanden gewesenen Bedingungen (gemäss) den Kentnissen und Erwartungen, welche der Handelnde hegte, auch tatsächlich [der wirklichen damaligen Sachlage] entsprach: dies lehrt ja der faktische "Erfolg" des Handelns.' M. Weber, *WL* (1973), p. 267. However, one should not conclude from this that teleology and finalism are conflated according to Weber. For Weber, too, finalism is something other than teleology.

18. 'Ein Idealtypus bestimmter gesellschaftlicher Zustände, welcher sich aus gewissen charakteristischen sozialen Erscheinungen einer Epoche abstrahieren lässt, kann – und dies ist sogar recht häufig [italics, HJ] der Fall – den Zeitgenossen selbst als praktisch zu erstrebendes Ideal oder doch als Maxime für die Regelung bestimmter sozialer Beziehung vorgeschwebt haben': ibid., p. 196. See also p. 201.

19. 'Auch Entwicklungen lassen sich nämlich als Idealtypen konstruieren, und diese Konstruktionen können ganz erheblichen heuristischen Wert haben.' Ibid., p. 203.

20. 'Hier sei nur noch bemerkt: die "Möglicheit" ist eine "formende" Kategorie, d.h. sie tritt in der Art in Funktion, dass sie die *Auslese* [italics: HJ] der in die historische Darstellung aufzunehmenden kausalen Glieder bestimmt': M. Weber, *WL* (1973), pp. 269–70 note 3. Stegmüller also considers the fact that different possible causal series can lead to the same result to be the most remarkable characteristic of 'verhaltenplastische Systeme' [systems which change according to the behaviour of their participants]: *Wissenschaftliche Erklärung und Begründung*, p. 588. Here also the paradigm of chaos is involved. Inside the system of possibly-causal links we have to search for small consecutive intervals of time in which acts and intentional and mechanical black boxes interfere. This is what Reisch and Shermer

call a chaotic process. See: G. Reisch, 'Chaos, history and narrative', *History and Theory* 30 (1991): 1–20, esp. 19–20 and M. Shermer, 'Exorcising Laplace's demon: chaos and anti-chaos, history and metahistory', *History and Theory* 34 (1995): 59–83, esp. 65–6. See also Chapter 4 of this book.

21. We are concerned here with what are referred to as INUS conditions. These conditions are individually insufficient [to produce an effect], but non-redundant; however, in conjunction they are unnecessary but sufficient. 'In conjunction' from my perspective means: in the form of a closed system, for example, the process from a single contamination to a flu epidemic. See J. L. Mackie, *The cement of the universe. A study in causation* (Oxford 1974) especially p. 62, and Chr. Lorenz, *De constructie van het verleden. Een inleiding in der theorie van de geschiedenis* (Meppel, Amsterdam 1987), pp. 153, 159–60, 180 and 197.

22. W. Dray, *Laws and explanation in history* (Oxford 1970 [1957]) pp. 70–3 and 98–104.

23. Ibid., p. 104.

24. M. Weber, *WL* (1973), pp. 273 and onwards.

25. Theda Skocpol's comparative method and Stuart Mill's comparative method of agreement and difference, which consist of pointing out causes through agreements and differences, show great resemblance to Weber's possibilism and discovering the adequate cause. Weber himself refers to Stuart Mill in *WL* (1973), p. 270 (note 3 of p. 269). See also H. S. J. Jansen, 'De voorwerpen van vergelijking. Op zoek naar een nieuwe vergelijkingstypologie', in *Tijdschrift voor Geschiedenis* 110 (1997): 329–56, especially 342–5.

26. Weber uses the term 'Wahlverwandschaft' for this.

27. P. Ricoeur, *Temps et récit*, p. 268.

28. Another Popperian aspect of black boxes can be illustrated by this example. Popper claimed that a regular or law-like relationship held as long as no evidence to the contrary was found. The black box 'all ravens are black' is valid as long as no white ravens have been discovered. If white ravens are discovered, this does not mean that regular or law-like explanatory constructions as a whole need be abandoned. When the classical historian Demandt claims that a Persian victory is more likely to have accelerated the introduction of rationalistic traditions in Western culture than to have rendered them impossible, it seems the time has arrived for opening the black box 'Greek victory at Marathon and rationalism'. Discovering that the effects Meyer and Weber imputed to the battle of Marathon are

no longer valid does not mean that working with 'law-like' relation-ships in the form of black boxes is illegitimate: Lorenz, *De constructie van het verleden* [The construction of the past], pp. 127–30, especially 128–9. After all, law-like generalizations are an indispensable instrument in Weber's explanatory procedure. In the form of black boxes they are a legitimate element in his possibilistic and contra-factual method of explanation. See also: H. S. J. Jansen, 'De beperkte ruimte in Lorenz' geschiedtheoretische atelier' [The limited space in Lorenz' workshop of historical theory], *Theoretische Geschiedenis* 20 (2) (1993): 139–57, especially 153–4.

29. W. H. Mitchel, *Relevant neoscientific management notions*, p. 311. Besides the three activities mentioned he also names: (d) obtaining and processing input as efficiently as possible. This characteristic is unimportant for the closed-systems analysis and its comparison to continuing entities is dealt with in what follows.

30. P. Ricoeur, *Temps et récit*, pp. 275–6. In the English translation of Ricoeur's book (*Time and narrative*) 'appartenance participative' is translated as 'participatory belonging'. I prefer the term 'collective participation'.

31. H. P. Bahrdt, *Die moderne Grossstadt, Soziologische Überlegungen zum Städtebau* (Munich 1974), pp. 58–95.

32. These three forms of action do not always imply that participants in such actions are unified towards outsiders. *Gemeinschaftshandeln*, such as the behaviour of people in the market or participation in a linguistic community, often implies that they wish to engage foreigners in the action. Acting according to consent does not by a long shot imply solidarity, nor does *Gesellschaftshandeln* imply avoiding contention. *Anstalt* and *Verband* are for Weber *Zweckvereine*, because they are continuing entities (*perennierende Gebilde*) that have risen out of *Vergesellschaftung*: M. Weber, *WL* (1973), pp. 439 and 461–74, especially 462, 463, 465 and 466.

33. 'Ursachen denen die "gewertete" Eigenart jenes "Individuums" im kausalen regressus zugerechnet wird': M. Weber, *WL* (1973), pp. 255–61, especially 261.

34. In addition to the work of Weber and Mumford, the following works were treated in the original study but left out of this text so as not to inundate the reader with my research results: L. Benevolo, *The city history of the city* (Cambridge, MA 1980), Bahrdt's *Die moderne Grossstadt* (already mentioned), K.-H. Blaschke, 'Qualität, Quantität und Raumfunktion als Wesensmerkmale der Stadt vom Mittelalter bis zur Gegenwart', *Regionalgeschichte* Bd. III (1968), pp. 34–50,

and the same author's 'Die periodisierung der Landesgeschichte', *Blätter für Deutsche Landesgeschichte* 106 (1970): 76–93. See also H. S. J. Jansen, *De constructie van het stadsverleden* [The construction of the urban past]. *Een systeem theoretische analyse van het stadshistorish onderzoek ter bevordering van de synthetiserende geschiedschrijving* (Groningen 1991), pp. 112–18, 130–2, 133–6, 256–8, 259–60, and 279–80.

35. M. Weber, *WuG* (1972), pp. 727–815. See also G. Abramowski, *Das Geschichtsbild Max Webers. Universalgeschichte am Leitfaden des okzidentalen Rationalisierungsprozesses* (Stuttgart 1966), pp. 85ff.

36. M. Weber, *WuG* (1972), p. 728.

37. H. P. Bahrdt, *Die moderne Grossstadt* (Munich 1974), pp. 58–63, 86 ff.

38. Ibid., p. 732.

39. B. Tromp, 'De sociologie van de stad bij Max Weber', in H. P. H. Goddijn (ed), *Max Weber. Zijn leven, werk en, betekenis* (Baarn 1980), pp. 113–33, esp. 118–19.

40. 'Coerced reallotment, regulation of common pastures, and the prohibition of the export of wood and straw': Weber, *WuG* (1972), p. 731.

41. The classical and medieval cities are differentiated from other cities 'as institutionalized associations of citizens with special and characteristic organs, who as such are subjected to common law and hence are members of the same legal community' ['als eines anstaltmässig vergeselschafteten, mit besonderen und charakterischen Organen ausgestatteten Verbandes von "Bürgern", welche in dieser ihrer Qualität einem zur ihnen zugänglichen *gemeinsamen Recht* unterstehen, also ständische "Rechtsgenossen" sind']: M. Weber, *WuG* (1972), p. 743.

42. Ibid., p. 736.

43. Ibid., p. 736; see also *WG* (1924), pp. 273–4. See also A. Edel, *Analyzing concepts in social science, Part 1: Science, ideology and value* (New Brunswick, NJ 1979), pp. 95–6.

44. N. J. Smelser, *Methods in the social sciences* (Englewood Cliffs, NJ 1976), pp. 143–50.

45. M. Weber, *WL* (1973), pp. 190–7 and 559–62; N. Nelissen, *De stad. Een inleiding tot de urbane sociologie* [The city. An introduction to urban sociology] (Deventer 1974), p. 45. When a conceptual differentiation is made in the above between the city and the countryside, it should be taken as widely as possible. 'Countryside' in this context not only means an agrarian economy and a village society, but also

the political power, based on agriculture, of feudal or patriarchal lords.

46. M. Weber, *WuG* (1972), p. 736.
47. Ibid., pp. 737–41. It is true that Italian cities still have quarters, but these operate in the context of an encompassing municipal government.
48. G. Abramowski, *Das Geschichtsbild Max Webers*, pp. 102–3. See also: J. Love, 'Max Weber and the theory of ancient capitalism', *History and Theory* 25 (1986): 152–72.
49. M. Weber, *WG* (1924), p. 281.
50. Ibid.
51. M. Weber, *WuG* pp. 746 ff. See also G. Abramowski, *Das Geschichtsbild Max Webers*, pp. 95–6.
52. M. Weber, *WG* (1924), p. 275; M. Weber, *WuG* (1976), p. 744; G. Abramowski, *Das Geschichtsbild Max Webers*, p. 96.
53. M. Weber, *WuG* (1976), p. 745; M. Weber, *WG* (1924), p. 276.
54. M. Weber, *WG* (1924), p. 273.
55. M. Weber, *WuG* (1976); G. Abramowski, *Das Geschichtsbild Max Webers,* pp. 92–3.
56. This term comes from J. Romein. Its explanation by him clearly shows him to be influenced by Weber's ideas about the unique European development with regard to bureaucratization, capitalization, the disciplining of labour, and rationalization: J. Romein. 'De europese geschiedenis als afwijking van het Algemeen Menselijk Patroon' [European history as diverging from the common pattern of humanity], in idem, *Historische lijnen en patronen* (Amsterdam 1976 [1952]) pp. 417–45.
57. M. Weber, *WuG* (1976), pp. 775 and 788–93; G. Abramowski, *Das Geschichtsbild Max Webers*, p. 90.
58. L. Mumford, *The city in history. Origins, its transformation and its prospects* (Harmondsworth 1979 [London 1961]), p. 40.
59. Ibid., p. 42.
60. Ibid., pp. 42, 47 ff.
61. Ibid., p. 40.
62. Ibid., p. 113.
63. L. Mumford, *The culture of cities* (New York 1938), p. 6.
64. Mumford formulates this consideration as follows: 'Or to put it in more *organic* [italics: HJ] terms: little communal village cells, undifferentiated and uncomplicated, every part performing equally every function, turned into complex structures organized on an axiate principle, with differentiated tissues and specialised organs, and with one part, the central nervous system, thinking for and directing the whole': L. Mumford, *The city in history*, p. 46.

65. 'What I would suggest is that the most important agent in effecting change from a decentralized village economy to a highly-organised urban economy was the king, or rather, the institution of kingship': L. Mumford, *The city in history*, p. 47.
66. 'One by one the privileges and prerogatives of kingship were transferred to the city and its citizens': ibid., p. 132.
67. Ibid., p. 113. One could call Mumford's organological thought Rousseau-ian. Rousseau is an exemplar for Mumford with reference to his voluntaristic notions with regard to the relationship between people and community as well as his organological notions with regard to the relationships between man and nature. Cf. Mumford's essay 'Rousseau, insurgent Romanticism', in: L. Mumford (ed.), *Interpretation and forecasts 1922–1972* (London 1973), pp. 187–93.

This perception of the city as consisting essentially of its citizens is however far older than Rousseau: it is articulated perfectly clearly, for instance, in the following two fragments of Alcaeus (Bergk 23n) from the seventh century BC:

Not villas crowned with rich and resplendent roofs;
nor stone-set walls, well fitted and stoutly made;
not ship-canals and naval dockyards
build up a city, but men prepared to
make use of any chances that come to them.

and:

Not stones and timber, not the craft
of joiners makes a city, but
wherever there are men who know
what way to save themselves, then there
are walls, and there a city is.

And in the case of the classical (or indeed the pre-classical) *polis* this is certainly not merely a matter of theoretical sentiment: I suppose the classic case of its being put into practice would be the story in Herodotus (I 162-7) of how the Phokaians, when besieged by the armies of the King of Persia, uprooted themselves *en masse* from their original city on the seaboard of Asia Minor and sailed off to refound a new city on the shores of Corsica.

68. L. Mumford, *The city in history*, *passim*, esp. p. 653.
69. Ibid., p. 296.

70. Ibid., p. 117: 'For a greater part of urban history, the functions of the container remained more important than those of the *magnet*; for the city was primarily a storehouse, a conservator and accumulator. It was by its command of these functions that the city served its ultimate function, that of *transformer*' [italics: HJ].
71. Ibid., p. 101; see also p. 117.
72. W. Dray, *Laws and explanation in history*, p. 85.

−6−

Uncovering an Urban Biography
Closed-System Constructions of
Individual Cities

In this chapter I shall examine closed-system constructions in the histories of individual cities and comparative urban histories. The same questions must generally be posed as in the case of the long-term studies. First among these is whether a city is involved in an internal, finalistic development and in this way integrates a number of sub-systems, to wit: structures of actors and black boxes. Secondly, it is important to ascertain if one may speak of collective participation in urban life. Thirdly: Is the city conceived as a quasi-subject enabling it to act as an independent variable? The question of whether a city has the appearance of a continuing entity, arising from dichotomous definition or otherwise, is actually superfluous in the case of studies of individual cities. After all, the cities do not need to be defined in these cases. That this often occurs anyway is one more argument for the constructivistic nature of urban historiography.

The questions mentioned are applied to Mack Walker's *German Home Towns*,[1] Blumin's *The urban threshold*, a book about nineteenth-century Kingston (New York)[2] and two studies by Frisch on Springfield, Massachusetts.[3]

The latter two works put us on the scent of the disintegrating or incoherent systems alluded to in Chapter 3. We have seen that amongst coherent systems the ideal type of the output and the teleology of actors and intentional black boxes fulfil an important function. In the case of disintegrating systems, the ideal type of the input and the quasi-teleology of (especially mechanical) black boxes play a dominant role. This will appear clearly from Frisch's studies on Springfield. Coherent and disintegrating systems are often linked to one another in urban historical studies. In Frisch's case links are made from disintegrating to coherent; in Mumford's work − he returns for a moment in this chapter − these links are different.

German Home Towns: Mack Walker's comparison

The goal-directed system construction, in which cities take the guise of continuing entities and quasi-subjects, is notably encountered in Mack Walker's comparative study *German Home Towns. Community, state and general estate 1648-1871*. Walker reserves the term 'German home town' for a specific type of German city. He uses it as a collective name for middle-sized and small towns from the middle of the seventeenth century to the end of the nineteenth-century. The populations of these towns vary from 750 to 15,000 inhabitants. The German home town is neither pre-industrial, nor late-medieval nor modern-industrial in character, nor is it a hybrid of these. It is a city with its own character, which is especially expressed in the nature of its constitutional, administrative and social constellation.

Continuing entities

Walker conceives the home town as a closed system in the following dichotomous way. In contrast to a village, the German home town or 'Heimatstadt' is economically differentiated, has walls, a market, guilds, and administrative autonomy. In contrast to large cities, the home towns do not have an administrative patriciate and do have a relatively large class of non-citizens. The *Bürgerschaft* thereby has a special social economic status, which the 'bourgeoisie' in the big cities lacks. In contrast to both the village and the big city, the citisenry of the German home town is not very mobile. One of the major reasons for this is the large involvement of the population in urban communal life. Here public and private spheres are in balance and bound up in each other. Walker therefore makes a sharp distinction between village- and city-dwellers on the one hand and hometownsmen on the other. This distinction arises mainly from the strong feeling of community of the latter. This feeling is marked by a combination of the participatory tendencies present in cities and those present in villages. Characteristic of the agrarian classes in their villages is the fact that they maintain close relationships with their neighbours, and that they are economically independent and show little political awareness. The urbanite, on the other hand, is economically more dependent on his fellow citizens, but is also more aware than the villager of political matters. He, however, experiences politics as something abstract because he barely knows his fellow citizens and their problems. The inhabitant of the home town knows his neighbours, just as villagers do, and is economically dependent, just like an urbanite. Because of this combination he finds himself in the fortunate circumstance that politics constitute a very concrete and clearly-delimited area for him.[4]

Finalism

On the basis of these characteristics the German *Heimstädte* have their own will, their own *telos*. This is directed towards maintaining a 'small town' way of life and the accompanying intense engagement of the individual in urban communal life. Tönnies has described such a finality as *Wesenswille*. In economic domains this is expressed in the will to maintain guilds and corporations; in social domains it expresses itself in strong social control, and in political domains in an extensive system of patronage. The finality of Walker's study lies especially in the *Heimatrecht*, which achieves the culmination of the ideal type 'home town' in the forties of the nineteenth century.

Collective participation

The home town can be described as a 'communarchy' when seen in the light of the system of patronage and the strong bond between the citizens and their administration. This term expresses the great involvement of all the populace in administrative matters. It also implies animosity towards the urbanite population of merchants, free artisans and government employees. The inhabitants of home towns refer to these more progressive, urbanite sectors of the population by the label 'movers and doers' or by the Hegelian term 'general estate'. (See the title of Walker's book. Hegel considered government employees to be the *allgemeine Stand*, whose closest English equivalent would be the term 'general estate'.) The contrast between home town citizens and the 'movers and doers' was still mainly a passive cultural opposition in the eighteenth century.[6] In the nineteenth century, however, this became an active political opposition between two different continuing entities with distinct forms of collective participation. The pre-eminent aim of the participatory activity of the home-town inhabitant is maintaining 'mediocrity'. This description is not meant derogatively. It should be seen as an attempt to avoid extremes with regard to number, wealth and power:

> Of course the community knew clear gradations of wealth, influence and social standing within itself. It expected different things of different people. But it did not tolerate too wide a spread or too rapid a shift, nor did the gradations make differences among hometownsmen even comparable to the differences

between themselves and the other castes. The home town maintained a steady pressure on all members toward the median.'[7]

Quasi-subject

From the above passage it is also clear that Walker's German home town sees itself as an acting subject: the home town knows something, it tolerates and maintains. It has the nature of a quasi-subject. Walker emphasizes that every home town should be considered an individuality.[8]

Home towns are, as quasi-subjects, part of another, more encompassing quasi-personage: the state. The relationship between these two is, according to Walker, not invariably amicable.[9] Especially in the nineteenth century, town and state developed completely different finalities. The home town endeavoured to maintain itself (*Wesenswille*); the state tried to achieve new rational goals, usually on the terrain of power and wealth. The home town is a way of life; the state considers itself more and more a means to an end. The idea of community in the German home town takes the guise of conformism. The collective participation of the state is based on rational consensus regarding 'calculated' goals. But in achieving this, a great deal of non-conformism remains possible. Sanctions are applied by professionalized government institutions, such as judges. The goal here is the mediation of conflicts, and the judges themselves are not involved in the conflict. Thus the state personifies Tönnies' *Kurwille*. That is why Walker puts the opposition between home town and state in the context of Tönnies' opposition between *Gemeinschaft* and *Gesellschaft*.[10]

Home town:	State:
• Strives to maintain itself.	• Has rational goals and is active.
• Represents a way of life.	
• Seeks preservation of that way of life.	• Considers itself an instrument, a means to an end.
• Collective participation takes the guise of conformism achieved through social control.	• Seeks wealth and power.
• *Wesenswille* (Tönnies)	• Collective participation on the basis of consensus with regard to calculated goals; non-conformism is possible. Sanctions are administered by professionalized government institutions; mediation of conflicts is their goal and the

judges themselves are not
involved in the conflict.
- *Kurwille* (Tönnies)

In the conflict with its internal and external enemies – the continually-resurgent urban patriciate in the seventeenth and eighteenth centuries and liberalism and bureaucratism in the nineteenth century, respectively – the communarchy continually changes its collective participation without giving up its core, the *Wesenswille*. In the nineteenth century this separate participation-ideology received a helping hand by way of the *Heimatrecht*. As the free traffic of goods and persons became more common in the rest of Europe, the home towns obtained the right to regulate the import and export of products, to refuse immigrants access to their territory, to forbid marriages, and so on. This politico-cultural dichotomy between town and state (two autonomous continuing entities) does not cause the home-town inhabitants to recalibrate their conception of community, but leads to a politically more aware and more aggressive defence of the home town ideology. Instead of a *Kurwille* based on rational consensus, the inhabitants clung to the traditional exclusive – because it excludes strangers – communarchal *Wesenswille*. The nature of the home town as subject now becomes very evident. Hence Walker also considers these towns to be the principal effectors of the 'Biedermeier' culture, and he considers Tönnies' concept *Gemeinschaft* to have originated in the communarchal nature of German home towns.

The most important function of the home town as explanatory subject concerns the genesis of the *petite bourgeoisie* or lower-middle class. The German *Kleinbürgertum*, in Walker's opinion, does not emerge abruptly but is the product of a process taking centuries. The factors contributing to this genesis are not so much objective factors regarding class, but factors of a politico-cultural and socio-mental nature. In the seventeenth and eighteenth centuries the *petite bourgeois* mentality was formed by a high degree of involvement in the political and cultural life of the town, a strong sense of class and discrimination against non-citizens. In the nineteenth century the home-town citizen disengaged himself even further from the Western bourgeoisie and, using among other things the *Heimatrecht*, took to a xenophobic ideology. In 1871 the home town went under in Bismarck's second empire, but the home-town ideology stood fast. The *petite bourgeoisie* continued to exist as a separate social group as a result of its mentality. Hereby Walker gives an internal finalistic explanation for the phenomenon of the German *petite bourgeoisie*.[11] The analysis of the German home towns also explains the genesis of the German lower-

German home town 1.

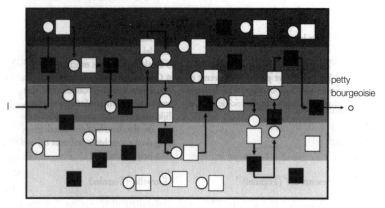

German home town 2.

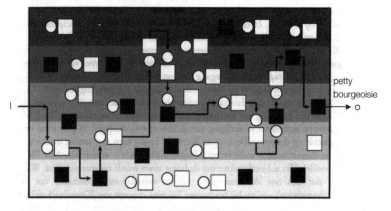

○ actors

■ intentional black boxes

□ mechanical black boxes

→ connecting line of singular causal imputation

I input = the genesis of the German home towns

O output = origin of the German petty bourgeoisie

Figure 8. German home towns

middle class. It should be noted here that this lower-middle class developed differently in the seventeenth century (a larger amount of political engagement and an aversion for the urban patriciate) than in the nineteenth century (*Heimatrecht*) (see Figure 8).

In this figure the rectangles (actually cylinders) represent the closed systems with which the German home towns can be compared. Every home town keeps its individuality, which is why there are various distinct cylinders.[12] Within the closed system – in other words, through the development of every home town individually – the lower-middle class emerges. After 1871, when the home town disappeared as a politico-judicial institution (quasi-subject), this *petite bourgeoisie* continued to exist. It retained its home-town mentality and hence became an easy prey for National Socialism. Walker and Gillis have called this explanation for the emergence of the *petite bourgeoisie* 'vertical' stratification. The term 'vertical' stems from the position of the cylinders in their diagrams, as a result of which the output emerges from the top of the cylinders.[13]

Studies of individual cities. Blumin's threshold

The American urban historian Blumin wrote *The urban threshold. Growth and change in a nineteenth-century American community*.[14] Blumin's book treats the history of the city Kingston (New York) from 1820 to 1860. Although Blumin acknowledges the possibility that the city can only be seen as a 'site' or, as he personally prefers to say, an 'archive', he wishes to examine Kingston as a 'community'.[15]

Continuing entity

Blumin takes Wirth's definition of a city as a starting-point. Wirth describes the city as a place with a large, dense, permanent and hetero-geneous population. This is a dichotomous definition of 'city', because Wirth assumes villages have the opposite characteristics. Blumin opposes this trite conception of villages as opposed to cities. He does not want to proceed from the assumption that villages are isolated and integrated (a 'community') and cities are open and anomic. Kingston the village in 1820 is actually less coherent than the urban Kingston of 1860. Kingston in 1860 is a 'community', whereas in 1820 it had not yet become one. To Blumin this indicates that cities are autonomous systems:

> Communities are not merely archives offering, in varying degrees, the specific
> phenomena, political, social and economic historians happen to be looking

for. They are themselves phenomena shaping and shaped by the lives of those who reside within them and interacting in various ways with other forms of social organization lying partly or wholly outside them.[16]

Finalism

Blumin hereby conceives the city as a closed system, which strives towards the integration of political, economical and social phenomena (partial systems). The development occurring in Kingston between 1820 and 1860 is internally finalistic and structured by a clear input and output. Around 1820, Blumin thus characterizes the ideal type of the 'input', Kingston as a 'country town', a village society, which is marked by a strong individualism and a weak local identity. Blumin credits this to the agrarian character of the inhabitants and their Dutch descent. Villagers lived fairly isolated in self-contained households, and the Dutch were greater individualists than the English, according to the author.[17] The role of the Nederduyts Gereformeerde Kerk (Dutch Reformed Church) was greater than that of the urban community and its administration.[18]

The ideal type of the 'output' looks different. In 1860 Kingston has a stronger identity as a community than in 1820.[19] The population growth and social economic changes '[. . .] served to strengthen the community where it had been weakest and helped turn the attention of cosmopolitan minds inward on the town'.[20] Spatially as well as associationally Kingston developed from a town with a weak coherence to a coherent community. Kingston's finality can in this regard be compared to the development of Weber's classical polis. There we found a process from feudal clan relations to (military) citizenship in the polis. We could also apply Mumford's term 'urban implosion' to Blumin's perspective on Kingston's increasing coherence. In the rural phase (around 1820) the attention of the 32 most important families was concentrated on the corporative structure and developments elsewhere in the region. There was little participation in associations, and the militia and fire department barely functioned. 'The general weakness and inactivity of Kingston's formal organisations [. . .] may well reflect the orientations of many of her residents to systems both above and below the community.'[21]

Collective participation

This externally-directed attention of the urban community slowly turned inward. This participatory implosion 'provided Kingston with a group life and even a collective awareness and *identity* [italics: HJ] that seems to have been but weakly developed in the country town of the previous generation'.[22]

Here Blumin is barely concerned with factors concerning objective growth, but with the 'actors' perceptions of community'. With this remark he indicates that he wishes to examine the collective participation of the inhabitants of Kingston. This apparently has not remained constant. The participation of the inhabitants develops from a more or less incoherent, rural participation to a more coherent urban one.

Quasi-subject

Blumin conceives the town as quasi-subject. He tries, as is evident from the quotation above, to map the development of urban identity as it emerges between 1820 and 1860 in Kingston. Blumin illustrates coherence, participation and urban identity with the aid of the following arguments.

• In 1860 Kingston no longer has any ethnic sub-cultures or sub-communities.
• The activities of associations are no longer in the hands of the elite, but in those of a broad middle class.
• Middle-class immigrants are quickly integrated by means of associations in urban communal life.
• The activities of associations have become larger, more intensive and more regular.

A reviewer of this book, Doyle, formulates a remarkable point of criticism towards Blumin's methodology. Despite his admiration for the research with regard to participation, he states: 'The vigorous associational life that flourished among the middle class after 1845 is demonstrated but never precisely explained.'[23] Doyle thinks that Blumin has missed a chance to clarify an implicit presupposition of the book, namely that 'the increasing economic interdependence of the community, and particularly its middle class, now required more formal mechanisms to integrate and organize its collective activity'. Doyle regrets that Blumin does not highlight the fact that associational life helps individual members of the middle class to build a reputation in business or strengthen it, to obtain credit or business contacts or expand them, and so on. Associational life is an exponent of economic and social life and not merely a mental–cultural phenomenon, according to Doyle.[24] Blumin does not make use of the integration of more material data, and credits everything to collective participation.

This not wholly unjust criticism indicates that although Blumin does involve the social, political and cultural–mental partial systems in his study, he does not involve the economic one. With his criticism Doyle emphasizes the fact that, in this kind of integral urban history, the partial systems of culture and mentality (in Marx's terms the superstructure) in many cases receive more attention than the material and economic (partial) systems. Blumin shows – consider what has been said of the possibilities for integrating partial systems, as summed up by Briggs and Lampard – more resemblance to Briggs than to Lampard. Blumin's work is an explicit example of a subjectifying approach; the author is writing an urban biography. He shows the internal finality of Kingston from 'Dutch' village to American town. The village does not have a particular identity; the town does. Just as in the cases used as examples from the long-term studies, the ideal-typical methodology is noteworthy. The ideal types in these cases have been formed around two different forms of participation.

Intermezzo: Incoherent systems

Coherent systems are dominated by the intentions of actors and the intentional black boxes linked to them. Disintegrating systems appear when intentional black boxes are dominated by mechanical ones. In other words: the black boxes are no longer controlled by the actors. In these cases we are concerned with systems in which the unintended effects of collective action in particular have gained ascendancy over the intended effects.[25] Such incoherent closed systems show a very different concatenation of actors and black boxes than is evident in the coherent systems described above. In the article 'Autonome historische Prozesse – kybernetisch betrachtet' Hoyningen-Huene shows the constitution of such systems. The goal of the article is 'tracking down the nature of necessity in an autonomous process'. In other words: Hoyningen-Huene asks himself to what extent mechanical black boxes can obstruct the intentions of the actors, causing the teleology to be transformed into a quasi-teleology. In the footsteps of the German theoretician of history, Meier, Hoynigen-Huene concludes that the autonomous efficacy or direct linearity of a process emerges because unintended side-effects of actions – namely: mechanical black boxes – gain ascendancy over conscious intentions.[26] As a result of this processes become more or less irreversible.

His clearest example is the replacement of horsepower by motorized transport. The intention to transport oneself by the use of motors was a consciously desired aim of a growing number of actors. In the initial phases of the use of motors it was still possible to transport oneself by means other than the automobile or the motorcycle. The wish for faster and more comfortable transportation was an incentive for further motorization. Mechanical black boxes in the end won out over reversible intentions. This occurred mainly through the adaptation of living and work places to the possibilities of motorized transport. Industrial and residential areas increasingly became separated from one another. This separation was based on the mechanical black box concerned with speedy motorized travel. Non-motorized alternatives became increasingly less expedient. The black boxes even won out over intentions when it was discovered that traffic jams and environmental pollution made alternatives to motorized traffic more and more desirable. This can partially be imputed to the separation of residential and working quarters, partially to the attraction of more comfortable transportation. Unintended side-effects gained ascendancy over intentions that were directed elsewhere.

This is a case of what is known as a positive feedback system. Such systems are characterized by the output of the first phase of the system's functioning as the input for the second phase and so on. The output of the closed system A1–B1 functions as the input of the closed system, B1/A2–B2 and so on. Just as the thermostat of a heating system takes the output of the heating system as input for the on–off mechanism, B1 functions as a 'thermostat' for A2. Here attention should be paid to the fact that the input of every new closed system continually shifts towards a weakening of the intentional acts of the actors and a reinforcement of the side-effects of the black boxes (see Figure 9). As we have seen, this can go so far that there comes a moment in which the intention to motorize is lost or even when action is undertaken against motorization, without the side-effects being susceptible to containment. See also the example of the butterfly's wing in Brazil's causing a storm in Texas, while a million of the same wings are incapable of breaking off the stormy effects. Intentions no longer do the sorcerer's apprentice any good; the spells have gone over his head.

As we look for a historical example of such disintegrating systems we arrive, I would almost say self-evidently, at the fall of the Western Roman Empire. In the analysis Max Weber gives of this problem, we find almost all elements of closed systems in evidence. First of all we have the explicit statement by Weber that the decline was not effected externally, but was the result of an internal process. In a lecture held in 1896 regarding 'Die soziale Gründe des Untergangs der Antiken Kultur' he stated:

> The Roman Empire was not destroyed from outside through the superior numbers of its opponents or the incompetence of its political leaders (. . .) the

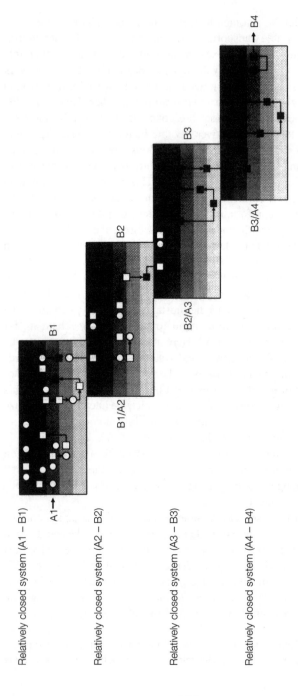

Figure 9. 'Positive' feedback system

Empire had not been itself for a long time; when it fell, it did not collapse suddenly under one thundering blow. The *Völkerwanderung* was rather the result of a development that had for a long time been in flux.[27]

Regarding the closed character of the process described here, no doubt need exist.

In Weber's opinion the finality of the Roman Empire rested on three pillars:

1. The black boxes of an urban economy and administration.
2. Grain speculators, war profiteers, tax overseers and slaveholders as the most influential actors.
3. A collective participation, consisting of intentional black boxes, directed towards the conquering of rich coastal areas around the Mediterranean Sea, which emerged from 'private' capitalism and imperialism.

The state as quasi-subject maintained all these because capitalists, imperialistic administrators and urbanites all participated in them. When in late republican and imperial times conquering rich coastal areas was followed by the conquering of poorer areas inland (Gaul and Germany), the urban nature of administration and culture slowly disappeared. Hence the state had less opportunities for exercising its encompassing functions. By bureaucratizing the state, Emperor Diocletian and his successors tried to turn the tide. This, however, entailed that 'private' capitalism had to make way for state capitalism with its mandatory fees and guilds, binding peasants to their land and replacing the tax-farmers by government tax officials. With the decline of private capitalism the urban structure of the empire disintegrated even further; the late Roman feudalization of the state emerged, and in this manner the urban, private capitalistic and Mediterranean-imperialistic participation upon which the empire was based was continually undermined. The main intention of maintaining the empire had as an unintended side effect the erosion of the main pillars upon which it rested. These intentional manoeuvres generated black boxes with an adverse effect.[28]

In the discussion of the 'fulfilment' of the ideal type of the classical polis as well as in that of the fall of the Roman empire, one should not speak of respectively one goal-directed and one disintegrating closed system, but of a concatenation of several closed systems.

The question now, naturally, arises of whether goal-directed and incoherent systems can also be linked. This question can be answered affirmatively. It will not be difficult for the reader to link the previously-mentioned closed system of the classical polis, which can certainly be applied to Rome,[29] to the incoherent systems of the later Roman empire. In this manner the possibility of a 'rise and fall' development in a closed system can be shown.[30]

It is also possible to link systems in the reverse direction: not moving from a goal-directed system to a disintegrating one, as in the case of Weber's rise and fall of the classical polis, but from a disintegrating to a goal-directed one. The following examples from urban historiography serve to illustrate this situation.

Application of the concept of incoherent systems to urban historiography: Frisch and Mumford

Here we are firstly concerned with two studies by the American historian Frisch, who examined the developments in the town of Springfield between 1840 and 1880. His process analysis is based on the construction of two ideal types: one concerning Springfield up to 1840 and the other concerning Springfield in 1880, which he calls respectively 'town' and 'city'. I will first deal with the ideal type 'town', and after that with the development of the incoherent system that illustrates the demise of this ideal type; then I will discuss the model 'city', and finally I will discuss the goal-directed system that deals with the creation of the ideal type 'city'.

Springfield as 'town' (1840) was an urban community in which the mutual ties between its members were personal and confidential. The sense of community was concrete and not subject to reflection. It manifested itself in a flourishing associational life with fancy fairs, local parties, an active voluntary fire corps and the like.[31] Although artisans were fairly well represented in the town council, the town administration itself formed a closed, elite corporation. The pre-eminent goal of this administration was representing the interests of the taxpayers. This meant that for the administrators there was no clear distinction between the private and the public spheres, that the administrative tasks were limited in size and were fulfilled as side functions, and that the lower strata of the urban community were not represented and hence held a position somewhat similar to that of metics (resident aliens).[32]

The elite character of the town administration had been under pressure from the beginning of the century. The large geographic and vertical mobility continually caused new faces to appear amongst the elite. This, however, did not lead to democratization or greater openness within the administrative corporation. The newcomers did strive for administrative renewal but quickly adapted themselves to the old elitist mentality as soon as they were *arrivé*. In a certain sense, the elitist structure of the administration was reinforced as the participation of artisans dropped from 32 per cent to 4 per cent between 1840 and 1880.[33]

Despite conscious attempts to change course – I shall return to this point later – here barely-controllable black boxes are clearly in evidence. The elitist character also obstructed the city administration in dealing with the problems of the new times arising in Springfield. An illuminating example is the idea of 'true economy'. This notion entailed that communal funds should be carefully managed. This at first sight admirable goal was mainly based on the interests of the taxpayer and thereby the interests of the members of the urban corporation (lower groups of the populace barely paid direct taxes). For this reason a great many administrators advocated high sewer taxation in the 1870s. Sewers would in this manner remain restricted to their circles. Those who lent more weight to considerations of general well-being and hygiene demanded a low sewer tax. That would, after all, lead to a greater number of fixtures. These more-modern notions did not simply vanquish the traditional conceptions regarding what are referred to as fiscal integrity and individual profit, even when it was clear to everybody that 'true economy' no longer existed.[34]

Not only did the black boxes function among the administrators, but they were also efficacious among the citizens themselves. The elitist administration had, in the course of time, aroused so much suspicion that any change – even if it was to the advantage of the citizens – was regarded with suspicion. The most spectacular example of this is the acceptance of a new communal charter in 1877. This charter, which was aimed at modernizing the administrative structure, the corporative nature of which was meant to be abolished, was dismissed by the citizens because of traditional suspicion of the 'regents' (black boxes!).[35]

As output for the complex closed system he sketches, Frisch designs a new ideal type, the 'city'. This type is marked by a more-formal form of participation amongst the inhabitants of the city and a growing sense of mutual dependence as a result of the increasing number of communal utilities such as sewers, water mains, public services and so on.[36] The need to arrange administration more efficiently became stronger as a result of these factors, and furthermore the notion that administration not only serves the taxpayer but also serves the common good gained ascendancy. The conception of community hence became more abstract. Politics was seen more and more as the systematic opposition of social polarizations. The opposition between the private and public spheres sharpened.[37]

The second ideal type directs the black boxes and actors previous to it. It creates a goal-directed closed system, which is characterized by 'city' – instead of 'town' – thinking. Especially the communal utilities mentioned above and the wish fundamentally to renew the city administration by way of the Charter of 1877 illustrate the goal-directed and collective wish to change the urban community fundamentally. The tensions between the old and the new conceptions of the city led to a crisis in the years 1870–1877. According to Frisch, a local newspaper formulated this crisis in the following way: 'we are just discovering the difference between a city and a town'.[38]

Schematically, Frisch distinguishes between the following periods:

1840–1860   The 'town' conception is still very much alive.
1860–1865   Enlargement of scale without adaptation.
1865–1870   The emergence of the new conception and the first conflicts between old and new conceptions of community.
1870–1873   Escalation of conflict, especially with regard to the 'true economy'.
1873-1877   An economic crisis leads to a complete crisis in the community.
1877–1880   Firsts attempts at and results of the new 'city' conception.

In this manner Frisch creates two different types of closed systems through the use of ideal types; the first of these – the incoherent system – is driven along by hard-to-control mechanical black boxes emanating from the ideal type 'town', while the second goal-directed system encompasses all the possible actions and 'drives' for the achievement of the ideal type 'city'. This can be depicted graphically in the following way.

Not all cases involve a link between an incoherent and a goal-directed system, such as the one elucidated by Frisch. Mumford reveals an opposite sequence in his *The city in history*. He sketches the development of cities (after antiquity) as a goal-directed, collective process that achieves its climax in the medieval city. After 1500 steadily-increasing disintegration is in evidence. In contrast to Walker's *German home towns*, which managed to develop their own identity in their conflict with the state, the cities described by Mumford continually suffer defeat at the hands of the state, as a result of which they sink deeper and deeper in a swamp of impotence. This process is reinforced by the fact that the new heads of state create a mentality in the cities in which credence is given to megalomaniac concepts such as Divine Rights and Absolute Sovereignty,

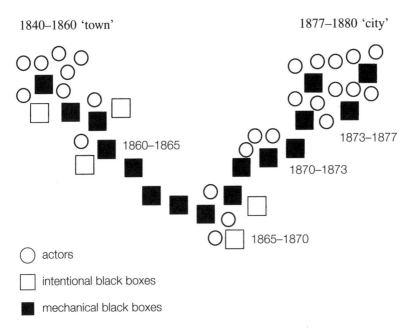

Figure 10. Disintegrating system 1840–1865 and goal-directed system ca 1870–1880

according to Mumford. This is why a new urban consciousness arises in the cities in which increased scale, large numbers and territorial expansion are considered important. 'The merchant cannot be too rich; the state cannot possess too much territory, the city cannot become too big.'[39]

The harmony of the medieval city is continually undermined, and the Baroque city, with its 'quest for financial and political power' takes its place. The nadir is formed by the nineteenth-century industrial city, in which the urban fate seems completely subjugated by the black boxes concerning capital, coal, dust and stench. Mumford synthesizes the European – especially the English – industrial city in the ideal type 'Coketown'. This is a name taken from Dickens for the prototype of an English industrial city: Manchester. This city of cotton and capitalism is used by Mumford to illustrate the disintegrating character of all nineteenth-century cities. He formulates this incoherent character by describing the participation in nineteenth-century industrial cities as purposeless. He therefore calls the Victorian cities themselves 'man-heaps, not agents of human association'.[40] The sequence described by Mumford runs from the ideal type of the medieval *communitas*, which he evaluates positively, by way of the incoherence of an increasingly capitalistic mentality and uncontrollable increases of scale, to the nadir of 'Coketown'.

In this third Part I have analysed two types of systems: goal-directed systems, of which Weber, Walker and Blumin offer examples in their studies, and incoherent systems, which form the reverse of goal-directed systems and which therefore can (partially) be found in the work of Mumford and Walker, but of which Frisch offers the most explicit example. In the case of goal-directed systems, as ideal-typically described, incoherent input is in evidence as well a decline of the influence of black boxes, an increase in the influence of actors and a coherent output, which can also be described as an ideal type. Incoherent or disintegrating systems form the mirror image of goal-directed systems. They consist of an ideal-typical input with the coherence of urban life as its main feature. However, in the course of time the influence of mechanical black boxes starts to increase and the influence of actors declines. In the end there is only incoherence in the ideal type of the output.

Closed systems have as common properties an input, intentional black boxes, actors, mechanical black boxes, partial systems and an output. By constructing input and output on the basis of ideal types, three types of closed systems can be constructed: goal-directed, disintegrating and combined systems. The goal-directed system will effect an integration of partial systems by showing how a coherent urban life founded on strong participation can emerge from an anomic and incoherent situation. The disintegrating system reveals the opposite development. The combined system is characterized by the different possibilities for linking both other systems.[41] With the aid of Weber's procedure for singular causal imputation, the specific tracks of mechanical and intentional black boxes on the one hand and actors on the other can be discovered. In this manner adequate explanations can be constructed for encompassing developments.

In Chapter 4 I indicated the importance that Briggs assigned to the politico-institutional, social, and cultural–mental partial systems in urban historical research. The importance of 'civic pride' within his research also came to the fore. In the light of what has been said regarding the finality, participation and identity of closed system constructions in this chapter and in Chapter 5, I hope it has become clear to the reader why Briggs has a preference for such partial systems.

Notes

1. M. Walker, *German home towns. Community, state and general estate 1648–1871* (London 1971). In the original Dutch version of the present monograph the following studies have also been included: A. Briggs, *Victorian cities* (Harmondsworth, 1968), S. B. Warner, *The private city. Philadelphia in three periods of its growth* (Philadelphia, PA 1968) and D. Fraser, *Power and authority in the Victorian city* (Oxford 1979), and from the hand of the same author: *Urban politics in Victorian England. The structure of politics in Victorian cities* (London 1979). See also H. Jansen, *De constructie van het stadsverleden. Een systeemtheoretische analyse van het stodshistorish onderzoek fer bevordering van de synthetiserende geschiedschryving* (Groningen 1991), pp. 139–40, 148–50 and 157–63.

2. S. Blumin, *The urban threshold. Growth and change in a nineteenth-century American community* (Chicago 1976).

3. M. H. Frisch, *Town into city. Springfield Massachusetts and the meaning of community 1840–1880* (Cambridge, MA 1972) and M. H. Frisch, 'The community elite and the emergence of urban politics', in S. Thernstrom and R. Sennett (eds), *Nineteenth-century cities: essays in the new urban history* (New Haven, CT 1976 [1st edn 1969]).

4. M. Walker, *German home towns. Community, state and general estate 1648–1871*, pp. 26–33.

5. Ibid., p. 56.

6. Ibid., pp. 112–20.

7. Ibid., pp. 133–4.

8. Ibid., pp. 1–5.

9. Ibid., pp. 190 ff.

10. Ibid., pp. 191–2.

11. Ibid., pp. 417 ff. Here we encounter a clear example of Von Wright's 'causal analysis' and of Weber's singular causal imputation.

12. Here one can speak of multiple causes. Smelser has noted that in Weber's *verstehende* [interpretative] sociology identical effects can have different causes. This in contrast to what Smelser calls nomothetical sociology, in which identical effects can only be achieved by identical causes: N. J. Smelser, *Methods in the social sciences.* (Englewood Cliffs, NJ 1976), pp. 141–9.

13. J. R. Gillis, 'German home towns', *Journal of Social History* (abbr. henceforth *JSH*) VI(3) (1973): 367–70.

14. S. Blumin, *The urban threshold. Growth and change in a nineteenth-century American community* (Chicago, Illinois 1976).
15. Ibid., p. 8.
16. Ibid., pp. 44–5.
17. Ibid., p. 48.
18. Ibid., p. 27.
19. Ibid., p. 220.
20. Ibid., p. 218.
21. Ibid., pp. 47–8.
22. D. H. Doyle, 'Nineteenth-century cities. Evolutionary and instantaneous', *Journal of Urban History* (henceforth abbr. *JUH*) V(1) (1978): 109–17, esp. 112.
23. Ibid., pp. 112–13.
24. Ibid., p. 113.
25. Lorenz is aware of the problem that in history not all phenomena can be reduced to individual or even collective intentions. He does not, however, explain the consequences that the transition from intended to unintended results of actions has for the writing of history: Chr. Lorenz, *De constructie van het verleden. Een inleiding in de theorie van de geschiedenis* (Meppel, Amsterdam 1987), p. 94.
26. P. Hoyningen-Huene, 'Autonome historische Prozesse – kybernetisch betrachtet', *Geschichte und Gesellschaft* 9 (1983): 119–23, esp. 120.
27. 'Das Römische Reich wurde *nicht* [italics: HJ] von aussen her zerstört, etwa infolge zahlenmässiger Überlegenheit seiner Gegner oder der Unfähigkeit seiner politische Leiter [. . .] das Reich war längst nicht mehr es selbst; als es zerfiel, brach es nicht plötzlich unter einem gewaltigen Stosse zusammen. Die Völkerwanderungen zog vielmehr nur das Fazit einer längst im Fluss befindlichen Entwicklung': Max Weber, *SWG*, p. 289; G. Abramowski, *Das Geschichtsbild Max Webers. Universalgeschichte am Leitfaden des okzidentalen Rationalisierungsprozesses* (Stuttgart 1966), p. 112.
28. G. Abramowski, *Das Geschichtsbild Max Webers*, pp. 111–13.
29. Ibid., p. 98.
30. R. P. Appelbaum, *Theories of social change* (Boston 1970), pp. 99–115. Appelbaum discusses several sociologists who have used such a 'rise-and-fall' construction. He counts Weber among these.
31. M. H. Frisch, *Town into city*, pp. 32–50.
32. Ibid., p. 242 and M. H. Frisch, 'The community elite and the emergence of urban politics', pp. 277–96, esp. 280–3.
33. M. H. Frisch, 'The community elite and the emergence of urban politics', pp. 279 and 284–5.

34. M. H. Frisch, *Town into city*, pp. 183–4 and 200. The city put itself deeply into debt during the seventies by spending on expensive communal facilities such as water mains, railroads, public buildings and so on.
35. M. H. Frisch, *Town into city*, pp. 215–18.
36. M. H. Frisch, *Town into city*, pp. 165, 219, 247 and M. H. Frisch, 'The community elite and the emergence of urban politics', p. 286.
37. M. H. Frisch, *Town into city*, pp. 174, 217–18, 225, 229; M. H. Frisch, 'The community elite and the emergence of urban politics', pp. 283–85 and 291.
38. M. H. Frisch, *Town into city*, p. 214.
39. L. Mumford, *The city in history. Origins, its transformation and its prospects* (Harmondsworth 1979 [London 1961]), p. 420.
40. Ibid., p. 512.
41. In the case of a switch from a disintegrating to a goal-directed system, a transition also occurs from a coherent input–output to a coherent input–output mediated by a process of disintegration and reintegration. In case of a switch from a goal-directed to a disintegrating system, beginning and end phases will display incoherence, with an ideal type in between marked by a great deal of participation and coherence.

Part IV
Half-Open System Constructions in Urban Historiography

'[. . .] the explanations found in history books are a logically miscellaneous lot.'

W. Dray, *Laws and explanation in history*, p. 85.

7

Babushkas of City Systems: Macro Levels in Long-Term Urban Studies

In a regatta, there are two types of spectators. The first chooses a fixed spot to watch the race (for example in the stands), the second takes a bicycle and follows the exertions of the participants from start to finish. This last type of spectator can be compared to what Mitchel has called 'performance' systems and for which I have used the term 'relatively-closed systems' in this study. They follow the exertions of historical actors by observing them from beginning to end. The behaviour of the people in the stands is representative for researchers of what Mitchel calls 'structural' systems,[1] or in this study for those historical researchers who work according to the half-open system model.

The spectators on the stands cannot follow the exertions of their heroes from beginning to end from their fixed spot, yet they compensate for this disadvantage by examining the condition of the course. For example, they consider the undulation of the water, the force and direction of the wind, the relative humidity and so on. The bicyclists can, at the end of the race, say the losers had 'arms of lead', having seen this from the bank. Those in the stands can explain that the losers had the misfortune to be on the lee side of the river and hence encountered less advantageous wave patterns. These latter spectators partially miss the 'actor's point of view' of the cyclists; the cyclists are less able to view the boats as sub-systems of natural conditions. The spectators in the stands are in a better situation to give 'contextual' explanations because of their knowledge of conditions. They take an 'observer's point of view'.

The distinction made in the half-open system approach between macro-levels or system levels and micro-levels or sub-system levels implies a partition in this part of urban historiography. There are urban historical studies that analyse the encompassing system and there are studies that are referred to as 'sub-system studies'. I shall refer to the studies that analyse the system, for reasons of convenience, as 'macro-studies', because the term 'system studies' might evoke associations with urban studies of closed systems, as well as the systems-theoretical approach towards urban historiography in general. The term 'sub-system studies' will be maintained, although the synonym 'micro-studies' will also be used. One should bear in mind here that, although macro-studies do not ignore urban sub-systems completely, to the extent that sub-systems are considered, they serve only to elucidate the system as a whole. For micro-studies the reverse holds true. In this chapter the macro-level will be scrutinized by way of several long-term studies. In the next chapter the micro-level will be dealt with.

Just as in the case of closed systems, the justification of the half-open system construction is important for the recognition of its meaning for historical writing in general. It is for this reason that notions from the theory of history underlying the distinction micro-level/macro-level will be examined. That these notions will be tested in the same manner as closed systems through the use of urban historiography goes without saying.

The nature and structure of macro-systems

Macro-systems, as present in urban historiography, are urban, non-urban or mixed. If the system is urban, it consists of one or another aggregate of urban phenomena, for example a network of cities or a – possibly quantified – agglomeration of cities. In the studies of Rozman and De Vries discussed below, urban networks are considered; Lampard uses a mixed system of city–countryside relationships.[2] It goes without saying that a non-urban macro-system will not be discussed here. (For this see the analysis of Sjoberg in the next chapter.)

In addition to consideration of the nature of macro-systems, some attention must be given to their structure. With regard to the latter, macro-systems are similar to babushkas, the well-known dolls shaped like a Polish or Russian (grand)mother, each of which contains a smaller babushka, which itself again contains a babushka, and so on.[3] The systems theoreticians McGrath, Nordlie and Vaughn express this 'nested' character by means of the proposition that every system capable of being studied is part of a larger system and consists of more than one 'molecular' system.[4] Schmal distinguishes between four 'babushkas' in urban research at a macro-level:[5]

a. An international or national system dominated by several metropolises, and further marked by an incremental, regularly-descending hierarchy of cities determined by size, with an increasing number of centres of decreasing populations at the lower levels.

b. A regional system, sometimes embedded in a national system, which is less clearly hierarchically structured, and is usually organized around one metropolis, and in which the towns at the lower levels are smaller and decrease more quickly in size than at the national level.

c. Cities as sub-systems, which form the living space of the inhabitants and which absorb and reorganize the encircling countryside.

d. Sometimes sub-systems that are internal to the city.

Because these systems and sub-systems have the same structure in principle, we can see here how the *fractalization* that was discussed with regard to chaos theory takes shape at the macro-level.

In his study 'Cities as systems within systems of cities' Berry posits that two routes in urban research have arrived at systems theory. The first route he calls that of the 'inductive generalisation'. This route pertains to generalizations that have been obtained by statistical analysis of data. An example is 'rank-size' research, which concerns itself with constructing hierarchies of cities with regard to the size of the population. Concerning this Berry remarks that '[. . .] the distribution of population within cities is a function of the position of these cities within the entire system of cities at some point in time, and the period of time for which they have been within the system'.[6] This route of 'inductive generalization' leads to the conception of the macro-level of half-open systems. The second route he calls the 'logical construction'. Here the location of cities is at issue. As example Berry gives the discussion over 'central place theory' as it has ignited around the work of Christaller.[7] At issue here is a theory that also pertains to the macro-level of half-open systems, and that concerns itself not with a hierarchy of cities formed on the basis of population density but with one based on practical functions (such as a market, shops, and administrative and cultural facilities). In both cases cities or parts of cities are viewed as sub-systems of systems. Berry is not a historian, and the urban studies he mentions cannot be considered historiographical. Nonetheless, approaches can be found in urban history that can be counted under the rank-size model and the theory of central places. A historical study according to the rank-size model is given by J. de Vries in his *European Urbanisation 1500–1800*.[8] In various studies Rozman has examined the hierarchies of central places in Japan, Russia, England, and France. Studies by both authors will be discussed in this chapter.

The explanatory function of the macro-level

In the preceding chapter we have seen how closed systems, through the construction of quasi-subjects, succeeded in achieving tight-knit urban syntheses. In the case of half-open systems analysis, the opposite often occurs. The subjectification is replaced by objectification, because the macro-systems put the sub-systems in a context and also because the macro-systems are in turn sometimes theoretically 'highlighted'. This last is done by comparing the specific relationships between the partial systems (or partial system elements or variables) as they occur in the macro-system with universally valid relationships in a super-system or theory. The synthesis of half-open systems is characterized by a receding theoretical horizon.

Hereby the macro-systematic babushkas take a route opposite to that of Hempel's Covering Law Model (CLM). Hempel formulated a rigid law, the pretensions of which have been continually moderated in its application, until he arrived at 'explanatory sketches' or other such modifications.[9] The theory of half-open systems gives us a plausible explanatory construction without necessarily involving a law. A nomo-thetical or theoretical explanation can serve as a context, but is not essential. If a theory is used, then the babushkas of macro-systems ensure a gradual moderation of the theoretical aspect. In this context Jerzy Topolski speaks, in the footsteps of L. Nowak, of a 'sequence of concreti-sations'.[10] Such a sequence runs from less to more direct causes.[11] This hierarchy of conditions indicates that explanation also has a topological aspect. That is to say that certain causes must be given a place in the totality of possible explanations. In the case of half-open systems, it is mainly the ordering of macro-systems and sub-systems to organize an explanation that is at issue, rather than the use of a law to justify an explanation.[12] That such an organized explanation can have more force than a law or a theory I hope to justify in what follows.

Systems instead of explanatory sketches

In answer to the question why a particular perch has died of lack of oxygen, the advocate of CLM can only answer that all living organisms – including perches – die if they do not get enough oxygen. This follows from the law that organisms need oxygen to survive. This CLM explana-tion, however, does not answer the question why this particular perch has died from lack of oxygen.[13]

In order to answer this question, we must not only subsume the concrete case under a law, but especially also subsume it under a concrete and analysable system. Hence we consider the above-mentioned perch to be a sub-system of a certain ecosystem, for example Lake Michigan. The water in this lake has been polluted with industrial effluents; hence it contains barely any oxygen, and that is why our perch has expired from suffocation.

We have done the following by means of such a system/sub-system construction:

a. We have created a system that can serve as an explanation, namely Lake Michigan as explanans.
b. The explanandum – the perch – has been further explicated, that is to say it has been described as a sub-system of the system Lake Michigan..

Although the explanans – the ecosystem 'Lake Michigan' – is not a covering law, it can be related to several covering laws. As a sound ecosystem, Lake Michigan can serve to effectuate the law that all living creatures require oxygen. As such, this lake can serve as explanans for a rich and easy piscine existence. However, the lake can also be conceived of as the explanans of the law that fishes – as living creatures – die if they do not have enough oxygen. This role as explanans can be assumed by Lake Michigan if it is polluted.

In both cases Lake Michigan is an acceptable explanation for the life and death of a particular perch. Yet it does not function as a covering law. These system explanations do, however, offer something more than, or rather something different from, a purely narrative correlation. The system can, after all, be coupled to a covering law without being one itself. Such a law can serve as justification (in retrospect) of the functioning of the system. For this reason, the system may have the 'holes' that Gardiner wanted to close with his covering law.[14] Schmal has pointed out that (half-open) systems can act as a handy explanans because of their non-rigid character.[15] The half-open systems explanations actually solve the problems that are insoluble for CLM. Hempel himself and Gardiner too have noted that it is not always possible for historians to indicate the law on which their explanation rests. Such a law may take such trivial forms that it is better to use an explanatory sketch instead of a law, through the underlying law should, of course, be identifiable.[16] Systems, in my opinion, are a better solution than Hempel's explanatory sketches. Systems on the one hand are more specific than laws, and on the other hand they embody recurrent patterns, as a result of which they show a great deal of reliability of their very nature. Explanatory sketches obtain this reliability only thanks to an identifiable underlying law. It is possible for systems to, at the least, exercise the same mediating function between laws and the explanandum as Hempel's explanatory sketches. In many cases the explanatory effect is even greater. As an intermediary link, the system often gives a further explanation of a law (see the example of the magnet in note 13), while an explanatory sketch exists only thanks to the law that has been left out. On this basis it may be posited that a system as the link between a law and a concrete case has more explanatory and, especially, more synthesizing force than an explanatory sketch.

The half-open systems explanation is also in accordance with a probabilistic syllogism. A probabilistic syllogism can have the following form:

(1) x (a1, a2, a3. . .) Pxb
(2) J (a1, a2, a3. . .)
==============================
(3) Jb

The first premise states that if a phenomenon (x) has properties (a1, a2, a3. . .), it is probable (*P*) that the phenomenon also has property (b). An example: x is a variable over the domain of Dutch Roman Catholics, furthermore *if* x has the following properties: x regularly goes to church (a1), listens to the KRO (a state-sponsored orthodox Catholic broadcasting association with membership) (a2), reads a Catholic newspaper (a3), lives in the fifties (a4), is married (a5), *then* x *probably* (*P*) has a large family (b). This is the first premise. The second premise is concerned with one particular substitution for x, for example an imaginary family Johnson (J), which possesses properties a1 to a5. The conclusion tells us that the Johnson family (J) has 9 children (b). The double line expresses the probabilistic nature of the conclusion.

The second premise pertains to a particular correlation frequency of two phenomena, namely: a specific Catholic with all the properties that accrue to him or her. In the first premise – the probabilistic law – a causal relationship is expressed between being Catholic and having many children. Of that causal relationship, it is stated that the relationship is not absolute but probable. The question now is whether one may equate a strong correlation in reality with the probable existence of a law. Ankersmit considers this an inappropriate identification of correlated phenomena with a probabilistic statement regarding laws. The latter is, after all, a statement regarding the extent to which an explanation is correct and the former – the correlation – is an observation with regard to real phenomena. These two cannot be linked, according to Ankersmit.[17]

From a systems-theoretical point of view, however, correlation and causality can be linked to one another. Systems are, after all, recurrent patterns and not laws. Systems are not required to fulfil conditions of universality and therefore are not on a completely different level from the concrete phenomena in reality that they describe. Furthermore, and this is most important in this case, the system can be investigated at greater length with regard to its causal operation; and that is impossible with a probabilistic explanation. Systems can do this because of their distributive properties and on the basis of the associative behaviour of sub-systems. If we stay with the example of the Catholic Johnson family with 9 children, then the following construction is possible. In a certain region, for example the south of the Netherlands, Catholic families with more than for example 7 children are selected. This selection is examined with regard to membership in a parish, membership of the KRO and the reading of a Catholic newspaper. Memberships and subscriptions prove to be in evidence in 90 per cent of the large families. There is therefore a strong correlation between a certain type of Catholicism and large families.

The question remains, however, whether there is a causal relationship in evidence here. We have, as it were, done nothing but examine the sub-system 'large family' with regard to associative characteristics. The sub-system is now placed in a system. This happens by means of research of the southern Dutch Catholicism in the period between 1950 and 1955. This can proceed by means by examining the Catholic newspapers of the region, KRO broadcasts, episcopal injunctions with regard to family size and birth control, and so on. These institutions of communication are intended to distribute their opinions among Catholics. This distributive property of the system corresponds to an associative property of the large family as sub-system, namely membership of the KRO and the parish and a subscription to a Catholic newspaper. Southern Dutch Catholicism cannot be considered a theory or law, but should be seen as a cultural system whose characteristics move from system to sub-system. Through association and distribution system and sub-system are engaged towards one another. What was first merely a correlation has become a full-fledged causal explanation by being subsumed in a system. Where the probabilistic law failed, the half-open systems explanation succeeds. This is because the gap between a correlation and a probabilistic law seems impassable, while the distance from the sub-system to the system can be kept as small as possible.

The example of the Johnson family also clarifies how we can place the actions of individuals or collectives in the context of a half-open system explanation. The reproductive behaviour of Mr and Mrs Johnson is not viewed from an actor's point of view, despite the pornographic possibilities that this throws open, and therefore cannot be qualified as being teleological. By way of the system the Johnson family is impressed with certain properties by which its behaviour can be dispositionally explained. Dispositional explanations clarify individual phenomena by imputing properties (dispositions) to them that belong to a more general class of phenomena. Thereby the individual phenomenon is subsumed into something less specific, the properties of which are known or in which a logical coherence can be observed. Insight into the class can hence lead to insight into the phenomena belonging to that class that are being researched.[18] The reverse is also possible: insight into the individual phenomenon can also yield new knowledge of that which is more general. The Johnson family can lead us to the reproductive behaviour of Catholics in the Brabant region in the fifties. What Topolski says regarding dispositional explanations can be applied to half-open system explanations in this light: 'It is [. . .] worth noting that when advancing explanations by reference to dispositions we may be interested either in the structure of the system [. . .] which we treat as the cause, or in the structure of the system [. . .] upon which a given cause, as we suppose, had acted.'[19]

Although dispositional explanations still show positivistic characteristics, this is much less so in the case of half-open system explanations. Precisely the wish to accentuate the synthetic element in half-open system explanations makes rigid positivism impossible.

Systems theory is not historism

Now that we have pried half-open system explanations somewhat loose from the CLM – and hence from positivism – the question arises whether we have not accidentally run into the arms of historism. Much can be said for this point. In several aspects the half-open system explanations that have been presented here do not appear to be a theory in the sense of a proposition that expresses a universal relationship between variables, which hold *ceteris paribus* and is falsifiable.[20] Indeed, such explanations more closely resemble presuppositions explicated in the context of synthesis, by which one can order data and relate them to one another.[21] The half-open system explanation is also directed towards synthesis in historical writing, something for which a positivistic theory is unsuitable.[22]

But doesn't this mean that systems theory is nothing more than narrative schemes or intrigues, as Peer Vries formulates the alternative to positivistic covering laws?[23] I do not think that this is the case. Comparison of the half-open system explanation presented here and Ankersmit's narrative substances can assist us here. Ankersmit considers his narrative substances to be interpretation categories of that part of historiography that occupies itself with synchronizing historiography. The examples that Ankersmit uses in most cases involve historical concepts that indicate a (stylistic) period, a culture, a nation or an intellectual movement, such as the Renaissance, the Enlightenment or the French nation. Ankersmit is not concerned with studies that, for example, have constitutional developments in England from 1688 to 1830 as their subject-matter.[24] Closed-system studies, as I have described them in the preceding chapter, are apparently not what Ankersmit had in mind in his study on the narrative character of historical writing. For that reason his ideas and mine concerning half-open systems can be compared reasonably well.

Ankersmit emphasizes that narrative substances do not originate through the application of concepts or ideas developed by others, but through the fabrication of an image by means of a configuration of facts, which is unique for every historian and every historical study. Every historian does unique research, because he forms his own point of view in the history he writes. This is different in the natural sciences, according to Ankersmit. There it occurs that one phenomenon (for example system S1) is explained in terms of another phenomenon – system S2 – that is better known. Such an explanation is possible in the natural sciences but not in history. Because the historical sciences are interpretative, whereby every historical narrative has its own *Gestalt*, that narrative cannot possibly be compared to other historical narratives,[25] according to Ankersmit. In my opinion, this contradicts the *modus operandi* of the historian. Every historian starts his study by broadly orientating himself using the historiography regarding his subject. This orientation does not serve solely to gather facts regarding the subject of study, but also serves to find comparable situations and structures that can explain the facts to be examined. Weber's ideal types have been so used by many German historians.[26] In the following discussions regarding urban historiography, we shall see that precisely in their manner of explanation and their use of time historical researchers often adopt each other's tactics. Their interpretations, though unique in their superstructures, are often not constructed as uniquely as Ankersmit would have us believe.[27]

Half-open system explanations, in my opinion, approach more closely the positivistic practice of science advocated by Vries than the narrativism of Ankersmit. These explanations are, after all, based on a research strategy consisting of a clear way of defining the research subject, a sharp explication of explanans and explanandum, 'systematic' and verifiable analysis, deductive reasoning from hypotheses, and explicit comparison. Doing research by way of a half-open systems approach implies dealing with the historical sciences in a problem-directed manner on the basis of a broad historical orientation, in which progress of knowledge is possible so long as that progress is sought in more explicitly formulated questions, more detailed analysis and more grounded answers. All of which are conditions Vries posits for a more positivistic approach towards the historical sciences.[28] In some cases one can even speak of the subordination of a system to a theory. The relationships explicated at a systems level then acquire a pretence to universal validity. Accumulation of knowledge, in the sense of encompassing more facts in one theory, then becomes possible. Sometimes it is even possible to formulate a new theory covering more and more diverse facts. These cases are, however, exceptional.

In this context it is important to know that urban historians who work with explanations in the form of half-open system constructions often enter into polemics against individualizing approaches, which are considered historistic. The use of macro-systems in urban historiography hence originated in positivist circles.

Partial systems and sub-systems in macro-systems. Organization and operation

The organization and operation of systems is rather complicated. Especially with regard to the effect of systems on sub-systems as they occur in urban historiography, some clarification is due. This effect occurs, as we have seen in Chapter 4, through the distributive influence of partial systems. These partial systems are used in a fairly general manner in some urban historical studies, but in most they are specified. The term 'variable' is used in cases of a very explicit operation of the partial system on the sub-system or vice-versa.

Half-open systems consist of the following parts:

a. *Systems* that encompass all the other parts mentioned hereafter of the system. These have boundaries just like closed systems, but these boundaries – in contrast to those of closed systems – do not have individualizing tendencies.

b. *Sub-systems*, which, in the context of this study regarding urban historiography, represent urban phenomena. Hence sub-systems here are cities or aggregations of cities. They function associatively, that is to say: they show tendencies towards being subsumed in the system.[29]

c. *Partial systems*, which represent areas of human action, such as the economy (also called 'labour'), demography (also called 'population'), technology, organization or that which is social in a more narrow meaning of the term, politics or administration, culture, mentality, and so on. Partial systems function distributively, that is to say: they exercise a general effect from the system on the sub-system. For this reason they form the basis of retrodictive causal explanations. Partial systems are bordered by other partial systems (see Chapter 4).

d. *Variables.* These are specifically-mentioned elements of the partial system (independent variables) or the sub-system (dependent variables). Their *values* can *vary*.

e. *Parameters.* These are values of independent variables, determined by the historian, that indicate transitions from one state to another. They can therefore serve as unitary measures for the analysis of processes.[30] For example: within Sjoberg's work, a particular state of technology can function as a parameter in the transformation from the pre-industrial to the industrial city.

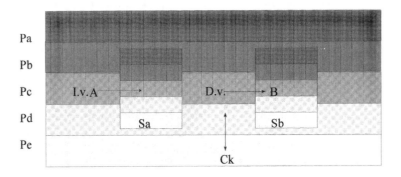

Figure 11. A half-open system

The half-open system represented above (Figure 11) consists of the following parts:

(1) the partial systems Pa, Pb, Pc, Pd, Pe
(2) the sub-systems Sa and Sb
(3) the variables A and B, A being an independent variable (abbr. i.v.) of partial system Pc, and B being a dependent variable (abbr. d.v.) of sub-system Sb.
(4) Ck is parameter k, which separates Sa and Sb.

One should be careful – I have noted this before – not to confuse this systems model, designed with epistemological intentions concerning urban historiography, with the systems used by the authors discussed further on themselves. They are concerned with an explanatory system, pertaining to states of affairs in the past itself; I am concerned with a more general theoretical systems model, which intends to show why the system models used in urban historiography can have an explanatory and synthesizing effect.

Half-open systems in urban historiography: questions for analysis

These theoretical expositions[31] concerning macro-systems lead to an analysis of a sizeable part of the long-term studies in urban historiography presented here. As a consequence, the following four clusters of questions are of import:

1. What does a macro-system look like? How is it distinguished from a sub-system? To what extent can one speak of a hierarchy of urban and, possibly, non-urban levels with regard to the nature of the macro-system? How is it delimited?
2. Because the sub-system in macro-studies cannot completely be ignored, questions arise concerning the role and definition of that sub-system. The questions linked to this are: How is the (limited) identity of the sub-system described? Is the prior existence of the system with regard to the sub-system formulated? Is the sub-system considered to be replaceable (commutative)? If this last question can be answered affirmatively, then this forms one more argument for the limited identity of the sub-system.
3. The effect of the macro-system on the sub-system occurs, as we know, by way of distributive partial systems. Hence an important question

is how those partial systems are described and in what manner they influence the sub-system. Which variables are mentioned?

4. In the light of the distinction advocated above between systems and laws or theories, it is important to consider to what extent the authors of urban historical macro-studies impute a universal or recurrent meaning to the systems they have designed. Although these systems, in most cases, lack the universality of laws, they will nonetheless not be completely bound to time and place. Otherwise they could not be distinguished from a closed-systems approach. If the authors themselves oppose the subjectifying approach, it will be examined whether this opposition emanates from a desire to transcend bondage to a specific place and time in order to be able to compare situations from different regions and periods with each other.

The treatment of these questions will occur in the same manner as that of urban historical studies with a closed system approach. This implies that only long-term studies will be discussed in this chapter.

Against a legalistic approach: Rozman

In several studies Rozman has described the genesis and development of national urban systems. In 1973 a comparative study on the history of urban systems in China and Japan was published.[32] In 1976 he published a study on Russia in the last phase of the pre-industrial urban system in the period 1750 to 1800.[33] In an article in 1978, 'Urban networks and historical stages', Rozman summarizes the development of urban systems in China, Japan, Russia, England and France.[34] In all these countries, cities develop into central places of an encompassing system. The borders of the states themselves also form the boundaries of the macro-system for Rozman.

The macro-system

In the macro-system, Rozman distinguishes between seven levels of central places. Levels 1 and 2 are, respectively, national or provincial administrative centres of more than 300,000 inhabitants; levels 3,4 and 5 are lower administrative centres (sometimes also having commercial functions, for example a harbour) with respectively 30,000 to 300,000, 10,000 to 30,000, and 3,000 to 10,000 inhabitants; levels 6 and 7 are respectively regional and local market centres with less than 3,000 inhabitants. The central places on levels 1 to 5 can be considered towns;

the central places on level 6 are semi-urban, and those on level 7 are non-urban.[35]

The hierarchy of central places thus formed is, naturally, a strong example of urbanization theory which is based on the genesis and development of urban networks. The first phases of urbanization are marked by the existence of a limited number of levels of central places; the last phase of urbanisation – for Rozman this is the last phase before the industrial revolution – possesses a fully-grown urban system with central places on all seven levels.[36]

The sub-systems

In 'Urban networks and historical stages', Rozman also makes a statement on the identity of the sub-discipline urban history that indicates not only that he attaches great importance to the systems-theoretical and demographic-quantitative aspects of urban history, but also that he considers the analysis of sub-systems to be of secondary importance. He states that the size of the population of a settlement is the only criterion in urban study on the basis of which cities can be distinguished from other research subjects. With the exception of the quantitative criterion, cities lack all identity.[37] Beyond this, a city is merely a 'locus', because 'practically every behaviour can take place in an urban setting'.[38] This very limited identity once again illustrates that he proceeds from a half-open system construction, and that the sub-system is hardly a subject of study. Rozman directs his attention completely towards the analysis of the macro-level. He is not concerned with the separate cities or the relationship between the separate cities and the urban network, but with the operation of the macro-level: the urban network itself. From this it follows that there is little explication beyond the statement that the network consists of a hierarchy of cities.

The partial systems

Three partial systems, namely population, economy, and administration, play a role in Rozman's studies. After all, population size, administrative functions and market functions determine the levels of the urban sub-systems. More and lower levels are included in the system as it matures. Levels and parameters determine the phases in the development of the system. Variables have not been further specified. In Chapter 10 I shall return to this problem.

Opposition to a subjectifying approach

Rozman starts one of his studies by registering his opposition to autonomous urban historiography. He does this by renouncing authors such as Marx and Weber who, according to Rozman, consider the city to be the cradle of civilization, capitalism, or revolution.[39] Weber, especially, is castigated severely. His 'legalistic approach', as Rozman terms Weber's typology, accentuates 'freedom' in the sense of autonomy as the determiner of urban growth. But countries such as Russia and Japan, which have known periods of rapid urbanization, have never developed a high level of urban self-administration in the European sense of the word. Dramatic urban growth in Japan occurred precisely at the moment that the first attempts at urban autonomy had been smothered. The 'legalistic approach' has not been able, according to Rozman, to find an explanation for the most important phenomena in urban history.[40]

Another objection to Weber's approach to urban history is his definition of cities as institutions leaning on a class of merchants, equipped with self-administration, that can maintain themselves against rural authorities. This definition is highly contingent on time and place, according to Rozman. It would be better to base the definition of cities on population size on the one hand and on commercial and administrative functions on the other. Such a definition is more readily applicable to many periods and large numbers of countries.[41] Here Rozman has a more or less universal or in any case recurrent pattern of urban development in mind.

A historical rank-size distribution model: De Vries

Like Rozman's study, that by De Vries on patterns of urbanization in pre-industrial Europe between 1500 and 1800 is based on the systems-theoretical construction of an urban hierarchy and the analysis of changes that have occurred in that hierarchy during the course of time.[42] As with Rozman, here we are concerned with a study that aims to examine the macro-level of half-open systems.

The macro-system

De Vries does not delimit the area of his studies, as Rozman did, on the basis of national borders, but he chooses the Europe of 'Latin Christianity' (with a few exceptions) as his research domain. The period between 1500 and 1800 is examined by ascertaining for every interval of fifty years whether new cities have arisen or extant cities have grown significantly.

On this basis De Vries has as his subject of study 154 cities with a total of a little less than 3.5 million inhabitants in 1500, and 363 cities with a total of more than 12 million inhabitants in 1800. These cities are classified according to the following six size categories ('ranks'): categories I to V encompass cities with, respectively, 10,000 to 19,900 inhabitants for category I and 160,000 to 319,900 inhabitants for category V, where the upper border of a category is set at double the number of inhabitants of its lower border; category VI encompasses those cities with more than 320,000 inhabitants.[43]

This abstract quantitative system is made more concrete by distinguishing regional sub-systems within the total European network, namely:

- supra-national systems, such as Northern Europe, Central Europe, Mediterranean Europe;
- national urban systems, such as those of England, Italy, the Dutch Republic; and
- sub-national, regional systems, such as the provinces of the Dutch Republic.

For the measurement of the changes in these systems, De Vries uses the 'rank-size distribution model' mentioned earlier. This model, in its simplest form, boils down to the following: the second largest city in an urban system is half the size of the largest city, the third largest city is one-third the size of the largest city and so on. This mathematical regularity can be graphically represented as a line declining to the right, where the largest and therefore highest-ranked cities are found on the left and smallest and therefore lowest-ranked cities are found on the right.[44] With the aid of several large adaptations De Vries uses a similar rank-size model to measure changes in the European hierarchy of cities.[45] On the basis of deviations from the hypothesized slope, De Vries establishes phases for the urban history of Europe between 1500 and 1800.[46]

The sub-systems

Like Rozman, De Vries proceeds from an almost completely quantitative-demographic definition of cities. He does not involve urban functions in his research into the nature and operation of urban networks. (The nature and function of cities are considered as soon as De Vries starts interpreting the changes he has discovered, on the basis of his quantitative-demographic research, in the urban network.) For De Vries, cities as sub-systems are not much more than settlements of more than 10,000 inhabitants.[47] This is because he wishes to accentuate the analysis of the connections between the central places and the urban network *as a whole* rather than the individual cities themselves. De Vries's book '[. . .] calls attention to the links among the nodes [i.e. cities as central places: HJ] and the interaction of this complex – i.e. of cities as a collective entity – with the society, economy, and government. In other words, while the city may have become less than it had been, the system of cities became more'.[48]

The partial systems

The curious circumstance presents itself that De Vries uses two partial systems in his analysis – demography and economy – but approaches these solely quantitatively. His urban network is an empirical, arithmetical construction on the basis of rank-size analysis. Because in this construction the only 'effect' of the system (the urban network) on the sub-systems is through migration figures, De Vries's urban network only has an observational and not an explanatory meaning.[49]

Opposition to the subjectifying approach

De Vries attacks several methods of historical urban research. First he rejects the interpretative and subjectifying approach. This urban-historiographical tradition emphasizes the innovative dynamics of the medieval and nineteenth-century cities on the one hand and the static, even parasitic, character of the early modern city on the other. De Vries observes that these different perspectives are contradictory. If the early modern city had such a strongly-consumptive, unenterprising nature, then it would not have been able to engender the dynamic nature of the industrial city. Some roots of that dynamic nature must have been present in the early modern city.[50] Because of these inconsistencies in the individualizing approach, De Vries prefers to consider cities as parts of urban systems.

Rozman, De Vries and Weber: a comparison

I observe the following differences between Rozman and De Vries:
Instead of a conglomerate of states – De Vries examines the urban network of Latin Europe – Rozman uses individual states as the context for his urban networks. Rozman uses political borders to delimit his system where De Vries uses cultural ones.

De Vries assumes that the territory he is examining is becoming more and more an economically integrated whole with a coherent urban network during the course of the sixteenth and seventeenth centuries. In Rozman's work, economic integration of the urban network is limited. Only the market places fulfil economic integrational functions for a part of the system – especially the lowest levels. He starts out from national borders, and hence studies national urban networks of a mainly political and administrative nature.

The most important difference between Rozman and De Vries, in my opinion, is that De Vries does not use the number of levels as the parameter for changes, as does Rozman, but a deviating rank-size order of cities.

Without wishing to trivialize these differences between De Vries and Rozman, their similarities are, for the purposes of this study, more important than the differences mentioned:

a. Both start from a systems-theoretical perspective and use a half-open systems construction, as well as exploring its macro-system.
b. Both their studies hardly consider the problematics of individual cities.
c. Both proceed from urbanization theory because they give a central role to the genesis and development of a system of cities.
d. For both quantitative elements play a major role.
e. Although Rozman has objections to the application of a rank-size approach to Russia, this is by no means a principled rejection. He only observes that in Russia the two central places, St Petersburg and Moscow, are many times larger than (and hence more than twice as large as) the second-level cities, which for example in 1782 did not amount to more than 35,000 inhabitants. Russia is so divergent that rank-size analysis has no point.[51] De Vries, who directly compares his research with that of Rozman, is less friendly towards Rozman's model. He calls it 'oddly abstract'.[52] Nevertheless, he observes with pleasure that Rozman advocates the existence of fully-matured urban networks even before the industrial revolution.[53]
f. A last point of similarity between Rozman and De Vries is especially important because it puts us in a position to compare both systems-theoretical approaches with a certain aspect of Weber's method. This aspect is the comparative method. As we have seen, Rozman uses his analysis to compare a number of pre-industrial societies: China, Japan, Russia, England, and France. De Vries observes that the rank-size distribution method is suitable for comparing, for example, Europe and China at the end of their pre-modern development. Both proceed from a definition of city applicable in many different situations.

Rozman defines cities as central places with certain functions and a certain size; De Vries maintains a universally-applicable, quantitative description, where the idea of the city as node (or nexus) also plays a role.

The differences between De Vries and Rozman on the one hand and Weber on the other are more remarkable. Although Weber proceeds from one more or less general working definition, his real definition of city is coupled to a unique historical phenomenon: the medieval city. That which is individualizing in Weber's case is, in a sense, already an assumption of his research. Rozman and De Vries, too, observe differences between the situations they compare; but these differences are not the premise, but the results of the research.[54]

At the end of his article De Vries makes several statements which, in my opinion, are characteristic for the differences between the comparative approach of the closed and the half-open systems theoretical methods of explanation. According to De Vries, the pre-modern urbanization process had no random – read: individual – development. It is a process that can be described as the destruction of an old urban structure and its replacement by a new one. The individual history of different cities is determined by seeking a place in an urban network that continually forms itself anew. By achieving a new economic function, and thereby increasing population figures, individual cities must continually try to conquer their place in the sun, or rather under the umbrella of the urban network. Often they encounter failure, which means that the city in question descends one or more levels. This is important for the following reason: De Vries here describes the histories of individual cities in a manner rejected in the closed-systems approach. The history of the individual city is, after all, viewed as a struggle to achieve a higher place in the system as a whole. He therefore pronounces the system to be extant prior to the individual city. This is characteristic for a half-open systems conception, in which the city is posited as sub-system.

Cities in a 'human ecological framework': Lampard

Macro-systems

In his 'Historical aspects of urbanisation', Lampard states that he views the city as a sub-system of the process of urbanization. The study of the process of urbanization, in his view, forms a central part of the research into processes of modernization in general.[55] Urbanization should be formulated in such a way that it forms a substitute for social change.[56] He considers the process of population concentration, as it occurs through growth of cities with regard to number and size, to be urbanization. Lampard wishes to examine this process in the context of questions regarding the how and why of modernization. His urbanization theory wishes to examine the relationships between the phenomenon population concentration and certain developments in social organization, structure and behaviour of people.[57] In other words: for Lampard, the history of urbanization is that form of social history occupying itself with the social and spatial distribution of people and the mental consequences thereof. On this basis one can distinguish three levels in the macro-system in Lampard's work:

1. A highest level of general social phenomena, which can be indicated by the term 'urbanization'. This urbanization takes place at the level of states, nations, federations of states or empires. In this manner urbanization can be considered as part of a supra-urban system. What is remarkable about Lampard's supra-urban systems is that they are political and not economical.[58] In this regard his systems-theoretical ideas are closer to those of Rozman than those of De Vries.

2. A second level is formed by hierarchies of cities. Such hierarchies develop in different places in the world at different periods; in Europe this period is the Middle Ages. The urban network that then originates has a relatively stable structure and is comparable to the urban network formulated by Rozman.[59] In contrast to Rozman and De Vries, Lampard does not define this hierarchy quantitatively, but qualitatively. He mentions them from bottom to top: hamlets, villages, cities, metropolises, and capitals.[60]

3. A third level of separate cities, of which he considers individuals and families to be the lowest form of sub-system.[61]

The sub-systems

Although the emphasis in Lampard's work lies on these macro-aspects, he nevertheless pays some attention to the micro-level. The remarks he makes about it are appropriate to the distinction between closed and half-open systems forms of urban history. By this I refer to the fact that in macro-studies the system is considered to be extant prior to the separate cities. 'The presence of cities presupposes a more or less attendant societal process of urbanization.'[62] Research about and in individual cities is considered possible by Lampard – in contrast to Rozman and De Vries.

However, to avoid this research's happening in an individualizing manner, he re-emphasizes that cities are the products of urbanization. 'Thus urbanisation is a societal process that necessarily precedes and accompanies the formation of cities.'[63] Individual cities should be studied as concentration points of people and activities. This concentration originates because cities fulfil the function of central place for a regional system. Such a function is sometimes also called an 'axial function' or a 'nodality'.[64]

The partial systems

The examination of the process of urbanization (the highest macro-level) is accomplished by Lampard with the use of what he calls a 'human ecological framework'. This term indicates a theoretical context, which consists of four partial systems from which the most important changes in the urbanization process emanate. As we know, Lampard distinguishes more partial systems (see Chapter 4), but those mentioned here are essential to the process of urbanization.

1. Population. Within this partial system Lampard distinguishes as variables: increase, decrease, composition and distribution of the population. Although the partial system 'population' gives us a further definition of the process of urbanization and therefore forms the basis of every study regarding urbanisation, it does not explain the process of urbanization. That is why it should be supplemented with other partial systems.
2. Technology. This partial system is a *conditio sine qua non* for the process of urbanization. Changes in technology automatically bring changes in the process of urbanisation. Technology, however, is not an exclusive characteristic of urbanization. Technical developments manifest themselves in all regions of society. Lampard's theory of urbanization therefore shows an opening here to a non-urban explanans.
3. Organization. This is the form in which the populace adapt themselves to the environment with the aid of the technological means at their disposal.
4. Environment. This is the most enduring partial system, although due to the influence of technology and organization it cannot be wholly viewed as an immobile force.[65]

The operation of partial systems occurs, according to Lampard, along a route of three parameters: a demographic one, which encompasses the growth and distribution of the population; a structural one, which is actually a combination of technological and organizational elements; and a 'behaviourist' parameter. This last parameter mainly concerns itself with mental issues, such as the difference in behaviour of parents and children with regard to migration, choice of work, social mobility, and family structure. It is noteworthy that these parameters are not specific to one partial system, but overlap several. This also holds true for the distributive force as the 'rationalising central movement of industrialism', a force that Lampard sees at work even before industrialization and that is composed of technological as well as organizational elements, and in which the behaviourist parameter is also at issue.[66]

Opposition to a subjectifying approach

In an article from 1970 'The dimensions of urban history', Lampard recommends a strategy reverse to the one customary for urban historical research. This 'reverse strategy' is in fact an attack on the individual-izing form of urban history. He reproaches this approach for making an ungrounded leap from the particular to the general when generalizing. Moreover, the illustration of something 'general' with the aid of the familiar 'for example' is often a hollow gesture, according to Lampard, because the author of such a case-study usually knows nothing of the process of urbanization in general, and hence the 'for example' lacks any relation to logic. Lampard prefers the reverse route, from that which is general to the particular, 'from the study of urbanisation to the cities'.[67] Elsewhere Lampard states that every urban situation is different from every other, but this distinction is of a gradual and not an essential nature: it is not an exception to a rule, but a digression from a trend.[68] 'The point is that, if the same sets of terms are used, similar techniques of analysis may be applied to both micro- and macroscopic situations and there is every reason to believe that the little world will illumine the large.'[69]

Lampard's conception of 'nodality' mentioned above can be considered an adstruction of this claim. The 'node' forms the core of an urban network, according to Lampard. The genesis of such nodes, or as Christaller and Lösch called them 'central places', refers to Lampard's whole theory of urbanization and the manner in which this approach and the subjectifying approach to urban history are different. Lampard assumes a certain area or region as a regional system, in which a more specialized core, a central place, slowly develops. Within such an urban centre, specialization and social differentiation arise, and hence differences in power and social status.[70]

Lampard's concept of 'nodality' at first sight shows great resemblance to Mumford's 'crystallization' conception of the origin of cities. Hence Lampard does not hesitate to use Mumford's expression 'the implosion of energies', which deals with the bundling of administrative, religious, and other such functions in one community. The city therefore becomes not only the caretaker of tradition, but also the place where innovations come from. Lampard himself states this as follows: 'As the pool of the system's specialised skills and cultivated intelligence, as depository of its surplus and the storehouse of knowledge, the node became the primary consumer of differentiated goods and services and in this way a creator of new values.'[71] Isn't this statement almost identical to Mumford's description of the *agens*-function of cities? Doesn't Lampard make the leap here towards a closed-systems approach to the phenomenon 'city'? These questions must be answered negatively for two reasons:

1. The position of power fulfilled by cities in a region or urban network does not devolve from themselves, but from their function as central place. Lampard's city as *agens* fulfils its innovating function as a sub-system of an – in this case regional – system.[72]
2. Lampard expressly distances himself from Mumford's explanatory method. He denounces this method of personifying cities and pronouncing them organisms. This would mean, according to Lampard, that the constitutional parts of a city have a strong mutual dependence and hence cannot or can only with great difficulty be replaced. (A consequence that, as we have seen, must be accepted with closed-system constructions –consider Weber.) The constitutional parts of a city are, however, in Lampard's opinion mobile and interchangeable, in other words commutative. Here we indeed find several essential differences between closed and half-open systems juxtaposed.

Creative functions of cities may not lead to the city's being considered an organism or person. 'Hence any extended analogy between persons and organisations, their "biographies" and "personalities" is a literary convention, a metaphor. People are organisms and cities are organisations.'[73] In contrast to an organism, an organization has no inherent boundaries to its growth and its life span. Constraints are placed on cities from without; these are ecological in nature. In order to emphasize his anti-organological conception, Lampard eventually arrives at an encompassing systems-theoretical conception, as we have discussed above.

In this chapter the macro-level of half-open systems has been examined. While doing this it has been concluded that macro-systems at first sight show a great deal of resemblance to closed systems, but that they have a totally different effect. While the closed systems in Chapter 5 displayed a 'horizontal', causal-finalistic operation, the macro-systems display a 'vertical', causal-functionalistic operation. Macro-systems, after all, function as antecedents of phenomena to be explained, and as such coincide with covering laws. However, they also distinguish themselves from them. One of the most important differences is the lack of universality, owing to which macro-systems at first sight seem less reliable than laws or theories. This lack is compensated for by the greater capacity of systems for specifying, analysing, and synthesizing. It is not without reason that, for example, Schmal prefers (macro-)systems to laws as explanatory entities in urban historiography. They are more specific and hence less rigid in his eyes.[74]

The work of Rozman, De Vries and Lampard has been examined for characteristics and boundaries of the macro-systems, the distinction between macro-level and micro-level, the nature and role of sub-systems with regard to the macro-system, and the distributive functioning of the macro-system on the sub-systems it contains. Furthermore, attention has been paid to the hostility of the three urban historians discussed in this chapter towards authors of urban historical long-term studies working according to the closed-system model.[75]

Several questions have not been touched upon in the discussions in this chapter. Whether it is also possible to discover half-open system models in studies of individual cities is one such question. The functionality and the related activity of sub-systems with regard to systems must also be reconsidered. Lampard's concept 'nodality' has already suggested that sub-systems don't always function as purely passive entities completely dominated by macro-systems. These questions will be dealt with in Chapter 8.

Notes

1. He describes such systems as consisting of people and non-human means of subsistence and resources compounded to sub-systems, which are connected mutually as well as to the environment. They are subject to certain values and to a central system, which leads them and provides them with possibilities for future action. W.H. Mitchel,

'Relevant neo-scientific management notions', in S. Optner (ed.), *Systems analysis* (Harmondsworth 1973), pp. 305–24 at p. 311.

2. See for an extensive analysis of regional systems of city-countryside relationships G. A. Hoekveld, 'Theoretische aanzetten ten behoeve van het samenstellen van maatschappijhistorische modellen van de verhouding van stad en platteland in de nieuwe geschiedenis van Noordwest Europa' [Theoretical preludes for compiling social historical models of the relationship of city and countryside in the recent history of Northwest Europe], in: *Economisch en Sociaal-historisch Jaarboek* 38 (1975): 1–47.

3. A number of people have pointed out to me that these nested dolls should not be called after a Polish grandmother, but after a Russian mother. The correct name is not *babushkas* but *matreshki* (Jan De Vries), *matrijoskas* (Dorothée Sturkenboom) or *matruschkas* (Maarten Evenblij in the *Volkskrant* of 30.3.1991). Dictionaries and encyclopaedias both foreign and domestic remained inconclusive. 'Babushkas' scored highest in an empirical study in different layers of the populace. Hence this appellation has been retained in the text. In the UK they are perhaps most often known simply as 'Russian dolls'.

4. J. E. McGrath, P. G. Nordlie, and W. S. Vaughn jr, 'A descriptive framework for comparison of system research methods,' in S. L. Optner (ed.), *Systems analysis* (Harmondsworth 1973), pp. 73–86, esp. 73. The 'nested' character of macro-systems is also posited by W.H. Mitchel, 'Relevant neo-scientific management notions', pp. 311–12; and A. D. Hall, 'Some fundamental concepts of systems engineering', in S. Optner (ed.), (Harmondsworth 1973), pp. 106–7.

5. H. Schmal, 'Epilogue: one subject, many views', in idem (ed.) *Patterns of European urbanization since 1500* (London 1981), pp. 287–307 at p. 292. B. J. L. Berry, 'Cities as systems within systems of cities', *Papers of the Regional Science Association* 13 (1964): 160–1. Although Schmal and Berry do not use the term, they of course deal with systems-theoretical approaches towards the half-open system construction.

6. B. J. L. Berry, 'Cities as systems within systems of cities', p. 151.

7. Ibid., pp. 152–5.

8. J. De Vries, *European urbanization 1500–1800* (London 1984), *passim*.

9. See for this last point: A. A. van den Braembussche, *Theorie van de maatschappijgeschiedenis* [Theory of social history] (Baarn 1985), pp. 45–62.

10. J. Topolski, *Methodology of history* (Dordrecht 1976), p. 568.
11. As an example Topolski gives the explanation of the rise of large agrarian enterprises in Eastern Europe at the end of the sixteenth century. These large farms were – in contrast to such companies in Western Europe, which had salaried labour – based on serfdom. To explain this phenomenon Topolski first refers to a rather theoretical, and therefore less direct cause: the nature of class relations east of the Elbe. This was marked by the weak position of cities. A second, more direct cause was the decisive influence the rural aristocracy acquired in the constitutional system during the course of the sixteenth century. As very direct causes, Topolski mentions: (a) the sharpening of traditional seigniorial rights and (b) the emergence of an extensive market for agrarian products in Western Europe, especially for grain. The explanation by way of the weak position of the cities forms as it were the outer macro-system that borders on theory (that of feudalism). The influence of the rural aristocracy on the political system in the sixteenth century is a fact from the macro-system that is somewhat more distant from theory and does not necessarily emanate from it. The (international) grain market and the sharpening of seigniorial rights form the most influential variables. Their effect achieves greater clarity when seen in the light of less direct causes.
12. Such a typology shows remarkably many similarities with the INUS-explanations. As separate causes they are neither sufficient nor necessary conditions, but they are also non-redundant and together and *in a certain pattern* they do form a sufficient explanation. See, for the INUS conditions, Chr. Lorenz, *De constructie van het verleden. Een inleiding in de theorie van de geschiedenis* (Meppel, Amsterdam 1987), pp. 117–18.
13. Dray gives another example. Suppose one answers the question of why iron is attracted to a magnet with the statement that magnets attract iron: then that is a covering law, but not an acceptable explanation. See W. Dray, *Laws and explanation in history* (Oxford 1970 [1957]), pp. 29 and 61. See also F. R. Ankersmit, *Denken over geschiedenis. Een overzicht van de moderne geschiedfilosofische opvattingen* (Groningen 1984), p. 114. A half-open systems analysis does render an acceptable explanation. Such an analysis explains how the magnetic system works by telling that magnets (system) create a magnetic field (distributive effect) in which north and south poles occur (partial systems), and that such magnetic fields cause similar partial systems to emerge (symmetry) in iron (the sub-system)

as in the magnet itself. That the orientation of the north and south poles in the iron (the sub-system) is precisely the opposite of their orientation in the magnet itself (the system) is a sign that the sub-system still maintains its identity, despite the fact that it has become part of a more encompassing system, in this case the magnetic field of the magnet.

The half-open systems explanation presented here has more explanatory power than the 'covering law' that magnets attract iron. How can this be? This is because the explanatory power of the law can only be sought in its reliability. Only an explanation's universal and predictive nature carries this reliability; only the fact that something holds always, independent of location and time, yields the seal and anchor for the explanatory power. Half-open systems possess not only a relative consistency, but also analytical capacities, specificity and coherence.

14. F. R. Ankersmit, *Denken over geschiedenis*, p. 113.
15. H. Schmal, 'Epilogue', p. 294.
16. F. R. Ankersmit, *Denken over geschiedenis*, p. 115.
17. Ibid., p. 118.
18. In particular S. Strebbing and W. Kneale have called attention to the explanation of a phenomenon through a comparison with phenomena, of which one has some knowledge or with which one is familiar: S. Strebbing, *Modern introduction to logic* (London 1933), p. 389; W. Kneale, *Probability and induction* (Oxford 1949), p. 91. See also W. Dray, *Laws and explanation in history*, p. 75. Stegmüller makes several objections to explanations that consist of 'Zurückführung auf Bekanntes und Vertrautes' [Reduction to that which is known and familiar]. Scientific explanation precisely occupies itself with problematizing that which is familiar and known. Nor can explanations based on analogy find any mercy in Stegmüller's eyes. If certain phenomena are analogous in the sense that they are completely or partially nomological or syntactically isomorphous, then they can both be explained by subsumption under one and the same law and the analogy is unnecessary: Stegmüller, *Wissenschaftliche Erklärung und Begründung*. pp. 131–5. Lorenz, however, considers analogous explanation to be very suited to historical practice, with his 'comparative causal explanation'. He assumes the presupposition that comparable causes will have comparable effects and that regularity can be encountered in reality. In this context he also posits the proposition that 'sufficient resemblance' between two causes does not mean that both cases 'can be *reduced* to the same *law*' (italics: Lorenz):

Chr. Lorenz, *De constructie van het verleden*, pp. 140–2, especially 140.

He also refers to the objections of hermeneuticians, who reject comparability because the comparison of historical phenomena often means that those phenomena have to be taken out of their context. Without judging whether the hermeneuticians or the comparative historians are in the right, it should be noted here that the context of a phenomenon should not only be posited but also explicated. The system–sub-system constructions presented here are intended to explicate the relationship between phenomena and their context. Comparison is therefore a question of construction, and, since this is so, there can be little objection to explanation by way of analogies.

19. J. Topolski, *Methodology of history*, p. 555.

20. P. H. H. Vries, 'Geschiedbeoefening, historisme en positivisme' [Historical practice, historism and positivism], *Theoretische Geschiedenis* 12(2) (1985): 147.

21. Ibid., p. 151.

22. Ibid., p. 152.

23. P. H. H. Vries, 'Geschiedbeoefening, historisme en positivisme', p. 153.

24. F. R. Ankersmit, *Narrative logic. A semantic analysis of the historian's language* (Meppel 1981), p. 11.

25. Ibid., p. 96.

26. O. Brunner, 'Stadt und Bürgertum in der europaïschen Geschichte' [City and citizenship in European history], in idem, *Neue Wege der Sozialgeschichte* (Göttingen 1956), pp. 80 ff, especially 81; O. Brunner, 'Die Stadt', in *Historia Mundi* VI (Berne 1958), p. 344 ff.; Franz Steinbach, 'Stadtgemeinde und Landgemeinde. Studien zur Geschichte des Bürgertums' I, *Rheinische Vierteljahresblätter* 13 (1948); E. Ennen, *Frühgeschischte der europäischen Stadt* (Bonn 1953); Joh. Hasebroek, *Griechische Wirtschafts- und Gesellschaftegeschichte* (Tübingen 1931); pp. 202 ff., especially 209; A. Heuss, 'Max Webers Bedeutung für die Geschichte des griechisch–römischen Altertums', *Historische Zeitschrift* 201 (1965): 529 ff.; G. Abramowski, *Das Geschichtsbild Max Webers. Universalgeschichte am Leitfaden des Okzidentalen Rationalisierungsprozesses* (Stuttgart 1966), pp. 86–7.

27. See Note 18.

28. P. H. H. Vries, 'Geschiedbeoefening, historisme en positivisme', pp. 165–8.

29. Some sub-systems have a tendency to dissolve completely in the system. They show hardly any tendencies towards maintaining their own identities, and are therefore called 'passive sub-systems'. Others strive more towards maintaining their identities, and on that basis they can serve as explanatory variables for other phenomena in the system. On that basis we speak of 'active sub-systems'. In Chapter 8 the distinction between active and passive sub-systems is further explained.

30. This description has largely been derived from the following definition: 'Nombre figurant comme une variable dans une expression ou dans une équation et qui peut être fixé à volonté', in *Grand Larousse encyclopédique* 8 (Paris 1963), p. 157. See further: *De grote Nederlandse Larousse encyclopedie* 18 (Hasselt, The Hague 1977), p. 475 and *De grote Oosthoek encyclopedie en woordenboek* 15 (7th edition, Utrecht 1979), p. 428.

31. In the original monograph the following studies were also included: P. M. M. Klep, *Bevolking en arbeid in transformatie. Een onderzoek in Brabant 1700–1900* [Population and labour in transformation. A study in Brabant 1700–1900] (Nijmegen 1978); idem, 'Urban decline in Brabant: The traditionalization of investments and labour (1374–1806)', in H. Van der Wee (ed.), *The rise and decline of urban industries in Italy and the Low Countries* (Louvain 1988), pp. 261–86 and K. Czok, *Die Stadt. Ihre Stellung in der deutschen Geschichte* (Leipzig, Jena, Berlin 1969) and idem, 'Forschungen aus Regionalgeschichte', *Historischen Forschungen in der DDR 1960–1970* (East Berlin 1970).

32. G. Rozman, *Urban networks in Ch'ing China and Tokugawa Japan* (Princeton, NJ 1973).

33. G. Rozman, *Urban networks in Russia 1750–1800 and premodern periodization* (Princeton, NJ 1976).

34. G. Rozman, 'Urban networks and historical stages', *Journal of Interdisciplinary History (JIH)* 9 (vol. 1, Summer 1978): 79. In his *Urban networks in Ch'ing China and Tokugawa Japan* (p. 4) Rozman makes yet another statement on the comparison of urban networks in pre-industrial societies that is of import to our study: 'The urban sociologist is usually concerned with the history of individual cities, not with the history of networks of cities. He rarely asks how city plans are meaningful representations of their societies and generally ignores how a map of all cities divided according to their population levels is a spatial depiction of a society.'

35. G. Rozman, 'Comparative approaches to urbanization: Russia 1750–1800', in M. F. Hamm (ed.), *The city in Russian history* (Lexington, KY 1976), p. 70.
36. Ibid., p. 79.
37. In practice Rozman does recognize that cities have economic and administrative functions.
38. G. Rozman, 'Urban networks and historical stages', pp. 80–1.
39. Ibid., p. 67.
40. 'Although it is probably the most widely-applied of any comparative methodology, the legalistic approach has been unable to account for many of the major phenomena in the history of urban population': G. Rozman, 'Comparative approaches to urbanization: Russia 1750–1800', pp. 70–1.
41. G. Rozman, 'Urban networks and historical stages', pp. 68–9.
42. J. De Vries, *European urbanization 1500–1800* (London 1984) and J. De Vries, 'Patterns of urbanization in pre-industrial Europe 1500–1800', in H. Schmal (ed.), *Patterns of European urbanization since 1500* (London 1981), pp. 79–109.
43. J. De Vries, *European urbanization 1500–1800*, p. 27
44. Ibid., pp. 49–54 and 85–120.
45. An important adaptation made by De Vries is, for example, that he does involve the largest cities in his study, but does not count them when determining the slopes of his urban hierarchy. This 'least square" regression method is more empirical than mathematical: Ibid., pp. 52 and 92.
46. J. De Vries, 'Patterns of urbanization in pre-industrial Europe', pp. 79–95, especially 80; idem, *European urbanization*, p. 256.
47. 'Cities [. . .] are places that have populations, population densities, percentages of the workforce in non-agricultural occupations and a measure of diversity in the occupational structure, all of which are *sufficiently large*.' For his study De Vries restricts this definition to size and density: 'As a practical matter our definition of a city will be based on size and density': J. De Vries, *European urbanization 1500–1800*, p. 22.
48. Ibid., p. 9.
49. This was pointed out in 1979 when De Vries offered a first glimpse of his research at the urbanization congress in Amsterdam: H. Schmal (ed.), *Patterns of European urbanization since 1500*, p. 107.
50. J. De Vries, *European urbanization 1500–1800*, pp. 4–9 and 254–5.

51. G. Rozman, 'Comparative approaches to urbanization: Russia 1750–1800', p. 79. De Vries, as I have noted earlier, also has objections against a simple rank-size ordering: J. De Vries, *European urbanization*, p. 52.
52. J. De Vries, *European urbanization*, p. 10.
53. Ibid., p. 9.
54. Ibid., pp. 262–3.
55. L. F. Schnore and E. E. Lampard, 'Social science and the city', in L. F. Schnore and B. M. Fagin (eds), *Urban research and policy planning* (Beverly Hills, CA 1967), p. 45.
56. 'Efforts should be made to conceptualize urbanization in ways that actually represent social change': E. E. Lampard, 'Urbanization and social change; on broadening the scope and relevance of urban history', in O. Handlin and J.Burchard (eds), *The historians and the city* (Cambridge, MA 1963), p. 233.
57. Ibid., pp. 233–5.
58. E. E. Lampard, 'Historical aspects of urbanization', in P. M. Hauser and L. F. Schnore (eds), *The study of urbanization* (New York 1965), pp. 543–5.
59. Ibid., p. 546.
60. Ibid.
61. Ibid., pp. 543–5.
62. Ibid., p. 519.
63. Ibid., p. 521.
64. See also P. Kooij, 'Urbanization. What's in a name', in H. Schmal (ed), *Patterns of European urbanization since 1500* (London 1981), pp. 33–47.
65. Lampard gives a concrete exposition of this human ecological framework in E. E. Lampard, 'Urbanization and social change', pp. 237–47.
66. Ibid., pp. 234–43.
67. E. E. Lampard, 'The dimensions of urban history, a footnote to the "urban crisis"', *Pacific Historical Review* (1970): 261–78.
68. 'Urbanization is the societal process that creates cities but each city is an accommodation of the general movement to a particular set of demographic, institutional, technological, and environmental circumstances – including the contingencies of events and personalities': E. E. Lampard, 'Urbanization and social change', p. 237.
69. Ibid., pp. 236–7.
70. E. E. Lampard, 'Historical aspects of urbanization', pp. 540–2.
71. Ibid., p. 543.

72. See for this point what is said in Chapter 8 about active sub-systems.
73. E. E. Lampard, 'Historical aspects of urbanization', p. 543.
74. H. Schmal, 'Epilogue: one subject, many views', p. 294.
75. For Rozman and De Vries that meant Weber; for Lampard it meant Mumford.

8

Uncovering the micro-Level: Sub-System Constructions in Urban Historiography

In Chapter 6 studies of individual cities were examined as urban biographies. In this chapter individual cities will be dealt with as half-open systems. We are not concerned here with discovering urban or semi-urban macro-systems as in the previous chapter, but with uncovering sub-systems.[1] Not all studies, however, that are analysed by way of a half-open systems construction explicate that construction. It is even the case that most of the studies presented here actually do not do this. This is naturally all the more reason to examine them.

Just as with systems, sub-systems can be described in many different ways. In the simplest case the sub-system is formed by an individual city. Here we are concerned with research in which the city is situated as a sub-system of a macro-system, and that tries to explain development in the sub-system through 'retrodiction' to the encompassing system.

Yet sub-systems do not always pertain to individual cities. Sometimes they are concerned with an aggregation of cities or, to put it differently, a sub-system construction of the *phenomenon* 'city'. Sjoberg's *Pre-industrial city* is an *explicit* example of this approach. The distinction with studies concerning macro-systems threatens to become extremely diffuse. Yet the difference between Sjoberg's work and that of Rozman, De Vries and Lampard is easy to point out. In contrast to the latter authors, Sjoberg does not intend to clarify the system as a whole through his analysis, but only wishes to show the effect of the system on the sub-system.

As a comparative study Sjoberg's work can, to an extent, be compared to Walker's book about German home towns. Sjoberg's comparative analysis of pre-industrial and industrial cities leads to what Skocpol and Somers have called the parallel comparison, an appellation that can be applied to Walker's work as well. In other words, Sjoberg shows what a great many cities, spread out over the world, have in common. On the basis of this cross-cultural analysis he arrives at a model of the phenomenon 'pre-industrial city'. However, the difference between Sjoberg's half-open systems analysis and Walker's closed systems analysis is not negligible, and can be compared with the difference between Sjoberg and Weber as it was briefly discussed in Chapter 4 Numbers of sections and paragraphs are not mentioned (Section 2). Furthermore, the distinction between Sjoberg's sub-systems analysis and the (macro-)systems analyses of Rozman, De Vries and Lampard will need to be clarified in this chapter.

Scokpol and Somers, as we know, distinguish, not only by parallel and other types of comparison, but also by contrasting comparison. Of this, too, a representative example has been included in this chapter. Foster's comparison of three English industrial towns in the middle of the nineteenth century, each generating a different form of class-consciousness, has been included as an example of contrasting comparison. The comparative study of Foster evokes the interesting question of to what extent sub-systems can have such an identity that their behaviour develops divergently from that of the system of which they are part. This problem, which deals with the distinction between what I have called passive and active sub-systems, is also dealt with in this chapter.

Before all this, we must first consider the 'normal' urban biographies and the comparative studies of Sjoberg and Foster in the light of their being half-open system constructions in which the analysis of the micro-level is primary. This will occur by way of the following questions:

1. How does the sub-system distinguish itself from the system or, in other words: What comprises the (limited) identity of the sub-system itself? In systems-theoretical terms: How coherent is it? In most cases these questions will be most easily answered by exposing the difference between the macro-system and the micro-system.
2. Which partial systems on the macro-level influence the micro-levels? The distributive effects of the partial systems from the system form the basis for the explanation of certain phenomena in the sub-system. Tracking these partial systems down, or certain elements or variables from them, clarifies the structure of different methods of explanation in sub-systems.
3. Because sub-systems are constructed as parts of a macro-system, the sub-systems studies will often have a 'family tree' structure. By this I mean that in many cases the sub-system is analysed as a variation on a macro-systems study or another sub-systems study. In no case will the studies of individual cities, despite their (limited) particular identity, take on the guise of a unique individual life, as was the case with the urban biographies discussed above. The problem of the replacability (commutativity) of the sub-system will therefore play a major role in the analyses presented here.

This is also related to questions regarding the cumulative nature of urban historical research. Very often urban historians present their own research as a part or an amendment of research done by others. This would seem to indicate possibilities for synthesis. As we searchingly try to place a piece of the puzzle in the right place with regard to the whole, we should place the half-open systems studies of individual cities in the macro-system. This can be done in different ways. The urban historical context is explored by way of macro-systems studies; sub-systems studies form the pieces of the puzzle themselves or these studies put them in the right place. Sometimes sub-system studies form a kind of mould with which other sub-system studies can be formed and perfected. If such a study succeeds in becoming an example for other urban studies, then we can perceive the genesis of a 'family tree' of research. The 'mould' study then functions as the trunk, the amending studies as the branches of the urban historical tree of syntheses.

Sjoberg's work clearly functions as a historiographical trunk. In other words, his pre-industrial and industrial city is in many cases an example for the analyses of other authors. That is why I shall begin with an extensive account of his ideas.

Sjoberg's parallel comparison of pre-industrial and industrial cities

For a good understanding of Sjoberg's work, both his – barely elaborated – macro-level as well as his – completely worked-out – aggregated urban sub-system warrant closer inspection.[2]

Macro-system and sub-system

In Chapter 4 we already observed that Sjoberg was occupied with the construction of types of cities. Just as Weber describes an Asiatic, a classical and a medieval ideal type of city, Sjoberg analyses the pre-industrial, the transitional, and the industrial city.[3] Because he unfolds a structural-functionalistic theory regarding societies as wholes before he considers cities themselves, these three types of cities are not purely historical constructions, but also more or less deductively constructed models. The theory behind them implies that he views society, as a 'whole', as a system. Sjoberg does not answer the question of how that system works. In contrast to Rozman, De Vries and Lampard, who all extensively consider the operation of the macro-level and barely deal with the sub-system, Sjoberg mainly concerns himself with the effect of the system on the sub-system. He deals especially with generalized pheno-mena *in* the cities, not with the operation of an urban network or a system of countryside–city relationships. The phenomena are discussed at the level of the sub-system with an occasional reference to the system by way of explanation

The partial systems and their operation

Sjoberg becomes a little more explicit when dealing with the operation of partial systems. However, here this operation must also be reconstructed from the phenomena they influence at the sub-systems level. Sjoberg distinguishes between a large number of partial systems: ecology, social differentiation and stratification, family, economy, politics and finally various systems of values and the instruments by which they are communi-cated. One variable is most important amongst all these: technology. As a parameter, technology determines the identity of the pre-industrial, the transitional and the industrial city. The simple technology of pre-industrial society leads to a lack of specialization, a limited division of labour, a large working populace and a small elite. This upper stratum can only maintain its position of power through rigid coercive measures of an external political and an internal religious nature. The social integration of pre-industrial societies is therefore marked by sharp antagonism. In contrast to Marx, who thought that class oppositions undermine the system, Sjoberg views social antagonism as supporting the system. Technological innovation is stymied by the superiority of a small elite with a strong sense of class and little appreciation for manual labour. This has as a consequence on the use of space in the pre-industrial city, in that the wishes of the elite are reflected in that use of space. The centre of the city is dominated by the church, the town hall, and the stately manors of the urban patriciate. The lower classes are pushed out to the periphery.

The limited transportation technology of the period naturally has a great deal to do with this social division of space. The pre-industrial city, as a consequence of all these factors, has a centre in which the residential, administrative, and religious functions dominate.[4]

Sjoberg places industrial society in opposition to pre-industrial society. As a result of more complex technology, there is more specialization in industrial society and a more elaborate division of labour. This entails a greater economic interdependence of social groups, because of which – and here Sjoberg follows Durkheim – a larger social coherence arises. (Durkheim uses the term 'organic solidarity' for this phenomenon.) Four issues seem in conflict with this solidarity: (1) the formation of more encompassing social superstructures such as national states and supranational organizations (for example the European Common Market); (2) the formation of more formal organizational structures; (3) the acquisition of positions of power in the new organizational structures by a (new) elite; and (4) secularization, which seems to point in the direction of estrangement rather than homogenization.

The greater social coherence of modern society forms itself despite all these factors, first of all through the economic interdependence mentioned above, secondly though the ascendancy of various intermediary persons and groups (such as social workers, teachers, researchers and so on) between the elite and the deprived, thirdly through a greater fluidity between the classes, and, finally, through a more open, democratic political system.[5]

This industrial social system leads to the following properties of the industrial city as sub-system. Cities are primarily commercial and industrial by nature, and are larger than the pre-industrial city with its 10,000 inhabitants. Spatially speaking, the residential function of the centre of the city has largely been replaced by a financial/administrative function. The elite no longer live there, and have made way for office buildings and banks. In American urban studies 'Central Business Districts' (CBDs) are spoken of in this context. Industry has concentrated itself in certain districts, often located on the periphery. All this is accompanied by a separation of residential and working areas. Because of the emergence of urban transport organizations, and especially cars, such a separation is no longer a problem. This all has led to suburbanization, as a result of which new shopping centres and service companies have arisen in suburbia. The spatial separation of different classes has become diffuse, although it has not completely disappeared.

The economic structure is marked by continuing division of labour, more competition, and also greater prosperity and more spare time, especially in the lower classes. Politically speaking, there is more democracy, because knowledge and authority have been distributed over broad layers of the social system thanks to the larger number of experts. Conflicting interests are harmonized through a democratic process.

The system of patronage has been replaced by a bureaucracy, working according to formal rules and therefore rationalized and specialized. With democracy, ethnic, religious and class barriers become more vague. Secularization grows, especially through mass communication and the intensification of upbringing and education.

The shift between these two types of cities yields a new type, called a 'transitional city' or an 'industrializing city' by Sjoberg. He does not mention any characteristics belonging to this type of city. He does distinguish between four transitional phases between the pre-industrial and the industrial social systems. These will be mentioned in Part 5, which is concerned with time and temporal arrangement.

The commutativity of sub-systems and its historiographical implications

Sjoberg's study is particularly well suited to serve as a starting-point for the study of individual cities according to the sub-system method. His pre-industrial city can function as heuristic model for sub-systems in the form of individual cities. In the following paragraphs we shall see that his study has indeed had this effect.

Studies of individual cities. The commercial city of Katz *et al.*

Urban historians have developed a kind of love–hate relationship with Sjoberg's studies. They have criticized him severely because of the generalizing character of his urban types, but many of them have used those same types as a basis for their own research. Thus Rozman and De Vries have criticized Sjoberg for his static notion of pre-industrial cities and societies. With his seven-phases theory Rozman, for example, wanted to show that both of these were far more dynamic than Sjoberg suggests.[6]

Another point of criticism was the vagueness of Sjoberg's conception of the transitional city. A real analysis of this type of city had not been given by Sjoberg, according to his critics. All he claimed regarding the industrializing city was that in the beginning of the transition traditional properties manifested themselves more forcefully and that towards the end the new industrial properties appeared more quickly.

The Canadian urban historians Katz, Davey and Doucet are interested precisely in examining the transitional city more closely, thereby giving it its own face. Emulating Bowden and Ward, who discovered that seventeenth-century London is more accurately described as a commercial city than as a pre-industrial city, they too think that the nineteenth-century transitional city should be considered a commercial city rather than an industrializing one.[7]

Macro-system and sub-system

They demonstrate this thesis using the Canadian city Hamilton (Ontario) between 1851 and 1861 as an example. They describe it as 'an ambiguous little city', lying on Lake Ontario 40 miles west of Toronto. The population (in 1851 14,000 inhabitants) is culturally and ethnically heterogeneous, yet reasonably integrated. Racial antagonism, such as occurs in many American cities, is absent. Festivities, parades of local artisans, the hierarchical political structure and the conservative 'Tory' tradition in local and provincial elections indicate the continued existence of an old 'civic order'.[8] This description of the nature and degree of cohesion in Hamilton could indicate that here we are dealing with a study centred on collective participation. Yet Katz *et al.* definitely do not have a community study in mind. Katz states: 'Ultimately my interest extends beyond the history of Hamilton to the way in which the complex set of structures and organizations that make up the modern world emerged from the quite different features of traditional society.'[9] The authors perceiving Hamilton as a commercial city note three important differences from both Sjoberg's pre-industrial and his modern industrial city.

a. Sjoberg's pre-industrial city is marked by a rigid structure of inequality and its inhabitants lack geographic mobility; Sjoberg's industrial city did possess geographic mobility, but lacked the structure of rigid inequality. The commercial city of Katz *et al.* precisely combines an enduring and rigid structure of inequality with a large measure of geographic mobility.[10] The variables 'geographic mobility' and 'social inequality' do not show the correlations predicted by Sjoberg for the pre-industrial and industrial cities.

b. Sjoberg's pre-industrial urban centre was socially homogeneous, namely elitist, and had predominantly religious and administrative functions. The centre of the industrial city was, in his opinion, primarily commercial and not industrial (CBD); the residential function of the centre was minimal. According to Katz *et al.*, the urban city centre of the commercial city has a socially-heterogeneous residential function and a mixed commercial–industrial work function.[11]

c. The commercial city in general and Hamilton in particular is small and compact – in this it resembles Sjoberg's pre-industrial city – but therein it is strongly specialized and is marked by a highly-differentiated use of space, which seems to qualify it as 'modern'.[12] Hamilton as 'commercial city showed an urban order fundamentally different from that of today, neither fully traditional nor modern,' write Katz,

Davey and Doucet.[13] Hamilton fits, according to them, neither in the pre-industrial nor in the modern urban types described by Sjoberg. On this basis Davey and Doucet conclude: 'The commercial city must be studied on its own terms.'[14]

The three Canadian historians do not decide on a rejection of Sjoberg's models, but continue in his footsteps and replace his vague transitional city with a new urban type, the commercial city. They assume a mercantile capitalistic economy during the nineteenth-century. Hamilton forms an urban sub-system of that economy. The Hamilton analysis of these Canadian historians is therefore a clear example of the application of the system/sub-system analysis to an individual city. We shall see that in the works of Blumin and Friedrichs, to be discussed in what follows, a similar line of thought is pursued. Katz *et al.* consider the commercial city to be a 'dominant urban form',[15] just as Sjoberg did the pre-industrial city. Despite their criticism the Canadian historians found inspiration in Sjoberg's way of thinking (Numbers of sections and paragraphs are not mentioned see also Section 2.3).

The partial systems and their operation

Katz, Davey and Doucet do not treat Hamilton completely, and mainly restrict themselves to the economic and social partial systems. They examine these for variables such as occupation, social mobility, property, geographic and social mobility, residential patterns, the nature and composition of the household, and so on. These analyses aim to ascertain what influence the variables mentioned above have on the behaviour and mentality of the inhabitants of Hamilton.

Katz *et al.* want to find a number of relationships applicable between structures, behaviour and mentality, having 'enduring' (not universal) validity.[16] The main relationship Katz discerns in his part of the book is that between rigid social inequality and large geographic mobility. This theory, which he derives from Laslett,[17] is illustrated with Edward Bellamy's metaphor of the coach in which the rich sit on top and are pulled forward by the poor masses. The rich can fall off, and then are forced to help pull the coach, but it is very difficult for the poor to climb up on the moving coach. The moving coach illustrates geographical mobility; the difficult climb rigid inequality.[18] There is therefore some kind of a causal relationship, according to Katz, between the high geographical and low social mobility amongst the lower classes in nineteenth-century society.

The commutativity of sub-systems and its historiographical meaning

By conceiving Hamilton as a sub-system of a mercantile capitalist system, Katz *et al.* can find a retrodictive explanation. They thereby take a safe middle course between a 'covering law' and a specific phenomenon, or to put it in their own words: 'The task for social history is to seek a level of explanation that mediates between the particularistic specificity of social history and the generalisations of social theory'.[19]

The research concerning Hamilton could function as a hypothesis for further urban historiographical research. In this manner it offers historians the opportunity: '[. . .] to build upon one another's work in a systematic and cumulative fashion'.[20]

Such a research construction implies two things. First of all that Hamilton, although having specific characteristics, can be replaced as the research subject by another city (see p. 210 see paragraph 2.1). This fits within the commutative character of sub-systems in systems-theoretical analyses of a half-open nature. Secondly, Hamilton has several characteristics as a sub-system through which it can be fit into an encompassing mercantile capitalist system. This associative property consists of a group of commercial entrepreneurs, bankers, retailers, and whole-salers living in the centre of the city who are – and this is why this associative property is specific to Hamilton – native to the town, Protestant, and politically powerful. On this basis the group members have pre-eminent positions in social life, especially with regard to education, charity and culture. Thus a group of a specifically entrepreneurial composition forms an associative property of Hamilton, as a result of which this city can be positioned as a sub-system of the system constituted by the mercantile capitalist economy of Canada in the middle of the nineteenth century.

The ante-bellum Philadelphia of Blumin

Macro-system and sub-system

In the study 'Mobility and change in ante bellum Philadelphia' Blumin treats the social mobility of two typically urban classes – artisans and urban merchants – between 1820 and 1860.[21] In that period these two classes are involved in a development that is characteristic for commercial cities (Blumin is not explicit whether he means all or some commercial cities). As a result of quick expansion of the market because of the transportation revolution at that time (this does not refer only to the building of railroads, but also the opening up of the 'wild west'), the system of artisanship was dismantled and the large merchants gained growing control over the production of goods. Blumin sketches the development of Philadelphia as a sub-system of a more encompassing system explicated by means of the partial systems 'technology' and '(commercial) economy', which are compounded in the terms 'transport revolution' and 'merchant capitalism'. Although the contours of the macro-level become sharper in this manner than they did in Katz *et al.*'s study of Hamilton, the emphasis in Blumin's study also lies on developments in the sub-system, in this case Philadelphia itself.

Partial systems and their operations

Using the two partial systems mentioned above, Blumin observes an enormous downward social mobility among artisans between 1830 and 1860 with regard to both their working situation and their living conditions. Their participation in the professional population declines from 56.2 per cent to 47 per cent during that period, while the percentage of unskilled workers increases from 16.7 per cent to 23.6 per cent. To explain this Blumin uses the theory of John R. Commons, who has pointed out that in the period before the Civil War one could speak of an increase in 'mercantile' capitalism. Large merchants acquired increasing control over the production of goods. Commons directed his research to the decline of shoemakers and the ascendancy of shoe traders, who organized shoe production by way of a kind of putting-out system.[22] This did not so much involve merchants interested in trade on the eastern seaboard, where raw materials and fabricates traditionally came from Europe and then were transported further inland, as it involved the export of eastern products to the western United States and 'import' from the west to the east. In 1840 the dominance of the merchant-entrepreneur is evident, not only among shoemakers, but also in textiles, meat and so on: '[. . .] in each of these industries it is evident that the growth of a small number of large producers was accomplished with little mechanization of the manufacturing process'. The mechanization of the production process occurred much later, but the army of workers was already formed before the Civil War.[23]

The commutativity of sub-systems and its historiographical meaning

It is remarkable that Blumin observes a process of commercialization in the United States that Katz, Davey and Doucet observed in Canadian

Hamilton and that is known in Europe under various names, such as 'mercantile capitalism', 'original accumulation', 'the commercial revolution', 'production of manufactures' and 'proto-industrialization'. Friedrichs's study, which will be dealt with in the following section, concerning the German city Nördlingen at the end of the seventeenth and the beginning of the eighteenth centuries, shows great similarity to Blumin's analysis. I shall deal with this problem in that section. Blumin discusses the distributive effects of the system on the sub-system. In his study the sub-system does not have its own face and is extremely passive by nature. It is the case, however, that the system is only explicated through an analysis of the sub-system Philadelphia. This study therefore diverges vastly from his book concerning Kingston, discussed in Chapter 6. Blumin therefore seems a representative of both a subjectifying closed-systems approach and also an objectifying half-open systems approach. This raises the question of whether it is meaningful to emphasize the external relationships and influences of 'communities of scholars' to such an extent in paradigmatic research.[24]

Stedman Jones's nineteenth-century London

Macro-system and sub-system

Stedman Jones makes an analysis of nineteenth-century London. He, too, is concerned with a study of London as a sub-system of a macro-system, but the identity of the city is very strongly emphasized here. In contrast to the three authors mentioned previously, the sub-system in Jones's case only very partially reflects the nineteenth-century English macro-system. Victorian society is sketched as a mainly industrial-capitalist system largely sustained by the cities of Lancashire. That system is equipped with a progressive liberal ideology in which the labouring class and its organizations are considered an integrating part of society. How different from London. The labour market in London is more pre-industrial than industrial-capitalist. The industry in London remains entrepreneurial-artisan and is therefore subject to great economic fluctuations and recessions. This leads to large unemployment in the city, especially in the last quarter of the nineteenth century. The effect of the industrial revolution is precisely to accentuate London's pre-industrial character-istics.[25] Unemployment in London leads to tremendous problems of pauperization, analysed in different ways by researchers at that time, for which different solutions were devised. The organological degeneration perspective, as it was formulated by Park, Burgess and others of the

Chicago school, which considers the size and structure of the city itself to be the cause for urban degeneration, is already encountered among nineteenth-century observers of London's travails, according to Jones.[26] An important element in their considerations is the observation that the poor and the rich live completely separated spatially. The improvement of anti-social behaviour of the pauper is therefore sought in the resurrection of the 'community'. The rich and the poor should live amongst one another. According to the social problem-solvers, London should again become one huge village, remarks Stedman Jones somewhat ironically.[27] This kind of solution is doomed to fail because it is based on a false premise, namely the notion of a city as an integrated community.

As opposed to such an, in his opinion, antiquated 'community perception', Stedman Jones posits a sub-systems conception. He clearly formulates this in his comparison of London and Petrograd. This latter city possessed the most advanced industry of the capitalist world, with a very class-conscious factory proletariat in a country that, for the rest, was almost medieval. London lies in the most advanced capitalist country in the world, yet its economic and social structure is still strongly pre-industrial.[28]

The partial systems and their operation

Jones's study is built on the comparison of the three partial systems: economy, society and ideology, of the nineteenth-century English system on the one hand, and the sub-system London on the other.

The economy of London differs from industrial capitalism as present at the end of the nineteenth-century in England. Although industrial capitalism is already marked by standardized mass production, the production in London is still small-scale and manual. Despite production of capital goods and semi-manufactured articles taking place in industrial capitalism, London 'merely' produces goods for consumption. Although industrial capitalism has shrugged off seasonal economic weakness, in London it can still be observed, especially in winter.

Social oppositions are tightly interwoven with these economic ones. While job opportunities are created for the half-trained factory proletariat in industrial capitalism, there is still high unemployment among casual labourers and a strong contrast between a skilled labour aristocracy and unskilled paupers in London.[29]

To this the ideological problem is linked. Stedman Jones points out that the pauper from London in the nineteenth century is more or less the prototype of the English pauper in general, and that the solutions devised[30] by the upper and middle classes are part of the nascent liberal ideology of the Victorian era. Thus Jones makes London the 'explanans' for the problem of paupers, '[. . .] London [is] one huge magnet for the idle, the dishonest and the criminal'.[31] Stedman Jones is not only concerned with the explanation of the problem of pauperization, but also with understanding the ideology of nascent liberalism in the last quarter of the nineteenth century. This liberalism attaches great importance to the improvement of the proletariat, yet considers the pauper the unwilling dregs of society. A structural analysis of the dialectics between the industrial/capitalist system and the pre-industrial secondary sector in London offers Stedman Jones the answer to this conundrum.[32]

The commutativity of sub-systems and their historiographic meaning

Stedman Jones conducts an indirect polemic against the subjectifying approach to urban history by his rejection of the Chicago school and the community solutions of the pauper problem, as proposed by the nineteenth-century researchers. He clearly situates London after 1860 as a sub-system of the nineteenth-century English macro-system by pointing out the increasing importance of the service sector in the English economy at that time and London's role in it. London, still strongly pre-industrial with regard to methods of production, waxes into an administrative and financial world centre during the course of the second half of the nineteenth century. This raises the question of whether we are here dealing with a 'normal' sub-system. The enormous expansion of the commercial, financial, and administrative sectors (an associative property of the sub-system 'London' towards the industrial-capitalist system) is diametrically opposed to the degeneration of the production sector. The latter suffers extra blows because the technology of mass production also gets its grip on goods for consumption, the cork upon which an important part of London's small-scale industry floats. The growth of the tertiary sector leads to increased demand for building lots, as a result of which rents and land prices rise tremendously.

The malaise in London's secondary sector is accompanied by large-scale unemployment, and the high price of land and high rents accelerate the process of pauperization.[33] Stedman Jones sees the explanation for the problem of pauperization in London in the uneven development of the secondary and tertiary sectors.[34] This uneven development is typical for the relationship between the industrial-capitalist system as a whole and London as a sub-system. Schematically this can be represented as follows (Figure 12):

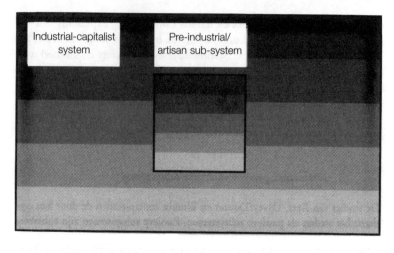

Figure 12. Jones's Victorian London

English Industrial-Capitalist System

This is divided into three partial systems:

- Economic partial system, with modern factory labour
- Social partial system, with the proletariat as the most important independent variable
- Ideological partial system, with nascent liberalism as the most important independent variable

London (as pre-industrial/artisan sub-system)

This has three partial systems variables:

- the pre-industrial artisan structure as the most important economic variable

- the problem of pauperization as the most important dependent social variable
- the ideology regarding poverty as the most important dependent ideological variable

Although Jones presents the antagonistic effect of uneven development as a kind of law, he certainly does not mean a covering law. Here we are concerned with the abrasive functioning of the system and the sub-system as a self-evident structural dialectic. London can in this context be exchanged for another city, in which case a similar functioning of the system and the sub-system will be in evidence (see industrial Petrograd by contrast with still-feudal Russia). In the following section we shall encounter several more examples of this 'law' of uneven development. Jones adds that all solutions proposed during the nineteenth century to the problem of pauperization were illusory, because it was not a cultural or a mental problem, but a structural problem. He thereby rejects an actionist analysis and points out objective-causal relationships as explanations for London's poverty problem. London distinguishes itself because of its pre-industrial character from the nineteenth-century industrial-capitalist system, but is closely tied to it as a commercial and administrative centre.

Thus Stedman Jones's study *Outcast London* is an excellent example of a half-open systems analysis, in which the active character of London as a sub-system is noteworthy. This naturally raises questions. How can sub-systems led by the macro-system of which they are a part initiate activities that are not immediately generated by the macro-system? Is this a case of the bankruptcy of the half-open systems analysis? Are sub-systems in the end nothing but closed systems?

Intermezzo: passive and active sub-systems

The studies by Katz, Davey and Doucet and Blumin conceived the cities examined as passive sub-systems. Passive sub-systems are sub-systems in which the sub-system does indeed possess some coherence, yet little opposition is offered to the distributive properties of the system and the imperialism of the partial systems (or variables). If we consider a car radiator as a sub-system of a very cold environment functioning as a system, then the system can destroy the radiator, but the radiator cannot in turn change the temperature of the system. In this case the car radiator must be considered a passive sub-system. Passive sub-systems can be tracked down by way of two questions. The first is whether the system influences the sub-system, and the second whether the sub-system can show divergent behaviour or even change the system. If the answer to the first question is affirmative and the answer to the second negative, we are dealing with a passive sub-system.[35]

If both questions can be answered affirmatively then the chance increases that we are dealing with an active sub-system. Stedman Jones's industrial London displays clearly divergent – in this case pre-industrial – behaviour with regard to the industrial-capitalist system. Sometimes active sub-systems can even change the system. Active sub-systems can in that case best be compared to feedback systems. Just as the thermostat of a heating system can actively effect the operation of the boiler, or the regulator of James Watt's steam engine can regulate the supply of steam, an active sub-system can influence the functioning of the system.

In the case of Jones's *Outcast London*, this is mainly the case with regard to the variable 'ideology'. The problem of pauperization in London led to a sharp distinction between labourer and pauper in the nascent liberalism of the nineteenth century. The contribution of the sub-system 'London' to the ideology of the industrial-capitalist system was an appreciation of the value of labourers and a depreciation of paupers.

It should be noted that the sub-system cannot independently exercise its influence when affecting the system. It can only do this as part of the system as a whole. An active sub-system is therefore not the equivalent of a goal-directed closed system.[36] This is not even the case with incoherent systems, which I have also compared to goal-directed systems in Chapter 7. Although this comparison indicates that the boundaries between the two types of systems are diffuse – in both cases one may speak of a quasi-teleological explanation – there is one major difference. In the incoherent systems the origin of the functioning of the system is teleological and can therefore always be connected to actors; in an active sub-system this need not always be the case. In the latter case the origin must in any case be found in the encompassing system.

The explanatory methods of active sub-systems are related to those of an abnormalist explanatory model. As sub-systems, active systems are subject to the functioning of the system. The system indicates what is a recurrent and hence a 'normal' method of explanation for a phenomenon. The contribution of the active sub-system itself represents that which is abnormal and therefore yields the most salient contribution to explanation. That is why that which is abnormal is often considered the cause in such an explanation. This, however, barely affects the 'normal' causes – 'the mere conditions', as they are called by Hart and Honoré – with regard to causal importance.[37] If we see that a well-kept garden, with a sprinkler system, is nonetheless desiccated under the hot summer sun, we do not consider the sun but the defective sprinkler to be the cause of this horticultural fiasco. Hart and Honoré, as well as Lorenz, all give more or less the same example for the abnormalist explanatory model. In their case it is, however, not a defective sprinkler, but a lazy gardener who effectuates the garden's demise.[38] Of import here is the relationship between the sun and the sprinkler system. A link can be made by equipping the sprinkler system with a hygrothermostat. This device activates the sprinkler if the moistness sinks below a certain minimum. Causally the broken thermostat forms an active sub-system (its mechanical inactivity leads to causal activity) with regard to the desiccated garden.[39]

At first sight the abnormalist explanation looks a lot like Weber's contrafactual argumentation and singular causal imputation. In both cases a 'normal' or regularly occurring state of affairs is replaced as cause by a specific one. In Weber's case the normal political behaviour of the Persians was replaced (as cause) by the political behaviour of the Greeks. In the case of the desiccated garden, the sun was replaced by a defective sprinkler (or lazy gardener). Lorenz hence counts both among the 'special' causal explanations.[40] Yet there is an important difference between the two methods of explanation. In the case of the singular causal imputation, that which is 'normal' is not a condition for the abnormal cause; this is the case for abnormalism. A Persian victory is not a condition for the political behaviour of the Greeks; on the contrary. Yet the sun is a condition for the operation of the sprinkler system. The explanation for the difference is simple. In Weber's case that which is normal is not a part of the abnormal developments. There are two different closed systems, each with its own internal development. The abnormality of one system is made clear by comparing it to the 'normality' of the other. In the case of the garden fiasco, one can speak of two types of (presupposed) conditions. Both the sun and the defective sprinkler effect the same (sub)system: the desiccated garden.

Active sub-systems are in evidence more often than is commonly supposed in urban historiography. Somewhat one-sidedly, only research such as that done by Robson concerning economic growth and the specialization of cities is considered. In that study Robson concludes that the most specialized cities show the greatest fluctuations in growth. From this he concludes that such cities are most independent of the macro-system.[41] The independence observed by Robson can only be interpreted as the operation of an active sub-system. In what follows we shall see that there are more examples of active sub-systems than Robson's alone.[42]

Active and passive sub-systems encourage the use of the mechanistic metaphor. Such a more mechanistic view is found in urban historiography in the notion of cities as central places. The city is then actually conceived of as an (active) gear in an enveloping whole, in which case the functioning of the gear is determined by the encompassing mechanism.[43] Lampard's ideas, discussed in the previous chapter, yield an excellent foundation for the theory of active sub-systems. His concept 'nodality' demonstrates how cities, as active points of concentration, are on the one hand system-dependent and on the other causally active.

Sjoberg, Katz, Davey and Doucet, and Blumin wrote urban studies in which the city, although it displayed an individual identity, did not have an active causal function. Stedman Jones's study of London led to the explication of the phenomenon 'active sub-system'. In the studies to follow, by Friedrichs and Foster, cities behave as active sub-systems.

In the above the following questions have been formulated regarding sub-systems studies in urban historiography: What distinguishes the sub-system from the system, or, in other words: what constitutes the (limited) identity of the sub-system itself? Which partial systems at the macro-level influence the micro-level? Are the sub-systems commutative? These questions should be supplemented with a fourth question, in the light of the problems concerning active sub-systems: In what manner is the phenomenon 'active sub-system' present in urban historiography? This question is dealt with in that part of the following analyses that deals with the identity of sub-systems (see p. 210 sections 6.1, 7.1 and 8.1).

Application of 'active' sub-systems theory to urban historiography. Foster's contrasting comparison of class formation in three industrializing English cities

Foster's comparative studies (see Note 1) deal with more or less the same problem as Jones's study on London. Foster raises the question of whether industrial-capitalism in England in the nineteenth century had the same social and political effect throughout England. To answer this question, he compares three English industrial towns in the period 1800–1860. Central to this study is the question of whether the labouring class present in these three cities developed the same level of class-consciousness.

Macro-system and sub-system

The first of the three cities treated is Oldham, located in the Pennine core of the industrial revolution. It is a centre of the cotton industry. The second is Northampton, in the Midlands, which industrialized during the Depression of the twenties and thirties. This event caused many immigrants from the countryside to offer themselves as cheap labour to the shoe industry established there. The third and last is South Shields in Northern England, equipped with extensive mining and shipbuilding industries. Although Foster assumes that the separate cities are 'never much more than an arbitrary geographical bite of a larger political system',[44] he still arrives at the conclusion that the dominant political-economical macro-system has had totally different effects on these three 'geographical bites'. Oldham was, according to Foster, under the continuous control of the working class between 1825 and 1850. Northampton was marked by a tumultuous yet superficial radicalism – in the last quarter of the nineteenth century it was the first city to send an atheist to parliament – but the workers themselves were barely organized and showed no interest in local politics. The working class of South Shields had close contacts with that of London. In the beginning of the nineteenth century it was well-organized and politically active; towards the end of that same century it became, despite the good organization, 'non-radical' and collaborative. These contrasting results of the comparison demand a closer examination of the macro-system and the partial systems active in it.[45]

The partial systems and their operation

The industrial-capitalist macro-system of England in the first half of the nineteenth century consists of an economic (partial) system marked by competition and success for the few. The discontent and conflicts that threaten to issue from this situation have to be combated through the social and economic (partial) systems. Politically speaking, this occurs through the maintenance of stability throughout the system, which demands a strong state; socially it occurs through the creation of sub-groups that start working as small-scale success systems. This last element from the social partial system plays a central role in Foster's explanation of the differentiated effects of a common macro-system. Industrial capitalism necessarily leads to the alienation of the working class, claims the author. In order to counter this estrangement, the workers themselves form sub-groups and sub-cultures with their own leaders and their own opportunities for success. As the formation of sub-cultures leads to internal divisions within the working class, the formation of sub-groups is advantageous for the capitalist and helps maintain the macro-system. Sub-cultures, however, can also increase the unity of the working class; and then they undermine the system. Whether the effect of the formation of sub-cultures affirms the system or undermines it depends on several variables issuing from the economic and social partial systems, which are let loose by Foster on the sub-systems he has chosen. From the economic partial system, he uses the economic structure and the spread of income as variables; as social variables he uses patterns of marriage and residence. These variables have especially divergent effects in Oldham and South Shields – Northampton lies in between these extremes – on the formation of sub-groups and therefore on the emergence of class-consciousness.

Variables	Oldham	South Shields
A economic variables		
1 economic variables	1 monolithic structure: only cotton industry	1 mixed structure: mines and shipbuilding
2 spread of income	2 little spread of income	2 large differences in income
B social variables		
3 marriage pattern	3 much intermarriage between partners from working-class and artisan backgrounds	3 fewer marriages between workers and artisans
4 residential pattern 4a mixed	4 residential pattern 4a mixed neighbourhoods of artisans and workers	4 residential patter 4a less mixed residential patterns
4b bourgeoisie living in the city	4b bourgeoisie living in the city	4b no bourgeoisie living in the city

A stronger class-consciousness emerged among the working population of Oldham for the following reasons: Oldham had a more monolithic economic structure (only the cotton industry), as a result of which the spread of income was less large than in South Shields; there was more of a mixed residential pattern in Oldham, as a consequence of which there were more 'mixed' marriages between workers and artisans; Oldham had a bourgeoisie that lived in the city, which South Shields lacked, as a result of which there was less formation of sub-groups in Oldham. This strong class-consciousness was expressed politically in Oldham between 1825 and 1850 in (1) the union's control of the local government; (2) the opposition of the people of Oldham to the new 'Malthusian' poverty law in 1834, which they did not implement for ten years; and (3) the fact that the radicals Cobbett and Fielden were chosen as members of parliament. Although the working class did not have voting rights because of the restricted franchise, they succeeded by various means in getting the middle class to take a radical political course. After 1860 the industrial-capitalist system changed socio-economically as well as politically, and Oldham was put back in its place in the macro-system.

The commutativity of the sub-system and its historiographical meaning

There is a relationship between the studies of Stedman Jones and Foster.[46] In both cases one may speak of an unorthodox Marxist 'family tree' of urban history. Although marked by a system–sub-system relationship, the effect of the system on the sub-system is differentiated. Thus Foster proceeds from a system–sub-system construction – cities were nothing but 'geographical bites' for him – yet he nonetheless arrives at a contrasting comparison. This is possible because of the abnormalist explanatory model he uses. A normal course of affairs (N1) would have been that the industrial-capitalist system would lead to class-consciousness. This can be compared with the 'mere conditions' mentioned by Hart and Honoré. In the example of the garden this would involve the effect of the sun. There is, however, also a specific normal course of events, which I would like to call N2. In the example of the garden this is the working sprinkler system or a diligent gardener. In this second normal course of affairs the desiccating effect of the sun is negated. In Foster's study N2 is constituted by the formation of sub-groups in most English industrial cities. The abnormalist explanation lies in the divergence from N2, which effectuates a partial return to N1. A broken sprinkler system or a lazy gardener leads to the flowers drying out anyway. In the case of Foster's study, the absence of the formation of sub-groups allows class-consciousness to emerge nevertheless. The abnormalist explanatory model implies a divergence from N2 and a partial return to N1.

It should be noted here that the capitalistic system forms a necessary condition for the class-consciousness in Oldham. Robson considers Foster's study of Oldham, Northampton and South Shields to be a good example of a differentiated system/sub-system approach on these grounds.[47]

Friedrichs'S early modern German city

Macro-system and sub-system

Friedrichs's book *Urban society in an age of war* and his article 'Capitalism, mobility and class formation in the early modern German city'[48] can be considered the antithesis of Walker's (closed-systems) study of German home towns. Both of Friedrichs' studies concern the German city Nördlingen from the sixteenth to the eighteenth centuries. Although Nördlingen could also be given the appellation 'German home town', Friedrichs objects to such a description. He restricts himself to the qualification 'early modern German city' on the basis of Maurice Dobb's theory on the development of early modern cities. Dobb – basing himself mainly on the situation in England and the Netherlands – claimed that in the period of mercantile capitalism artisans either ascended the social ladder to become capitalists or descended to a semi-proletarian level. Friedrichs wishes to amend this forked theory. For Germany, he claims, Dobb's theory is not completely valid: '[. . .] for there the decay of the economic position of the craftsmen took place in a political and social environment which protected them from proletarization and made them instead into the core of the emerging lower middle class.'[50]

As against the division within the medieval city between *Unterschichten* [the dregs of society] and *Bürgerschaft* [citizenry], a tripartition occurs in the seventeenth and eighteenth centuries under influence of the *Verlagsystem* [putting-out system]. The lower layer continues to exist, but the *Bürgerschaft* splits into the 'entrepreneurial bourgeoisie' and the *Kleinbürgerei*. It is this form of social stratification that is typical for the early modern German city, as a sub-system of the mercantile capitalist *Verlagsystem*. What is noteworthy here is that only a limited identity is attributed to Nördlingen. Friedrichs contents himself with the observation that he is concerned with a 'case study of urban society in early modern times'.

The nature of the macro-system in which Nördlingen functions as sub-system is non-urban. After the example of Dobb, Friedrichs considers early capitalism, explicated as the putting-out system, to be the macro-level. This well-known system of household industry, in which merchant entrepreneurs have the peasants in the countryside work for them as paid workers, as a result of which a first form of non-artisan production arises, already forms a threat for the artisans of Nördlingen itself in the early seventeenth century. They are, after all, bound to various guild regulations, which the merchants can easily avoid. Economically weakened, they are hardly represented in the town council. They have not yet completely lost their economic position because within the city the town council still maintains the system of *bürgerliche Nahrung*. This means that the citizens of Nördlingen are still obliged to buy their products from artisans in the city.

Only after 1712, as the merchant entrepreneurs get a firm position in the town council, is this traditional, urban artisan system abandoned and the victory of the *Verlagsystem* within the city walls consummated. With this Nördlingen loses its last medieval characteristics and the early modern German city is born.

If we reduce this exposition to its systems-theoretical structure, the developments in Nördlingen can be described as follows. Nördlingen, with its urban-artisan economy of *bürgerliche Nahrung,* forms a limited sub-system within a more encompassing system, which dominates the whole region around Nördlingen. Within the sub-system, developments occur, in this case the emergence of the *petite bourgeoisie*, that can only be explained by referring to developments within the encompassing putting-out system. This is a case of a retrodictive explanation.

The city as sub-system, however, possesses a limited identity and can therefore for some time resist developments outside. The *petite bourgeoisie* emerges both through the urban sub-system itself and through the external system, the entrepreneurial method of production.

The entrepreneurial system finally effects a symmetry between the macro-system (the early capitalist economy) and the retarded sub-system (Nördlingen). However, Nördlingen as sub-system distinguishes itself from the encompassing system through the *bürgerliche Nahrung* economy. Precisely because the sub-system resists the (entrepreneurial) system so strongly, we may consider Nördlingen to be an active sub-system, which after a vigorous struggle and crises is destroyed at the beginning of the eighteenth century. By positioning the sub-system Nördlingen in the explanatory *Verlagsystem*, Friedrichs does not give an internal analysis but rather, as it was called by Von Wright, an external causal explanation.

The resistance in Nördlingen to the system of mercantile capitalism can be compared to the sprinkler system or the diligent gardener. If the resistance disappears then the system (respectively the sun or mercantile capitalism) has free rein.

The partial systems and their operation

That we are here not concerned with a teleological explanatory chain in a closed system becomes evident when we consider the partial systems that Friedrichs examines for their explanatory (and hence distributive) effects. To do this he divides the history of Nördlingen into demographic, economic, social, financial, political, and religious partial systems. Two questions lie behind Friedrichs's exposition: 1. What influence do the various wars in the seventeenth century have on the social-economic development of Nördlingen? 2. What consequences did the rise of the *Verlagsystem* have for the social and political constellation of the city?

As to the first question, he arrives at the surprising conclusion that, in the long term, the wars had more of a conserving than of a dynamic effect on the city. The real transformation of late medieval Nördlingen into an early modern city takes place as a result of changes in the economy and social relationships.[52] The guild economy makes way for early capitalism and the social political influence of the guilds wanes in favour of that of the textile entrepreneurs.[51] What is noticeable here is that a singular, teleological explanation in terms of specific acts of war and violence is replaced by the recurrent, distributive effect of the economy.

The commutativity of sub-systems and its historiographical meaning

In order to emphasize this, Friedrichs once again points out the general character of developments as they occurred in Nördlingen. 'None of these developments, of course, was unique to Nördlingen: sooner or later virtually every European city experienced these things as part of the transition from a medieval to a modern outlook and social structure.'[52] Friedrichs describes Nördlingen as a case that functions as a model for similar changes elsewhere. Hence it is a matter of course that his conception of an early modern German city has a commutative nature.

The fact that Friedrichs's study concerns a city in a different continent and period than the ones discussed by Katz and Blumin can mean one of two things: either it is the case that everywhere in the (Western) world a commercial revolution (in which mainly the artisan class is depleted) precedes the industrial revolution, or Katz, Blumin and Friedrichs – without being aware of it – have used a similar model of analysis. In the first case one can speak of a general process occurring in reality that can be described in the form of a recurrent system. In the second case, one may speak of an identical model of analysis, an analogous paradigm.

Because of the epistemological premise of this study, the one possibility does not exclude the other. The model of analysis mentioned can be described as a half-open systems analysis, in which mercantile capitalism can be considered a system, and Hamilton, Philadelphia and Nördlingen can be considered (commutative) sub-systems. Mercantile capitalism, however, can also form a system in reality, which could indicate that there is a recurrent historical phase preceding the industrial phase in many places in the world. Ontologically or epistemologically, in both cases the possibilities for comparison are so large that they can lead to cumulative knowledge. The view that there is only space in history for that which is unique and specific and that generalizing research is the domain of the social sciences seems to me to be refuted by the systems–sub-systems studies analysed here.

A comparison of Walker's German home town and Friedrichs's early modern German city

We have now come to the end of the two parts of this study dealing with methods of explanation. To conclude and summarize, a comparison follows between Walker's German home towns and Friedrichs's analysis of Nördlingen as an early modern German city. These studies can be compared because Nördlingen falls under Walker's definition of a German home town and because both studies pay a great deal of attention to the lower middle class, which has had such an important influence on the course of German history. That Friedrichs calls Nördlingen an *early modern German city* and not a *home town* points out the difference in the operation of half-open and closed systems. This difference is best illustrated by the way that Walker and Friedrichs explain the genesis of the German *petite bourgeoisie*. Walker's German home towns explain this fact by showing the singular causal links of that genesis in a closed system. From Walker's viewpoint, the German home towns are equipped with a flow of internal causes explaining the emergence of the German *petite bourgeoisie* by conceiving that bourgeoisie as the output of a relatively-closed system construction. Friedrichs, on the other hand, explains that genesis by explicating the encompassing system and referring to it. Schematically the systems-theoretical interpretations of Walker's and Friedrichs' explanatory models can be represented as follows (Figure 13).

As we may recall, the cylinders depict the closed system, with which we have compared Walker's home towns. Every home town retains its individuality, which is why several cylinders are represented with different causal links. Within the closed systems – in other words, through the internal development of the German home towns – a *petite bourgeoisie* emerges that, after the disappearance of the home towns in 1871, maintains

German home town 1.

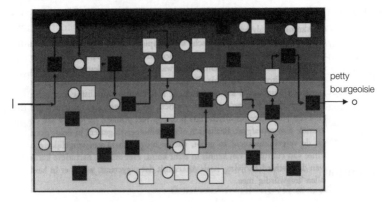

petty
bourgeoisie

German home town 2.

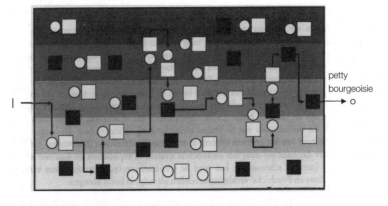

petty
bourgeoisie

○ actors

■ intentional black boxes

□ mechanical black boxes

→ connecting line of singular causal imputation

I input

O output

Figure 13. Walker's German home towns

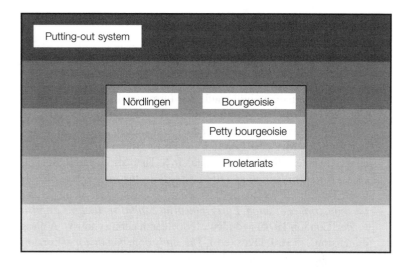

Figure 14. Friedrichs's Nördlingen as an Early Modern German City

its home-town mentality and therefore becomes easy prey for National Socialism. Walker and Gillis have called this explanation of the genesis of the *petite bourgeoisie* 'vertical' stratification. This term is comprehensible when we imagine the cylinders in a vertical position.

The large rectangle represents the putting-out system as the encompassing system. Within the sub-system of Nördlingen, which serves as a model for the early modern German city, the *Verlagsystem* splits the bourgeoisie into the entrepreneurial bourgeoisie and the *petite bourgeoisie*. In contrast to the vertical social stratification mentioned above, this is called 'horizontal' stratification.

What are the consequences of the differences in the methods of definition and explanation, in other words the differences between closed and half-open systems constructions, for the time and temporal arrangement used by historians when writing history? This question will be dealt with in the next chapter.

Notes

1. G. S. Jones, *Outcast London. A study of the relationships between classes in Victorian society* (Oxford 1971); C. R. Friedrichs, *Urban society in an age of war. Nördlingen 1580–1720* (Princeton, NJ 1979); idem, 'Capitalism, mobility and class formation in the early modern German city', in Ph. Abrams and E. A. Wrigley (eds), *Towns in societies. Essays in economic history and historiological sociology* (Cambridge, MA and London 1975); S. Blumin, 'Mobility and change in ante bellum Philadelphia', in S. Thernstrom and R. Sennett (eds), *Nineteenth-century cities. Essays in the new urban history* (New Haven, CT 1976), pp. 165–208; J. Foster, *Class struggle and the industrial revolution. Early industrial capitalism in three English towns* (London 1974) and idem, 'Nineteenth century towns. A class dimension', in H. J. Dyos (ed.), *The study of urban history* (London 1968), also appearing in M. Flinn and T. Stout (eds), *Essays in social history* (Oxford 1974). The original study also included: D. F. Crew, *Town in the Ruhr. A social history of Bochum 1860–1914* (New York 1979) and H. Van der Wee, *The rise and decline of urban industries in Italy and the Low Countries [Late Middle Ages – early modern times]* (Louvain 1989).
2. The following is derived from: G. Sjoberg, *The pre-industrial city. Past and present* (Glencoe, IL 1960) and idem, 'Cities in developing and industrial societies, a cross-cultural analysis', in P. M. Hauser and L. F. Schnore (eds), *The study of urbanisation* (New York 1965).
3. G. Sjoberg, 'Cities in developing and industrial societies, a cross-cultural analysis', p. 215.
4. Ibid., pp. 216–20.
5. Ibid., pp. 237–49.
6. G. Rozman, 'Urban networks and historical stages', *Journal of Interdisciplinary History* 9(1) (Summer 1978): 65–91, esp. 66; J. de Vries, *European urbanization 1500–1800* (London 1984), p. 5.
7. M. Katz et al., *The people of Hamilton, Canada West. Family and class in a mid-nineteenth-century city* (Cambridge, MA and London 1975), pp. 321–2.
8. Ibid., pp. 3–4.
9. Ibid., p. 14.
10. Ibid., p. 44.
11. Ibid., pp. 320–42.
12. Ibid., pp. 321 and 341.
13. Ibid., p. 316.

14. Ibid., p. 341.
15. Ibid., p. 9.
16. Ibid., p. 13. Here an observer's viewpoint is manifest. Deriving behaviours and mentalities from structures presupposes isomorphy (equality of form and structure) between reality on the one hand and human thought and action on the other. This presupposition of isomorphy itself is based on the notion that people are led in their behaviour by a rational analysis of pros and contras. M. Anderson ('Family and class in nineteenth century cities', *Journal of Family History* 4 (1979): 130–48, especially 147) has pointed out that this is typically an observer's viewpoint. It is concerned with a dispositional explanation.
17. P. Laslett, *The world we have lost* (London 1965), p. 148.
18. Katz *et al.*, *The people of Hamilton*, pp. 309–11.
19. Ibid., p. 316.
20. Ibid., pp. 10–11.
21. S. Blumin, 'Mobility and change in ante bellum Philadelphia', in S. Thernstrom and R. Sennett (eds), *Nineteenth-century cities. Essays in the new urban history* (New Haven, CT 1976), pp. 165–208, esp. 201.
22. J. R. Commons, 'American shoemakers 1649–1895', *Quarterly Journal of Economics* 24 (1909): 39–84.
23. S. Blumin, 'Mobility and change in ante bellum Philadelphia', p. 202.
24. See F. R. Ankersmit and A. A. Van den Braembussche, 'De huidige geschiedfilosofie onderschat de rol van de taal bij de vormgeving van ons inzicht in het verleden' [Contemporary philosophy of history underestimates the role of language in forming our insight into the past], *Groniek* 89/90 (1984) *Taal en geschiedenis:* 15–16. This, for example, can also be said of Warner if one compares his *Private city* with his *Streetcar suburbs. The process of growth in Boston 1870–1900* (Cambridge, MA 1962) and of G. Sjoberg if one compares *The pre-industrial city* with 'The rise and fall of cities', *International Journal of Comparative Sociology* IV (1963): 107–20.
25. G. Stedman Jones, *Outcast London. A study of the relationships between classes in Victorian society* (Oxford 1971), pp. 19–23.
26. Ibid., pp. 13–14.
27. Ibid., pp. 258–61.
28. Ibid., p. 346.
29. Ibid., pp. 23–33.
30. Ibid., pp. 241 ff.
31. Ibid., p. 12.

32. Ibid., pp. 13–14.
33. Ibid., pp. 153–4 and elsewhere.
34. Ibid., p. 349.
35. C. West Churchman, 'Systems', in S. Optner (ed.), *Systems analysis*, (Harmondsworth 1973), pp. 286–7.
36. V. C. Hare, *Systems analysis: a diagnostic approach*, pp. 43–5, and N. Jordan, 'Some thinking about "system"', in S. Optner (ed.), *Systems analysis*, p. 70.
37. Hart and Honoré do suggest something like this by making a distinction between the cause (the abnormal event) and the condition (the normal state of affairs). This distinction may be made as long as it is not forgotten that the normal state of affairs is the necessary condition for indicating the specific cause: H. L. A. Hart and A. M. Honoré, 'Causal judgement in history and in the law', in W. Dray (ed.), *Philosophical analysis and history* (New York and London 1966), p. 217.
38. Hart and Honoré, 'Causal judgement in history and in the law', pp. 213–37 and Chr. Lorenz, *De constructie van het verleden*, pp. 129–30.
39. One can, of course, also posit that a working hygrothermostat forms an active sub-system *vis-à-vis* the 'normal' desiccating effect of the sun. The distributive efficacy exercised by the sun, in this case on the sprinkler system, leads to a new, divergent distributive effect, namely: the watering of a garden ravaged by the sun. The system 'sun' with its distributive effect 'desiccation' is resisted by the sub-system 'sprinkler system' with its distributive effect 'moisturizing'.

 In this context one may think of a remark made by Berry with regard to the operation of urban networks and the second law of thermodynamics. This second law claims that the entropy – that is, the disorder – of an (in Berry's case – a relatively) isolated system never (in Berry's case – hardly ever) decreases. Berry remarks, following in Murayama's footsteps, that there are many examples of systems processes in which divergences are not corrected and homogenized, but in which these divergences are reinforced. B.J.L. Berry 'Cities as systems within systems of cities', *Papers of the Regional Science Association* 13 (1964): 160–1.
40. Chr. Lorenz, *De constructie van het verleden*, pp. 129–30 (in the 5th revised edition 155–7).
41. B. T. Robson, 'The impact of functional differentiation within systems of industrialized cities', in H. Schmal (ed.), *Patterns of European urbanization since 1500* (London 1981), pp. 113–30, esp. 117.

42. H. Schmal, 'Epilogue: one subject, many views', in H. Schmal (ed.), *Patterns of European Urbanization*, p. 300.
43. R. F. Berkhofer, *A behavioral approach to historical analysis* (New York, London 1969), p. 175. Although Berkhofer does make the distinction between organic and mechanical theories in the social sciences, he gives too little attention to the exact causal relationships playing a role in both types of theories. For this reason he has too little eye for the metaphorical nature of the terms 'mechanical' and 'organic'.
44. J. Foster, *Class struggle and the industrial revolution*, pp. 2–3.
45. Ibid., p. 2.
46. See: D. F. Crew, *Town in the Ruhr. A social history of Bochum 1860–1914* (New York 1979), pp. 6 and 226 Note 25.
47. B. T. Robson, 'The impact of functional differentiation within systems of industrialized cities', p. 115.
48. C. R. Friedrichs, *Urban society in an age of war. Nördlingen 1580–1720* (Princeton, NJ 1979); idem, 'Capitalism, mobility and class formation in the early modern German city', in Ph. Abrams and E. A. Wrigley (eds), *Towns in societies. Essays in economic history and historiological sociology* (Cambridge, MA and London 1975), pp. 187–209.
49. C. R. Friedrichs, 'Capitalism, mobility and class formation in the early modern German city', p. 189.
50. C. R. Friedrichs, *Urban society in an age of war. Nördlingen 1580–1720* , p. 294.
51. Ibid., p. 295.
52. Ibid.

Part V
Time and Temporal Arrangement

'No matter how valuable systems analysis may be to historical analysis, it is as nothing if it fails to take time into account.'

R. F. Berkhofer, *A Behavioral approach to historical analysis*, p. 209.

9

Time and Entities Subjectifying and Objectifying Conceptions

Time forms a central category in historical writing. For this reason the manner in which time is conceived in urban historiography plays an important role in this study. Therefore the Chapters 9 and 10 are dedicated to temporal problems. This chapter deals especially with the perception of time. In it I wish to show that historical works making use of the closed-system construction are marked by a subjectifying conception of time. In this light it is almost self-evident that historical works that explain by way of relatively-open systems use an objectifying conception of time. Because it may be interesting for the reader to partake now and then of other forms of historical writing than urban historiography, historiography concerning family and state will also be treated in this chapter.

In the general thinking about time, two traditions come to the fore. One tradition can be called objective or cosmological, the other subjective or phenomenological.[1] The cosmological tradition perceives time as a category of being, the phenomenological way of thinking categorizes time as a phenomenon that can be experienced by human consciousness. Neither of these two traditions exists in a pure form. Aristotle, Augustine, Kant, Husserl and Heidegger, to name the most important philosophers involved in temporal questions, experienced the difficulty of choosing one side or the other. For Aristotle these two temporal points of view were already interwoven. Although in his *Physics* Aristotle considered time to be an objective category of *being*, connecting it with 'the number of motion',[2] he also stresses that it requires a *soul* – thus a subjective element – to count intervals and distinguish instants.[3] Augustine approached the problem from what we now call the phenomenological side. For him time was an issue of the soul. It is a *distentio in anima*, that is to say time is something of the mind that distends itself in memory, attention and anticipation. Yet Augustine had to confess that time had a beginning along with all other created things, and thus an objective side.[4]

The impossibility of perceiving or conceiving time completely from a cosmological or a phenomenological point of view does not conceal the necessity of commencing thought about time from either an objective or a subjective presupposition. So instead of speaking of an objective and a subjective time, I prefer to speak of an objectifying and a subjectifying temporality.[5] These terms may also clarify – of course without offering solutions – the aporias in which thinking about time is involved.[6] A subjectifying time-conception will always run against an objective wall and vice versa. Kant, standing in the Aristotelian, objectifying tradition, considers time to be a structure of nature, but also one that resides in the *Gemüt* or intuition, the subjective constitution of our mind. Heidegger's temporal categories belong to the domain of *being there*, which is to say that they belong to the – subjectifying – domain of human existence, and not purely to *being*. However, he attempted to derive time from 'ordinary time', in which a cosmological element is undeniable.

Ricoeur has tried to clarify the subjectifying–objectifying time-aporia by lifting it up to a narrative level, although he was completely aware of the insolubility of the problem. Hence he conceived a threefold imitation of time-experience, called *mimesis*, on the level of language. In terms of *acting* time is prefigured (mimesis1), in *narrative* time is configured (mimesis2) and *in hearing/reading* time is refigured (mimesis3). Ricoeur thus defends a circular thesis that temporality is brought to language in the sense that language configures and refigures temporal experience.[7] Configured time plays a crucial part in this thesis, because it is the mediation between the two other temporal conceptions. The configured time is brought to life and language by the concept of 'emplotment'. Ricoeur did not borrow this concept from Hayden White, who also used it in his *Metahistory*, but from . . . Aristotle. Does this mean that Ricoeur employs an objectifying concept of time on a narrative level? Not in the least. The concept of emplotment is not derived from Aristotle's *Physics*, but from his *Poetics*.[8] As we shall see, it is much more a subjectifying than an objectifying temporal conception.

Ricoeur's configured time is a central category for analysing temporal constructions in historiography, and so is emplotment. I shall therefore return to these problems later on.

Nevertheless, it is a pity that Ricoeur does not pay any attention to the objectifying conception of time as it displays itself in language, especially in historiography. In this chapter I want to show that in historiography the objectifying conception of 'narrative' time deserves the same prominence as Ricoeur's subjectifying time of emplotment.

To explain the 'narrative' construction of objectifying time, we must initially return to Aristotle's *Physics*. Time as a form of being is, according to Aristotle, an infinite succession of 'presents'.[9] This endless stream of 'presents' actualizes itself in movement and extension and can therefore be measured and is objectifiable.[10] Here the past merely functions as a terminus *a quo* and the future as a terminus *ad quem*. In other words, future and past are nothing more than that which is before and after the present.

In its most simple form, we encounter objectifying time in historical writing in the form of time tables, annals, chronicles, or yearbooks, or in a more contemporary form in live accounts of (sports) events on television or radio. The chronological temporal scheme in this case consists of nothing more than a repeated series of 'presents'.

Kant considered time an *a priori* intuition (*Anschauungsform*), residing in the *Gemüt*, as we have seen. Although it seems that in this way Kant proposed a subjectified time, he stressed that in the field of appearance time is substance and permanence, which are objectifying categories. Substance and permanence entail, paradoxically, succession and simultaneity.[11] As a consequence, a more sophisticated conception of objectifying time can be developed. Ernst Bloch has done this in the form of a *Gleichzeitigkeit des Ungleichzeitigen*, and has thus grounded and justified an objectifying time-conception in historiography.[12]

Bloch's 'simultaneity of that which is non-simultaneous presupposes two points: first a time-scheme divided into phases, and second a constructed entity that can contain several phases simultaneously. An example of phased time can be found in Marx's periodization of history according to modes of production, starting with primal communism through a slave economy or an Asiatic mode of production to feudalism, early capitalism and industrial high capitalism. An entity encompassing several phases simultaneously is called by Marx a formation of society, but can, in more general terms, be called a system. Characteristic of some systems is, as we know, the fact that they are built up of sub-systems. Although sub-systems exist by grace of the systems to which they belong, they still possess relative autonomy. This is important for their temporal dimension. Thus the system, for example, can be modern and the sub-system can be traditional, or vice versa. Because the system and the sub-system exist simultaneously but are marked by different time phases, in this case we can speak of the simultaneity of that which is non-simultaneous.[13] Such a simultaneous non-simultaneity is also called compounded time. This appellation makes it clear that in addition to a phased conception of time, a certain constructed entity is also important, in this case the system–sub-system construction.

Although Heidegger uses three different descriptions of time, all three with very specific Heideggerian meanings, he clearly does not use a compounded time in the above-mentioned meaning of the word. In all of his three conceptions of time, *temporality*, *historicality* and *intra-temporality* (within-timeness), past, present, and future flow into one another. In the notion of *temporality* Heidegger formulated his most fundamental conception of time.[14] In statements such as 'This pheno-menon, the future that has passed in the present forms a *whole* (italics: HJ) which we call temporality', and 'Being there (*Dasein*) *temporalises itself* (italics: HJ) in the present as the *unity* (italics: HJ) of the future and having been.[15] Heidegger not only points out that the present already contains the design of the future, but also that temporality is a homo-genizing and subjectifying concept. Heidegger's temporal categories belong to the domain of *being there* or even to *Care* (*Sorge*), which is to say that they belong to the domain of human existence and not purely to *being*. He is neither concerned with *metaphysical time* in the Kantian meaning of the word, nor with *mathematical clock time*, but with *experienced* and *experiential* time. Birth, growth and death, flowering and demise, but also actions with an initial situation, an intended goal, and a result of the action play a central role in such an experienced and experiential time. Here we encounter not an objectifying and compounded conception of time, but a subjectifying and homogeneous one.[16]

The path from such an experienced and experiential time to time as it is used in historical texts is long. But some philosophers of history have explored it nonetheless. Some, such as Hayden White, Mink and Anker-smit, have found it to be a dead-end road; others, among them Carr and Ricoeur, discovered a beautiful vista at its end. A problem in the case of the subjectifying conception of time is that in many historical narratives not only individual subjects and their actions figure but also anonymous forces and apparently anonymous collectives. Which historical subjects should we be thinking of if historical writing does not concern individuals (and the time they experience)? Just as objectifying, compounded time is marked by specific entities in the form of system–sub-system construc-tions, homogenizing and subjectifying time also has its entities. These are what the American philosopher of history Mandelbaum has called *continuing entities*[17] and what the French philosopher Ricoeur called *entités de premier ordre*.[18] Ricoeur shows that such entities take the guise of quasi-personages in historical writing. In Chapters 5 and 6 I tried to make clear that relatively-closed systems form the skeleton of these quasi-subjects.

Hayden White, Mink and Ankersmit have made some relevant remarks concerning time.[19] White and Mink identify time with the objectifying conception of time in annals and chronicles, but, in their opinion, this conception of time is lost in the configuring nature of modern historical writing. Experiential time cannot, according to them, be identified with narrative time because life does not have a beginning, middle or end as narratives do. 'Life has no beginnings, middles and ends', as Mink puts it. Ankersmit claims that time is not a physical or philosophical term, but a cultural concept. This implies that it is not time that shapes history, as occurs in annals and chronicles, but that historical writing shapes time.[20] Ankersmit, however, seems to contradict this statement earlier in the same article when he remarks that determinations of time cannot be found on the level of interpretation, but '*always* [italics: HJ] are harboured "in" the statements of which the historical text consists (for example: "in 1789 the French revolution broke out"). This implies, according to Ankersmit, 'that time in historical practice can only be of secondary importance'.[21]

The purpose of this chapter, among other things, is to rebut Ankersmit's second claim. Time manifests itself most emphatically in historical literature, precisely at the level of interpretation (or representation, if one prefers) and only in a very limited – annalist – fashion at the level of separate statements regarding the past. I will not occupy myself here with the question of whether conceptions of time as they can be found in historical literature have their roots in a cosmological or a phenomeno-logical conception of time. I do want to show that both objectifying and subjectifying conceptions of time play a role in historiography, and especially that these conceptions of time are linked to certain conceptions of entities.[22] This concerns constructed entities, which are themselves either subjectifying or objectifying. In other words, the congruence between the nature of time and the nature of the entity whose temporal dimension is being examined plays a central role in this chapter. In the first case we encounter system–sub-system constructions and in the second supra-individual subjects. These are also called super-actors or, to use Ricoeur's terminology, quasi-personages. Precisely because we are not dealing with 'real' cosmological or phenemological temporality, but with temporality as it is depicted in narratives, the nature of the constructed entity determines the conception of time.

The same holds true for the historical studies concerning the family, cities and states that I shall shortly examine with regard to their temporal construction. I have opted for studies in these three areas in the hope of offering the reader as complete a picture as possible of the temporal constructions enclosed in historiography. In order to show that temporal construction is more dependent on the entity than on the nature of the topic chosen by the authors in each case I shall give two examples of which the topics are closely related but distinct as to their entities and that therefore differ vastly with regard to temporal construction.

There is one major difference between Braudel and Marx on the one hand and the authors whose work regarding family, city and state are analysed in the fourth part of this chapter on the other. The historical studies of Braudel and several Marxists speak in a rather confusing way about the narrative entities on which their stories are founded.[23] The authors of the studies concerning family, city and state are much more aware of the nature and structure of their narrative entities. They therefore use a clearer temporal construction.

Philosophers of history and time: Carr and Ricoeur

Carr and Ricoeur concerned themselves in first instance with the question of the extent to which there is a correlation between experienced and experiential time on the one hand and time in (historical) narratives on the other. Carr makes a direct link. Experienced time is the temporal experience of the acting subject and the temporalities of actions and of narratives show many similarities. Narrative time manifests itself in the plot of the narrative, and just as the narrative has a beginning, a middle, and an end, actions have these too. An action is, after all, a reaction to something that has happened in the past (however recent), with a change in the future in mind. The action itself is nothing but the *hodiecentric* mean between past and future. The question here remains to what extent Carr is correct with regard to the continuity and congruence between actions in reality and the plot of a (historical) narrative.[24] An important point of Carr's opponents is that there is a great deal of interference in the form of contingence and unintended consequence during action, while these elements are left out of the narrative as being irrelevant to the plot. This selectivity of the narrative, or rather its narrator, also occurs in the action, according to Carr, because prior to the action its goals have already been chosen. Action already possesses a form of narrative cohesion and hence it is certainly not contingent. He thereby affirms a remark made by the Finnish-English theoretician of history Von Wright, who posited that an action can only be understood (intentionally) if it can be fitted 'into a "story" about the agent'.[25]

A second argument against Carr's ideas is related to the first. The narrator has knowledge from hindsight, the actor does not. This is an interesting point, because it observes a perspective in historical research that takes the future into account. Carr addresses the problem of knowledge from hindsight, because of which the story differs from the action, with relative ease.[26] The actor continually asks himself before his actions what consequences they might have and chooses his goals according to these considerations. Carr forgets that there are different issues at hand here. The consideration of the consequences of actions continues to belong to the domain of finding goals of action and hence to teleology (*telos* is Greek for 'goal'). The hindsight of the historian pertains to finalism, that is to say to knowledge of the ends of processes. Finalism and teleology are often used as synonyms, but they are clearly distinguished concepts within the theory of history. Teleology cannot and finalism can take account of the unintended consequences of actions. Finalism as knowledge in retrospect was most palpably expressed by Hegel in his *Vorrede* for the *Grundlinien des Rechts* with his statement 'the owls of Minerva start their flight in the falling dusk'.[27] This could not be said of teleology.[28]

A third point of Carr's opponents is that stories and especially historical narratives do not always concern individual subjects, but usually involve collectives and individuals acting in a social context, such as an association, a nation, or a union. Carr answers this criticism with the remark that the we-subject is not in principle different from the I-subject.[29] In other words, Carr equates the subjectifying entity, the quasi-personage, to the human individual and subjectifying temporality to the temporality of action.

Ricoeur problematizes the relationship between experienced time and narrative time in history much more.[30] More than Carr, Ricoeur tends towards methodological and even ontological holism.[31] That is to say that not only persons but also suprapersonal organizations can act. This also explains why Ricoeur on the one hand gives much importance to causal relations alongside intentional ones, but on the other points out that, in addition to a we-perspective, a they-perspective is also possible in historical narration. The historian's striving towards objectivity demands this. Beyond that, the collective possesses far more autonomy than Carr's we-perspective suggests. Using Mandelbaum's continuing entities, Ricoeur develops an *entité de premier ordre* to which individuals can belong without completely identifying themselves with it.[32] The term *appartenance participative*, literally 'participatory belonging', does not merely imply a simple transition from an I-subject to a we-subject, because the participating individual can also resist the collective or be indifferent to it. Although Ricoeur also uses the term 'quasi-personage' for the *entité de premier ordre*, it would be inaccurate to equate the individual and the quasi-personage to one another. Precisely because causal and finalistic relationships play a role in the development of such a super-actor, as well as teleological ones, it is impossible to identify individual actions and those of quasi-personages with one another, as Carr does.

Also with regard to the retrospective perspective of the historian and the role it plays in historical writing, Ricoeur's opinions are more nuanced than those of Carr. Knowledge of the unintended consequences of both individual and collective actions gives historical narratives a finalistic element absent in teleology. Ricoeur in particular elucidates his understanding of the distinction between teleology and finalism in his discussion of the work of Danto and Mink. In particular the capacity of emplotment to foresee the end of a plot in the beginning of a story is of importance for this distinction. After all, this feature is absent in a teleological discourse, but present in a finalistic one, in a narrative.[33]

When constructing the plot of a historical narrative, the writer should keep in mind that the quasi-personage or quasi-personages figuring in the narrative develop from a beginning to an end. The events taking place in between carry the mark of these two elements. Distinguishing in events a beginning and an end (finalism) of a plot is what Ricoeur calls the *mise en intrigue* or emplotment. The construction of the historical plot involves more than merely placing events in the correct chronological order: it is a configuring act. The historical narratives are, after all, more than chronicles or annals.[34] The dimension leading from origin to finality of the *mise en intrigue* finds its grounds in the primary causal and intentional relationships that the historical writer instils in the separate statements of his narrative. This indicates that Ricoeur's subjectifying conception of time allows more objectifying elements than Carr's.[35]

In conclusion, we can distinguish three layers in Ricoeur's narrativism: 1. The first layer is on the micro-level and contains causal and teleological relations; 2. A middle layer puts events in place in the light of their meaning for the beginning or ending of the narrative in which they have been involved, the *mise en intrigue*; and 3. A layer comprising the macro-level, the level of the plot itself, exists in which quasi-personages or super-actors such as states, nations, associations, social groups and whole cultures interact and are subject to the vicissitudes of fate.

In particular, Ricoeur's analysis of the meso-level and macro-level yields useful insights for discovering the temporal dimension in historical studies. Through the use of studies from the French school of *les Annales*, Ricoeur shows how his method of reading can be elucidating when seeking the temporal dimension in historical writing. Hence we shall, at first, closely follow Ricoeur's footsteps during the following discussion of historians who have occupied themselves with temporal perspectives.

There is some difference between a philosophical and a theoretical interest in the problematics of time with regard to history. The philosopher of history is first and foremost a philosopher, and wishes to justify temporal constructions in historical writing, or in any case link these to the experienced and experiential time of the actors.[36] For the theoretician of history, it is more interesting to ascertain how time is formulated in historical writing. Furthermore, not every form of temporality is derived from the experienced time of (quasi-)subjects. We also know that objectifying time exists. This plays an equally important role in historiography. The pragmatism of the theoretician of history first leads to the question of the nature of temporal constructions in historiography. The theory of history pertains primarily to the examination of historiography, and only secondarily to eventual justifications.

Historians and conceptions of time

Few historians have written about the conception of time. Generally they are mainly interested in the phenomenon time in so far as it is linked to problems regarding periodization. Because I do not wish to deal with the problematics of periodization linked to the conception of time in this chapter – I am, after all, concerned with the relationship between time and entities – only those historians are significant who have problematized the temporal dimension. These can be divided into two groups: historians who are interested in a homogeneous conception of time and those who occupy themselves with compounded time. Given the above, it will be clear to the reader that I wish to show that historians who conceive time as being homogeneous will also use a subjectifying conception of time and the subjective entities accompanying it, while historians who prefer a compounded conception of time will construct objective entities. In the case of Braudel and some Marxist philosophers, both time conceptions are used next to each other, and sometimes even intermixed. This is rather confusing. That is why Braudel and Marx are the principal actors in the next few paragraphs.

The subjectifying, homogeneous conception of time

Braudel and stratified time   It might seem rather strange to seek a homogeneous conception of time in the work of Braudel. This French historian, after all, posited not a homogeneous conception of time, but a layered one in his *La Méditerranée et le monde méditerranéen à l'époque de Philippe II*.[37] Braudel distinguishes between seven partial domains with three different time strata in Mediterranean culture:

1. A geographic and ecological partial system, both with a very slow temporality, which he calls *presque immobile* ('almost immobile'). This means that, in a time-span of several centuries, little occurs in these domains.
2. Economic, social, geopolitical and cultural partial systems with a higher-paced undulating temporality.
3. A political system in which temporality is very fast and vibrating, because of the event-driven nature of politics. Thus Braudel presents an infrastructure in his narrative that is already very complex.[38] But this is only the beginning. At the end of the first part and in the second part he considers the cities in the Mediterranean area and observes that each of these is subject to its own development, leading to the construction of a particular identity by each city. In this manner every city has its own plot as quasi-personage and hence its own temporality. We thereby seem even further away from a homogeneous conception of time. Yet this is not entirely the case. After all, the stratified conception of time has been transformed into a conception of time as defined by intrigues or plots. Nonetheless, further homogenization must still take place. Braudel effects this by referring to economy: 'Les villes naissent, progressent, déclinent, suivant les pulsations mêmes de la vie économique'.[39] On this basis we may conclude, according to Braudel, that the meso-stratum should be sought in economic conjunctures. And indeed in his *L'Écriture sur l'histoire* we find the following passage: 'A new method of historical narrative presents itself, let us say the "recitative" of the conjuncture, of cycles, and even of intercycles which offers a choice from one of a dozen years, one of a quarter century and, at the most extreme limit, the halfcentury of Kondratieff.'[40]

Ricoeur, too, must admit that Braudel localizes his Mediterranean temporality in the conjunctural temporality of the economic meso-level.[41] Ricoeur, however, is not completely happy with this turn because actions, to which he lends much importance, are in danger of being marginalized. He therefore prefers to subscribe to a remark of Braudel's in which he calls the Spanish and Ottoman empires, and finally the Mediterranean area as a whole, super-actors.[42] The plot and hence the temporality in Braudel's study are determined by the conflict and (relative) decline of these two super-actors. After the battle of Lepanto, they increasingly ignore each other out of impotence. This also heralded the beginning of the decline of the Mediterranean system as a whole, a system that had formed the centre of the world for more than twenty centuries. Involving more than the departure of two empires from the stage of world affairs, this event also coincided with the decline of the phenomenon 'empire' itself. Put even more forcefully: Mediterranean culture gradually gave up its position to Atlantic culture. Ricoeur admits that Braudel holds to his three time strata for analytic and didactic purposes. But it is in the super-plot of the decline of the Spanish and Ottoman empires, and with them the fall of Mediterranean culture as a whole – a plot he calls virtual – that Ricoeur sees the true temporality of Braudel's study of the Mediterranean.

This analysis has three points of emphasis:

1. Ricoeur is right in his interpretation when he observes a subjectifying – as a result of its dealing with quasi-personages – temporality in Braudel's plot regarding the conflict of the two empires and the decline of Mediterranean culture.
2. From this finalistic perspective, Ricoeur has an eye for aspects concerning actions as well as the causal, in this case the economic, aspects of Braudel's analysis.
3. The three time strata identified by Braudel are homogenized by Ricoeur – and perhaps by Braudel himself – in an undulating middle form of temporality. This undulating middle temporality can be classed with what Ricoeur calls the *mise en intrigue* and what I would like to call the narrative *meso-structure*. In may opinion, this meso-structure is of primary importance for temporal constructions in historical narratives.[43]

This also is evinced by Braudel's other large work *Civilisation materiélle, économie et capitalisme, XVe–XVIIIe siècle*.[44] In the third part of his work, with the suggestive title *Temps du monde*, we see this meso-structural, undulating temporality back in the simultaneous increases and decreases of prices in different places in Europe. In Braudel's opinion, this proves the existence of a global capitalist economic system. These short oscillations of prices can be homogenized in a secular trend of which the years 1350, 1650, 1817, and 1973 form the apexes. In each of these years, a global economic system reached its zenith. Although there need be no precise simultaneity, undulation in social, political and cultural domains accompany these economic movements of the economic conjuncture. The *récitatif de la conjoncture*,[45] the undulating meso-structure, here too forms the actual temporality of narration.

In conclusion, we can say that stratified temporality is homogenized in the meso-structure of Braudel's historical narrative and that it takes the guise of an undulating conception of temporality. We find this undulating temporality present in cities, states, economic systems and cultures. Braudel's narrative concerning Mediterranean culture, with its plot of late flowering and decline, conceives this culture as a subjectifying entity, or quasi-personage.

Marx and ideal-typical time Ricoeur is not wholly content with how Braudel constructs conjunctural temporality. The *appartenance participative* plays too small a role in Braudel's temporal construction, in Ricoeur's opinion. According to Ricoeur 'conjunctural temporality' does not lie in economic undulations but in the waxing and waning of the collective participation (see Chapter 10). Through the use of ideal-typical constructions, this conception of time can be tracked down. Schlomo Avineri, the great expert on the thought of Marx and Hegel, elucidated this temporal construct in his *The social and political thought of Karl Marx*.[46] In this study, Avineri observes that Marx's modes of production should not be considered as real phases in history, but as ideal types, or heuristic models. Feudalism, mercantilism, and capitalism are attempts to 'grasp' a social process continually in flux.

Avineri gives the following example.[47] Before 1847, England did not fully comply with the ideal type of a capitalist society. This is because remains of the feudal-mercantile mode of production still existed. This especially pertains to the Corn Laws, because these protectionist laws worked in favour of (generally aristocratic) large landholders. Although not wholly applicable to English society because of the Corn Laws, the capitalistic ideal type is heuristically very profitable. When the Corn Laws were repealed in 1847, the capitalist ideal type was 'achieved'. In that same year the ten-hour workday was implemented, as a result of which an alienation from the capitalist mode of production immediately took place. The ten-hour workday, after all, anticipates a post-capitalist society, which we shall later call 'the welfare society'. This welfare society is far from being achieved, although the first symptoms of a path towards it are visible. Avineri himself formulates this as follows: 'Since all historical reality is always in a process of becoming the model is either a criterion for a reality developing towards it – or if adequacy has been maximized, internal circumstances have given rise to a reality that has overtaken the model and moves further and further away from it.'[48]

This Hegelian operation of alienation *Aufhebung* (achievement) and again alienation not only yields an undulating temporal construction, but also clarifies the finalistic nature of this ideal-typical heuristic. Here, too, the owls of Minerva only fly after twilight. The name Max Weber cannot be omitted when discussing ideal types. Unfortunately, Weber barely occupied himself with time. However, Guenther Roth has made a link between Weber's methods of analysis and Braudel's undulating conjunctural temporality. 'The correspondence between Braudel's and Weber's levels of analysis seems closest in the case of "conjuncture" and secular theory, since in most instances both concern medium-range historical changes.'[49] Roth's position seems somewhat strange, as Weber's ideal types have always been characterized as being somewhat static. Nevertheless, I think that Weber's epistemology of actions is strongly teleological (zweckrationales handeln), that ideal types play an important role in it, and that it also contains the finalism that goes along with teleology.[50] Ideal types may be constructions of a historian and not of the actors themselves – as such they must be considered finalistic – yet they may have functioned as goals of action for the historical actors themselves.[51]

Objectifying, compounded time

Braudel In addition to that of Ricoeur, another interpretation is possible of Braudel's Mediterranean study. In it the tripartite layering of time should not be interpreted teleologically or finalistically with quasi-personages as principals, but structuralistically as a history without people and as a historical explanation without actors. Topolski and Spilt interpret Braudel from the idea that he was concerned with the reconstruction of structures and processes, in which precisely those elements are important that take place outside the awareness of the historical actors.[52] For Topolski and Spilt the 'lowest' stratum, comprising the almost immobile and conjunctural forms of temporality, forms the explanatory apparatus for political and cultural phenomena on the 'middle' level and, especially, on the 'highest' event-driven level. This yields simultaneity of that which is non-simultaneous, which, as is known, we summarize by the term 'compounded time'.

A structuralist interpretation is also possible of the third part of Braudel's *Civilisation matérielle, économie et capitalisme*. This seems curious, because we observed above that Braudel also uses a conjunctural temporality, namely that of the secular trend. Nonetheless, Braudel also conceives a compounded temporality in this part with the significant title *Le Temps du Monde*. In this, Immanuel Wallerstein's *The modern world-system* served as example. Braudel especially seized on Wallerstein's idea of dividing such a system into a centre, a semi-periphery and a periphery. Braudel sees a sequence of seven world systems grouped around seven centres from the late Middle Ages. He treats them one by one: Bruges and the Hanse, Antwerp, Genoa, Amsterdam, and London. New York is mentioned but not treated. The three different regions of each of these world systems are linked to different characteristics and, what is most important in this context, different temporalities. The periphery vegetates at subsistence levels and therefore develops very slowly. The semi-periphery is marked by a *vie économique* with local markets, combined with yearly markets, merchants, fairs and so on, as a result of which this area is marked by a semi-modern time. In the centre large banks, merchant firms and exchanges dominate through a calculating and planned capitalism and manipulation of the 'underlying' economies. The *temps du monde*, or the most modern temporality of the world, therefore marks these centres. Within one world system there are three sub-systems, each with its own temporal order determined by the mode of production dominant in it, according to Braudel. World history, according to Braudel, should be seen as a '[. . .] cortège, une procession, une coexistence de modes de production que nous avons trop tendance à considérer dans la succession des ages de l'histoire. En fait ces modes de production différents sont accrochés les uns aux autres. Les plus avancés dépendent des plus arrières et réciproquement: le développement est l'autre face du sous-développement.'[53] The world even has parts that are completely outside every temporality. The interior of India, for example, is such a 'quiet' region.[54] Also 'pockets' may be present in the different sub-systems. Thus the central part of the world system has pockets of backwardness and vice versa: the periphery may contain 'stepping stones' of the capitalist centre. In the seventeenth-century world system, with the Dutch Republic as world centre, the province Drente formed a pocket of backwardness in the centre, while Batavia in the East Indies, with its factories and colonies of merchants, formed a 'stepping stone' of capitalism in the periphery.[55]

It should be clear that such a structuralist reading yields a form of temporality that mainly consists of temporal spaces not involving a subject. Such temporal spaces can lie end to end on a time chart, but also next to and in one another, although in different geographic locations.[56]

Marx   Just as a structuralist reading of Braudel is possible, Marx is also open to a structuralist interpretation. Two terms play a crucial role in doing this: mode of production and formation of society. A formation of society can be viewed as a society at a given moment conceived as a dynamic link between modes of production. In this manner, formations of society divide society into spaces with different modes of production. It is known that Marx divides the history of humanity into several phases that develop, albeit abruptly, from simpler to more complex modes of production: tribal communism, slave economy, feudal society, mercantile capitalism and high capitalism. These phases, seen together, have a connotation of primitive to modern, static to dynamic. On this basis, it is possible to distinguish between not only different modes of production, but also different temporal spaces. A clear example is given by J. L. Van Zanden, who describes the mercantile-capitalist formation of Dutch society in the seventeenth century as a building-up of trade networks and flows, of markets and institutions that enable market trade and production systems that work for this growing labour market. This process of construction is concentrated in relatively small towns, commercialized *islands* in the middle of a *non-capitalist sea* [italics: HJ].'[57] This statement is in accord with Marx, who, in the *Grundrisse der Kritik der politische Ökonomie*, not only views the city as a place where new divisions of property emerge, but also as a breeding ground for new forces of production.[58] On the basis of different compositions of their modes of production, formations of society are also marked by different temporalities. In the formation of society mentioned above, households, for example, form a non-capitalist mode of production.[59] This structuralist reading of Marx yields a compounded temporality. It was the French philosopher Althusser who called attention to this compounded time. On this basis he claims that there is no general history with a singular, homogeneous, linear time (as it was formulated by Mandelbaum),[60] but a succession of what he calls *historicity structures*. Such a historicity structure actually forms an encompassing macro-system, in which formations of society with their own temporal dimensions figure as sub-systems of which the modes of production, also with their own temporality, figure as sub-sub-systems.[61] The fact that more- and less-'modern' temporal spaces are arranged next to and in one another indicates a system-sub-system construction (babushkas!), with distinct temporal spaces and therefore an objectifying conception of time.[62]

Temporary conclusion

Braudel and the Marxist philosophers and historians display two types of temporal construction: a subjectifying, homogeneous temporality and an objectifying, compounded temporality. The first is brought about by increasing or decreasing coherence in what Ricoeur calls a first-rank entity. Ricoeur calls this increasing and decreasing coherence *apparte-nance participative*. In the above it was pointed out that the increase and decrease of coherence can be depicted through the use of ideal types. The following historiographical examples show how these ideal-typical constructions appear in historical literature. It will then, hopefully, also become clear that the temporal dimensions that emanate from these constructions are not called subjectifying only because experienced time plays a role in them, but also because the entity dominated by such a time itself is characterized as a subject. It was not without cause that Ricoeur called these entities quasi-personages. In order to discover these temporal constructions in historiography, it is important to examine the infrastructure of such super-actors. This investigation is called for not only with regard to the causal and teleological relations of the micro-structure, but also and especially with regard to the meso-structure (Ricoeur's *mise en intrigue*). This meso-structure is determined by the origin (initial ideal type) and finality (final ideal type) of the super-actor. Sometimes it is also necessary to consider the plot of the super-actors themselves.

The second temporality mentioned, possessing an objectifying and compounded nature, is used by historians who have no patience with finality, and as little as possible with historical thinking grounded on actions. They are aware that strong causal explanations cannot be achieved in historical writing, but system–sub-system constructions form an excellent alternative, in their opinion. This objectifying, compounded temporality is marked by an entity consisting of a system in a certain temporal phase linked to sub-(sub-)systems in other temporal phases.

By using examples from familial, urban, and state histories, I wish to show how the subjectifying, homogeneous temporality on the one hand and objectifying, compounded time on the other take shape in three different forms of historical writing. Family, city and state have been chosen because they yield histories involving entities of small, middle, and large sizes, respectively.

Two studies have been selected from each of these topics, one using a homogeneous, subjectifying temporality, the other a compounded, objectifying temporality. The identical topics allow coupled studies regarding family, city and state, in which each couple displays two different forms of temporality. In this manner I have tried to emphasize that the difference in temporal construction cannot be imputed to the themes or the content of a historical narrative. The difference in temporal construction primarily has to do with the distinct nature of the entity created by the author, often unconsciously, when dealing with families, cities or states. Within both subjectifying as well as objectifying temporality, three variations will appear to emerge. The finer nuances of all this will be dealt with in what follows.

The time of collapsing states

I first wish to demonstrate both types of temporal construction by way of two studies on the collapse of states in early-modern times. These studies are Skocpol's *States and social revolutions*[63] and Goldstone's *Revolution and rebellion in the early modern world*.[64] Both books concern revolutions in certain Eurasian countries. Both authors oppose Eurocentric and especially Marxist interpretations of revolutions. These interpretations view revolutions as a consequence of civil emancipation movements purporting to eradicate the more or less feudal obstacles to the free entrepreneurial mode of production. According to Skocpol and Goldstone, early-modern revolutions are not caused by social groups but by crises in the governmental apparatus, with, as a consequence, revolution among the populace.[65] Goldstone is a pupil of Skocpol, which explains their common interests.

Skocpol's *States and social revolutions* is the clearest example of Ricoeur's meso-narrative and macro-narrative temporal conception. First Skocpol views the state as an entity *sui generis*, 'as an organisation-for-itself'.[66] On this basis the state can act, through its representatives, against social interest groups such as the elite and agrarian communities as a (super-)actor. Skocpol clarifies this depiction of the state as super-actor or quasi-personage by attacking (supposed) theories of Marx and Tilly, in which the state is seen as a variable dependent on social and economic relationships.[67]

Skocpol primarily seeks the origin of the collapse of the Ancien-Regime states in international relationships. As to France, Russia, and China, the three countries she analyses for her examination of state breakdowns, she observes that an exhaustive war and, as a consequence, an empty treasury form the root of the problem. A conflict between internal super-actors issues from this external battle of titans: first, between a conservative elite belonging to the government and a non-government elite favouring reform. Because neither party wins the conflict between the elites, no reforms are undertaken, which leads to widespread revolts of a new quasi-personage, the agrarian communities. In the end, these manage to topple the government with the aid of new elite groups and found a new revolutionary state. This state is a threat to other states of the Ancien Regime, as a result of which a new phase of the struggle between states is initiated. The revolutionary government also has internal enemies, who are repelled by a *levée en masse*, as a result of which a new super-actor is created: the people or nation. Because this new quasi-personage succeeds in vanquishing both the internal and the external enemies of the new revolutionary state, the latter can endure.

It is possible to read Skocpol's book as an intrigue on the macro-level. For this there are two main reasons: the notion of the state as autonomous, and the important role played by international relationships in Skocpol's book. Because of these, France, Russia, and China become super-actors, interacting with other super-actors, as a result of which the actions of these quasi-personages can be examined as to their intrigues. The collapse of these quasi-personages causes new super-actors to emerge: elites, agrarian communities, nations and so on, each with their own histories of rising and falling. In this sense a strong analogy can be drawn between Ricoeur's analysis of the decline of the Mediterranean culture and Skocpol's decline of the Ancien Regime states. The Mediterranean culture collapsed as a result of the conflict between the Turkish and the Spanish quasi-personages; the French, Russian, and Chinese states collapsed because of conflicts within the elite and the struggle of that elite with the agrarian classes.

Nevertheless, I lean towards seeking the temporality of Skocpol's book at the meso-stratum, the level of the emplotment. This deals with the breakdown of the state of the Ancien-Regime type. Skocpol describes the ideal type 'Ancien Regime' as absolutist, incapable of liberal reforms, with an agrarian structure of large landholders and communities of peasants dependent on them.[68] Revolution, or rather state breakdown, entails that the state splits into its constituents, namely the elite and the agrarian communities. Because Skocpol almost exclusively attends to the internal developments in France, Russia, and China, much can be said for such a meso-narrative reading. It is of great importance here that the author makes the influence of international relationships on the actions of national entities operate through the person of the ruler. Here one can think of declaring war or making peace, for example.[69]

In addition to attending to such internal, actionist relationships between phenomena, Skocpol also seeks causal relationships. She especially discovers these by comparisons with countries or situations which seem revolutionary, but in which a state breakdown does not occur. (This is an example of the contrafactual analyses that yield singular causal imputations *à la* Weber, and to which Ricoeur attached such importance in his micro-structural analysis of narratives.) A state breakdown also has as a consequence that a certain form of *appartenance participative* disappears, while the state of the new regime creates a new form of collective participation. This clearly indicates that phenomena are seen in the light of their origin and/or finality. The new regime is described ideal-typically as more autonomous, stronger, more bureaucratic and more able to incorporate masses of people in the governmental system. The power of the large landholders ends in the new governmental system.[70] This description of the new-regime type of state seems to suggest that Skocpol is also occupied with the history of the construction of the new revolutionary state. This is, however, not the case. The disintegration and collapse of states of the Ancien-Regime type are central to her book. Skocpol does not use the term 'state breakdowns' without reason.

Goldstone's book lacks both the ideal-typical meso-narrative temporality and the subjectifying macro-narrative temporality. He stays much closer to the ideal of positivistic science in his analysis of revolutions. Goldstone is more concerned with the discovery of the conditions for action than with the actions themselves. A clear indication of his positivism is his use of terms derived from chaos theory, which hails from the physical sciences. Especially the term 'fractal' is important in this context. This term indicates that processes on a national level can also manifest themselves on a regional or supranational level. This mitigates the role of the state as central object of study, which is unthinkable in the case of Skocpol. Goldstone is concerned not with the examination of quasi-personages, but with social processes that can present themselves in analogous forms on different levels.[71] This implies, for his research subject, that the state is dependent on economic trends, on international relationships and on the tension between dominant and alternative ideologies. This dependence is effected by the causal operation of the structural demographic model Goldstone uses. This model actually posits a general social system or 'robust process', as Goldstone calls it, to which the state is to a great extent subjected. Goldstone considers demographic development the big motor behind revolution. In a pre-industrial economy with Malthusian tensions, demographic growth can lead to a decrease in real wages. This leads to a decline in tax proceeds, from which public servants in particular must be paid. Because of the population increase on the one hand and the diminished treasury on the other, the competition between the sons of the social elite, who qualify for government functions, becomes greater. Part of this elite will not get the jobs they want and will try to mobilize the masses by the use of 'democratic' ideologies. Because of the decrease in real wages, this mobilization becomes easier and easier.

All these issues regularly arise in the pre-industrial period, but do not lead to revolutions. Only in situations where all these elements come together at the same time, or as Goldstone expresses it, display *synergy*, does a revolution break out. England and especially London around 1640 is taken as example by Goldstone. There he observes the inability of the administrative system of London to solve problems emerging as a result of a sharp population increase:

> Unfortunately, for the early modern state it is difficult to measure the rate of administrative control; what we do know is that by 1640 [. . .] London has *outrun* [italics: HJ] its administrative machinery. For our purposes of examining early modern states, we can make as an approximation that the more *rapid* [italics: HJ] is a city's long-term growth, the more difficulty an administration will have in *keeping pace* [italics: HJ], so that mobilization potential is likely to increase.[72]

This quotation indicates that Goldstone's study is an example of accelerated time. This accelerated time is calibrated here by the immobile administrative system of London on the one hand and the cumulative growth of the population of London between 1500 and 1640 on the other.[73]

Temporality in familial history

The two works I shall use for the analysis of temporal conceptions in family history are Richard Sennett's *Families against the city*[74] and Angelique Janssen's *Family and social change*.[75] Both works coincide not only in their research into family development at the end of the nineteenth century but also in their opposition to Talcott Parsons's claim that there is a fit between the nuclear family and industrial society. According to Parsons, complicated industrial society demands more-specialized labour and therefore more education. Children are therefore subject to a longer phase of upbringing, during which they are taught to distinguish between more-particularistic and affective relationships with, and appreciation of, close family members on the one hand and more-general functionalistic and less-affective relationships with people outside the family (and also with members of the extended family). The difference between the role behaviour of the father with his orientation towards the outside world and the tasks directed towards the family of the mother is typical of this double-value system. On the basis of their longer course of upbringing, their better preparation for different social roles, and the larger mobility of the family in general and its members in particular, children from nuclear families are more successful socially, according to

Parsons. It is worth noting here that Parsons views the family as a sub-system of the social system.

Sennett and Janssens consider both the ideas of Parsons and also the criticism their structuralist-functionalist viewpoint has aroused. Among those critics Ariès especially is notable for not considering the nuclear family to be that functional for industrial society. Its closeness and cult of intimacy, and the late contact of the children with society, render it impossible for the children to identify with the different roles of the father and mother and to experiment with these roles. Therefore they are less prepared for their social functions and hence often less successful. Ariès clearly prefers the values and chances of success of the more-extended family.

Both Janssens and Sennett support Ariès more than Parsons in their debate, without completely abandoning the idea of a fit between the nuclear family and industrial society. The manner in which they both take position in the Ariès-Parsons debate is so different with regard to argumentation that vast differences in their conceptions of time emerge.

Sennett studies families in the Union Park neighbourhood of Chicago between 1872 and 1890. In this period families from the lower middle class lived there. Previously upper-class families had inhabited the neighbourhood, and after 1892 families of workers populated it. Owing to several external factors, but especially because of the actions of the family members themselves, the ideal type 'lower-middle-class family' develops in Union Park between 1870 and 1892.

After 1872 Union Park became a neighbourhood for families from the lower middle class, owing to bad transit connections with the centre of Chicago, lower land prices and a fire in 1871. Neighbourhood relationships in the form of philanthropic and religious gatherings and dancing evenings seen before 1872 disappeared. Sennett expressly does not want to credit this to the greater population density in the neighbourhood, nor to the class difference of the inhabitants, but to the *actions* of the family members themselves.[76] He thereby conceives the family as a *continuing entity*, as a quasi-personage. The role of the woman is especially important, according to Sennett. Although the man is usually in an economically-dependent position – he works for a boss or has a job in an office – he obliges himself, and is obliged by his often-younger wife, to pursue a career.[77] Despite the fact that the economy is reasonably expansive, these men often do not succeed at this career. Sennett attributes this to the fact that newlyweds had children at an early age, forcing them to forgo social risks, as a result of which they bound themselves to keeping one and the same job. The women usually did not work, so as not to disturb the pattern of authority in the family.[78] In 1886 and 1888 violence broke out in the neighbourhood. The violence itself was not so remarkable, says Sennett, but the reactions of the inhabitants of the neighbourhood were. An enormous fear of anarchy fed the already existing fear of the big, bad outside world, which had been acquired on the workfloor:[79] '[. . .] the family moulded *itself* (italics: HJ) as the mirror opposite of disorder and complexity in the city'.[80]

The title of Sennett's book might seem to indicate that it involves a real conflict between the family and the city. This could be an argument for seeking the temporal dimension of his work in the (macro-narrative) intrigue of the family and the city as quasi-personages. But the temporal dimension does not lie in the narrative macro-structure, but in the gradual development of the intimate nuclear family with its intensive-affective family life. There is no actual conflict between families and the city. The city only functions as enemy in the perception of the members of the family. It is the idea of an evil outside world that effects the intensification and the nucleation of the family.[81] On the basis of all this we can say that the temporal dimension in Sennett's case should not be sought in the macro-structure of an intrigue in which quasi-personages interact, but in the narrative meso-structure of the entity 'family'. He is concerned with the development of the ideal type of the intensive nuclear family. Continually Sennett refers to another ideal type, namely that of the extended and hence more robust family, when depicting this development. He considers its demise more or less a *fait accompli* at the beginning of the developments in Union Park. Evolutions within that family type are not in evidence. The temporal dimension in Sennett's study lies in the development of the nuclear family of the lower-middle classes to a cohesion that, although based on fear, gives this family type a clear ideal-typical identity. Hence the meso-narrative development of the intensive lower-middle class family between 1870 and 1892 forms the central theme of Sennett's book.

Sennett rejects Parson's idea of the intensive nuclear family's originating in flexibility, mobility, and individuality, but does accept the growing importance of the nuclear family in industrial society. Janssens sows more doubts regarding the relation between that type of family and industrial society, as formulated by Parsons. She does this in her study of the composition of families in the Dutch city Tilburg between 1849 and 1920. On the basis of the ideas of Parsons and his followers, the extended family type should quickly have disappeared in Tilburg and a nuclear-family system should have appeared almost immediately. After all, according to Parsons the sub-system, in this case the family, should conform as quickly as possible to the system, in this case industrial society. Janssens observes an opposite situation: 'My conclusion then is that the family bonds retained a considerable durability and were used actively and in an overall rational way in an attempt to overcome some of the problems facing nineteenth-century families. Moreover extended family arrangements, rather than being disrupted appeared to have been promoted in some instances by the social and geographic mobility engendered by industrial society.'[82] Janssens expressly links a question – that is the point I wish to make here – regarding the temporal dimension to this conclusion: '[. . .] is family change by definition slower than social structural change irrespective of the context, so that a *time lag* [italics: HJ] will always occur?'[83]

Although a problem of this type can never be solved completely, it does demonstrate the question of whether an internal-actionist explanation for the continued existence of the extended family should be sought or an external-causal, and therefore system–sub-system, explanation. With the term 'time lag' she clearly opts for the latter. Many similarities can be found between her line of reasoning and that of G. Sjoberg and R. Nisbet, who distinguish a phase in the transition from respectively a pre-industrial to an industrial society and a pre-modern to a modern society, in which traditional values become stronger.[84] Janssens's remark that processes of industrialization do not immediately destroy pre-industrial values such as family solidarity, but rather continue them, should be interpreted in this light. This is because they are an aid in confronting new situations and problems.[85]

This makes it even more evident under which conception of temporality her study takes place. At the beginning of her book she refers to the *gleichzeitige Ungleichzeitigkeit*,[86] which she prefers over the structuralist-functionalist *fit* between social changes and changes in family life. The model of social change offered by the concept of *time lag* [italics: HJ] certainly appears to be more attractive to historians than the one proposed by structural-functionalism.[87] Janssens here refers to Medick, who points out simultaneous non-simultaneity in families of peasants in the proto-industrial phase.[88]

By contrast with the accelerated time encountered in the work of Goldstone, in Janssens we find a *decelerated* time. Industrialization, modelled after Parsons's relatively quick systems temporality, turns out to be coupled to a much slower familial sub-system in Tilburg. Especially as a result of religious traditions and a certain manner of migration, structures and values of the extended family continue much longer than might be expected solely on the basis of the process of industrialization.

Urban historical temporality

Since Asa Briggs's *Victorian cities*[89] put the nineteenth-century city on the historical research agenda, many studies have appeared concerning English cities from that time. Briggs agitated against Mumford's image of 'Coketown' – Mumford's appellation for the nineteenth-century English industrial city – as a product of coal, dust and stench. A late echo of this discussion can be found in the three studies examined here with regard to their time conception. Derek Fraser is represented with *Power and authority in the Victorian city* and *Urban politics in Victorian England*; Steadman Jones wrote *Outcast London*.[90] Fraser supports Briggs's optimistic view and sees a reasonably-sunny future in store for the English city at the end of the nineteenth century. The Marxist Jones paints a far less rosy picture of London in the same period.

Fraser treats the institutional history of several Victorian cities between, roughly, 1830 and 1900 and the social and political culture developing in this period. The situation around 1830 is sketched on the basis of the ideal type of the corporate city. This ideal type is constructed by Fraser in his *Power and authority in the Victorian city* through seven incorporated cities, recognized by the British government (Liverpool, Leeds, Birmingham, Bristol, Leicester, Bradford and Sheffield). This ideal type depicts the situation in these cities before the Municipal Reform Act of 1835. In such corporations the power is in the hands of an urban patriciate consisting of a fairly-closed community of aristocratic and mercantile families. This refers to the domination of the old Whigs and Tories, who are usually members of the Church of England and who keep the town administration closed by only accepting new members through co-optation. This has the advantage that they do not have to be accountable to the urban community or its representatives. Against this administrative elite a middle class emerges, whose members, politically speaking, belong to the Whigs or the Radicals, and who are religiously often dissenters. This new middle class wants the abolition of corporate administration and the foundation of a representative municipal council.

With the aid of a second study by Fraser, *Urban politics in Victorian England*, this ideal type from 1830 can be completed. Institutionally speaking local councils and commissions are very important in the urban corporations. As the most important of these Fraser names: the parochial councils, of which the churchwardens have control; then the poor law commissioners, whose task it is to execute the poverty laws and who therefore have the largest municipal budget; and finally the office of the improvement commissioner and highway surveyor, which takes care of the upkeep of the roads and has jurisdiction over other modernizations. In the light of the above, the ideal type of the early nineteenth century English town is marked by a lack of social and constitutional cohesion. Socially, both the middle class and the proletariat stand in contrast with the small elite of the urban patriciate; but although these non-elite classes are populous, they have little mutual contact. The lack of constitutional cohesion can be attributed to the co-existence of the corporate town administration on the one hand and quite a number of fairly independent commissions and councils on the other.

The ideal-type of the Victorian city at the end of the nineteenth century is marked by another social-political system. The middle class now completely controls the stage of urban politics (although there are noticeably many aristocratic mayors.[91]) The role of commissions and councils has practically ended; the urban administration has become completely representative through the institution of free and secret elections.

The process of transformation from the initial to the final ideal type consists of the disintegration of the urban corporation and the construction of a representative urban government. Although the process of disintegration was initiated by the Municipal Reform Act of 1835, Fraser emphasizes that the reforms are achieved by the cities themselves. In the other words this is an internal process: 'The transformation of municipal government between 1835 and 1900 was achieved primarily by local legislation promoted by *local initiative* [italics: HJ].' Even though we may speak of a first external political impulse, individual and internal urban processes of disintegration are at issue here. The disintegration of the corporate system has what is called a quasi-teleological nature.[92] The process of modernization demanded that many new problems be dealt with. Therefore new commissions were continually founded under the supervision of a new representative urban government, according to the directives of the municipal law of 1835. Unfortunately the supervision of the community council failed, at least till 1870. The effect was, in the end, identical to the old corporate tradition of fragmenting the local administration.

After 1870 a change occurs in this continuing process of disintegration. The new municipal councils increasingly succeed in getting the previously more or less independent commissions to work under their authority. This process of *amalgamization*, as Fraser calls it, leads to quasi-teleology being transformed into a real collective teleology, causing a coherent local administrative system to emerge. Before the beginning of the 1870s '[. . .] a multiplicity of agencies were created on the principle of administrative specialization; after that a search began for a more uniform and coherent government system'.[93] Fraser's books are marked by an undulating temporality at the social and administrative levels of the nineteenth-century English city. The growing problems of industrialization and modernization at the beginning of the nineteenth century are at first impotently attacked by an increasing number of special commissions, which increasingly undermine administrative coherence. After 1870 the municipal councils continually get more grip on the work of the commissions. A more-coherent municipal government emerges as quasi-personage, addressing social problems in a goal-directed manner.

The cities Fraser examines do not interact or barely do so at all. This means that an overall English urban intrigue is missing in his study, and therefore also a macro-narrative temporality. Fraser is concerned with a meso-narrative analysis of the internal developments of urban entities.

As we know, Stedman Jones's study about London in the first instance depicts this city as a pre-industrial sub-system of an industrial-capitalist system. The nineteenth-century English system is marked by standardized mass production of capital goods and semi-fabricates, socially by the opposition of capitalists and half-educated proletarians, in politics by the abstention of the government from economic affairs, and ideologically by an unabashed liberalism that justifies the politics of abstention and reinforces it. How different is London. In London the production apparatus is still mostly small-scale and artisan, and is in the service of producing articles for consumption. The social opposition comprises well-educated artisans against unschooled labourers. Casual labour and unemployment are rife among this last group. Because pauperization threatens public security, all kinds of plans are conceived for fighting poverty, even though liberalism at that time was highly insensitive to this issue. Various arrangements, such as subsidized rents, old-age pensions, national insurance systems and so on, were conceived, and many historians have viewed these as presaging the later welfare state. Jones expressly rejects such a form of finalistic thought. He points out that solutions that do not point towards a welfare state at all formed an integral part of these social ideas, among which he mentions: segregation of paupers, forced migra-tion, separation of the children of paupers from their parents, sterilization, and confinement. These do not presage the welfare state, but are the excesses of the ideology of a retarded formation of society. At first sight Stedman Jones's manifest structural Marxism seems only to pertain to a decelerated time: a London time lag in industrial-capitalist England.

An accelerated time, however, is also in evidence. With industrializa-tion the service sector continually becomes more important. The harbour of London is the transportation hub of the British empire, and London is also the administrative centre of that empire. As such, London is the leader of industrial capitalism, with all the consequences that entails. The growth of the tertiary and quaternary sectors leads to a greater demand for building space, as a result of which land prices and rents soar. This double compounded time can only increase the problem of pauperization. Stedman Jones illustrates this problem with the enormous miscalculation of the Marxist-socialist labour organization in London, the 'Social Democratic Federation', in 1886. The economic depression, the harsh winters and the overpopulation of London in the middle of the 1880s give the socialists the impression that the end of capitalism is near. Because of growing unemployment increasing discontent amongst the population of paupers and the anxiety of well-to-do London, this seems imminent. Defying the prescriptions of the *Communist Manifesto*, the SDF directs its propaganda towards the paupers; this very much to the displeasure of Friedrich Engels, who wrote an angry letter to his comrades in London. Engels does not consider the riots of 1886 to be the beginning of a communist revolution, but rather examples of the usual, desperate food riots. He reproaches the SDF with directing its agitation too much towards the Gutter Proletariat, which, after some mayhem, returns to the East End singing *Rule Britannia*. Stedman Jones agrees with Engels. Unemployment, pauperization and ignorance did not disappear until London industrialized (cars and electronic equipment) after the First World War. However, it is not the SDF but the London Labour Party whose membership numbers increase because of these developments, observes Stedman Jones regretfully. He then concludes his book with a, for us, very important line: 'The law of uneven development had worked cruelly against its creators,'[94]

The simultaneous non-simultaneity of London has a double nature. As commercial administrative centre of a modern industrial-capitalist formation of society, it functions as catalyst of this formation; as a city with a backward pre-industrial artisan sector it slows down this same formation of society. Thus London has a double compounded time. A better illustration of Bloch's statement regarding compounded time is hardly imaginable.

Conclusion

A pragmatic theory of history[95] must take a much closer look at historiography than at the philosophy of history before making claims regarding the nature of historical science. Mink, White and Ankersmit claim that time is negated in historical configuration without consulting historiography itself. Even Ricoeur uses the historiography of the *Annalistes* more as an illustration than as a research domain for his views regarding historiographical time. Ricoeur does, however, offer the most links for an analysis of historiographical time. It is in particular terms such as 'continuing entity', *entité de premier ordre*, 'quasi-personage', and *appartenance participative* that clearly indicate the nature of the entities figuring most prominently in historical narratives, in his consideration. Moreover, it is clear that he distinguishes between the intrigue of the historical narrative and the *mise en intrigue* – which I have called respectively the narrative macro-structure and meso-structure – that have been of fundamental importance to my analysis of time.

The historiographical examples, however, have shown the weak points of Ricoeur's conception of time. First of all it must be noted that it is not so much the macro-structure but the meso-structure that determines the subjectifying temporality of the historical narrative. The diversion from and growth towards an ideal-typical construction of the entities conceived by the authors determine to a large extent the undulating course of that temporality. Finally, historiographical temporal constructions cannot be limited to their subjectifying form: there is also an objectifying, compounded, form of temporality in evidence in historiography.

In the historiographical analysis of studies regarding families, cities and states, I have repeatedly placed a subjectifying in contrast with an objectifying temporal construction. Gradually, it became clear that there are variations to be found both in the subjectifying and in the objectifying forms. Decreasing and increasing cohesion in the *appartenance participative*, or rather its ideal-typical formulation, constitute the singular form of subjectifying temporality. For the first of these (decreasing cohesion) Skocpol's state breakdowns stood as model; for the second (increasing cohesion) Sennett's core family. The double form of subjectifying time, which we encountered in Fraser's studies on Victorian cities, is marked by decreasing cohesion of the initial ideal type and increasing cohesion of the final one. A reverse order is also possible, and even combinations of both. With this subjectification, time gains an undulating nature.

Within the studies with an objectifying temporality, we encountered an accelerated and decelerated temporality in the works of Goldstone and Janssens, respectively. A double time lag was found in Stedman Jones's study of nineteenth-century London. It remains strange that Ricoeur does not involve this objectifying *gleichzeitige Ungleichzeitikeit* in his study of time at all.

In all this I hope I have made it clear that time does not so much manifest itself in the separate statements constituting a historical narrative (in 1789 the French revolution started), but rather precisely in its configurating middle layer. In configuration the temporal dimension is not abolished, as Mink, White and Ankersmit claim; on the contrary, it is established. Finally, I hope to have made it clear to the reader that there is a close relationship between method of explanation and temporal construction. The increasing and decreasing coherence of relatively-closed systems that we encountered in the work of Frisch and Mumford (Chapter 6, see p. 210 Section 4) lead to an identical undulating time as found in the studies of Fraser concerning the Victorian city. Jones's study on London has also, hopefully, clarified the relationship between compounded time and the method of explanation using active sub-systems. More will be said of this in the next chapter.

Notes

1. These terms are derived from Ricoeur, *Time and narrative*, Vol. 3 (Chicago, London 1988), p. 244.
2. Aristotle, *Physics*, 219a–220b.
3. Aristotle, *Physics*, 223a 21–29.
4. For the subjectifying part of Augustine's time-conception see: *Confessions* XI, xx, 26: 'There is, namely, a kind of trinity in the *soul* [italics: HJ] [. . .] consisting of the following things: the present memories of the past, the present contemplation of that which is present and the present expectation of the future'; for the objectifying part, see: Ricoeur, *Time and narrative*, Vol. 3, p. 244.
5. *Objectifying* should be interpreted here as tending to be *bound to objects, things or substantialities*; so subject-oriented elements do not necessarily have to be absent, but they are not dominant. The term objectifying should not be confused with objective or striving towards objectivity. See also: J. Fennema, 'Time a concept of growth', in P. A. Kroes (ed.), *Nature, time and history. Nijmegen studies in the philosophy of nature and its science II* (1985), pp. 105–19, esp. 109–110 and J. Dudley, 'Substance, nature and time: a criticism of Aristotle', ibid., pp. 69–84, especially 79–84. *Subjectifying* does not signify subjective or tending towards subjectivity here, but *bound to subjects*, without object-oriented elements being completely absent.

6. See for these aporias also Ricoeur, *Time and narrative*, Vol. 3, pp. 244–74 and P. Ricoeur, 'Narrated time', in M. J. Valdès, *A Ricoeur reader: reflection and imagination* (Toronto, Buffalo 1991), pp. 338–54.
7. Ricoeur, *Time and narrative*, Vol. 1, p. 54.
8. Ricoeur, *Time and narrative*, Vol. 1, pp. 31–52.
9. Aristotle, *Physics IV*, 11, 219a–220b.
10. Aristotle, *Physics IV*, 11, 221a and 223b.
11. See Ricoeur, *Time and narrative*, Vol. 3, p. 251.
12. E. Bloch, 'Ungleichzeitigkeit, nicht nur Rückständigkeit', in idem, *Philosophische Aufsätze zur objektiven Phantasie* (Frankfurt am Main 1969) pp. 41–8.
13. This simultaneous non-simultaneity does not completely coincide with that which Koselleck has in mind in his 'Geschichte, Geschichten und formale Zeitstrukturen'. Koselleck refers to the phases in the constitutional histories of the Greek *poleis*. These go through different phases at the same time, as is shown by Thucydides and others. Koselleck is not concerned with different temporalities in a system–sub-system construction, but in non-simultaneous simultaneity. See R. Koselleck, *Vergangene Zukunft. Zur Semantik geschichtlicher Zeiten* (Frankfurt an Main 1979), pp. 132 and 137. Ankersmit, in the wake of Spengler, denies any significance to Kant's objectifying conception of time for historiography: see Ankersmit, 'Over geschiedenis en tijd', in *De navel van de geschiedenis, over interpretatie en historische realiteit* (Groningen 1990), p. 113.
14. M. Heidegger, *Zijn en tijd* (trans. M. Wildschut, 1998) pp. 408–11, 494 and 530.
15. Ibid., respectively pp. 408 and 494.
16. 'The existential now is determined by the present of occupation, which is a "making-present", *inseparable* [italics: HJ] from "awaiting" and "retaining".' 'The making-present which interprets itself [. . .] is what we call "time".' This 'now' and as a consequence this 'time' is not an abstract instant it is an existential now and an existential time. This rather rough analysis of the highly-complex temporal analysis of Heidegger shows great resemblance to Ricoeur's in *Time and narrative I* (Chicago 1984), pp. 60–4, esp. 63.
17. M. Mandelbaum, *The anatomy of historical knowledge* (Baltimore, MD and London 1977), pp. 11 and 17–19.
18. P. Ricoeur, *Temps et récit*, Tome I (Paris 1983), pp. 273–5; see also P. Ricoeur, *Time and narrative*, pp. 199–200, in which the term *first order entities* is used.

19. L. O. Mink, 'History and fiction as modes of comprehension', *New Literary History* (1970): 557 ff.; Hayden White, 'the value of narrativity in the representation of reality', in W. Mitchel (ed.), *On narrative* (Chicago 1981), especially pp. 4 and 23; F. Ankersmit, 'Over de geschiedenis en tijd', in *De navel van de geschiedenis. Over interpretatie, representatie en historische realiteit* ['Regarding history and time', in The navel of history. Interpretation, representation, and historical reality] (Groningen 1990), pp. 108–25. Ankersmit rejects objectifying time for the following reasons: (1) he does not consider Kant's transcendental time applicable to history (p. 114), and (2) he does not consider chronological (clock time) to convey meaning for modern historical writing (p. 116). Ankersmit rejects subjectifying time by observing, with Mink and White and in contrast to Carr, a large discontinuity between the experienced time and the temporality of the historical narrative (pp. 119–24). Unfortunately, he does not involve Ricoeur in his exposition. The latter also sees a great distance between experienced time and narrative time, but still arrives at a subjectifying conception of temporality.

20. Ankersmit, *De navel*, pp. 123–4.

21. Ibid., p. 114.

22. See also Hayden White, 'The value of narrativity in the representation of reality', pp. 11–14.

23. For an exposition on this subject see, among others: A. G. Weiler, 'The fractured time of history', in Scheurer and Debrock (eds), *Nature, time and history. Nijmegen Studies in the Philosophy of Nature and its Sciences* 4(1) (1995): 55–66.

24. D. Carr, 'Narrative and the real world: an argument for continuity', *History and theory* 25 (1986): 117–31, at 122 and 125.

25. H. von Wright, 'Determinism and study of man', in I. Maninen and R. Tuomela (eds), *Essays on explanation and understanding. Studies in the foundation of humanities and social sciences* (Dordrecht 1976), pp. 414–35, esp. 423.

26. Carr, 'Narrative and the real world', pp. 123–6.

27. 'die Eule der Minerva beginnt erst mit der einbrechende Dämmerung ihren Flug': G. W. F. Hegel, *Grundlinien der Philosophje des Rechts oder Naturrecht und Staatswissenschaft im Grundrisse*, ed. H. Reichelt, Frankfurt a.M. 1970), p. 28. Hegel's *List der Vernunft* is based on such finalism. Hegel thought that the reasonableness of the actions of historical individuals only becomes evident when historical processes have ended and the philosopher has analysed and described them. What seemed unreasonable and meaningless to the actors turns

out to be a 'trick' of the World Spirit to achieve the progress of rationality. See also H. Fain, *Between philosophy and history. The resurrection of speculative philosophy of history within analytic tradition* (Princeton, NJ 1970), especially p. 275, and H. White, *The content of the form. Narrative discourse and historical representation* (Baltimore, MD and London 1987), especially p. 21.

28. Max Weber has elucidated the difference between finalism and teleology: 'Der Historiker nun ist seinem Helden [the historical actor: HJ] zunächst darin überlegen, dass er jedenfalls *a posteriori* weiss, ob die Abschätzung der gegebenen, äusserhalb desselben vorhandenen gewesenen Bedingungen [gemäss] den Kentnissen und Erwartungen, welche der Handelnde hegte, auch tatsächlich [der wirklichen damaligen Sachlage] entsprach: die lehrte ja der faktische "Erfolg" des Handelns' [The historian however is superior to his hero [the historical actor: HJ], in that he in any case knows *a posteriori*, whether the actor's evaluation of the circumstances according to his knowledge and expectations also truly expresses the state of affairs at that time: this also shows him [the historian: HJ] the factual consequences of the actions.]: M. Weber, *Gesammelte Aufsätze zur Wissenschaftslehre*, 4th edn (Tübingen 1973), p. 267.

29. Carr, 'Narrative and the real world', pp. 127–31.

30. He does maintain the relationship between the action and the narrative – he does not give an extensive analysis of Von Wright's teleological explanatory model without reason – but the relationship lies not so much in the temporal aspects and thereby in the narrative dimensions of the action, but in the mimesis or imitation in the narrative temporality of the time of action. The action possesses a certain coherence, but this coherence cannot simply be called narrative; at best one may speak of a pre-figuration of the narrative in the action. In action one may speak of a pre-figurative temporality, in the (historical) narrative of a configurative temporality. Ricoeur means by this that it is in the plot of the story that temporality takes its clearest shape.

Even though actions do form an important part of the infrastructure of historical narratives, Ricoeur also lends importance to causal relationships, in addition to teleological relationships between actions. Carr does not consider causal relation in his narrativism. Ricoeur does: in addition to Von Wright, Max Weber and Raymond Aaron with their singular causal imputation also play an important role in his study of the nature of the historical narrative. See Ricoeur, *Time and narrative*, pp. 182–92.

The concept *mimesis* is derived by Ricoeur from Aristotle – not the Aristotle of the *Physics*, but the author of the *Poetics*. We shall see that Ricoeur in no way seeks to follow Aristotle in his objectifying conception of time (ibid., p. 162).

31. See for example Ricoeur, *Time and narrative I*, pp. 131 and 171.
32. Ibid., pp. 193–200.
33. Ricoeur, *Temps et récit*, p. 207 ff., especially 222; *Time and narrative I* pp. 145–7, especially 157–8. Typical for finalism is Mink's statement 'we retrace forward what we already traced backward', quoted from Ricoeur, *Temps et récit*, p. 157.
34. Hayden White 'The value of narrativity in the representation of reality, in *The content of the form. Narrative discourse and historical representation* (Baltimore, MD and London 1987, pp. 2–25, especially 5 and 6.
35. Ricoeur is also more attached than, for example, Hayden White, Carr and Ankersmit, to the scientific status of history: Ricoeur, *Temps et récit*, pp. 162 and 175–82 and elsewhere.
36. See, for example, *Temps et récit*, p. 182.
37. F. Braudel, *La Méditerranée et le monde méditerranéen à l'epoque de Philippe II* (Paris 1949).
38. The three temporal strata of Braudel should be distinguished from the three narrative levels of Ricoeur. Ricoeur's micro-level consists of actions and the causal conditions and consequences of them. This is something different from the almost immobile time of Braudel, in which almost only conditions for actions figure and barely any actions themselves. Actions are important mainly in Braudel's quickly-vibrating event-driven time. There is, however, suggests Ricoeur, a relationship between his meso-level of the *mise en intrigue* and the the undulating, conjunctural time of Braudel. There is also a relationship between Ricoeur's narrative macro-level and Braudel's super-structure of Mediterranean culture as a whole. These issues will be dealt with in what follows, but as guidelines for the reader, a scheme follows:

		Vibrating political time	Micro-level	
	Infrastructure	Undulating conjunctural time	Meso-level	
Braudel		Temps presque immobile	(Micro-level?)	Ricoeur
	Superstructure	Mediterranean culture as quasi-personage	Macro-level	

39. F. Braudel, *La Méditerranée et le monde méditerranéen à l'epoque de Philippe II*, Vol. I, p. 295. In the English translation this is: 'Towns

rise, thrive, and decline according to the pulses of economic life: F. Braudel, *The Mediterranean and the Mediterranean world in the age of Philip II*, Vol. I, (Glasgow 1972), p. 322.

40. 'Un mode nouveau de récit historique apparait, disons le "récitatif" de la conjoncture, du cycle, voire l'intercycle qui propose à notre choix une dizaine d'années, un quart de siècle et, à l'extrême limite, le demi-siècle de Kondratieff': F. Braudel, *L'Écriture sur l'histoire* (Paris 1969), p. 48.

41. Ricoeur, *Temps et récit*, pp. 302–3.

42. Thus Braudel writes regarding the Mediterranean region as a whole: 'Nous saurons donc pas sans peine quel personage historique exact peut être la Mediterranée' and further '[. . .] son personage est complex, encombrant, hors série.' [We know without difficulty which exact historical personage could be the Mediterranean one [. . .] its personage is complex, encompassing and extraordinary]: *La Méditeranée* I, p. 13.

43. It is this homogenization of time that Mandelbaum has in mind when he says that even though a specialist historian has the right to periodize on the basis of one single aspect, a general historian must base his periodization on the integration of several cultural elements: M. Mandelbaum, *The anatomy of historical knowledge* (Baltimore, MD and London 1977), p. 166.

44. F. Braudel, *Civilisation matérielle, économie et capitalisme, XVe–XVIIIe siècle* (Paris 1979).

45. F. Braudel, *La Méditerranée I*, p. 214.

46. S. Avineri, *The social and political thought of Karl Marx* (Cambridge 1970).

47. S. Avineri, *The social and political thought of Karl Marx*, pp. 159–62.

48. Ibid., p. 160.

49. G. Roth, 'Duration and rationalization: Fernand Braudel and Max Weber', in G. Roth and W. Schluchter, *Max Weber's vision of history. Ethics and methods* (Berkeley and Los Angeles, CA and London 1979), pp. 166–94, esp. 180.

50. M. Weber, *Gesammelte Aufsätze zur Wissenschaftslehre* (4th edn, Tübingen 1973), p. 267.

51. 'Ein Idealtypus bestimmter gesellschaftlicher Zustände, welcher sogar aus gewissen sozialen Erscheinungen einer Epoche abstrahieren lässt, kann – und dies ist sogar recht häufig der Fall – den Zeitgenossen selbst als praktisch zu erstrebendes Ideal oder doch als Maxime für die Regelung bestimmter sozialer Beziehungen vorgeschwebt haben'

[An ideal type of certain states of society, which can be abstracted from definite social phenomena in an era, may – and this is often the case – be seen by contemporaries [=historical actors: HJ] as an ideal or a maxim for the organization of certain social relations]: M. Weber, ibid., p. 196; see also p. 201. See further: H. S. J. Jansen, *De constructie van het stadsverleden*, pp. 101–3, esp. 103.

52. J. Topolski, *Methodology of history* (Dordrecht 1976), p. 591 and P. Spilt, 'De annalesschool', *Ter elfder ure* 26(31) (Geschiedtheorie 1, 1982): 348.

53. F. Braudel, *Le temps du monde*, p. 55: '[. . .] the history of the world is an undivided procession, a cortege of coexisting modes of production which we are too inclined to think as following one another in successive historical periods. In fact the different modes of production are all attached to each other': idem, *The perspective of the world* from: idem, *Civilization and capitalism, 15th–18th century III* (London 1984), p. 70.

54. *Le temps du monde*, p. 8; *The perspective of the world*, p. 18.

55. *Le temps du monde*, pp. 29–31; *The perspective of the world*, pp. 40–2.

56. Note: the three temporal structures of a world system in Braudel's *Civilisation matérielle* are not identical to the three time layers in his Mediterranean study.

57. J. L. Van Zanden, 'Is het handelskapitalisme een aparte theorie waard?' [Is mercantile capitalism worth a separate theory?], *Tijdschrift voor Sociale Geschïedenis* (1996): 53–64, esp. 56. See also J. L. Van Zanden, *Arbeid tijdens het handelkapitalisme. Opkomst en neergang van de Hollandse economie 1350–1850* [Labour during mercantile capitalism. Rise and fall of the economy of Holland 1350–1850] (Bergen 1991).

58. K. Marx, *Grundrisse der Kritik der politische Ökonomie* (Berlin 1974, 1st edn 1857–1858) pp. 375–6. See also H. Lefebvre, *La pensée merxiste et la ville* (Paris 1972), pp. 80–6.

59. M. Benson *et al.*, *Politieke economie van de huishoudelijke arbeid* [Political economics of housework] (Nijmegen 1977), pp. 144–5.

60. See Note 39.

61. L. Althusser and E. Balibar, *Das Kapital lesen I* [Reading *Das Kapital I*] (Reinbek bei Hamburg 1972), p. 143. See also: M. Terpstra, 'Het geschiedenisbegrip bij Althusser' [Althusser's concept of history], in *Ter elfder ure* 2631) (1982): 443.

62. It should be said, in all honesty, that there is also a subjective element present, because 'past' and 'future' are present in the 'present'. Only a subject, here the historian, can observe this. The subjectifying

element is reinforced if the aspect of action is added to it. Ernst Bloch formulates, as Marxist, the mixture of subjectivity and objectivity when he explains the difference between the social 'contradictions' of *petite bourgeoisie* and paupers on the one hand and proletarians on the other. The first group uses a non-simulataneous (that is to say a past-oriented) and the second a simulataneous (that is to say an up-to-date) contradiction. The objective contradiction of the *petite bourgeoisie* and the paupers consists of an unprocessed (and hence still-present) past in the form of an opposition to the aristocracy and the urban patriciate; the subjective contradiction consists of unfocused rebellion and rage. The simultaneous contradiction of the proletarians is, subjectively speaking, a conscious (goal-directed) revolutionary act and, objectively speaking, an obstacle, in the present, for their future: 'Als subjektiver ist dieser ungleichzeitige Widerspruch gestaute, ungenaue, daher ablenkbare Wut; als objektiver ist er unaufgearbeitete Vergangenheit. Der gleichzeitige Widerspruch dagegen der echten revolution ist subjektiv die wache revolutionäre Tat des Proletariats und objektiv die im Jetzt enthaltene, verhinderte Zukunft': E. Bloch, *Philosophische Aufsätze*, p. 42.

63. T. Skocpol, *States and social revolutions* (Cambridge 1979).
64. J. A. Goldstone *Revolution and rebellion in the early moder world* (Berkeley and Los Angeles, CA and London 1991).
65. T. Skocpol, *States and social revolutions*, p. 4 and J. A. Goldstone, *Revolution and rebellion*, pp. 283–9. For a more extensive analysis of the similarities and differences between the books of Skocpol and Goldstone, see H. S. J. Jansen, 'Het vergelijken vergeleken: Skocpol and Goldstone' [Comparison compared: Skocpol and Goldstone], *Theoretische Geschiedenis* 24(3) (1997): 289–304.
66. T. Skocpol, *States and social revolutions*, p. 27.
67. Ibid., pp. 27 and 292.
68. Ibid., pp. 155–7 and 282–3.
69. Ibid., p. 24.
70. Ibid., p. 283.
71. J. A. Goldstone *Revolution and rebellion*, pp. 46, 345–7, 464.
72. Ibid., p. 140.
73. Ibid., pp. 140–5.
74. R. Sennett, *Families against the city. Middle class homes of industrial Chicago 1872–1890* (New York 1974).
75. A. Janssens, *Family and social change. The household as a process in an industrializing community* (Cambridge 1993).
76. Sennett, *Families against the city*, pp. 42–6.

77. Ibid., pp. 47–9 and 107.
78. Ibid., pp. 146–7.
79. See also R. Sennett, 'Middle-class families and urban violence: the experience of a Chicago community in the nineteenth century', in T. K. Hareven (ed.), *Anonymous Americans. Explorations in nineteenth-century social history* (Englewood Cliffs, NJ 1971), pp. 280–305, especially 281–91.
80. Sennett, *Families against the city*, pp. 42–6.
81. Ibid.
82. Ibid., p. 236.
83. Ibid., p. 242.
84. G. Sjoberg, 'Cities in developing and industrial societies: a cross-cultural analysis', in Ph. M. Hauser and L. F. Schnore, *The study of urbanization* (New York, London 1967), pp. 213–63, and R. Nisbet (ed.), *Social change* (New York, Evanston, ILl., San Francisco, London 1972), p. 29.
85. Janssens, *Family and social change*, p. 245.
86. Ibid., p. 21.
87. Ibid.
88. Ibid. See also H. Medick, 'The proto-industrial family economy', *Social History* (1976): 291–315, esp. 293.
89. A. Briggs, *Victorian cities* (Harmondsworth 1968).
90. D. Fraser, *Power and authority in the Victorian city* (Oxford 1979); idem, *Urban politics in Victorian England. The structure of politics in Victorian cities* (London 1979) and G. Stedman Jones. *Outcast London. A study of the relationships between classes in Victorian society* (Oxford 1971).
91. See among others D. Cannadine, *Lords and landlords. The aristocracy and the towns 1774–1967* (Leicester 1980).
92. Quasi-teleological relationships seem goal-directed but are actually causal.
93. Fraser, *Power and authority in the Victorian city*, p. 152.
94. Jones, *Outcast London*, p. 349.
95. See, for a pragmatic theory of history, A. A. Van den Braembussche, 'Historical explanation and comparative method: towards a theory of the history of society', *History and Theory* 28 (1989): 1–24, especially 1–3.

–10–

Time and (Dis)Continuity[1]
Arrangements of Time

In the preceding chapter we saw that subjectifying time is closely linked to a subjectifying entity. Ricoeur's quasi-personages functioned as a model for this type of entity. Ricoeur derived the idea of quasi-personages from Mandelbaum's continuing entities. In this chapter, I wish to determine how continuous these entities are. The preceding chapter also dealt with the homogeneous character of subjectifying temporality. In Braudel's analysis of the Mediterranean culture, we saw that the continuing entity 'Mediterranean culture' was composed of smaller continuing entities such as kingdoms, states and cities, each with its own temporality. These subordinate temporalities were, however, homogenized in a general Mediterranean temporality. Little attention was then given to the fact that both the Mediterranean temporality and also the subordinate temporalities of kingdoms, states and cities had an undulating nature. This undulating nature of subjectifying time will be examined more closely in this chapter. Undulating time in a continuing entity also implies that, despite changes, continuity is present in subjectifying temporalities. This has consequences for the classification of time, making it more difficult. How such difficulties can be addressed and solved will also be dealt with in this chapter. The traditional division of history into ancient, medieval, modern, and recent periods will play an important role in this solution. This periodization also has consequences for the question of whether a global history is possible on the basis of subjectifying time. The fact that it is based on a continuing entity raises the question of whether the world as a whole can be considered such an entity.

On the basis of these issues the following problems will be considered in the next chapter:

- Why is subjectifying time continuous and undulating?
- How are problems of periodization solved in this continuous and undulating time?

- Which problems are entailed by traditional periodization for the possibility of a form of global historical writing?

In the preceding chapter, we also observed that objectifying time is closely linked to an objectifying entity – the system–sub-system or half-open system construction. I then assumed that the sub-system is in an another temporal phase than the system. Thus objectifying temporality was linked to compounded temporality. This representation is not completely correct. System and sub-system can be in different temporal phases, but this is not necessary. If a system and a sub-system are in the same temporal phase, then it becomes unnecessary to track down both their temporal dimensions. Analysis of one is sufficient to determine their temporal construction and classification. If the system and the sub-system are both in the same temporal phase, the question arises of whether in that case one can speak of homogenizing time and hence conclude that the originally objectifying temporality has become subjectifying. A provisional answer could be that subjectifying time also possesses continuity and undulation, while these are absent in objectifying time. Such an answer is, however, not completely correct. Apparently, continuity also seems present in objectifying time. After all, one need only think of Sjoberg's pre-industrial and industrial urban phases and realize that the pre-industrial period sometimes spanned several centuries. Nonetheless, this is not a case of continuity in the sense that the subjectifying temporality mentioned above is continuous. That, after all, pertained to continuity in change. The continuity present in Sjoberg's and other objectifying studies has a much more static character. Temporality is divided into blocks or phases that are themselves fairly static. Between these there are moments of transition, which accentuate the discontinuity of objectifying temporality. Objectifying temporality is not undulating but static and often discontinuous. In contrast to the undulating nature of subjectifying temporality, objectifying temporality has discontinuous phases.

This phased temporality is examined by way of the following questions:

- Which phases can be distinguished in macro-systems studies?
- What do the transitional periods in half-open system studies look like? A distinction should be made here between studies describing active sub-systems with a compounded time and those describing passive subsystems not marked by compounded time.
- What implications does phased temporal classification have for the writing of global history?

Finally: I had planned to look beyond the borders of urban history in this chapter, as I had done in the preceding one, and involve other historical sub-disciplines, especially those concerning family and state. In the end, however, urban history proved to contain so many unexplored possibilities with regard to the temporal dimension that I returned to my first love, urban history, in this chapter.

Subjectifying temporality, continuous entities and periodization

Continuous and undulating temporality

Undulating temporality is a familiar phenomenon in historical writing. When Huizinga wishes to show his readers that the transition from the Middle Ages to the early modern area did not happen abruptly, he sketches the shift into the Renaissance as follows: 'The image of the transition from the Middle Ages to the modern era is (and how else could it be?) not one of [one] great upheaval, but of a long row of waves, which roll up the beach: each of these breaks at a different distance and at a different moment.'[1] Undulating temporality seems most manifest in economic history. Increasing and decreasing scarcity expressed in a conjuncture line in many cases constitutes the undulation of a historical narrative. As we shall see, undulating temporality can be exposed in different ways in urban historiography.

Increasing and decreasing cohesion: Blumin. In Chapters 5 and 6 we have seen that cities conceived as closed systems sometimes have a goal-directed and sometimes a disintegrating nature. This transition gives the temporal dimension of such systems an undulating character. Goal-directed systems improve the internal cohesion of the closed system because all actors and black boxes are directed towards the achievement of a communal output. Disintegrating systems are characterized by a relatively small influence of the actors and an excessive influence of the unintended side-effects of their actions. The ascendancy of motorized traffic and the fall of the Roman Empire are examples mentioned in this context. By way of the studies of Frisch, Mumford, and in a sense, Fraser, as mentioned in the preceding chapter, I have explained that goal-directed and disintegrating systems can also be linked in a series.

The alternation of goal-directed and disintegrating systems is interpreted by the systems theoretician Hall as an alternation between coherence and additivity. Both these extremes of coherence of systems were presented in Chapter 3 as properties of closed and open systems, respectively. It is, however, also possible that one and the same system is marked by gradations of coherence. This can be observed by comparing the coherence of the system at different intervals. The system may show greater coherence at one moment than at another. By examining the coherence or additivity of systems, one can expose the dimensions in them concerning time and change. If a system develops from coherence to additivity, having many parts that behave independently with regard to the whole, then such a system is subject to what Hall calls the 'progressive factorization' of its parts. If we consider the British Commonwealth of Nations as a system, then we may say that it has been subject to progressive factorization during the twentieth century. The reverse of this process of disintegration is 'progressive systematization'. This signifies that relatively independent parts, which nonetheless show a certain mutual affinity (Hall in this context speaks of 'pre-existing relations'), show increasingly strong ties. This integration reinforces the autonomy and identity of the system. Disintegration and integration alternate.[2]

Blumin sketches the development of Kingston in *The urban threshold* as a closed system with increasing coherence. The history of Kingston is conceived as the 'rise' from 'town' to 'city'. The 'town' Kingston of 1820 shows little coherence and can barely be called a community. The city of 1860 constitutes a community with a certain *appartenance participative*. Several cataracts can be observed in this process. Around 1820 the Dutch and the English parts of the populace are still in equilibrium. The government is a fairly closed club of notables. It is a 'regime of uncles', a description with which Blumin expressly refers to Mack Walker.[3] Walker uses this term to indicate a phase in the history of the German home towns in which the concentration of power in the patriciate damages the communarchy. However, Kingston, in contrast to the German home towns, has barely any *collective participation* during these years, according to Blumin. Starting from 1845 Kingston develops a flourishing associational circuit, through which the emergence of specifically ethnic sub-cultures and communities is prevented. Immigrants belonging to the middle class are quickly integrated in the urban community.[4]

In 1820, political life in Kingston is determined by people, problems, campaigns and affairs at the levels of state and nation. Around 1860 local politics starts playing a more important role. National problems acquire their own local identity.[5] This, too, indicates increasing coherence. At the end of his book, Blumin depicts the 'intrigue' of historical narrative concerning Kingston as follows: 'But the transportation revolution did not initiate contact between Kingston and an unfamiliar world and *did not bring about the disintegration of a previously self-sufficient community.* Indeed [. . .] the institutional development [. . .] *serves to strengthen the community where it had been weakest and helped turn the attention of cosmopolitan minds inward on the town.* [italics: HJ]'.[6] Kingston develops from a relatively-open system, which is not clearly delimited from the state and the region, to a relatively-closed system with a clearly recognizable 'personal' identity. Blumin's urban biography describes the coming of age of Kingston as an autonomous city.[7]

Increase and decrease of appartenance participative: Merrit and Walker. The consequences of coherence and additivity for the participants in a relatively-closed system lead us again to the *appartenance participative.* This property of Ricoeur's first-order entities also shows a surge from integration to disintegration. Patriotism and class-consciousness are examples of this *collective participation.* They can manifest themselves strongly, but they can also be forgotten, opposed, or denied. However, they do not thereby disappear. On the contrary: such a negation actually presupposes the existence of collective participation, according to Ricoeur.[8] He does not elaborate on the recognition or denial of this participation. Nor does he formulate a theory on this issue. Nonetheless, it is not hard to find one. Increase or decrease of the *appartenance participative* causes a tidal movement, which can be compared to the coherence or additivity of systems parts, respectively.

An example of such a tidal movement in *collective participation* is given by the American Merrit in two studies on the emergence of American nationalism in the middle of the eighteenth century. In opposition to historians who claimed that this identity grew slowly but surely during the course of the eighteenth century and to historians who claimed that it emerged swiftly and abruptly, Merrit shows both groups to be wrong. In order to do this he examined symbols, which concerned alliance to either the English political community or the American one. By way of the quantitative analysis of the use of symbols in five American colonial newspapers, he arrives at the conclusion that an undulating development of participation is in evidence.[9]

The communarchal developments that Walker sketches in 'home towns' between 1648 and 1871 are an example of a similar process in urban historiography. Walker starts his study with accounts of developments during the seventeenth and eighteenth centuries in several 'home towns'. His main theme here is that the communarchy of the home town is internally threatened by *Freund- und Vetterwirtschaft* (nepotism). One point worth noting here is that the state sometimes acts as a friend and protector and sometimes as an enemy of the communarchy.[10]

Almost immediately Walker notes the *emplotting, cyclic and internal* nature of these developments: 'In *stories* like these a pattern appears, a *cyclical pattern*, that shows why intervention by the territorial state and the persistence of the home town community were not only compatible in this political incubator. They were part of the *same process* [italics: HJ].'[11]

This first tidal movement is marked by three periods:

- a period of communarchy
- a period of nepotism and thereby of disturbance of participation
- a period of the re-establishment of the communarchy.[12]

In the second half of the eighteenth century the absolute state became more influential and its attitude towards the home towns became more ambivalent. Sometimes the communarchy is defended against the patriciate; yet the influence of the central government is also occasionally enlarged, to the detriment of both the patriciate and the adherents of communarchal participation.

An important attack on the urban autonomy of the home town occurred during the Napoleontic era. The individualistic ideals of equality of the French were diametrically opposed to the communautarian conception of equality of the home town citizens. In the twenties of the nineteenth century this attack was continued by the more or less liberal bureaucracy in Prussia and other German states ('the general estate').

After 1825 the resistance of the home towns to this policy became increasingly strong. The battle between city and state in this period concerns the question whether individuals have the right to freedom of movement and settlement, a right that is defended by the state and its bureaucracy and opposed by the home towns. On four issues differences concerning this matter continually cropped up: free trade, freedom to settle, freedom to marry whom one wishes and the general care for the poor. The home towns rejected these positions and acquired the previously-mentioned *Heimatrecht*. This system gave them the opportunity to protect their own entrepreneurs and workers against outside competition, to determine for themselves who is accepted into the town and who is given citizenship of the city, and finally to organize care for the poor and 'neighbourliness' for themselves.[13]

By this means the *appartenance participative* of the home towns reached its zenith in the thirties and forties of the nineteenth century. In the revolutionary year 1848 the parliament of Frankfurt seemed to be their ally in their battle against the state and the bureaucracy. In the end, however, this parliament showed itself in support of the freedom of the individual. The defeat of this parliament in 1849 led to a certain restoration of the home town, but at the end of that decade the Prussian government dumped the towns again, after which they were finally subsumed in the Second German Empire.

The changes that the home towns were subject to are changes in *collective participation*. Undulating time emerges through an evaluation of the nature and strength of the home town mentality. Walker continually asks himself whether the concrete situation in a number of small- and middle-sized German towns complies with communarchal togetherness. Its developments show ups and downs. There are moments of achievement and alientation in this participation. The battle for the communarchy between adherents and opponents thus forms both the intrigue and the temporal dimension of Walkers' book.

The increase and decrease of the intensity of ideal types: Weber. Although the importance of the ideal type for subjectifying time has already been dealt with in the preceding chapter – the same, by the way, holds true for *appartenance participative* – Weber's role has remained understated. It is for this reason that I briefly return to Weber's thought here. Weber's ideal types are, after all, extremely suited for showing the undulating effect of collective participation. His typology achieves this by comparing the actual participation in the urban past to the more or less logical correlations of the ideal types. In his description of ideal types, Weber often discounts the role of the historian. He is, after all, obliged 'in jedem Falle festzustellen, wie nahe oder wie fern die Wirklichkeit jenem Idealbilde steht . . .' [to ascertain in every case how close to or how far from reality an ideal type stands].[14] Cities comply better with ideal types at some moments than others. The ideal typology therefore leads to evaluative historical contemplation. Expressions such as 'eine Stadt-gemeinde im vollen Sinn des Wortes' [an urban community in the full sense of the word][15] and 'die vollentwickelte Antike und Mittelalterliche Stadt' [the fully-developed classical and medieval city][16] are examples of the evaluative effect of ideal types in urban history. Such expressions also indicate that there are also classical and medieval cities that have reached completion, as it is described in the ideal type. Thus market-places where large numbers of merchants and artisans live together are on their way to becoming a city, but cannot yet fully comply with the ideal type. They cannot 'fulfil the concept city'.[17] The ideal type is only fulfilled in cases of complete political and institutional autonomy. This also clarifies the heuristic intentions of the ideal typology. Historical 'reality' is continually examined for phenomena that comply best with the characteristics described in the ideal type. When those phenomena approximate the ideal type more closely, the coherence of those phenomena is greatest; when the phenomena become more distant from the ideal type, one may speak of either growth or decline. It is not without reason that Appelbaum counts Weber among 'the rise and fall' sociologists.[18]

In classical times Weber distinguishes undulating movements in the following urban types: (1) cities with a 'Burg- und Heerkönigtum' [a castle and a king, (2) 'Adelspolis' [aristocratic polis], (3) 'Hopliten-polis', (4) 'demokratische Bürgerpolis' [democratic civilian polis], (5) 'bürokratische Stadtkönigtum' [bureaucratic city kingdom], and (6) a city under the 'Leiturgiemonarchie' [liturgical monarchy].[19] In this series the aristocratic (*Adels*) polis and the hoplite polis are upward-directed ideal types leading to the 'demokratische Bürgerpolis'; the 'burokratische Stadtkönigtum' and the city under a 'Leiturgiemonarchie' are ideal types that, seen in the light of the civilian polis, indicate decline.

Continuous, undulating temporality and the problem of periodization

One of the most important instruments of the historian for synthesizing the results of his research is periodization. In his book *De periodisering der geschiedenis* [The periodization of history], Van der Pot writes:

> 'In periodisation we have the ability to summarise the whole course of history in the shortest way possible. If it fulfils all the conditions [. . .], then it offers *the last general synthesis of our historical knowledge.* We hence do not go too far when we claim, that *the division of history into periods is the actual core of the form which historical study imprints on the past* [italics Van der Pot]'.[20]

Van der Pot even claims that the periodisation of historians reveals their conception of the world. He shares this opinion with Jan Romein. Huizinga considers this too extravagant and mitigates the importance of periodization.[21] Yet he too states; 'It is clear that there is an active need for well-calibrated and clearly-determined terms of periodisation. They are necessary in order to understand history in its alternating phases.'[22] In a recent study Dorsman also pointed out the possibilities for synthesis present in periodization.[23]

Periodization is a relatively unexplored area within theory of history. Van der Pot's study *De periodisering der geschiedenis* – although written in 1951 – is still the only monograph extant on this subject internationally speaking.[24] Incidentally, Huizinga, the German philosopher and historian Troeltsch and some others have also occupied themselves with problems concerning periodization.[25]

Continuing entities as a foundation for periodization. Following the footsteps of Troeltsch, Van der Pot raises the question of the grounds for periodization. Troeltsch formulated this problem in the following manner: '[. . .] whether one must base periodisation on the great sociologically continuing patterns of living [. . .] or whether one should proceed from the last and deepest mental attitudes of the periods [. . .]'.[26] In his solution Troeltsch chooses for the 'great sociologically continuing patterns of living', which he also calls 'grossen soziologisch-ökonomisch-politischen Dauerformen' or 'sozialökonomisch-politisch-rechtlichen Unterbauten'.[27] As examples of such 'continuing entities' he mentions settlements, *poleis*, world empires, monarchies, feudality, cities, cultures, including the culture of capitalism, states, elites, and also races. In these he follows mostly Weber and Sombart.[28] Troeltsch hence assumes continuing entities in his periodization. According to Van der Pot, Troeltsch does not sufficiently consider the cultural appreciation of the historian in the choice between continuing entities and the cultural particularity of a period. He thinks the historian 'should proceed from that aspect of culture which one considers most important for one's own sake'.[29]

The opposition between Troeltsch and Van der Pot could be seen as an opposition between an 'exploratory' and an 'interpretative' approach towards periodization. Troeltsch's approach can be called exploratory because he proceeds from the continuing entities themselves and tries to indicate points of discontinuity in order to identify periods that are as homogeneous as possible. Van der Pot's approach, by contrast, can be conceived as interpretative because he proceeds from the historian's conception of the world. This opposition should not be seen too sharply. In the approach on the basis of continuing entities the historian, as architect of the closed system and as discoverer of homogeneity, still plays a major role. It is important in this context that Troeltsch pays a great deal of attention to mental–cultural factors in the genesis and existence of continuing entities: they are, according to him, units, which 'selbst wohl geistig bedingt sein mögen' [may themselves be mentally determined]. The 'mental attitudes' [*geistige Einstellungen*] form the foundations of Troeltsch's 'continuing entities' [*Dauerformen*] and also form its 'sociological actualisation' [*soziologische Gestaltung*] and the 'driving unifying force' [*treibenden Einheitskräfte*]. He thereby indicates that he is seeking a collective culture, a common conception, for purposes of periodization.[30] That the constructing historian plays an important role during such a quest is self-evident.

Van der Pot does not wholly relinquish periodization to the historian's activities of characterization. On the contrary: he even rejects aprioristic periodisation; in other words, he rejects divisions into periods that are based on a theory external to history. Periodization must always be the result of research, according to Van der Pot. But research into what? Van der Pot does not pose this question, because he assumes that the past, after the researcher has determined the characteristics of periods, will of itself yield the points of discontinuity.[31]

Because I deem the past incapable of doing this, I consider periodization the result of the examination of continuing entities moulded into closed-systems constructions. The methods of explanation and temporal conceptions that the historian himself has placed in the closed system will hence also play a role in periodization.

Characterisation and division into epochs: Weber and Mumford. Periodization concerns not only the subdivision of time but also discovering of the characteristics of the periods found. If one proceeds from continuing entities during this process of discovery, then one should take it into account that the various partial systems, each possibly having its own temporality – consider Braudel with his three layers of time – must be homogenized in one temporality. Berkhofer seeks this homogenization through the discovery of common attitudes and actions effective in such an entity. In other words: he searches for a configuration in time of common ideas, plans, and values and the actions that ensue from them. Such a 'shared ideation' permeates the various partial systems of a society during a certain time and thus yields the foundation or the unity of a certain temporal span.

> Periodization rests upon the belief, that at a given duration of time a cluster of characteristics permeates many areas of life and supposedly relates diverse trends and events in a society. [. . .] Periodization then would be based upon the *shared ideation* [italics: HJ] in a society. To the extent that such an ideation accounts for the actors' behaviour in a society, cultural periodization would unite the seeming diversity of a time in that society'.[32]

Berkhofer wishes to use concepts for the periodization of closed systems that permeate those systems completely. A period begins the moment an amalgamating movement is initiated in a single partial system, crosses its boundaries, and starts to control other partial systems. It ends in the event of a contraction in communal systems of belief. Thus periods can be identified with a clear and homogeneous cultural identity along with periods of less coherence. Berkhofer's method of periodization in this way resembles the undulating conception of time that I discussed in the previous section. This is especially pronounced when Berkhofer describes how one period should be linked to another in historical practice:

> The holistic problem involved in time settings is best seen in relating one period to another. In theory one period would bear little or no relation to another because each would be a whole [this holds for half-open systems constructions: HJ], but in the historical analysis of a society the second period must have been derived from the first because of the continuity of the society [i.e. continuing entity: HJ.] The question for the historian becomes in practice, when did the first period end and the second begin? In historical research there usually exists a time of transition that is blurred analytically but is nevertheless existent in the past of a society and important to the written history of the past.'[33]

Many periodizations are arrived at in the manner described here by Berkhofer. Yet it is open to some objections. Berkhofer, at least at times, seems to remove change from the course of history itself and to divide a historical process into static homogeneous blocks and dynamic, integrating or disintegrating phases. This can damage the teleological–finalistic and thereby dynamic nature of the closed-system construction. Dorsman also attaches value to retaining this dynamic nature in periodization and therefore proposes to take a common problem at issue as a criterion for a period instead of a common culture.[34] Different solutions on the basis of various values, mental attitudes, (sub)cultures and mentalities can then be integrated as a reaction to one and the same problem.[35]

For periodization in literature and the figurative arts, this is probably a solution; however, it does not apply to 'normal' history. Dorsman's example of the *fin de siécle* as a period of ambivalence shows how pale, vague and commonplace such a characterization of a period can end up being.[36] It is better, in my opinion, to consider, in addition to communal problems, the participation with which the members of a community attack the problems they encounter. Stated more simply: the *appartenance participative* examined in the previous chapters should be given a central role in the methodology of periodization. This already occurs in many urban historical studies. Clear examples of the conflation of *appartenance participative* with the characteristics of a period can be found in urban biographies. In the work of Frisch, for example, the division into periods is analogous to decline of the culture of participation in the 'town' and the ascendancy of the new 'city' culture.

Having said this, I realize that undulating temporality immediately evokes the question of how the exact beginning and ending of a period can be determined. Should a new period start at the beginning or the end of an ascending movement or, for example, in its middle? Or should it occur at the corresponding points of a descending movement?

In Weber we encounter another example of the conflation of urban collective participation and the qualification of historical periods. In his work, each type of city is marked by its own culture of participation, which serves as a common characteristic of a period. The Asiatic city is marked by the almost complete absence of *collective participation*. Here one can speak of a negative participation culture. The classical city has a culture of participation consisting of political self-determination, with, as a consequence, a military–civil urban culture. The medieval city can best be characterized as a city with economic–civil participation. That the culture of participation and the ideal type coincide in Weber indicates the great significance that both closed-systems constructions have for periodization. Weber's periodization can be described as follows:

ASIATIC CITY

A potentate rules the city; the urban inhabitants do not possess any administrative autonomy.

The inhabitants of the city have no citizenship status. They are politically silent and often lack personal freedom.

The city does not contribute to rational-capitalist development.

CLASSICAL CITY

The urban inhabitants possess administrative autonomy.

Many of the inhabitants of the city are *zôa politika*, that is to say citizens of the city.

The city does not contribute to a rational-capitalist development.

MEDIEVAL CITY

The inhabitants of the city possess administrative autonomy.

Many of the inhabitants of the city are citizens and *homines economici*.

The city yields a contribution to rational-capitalist development.

In Chapter 5 I examined the differences of opinions among historians regarding the nature of participation and the ideal typology to which it leads. The same differences of opinion can arise regarding periods. This fact manifests itself even more concerning the relationship between *appartenance participative* and ideal typologies on the one hand and periodization on the other. Weber's and Mumford's views regarding the medieval city can serve to illustrate this. Mumford determines the medieval city on the basis of three characteristics:

- The urban type succeeds in building a balanced economy through the achievement of a balance between individual and communal interests.
- It can establish a harmonious relationship with the surrounding countryside.
- It is capable of getting the four classes, nobility, citizenry, clergy and peasantry, to work together organically. Mumford sees the essence of the medieval culture of participation in the short-lived victory of 'communitas' over 'dominium'.[37]

Not one of these characteristics expounded by Mumford points to the role of the medieval city as the incubator of capitalism. He drops capitalism like a cuckoo's egg in harmonious medieval urbanity. It is an alien element.[38]

Weber's appreciation for the medieval city is no less than that of Mumford. His praise of that type of city is, however, based precisely on its large contribution to the genesis of the *homo economicus* and thereby to the capitalist mentality.

Berkhofer writes the following about such contradictions with regard to the content and meaning of the names of periods: 'Arguments over periodization are not so much about what events occurred, for most historians will agree about this, but rather over the meaning of those events for an interpretative unity of a certain time-span.'[39] This has as a consequence that periods with the same names can still display very different characteristics. This is also why Van der Pot calls such periodizations colourless and rejects them for this reason. Huizinga uses the same term, but considers such colourless periodizations very effective precisely because they are colourless.

Periodisation and the writing of global history

The subjection to a 'higher' periodization: Walker and Weber once again. Many urban historians solve the problem of periodization pragmatically. They direct themselves towards more-encompassing and therefore, hopefully, better-known continuing entities for periodization in long-term and comparative studies. In comparative urban studies such as those of Walker and Fraser, time is divided into periods pertaining to the country or kingdom that the cities being compared belong to. In Walker's case this is Germany; in Fraser's England. In long-term studies such as those of Weber and Mumford, attention is directed towards the continuing entity European culture. Many urban historians apparently feel a need to orient themselves towards 'higher' continuing entities when describing urban phenomena in the long term, because these have a better-known and more-familiar division into periods than the urban developments themselves.[40]

The clearest example of such a periodization, based on a better-known continuing entity, is used by Walker in his study regarding German home towns. He makes a periodization in which both the beginning (1648) and ending (1871) are determined by political events in a larger whole. In 1648 the Holy Roman Empire of the German nation collapsed and in 1871 the Second Empire began. In a sense, the German home towns owe their existence to the weakness of the former and their fall to the strength of the latter. The years indicating the beginning and end of his narrative indicate that Walker uses developments in a superordinate continuing entity (the German Empire) as temporal markers for his urban history. The same holds true for the temporal durations between 1648 and 1871: the absolutism in the eighteenth century, the Napoleonic era, the first half of the nineteenth century and finally the period 1848–1871. It is a periodization closely related to that of the German countries in the period between 1648 and 1871.

Weber does something similar. He positions the history of the city between the disappearance of the *oikos* and the emergence of the national state. This is natural in the light of his dichotomous, ideal-typical notions. The *oikos* disappears through the development of a local market, through which the inhabitants of the city satisfy an economically substantial part of their daily needs.[41] For Weber, the local market forms the first seed of urban development. Weber draws the curtain on urban history at the moment that the inhabitants of the city no longer satisfy their daily needs through the local market, but through a national economy. This occurs, according to him, around 1500 with the emergence of nation states.

When we examine Weber's periodization more closely, the political-institutional element proves to play a major role. This is, of course, not surprising, because Weber has precisely these political-institutional elements play a major role in his ideal typology. Weber uses *Asiatic* and

Greek culture and politics ('Burg- und Heerkönigtum', 'Adelspolis', 'Hoplitenpolis', 'demokratische Bürgerpolis'), the *Roman Empire* (bürokratisches Stadtkönigtum', 'Leiturgiemonarchie')[42] and *medieval German Empire* (südeuropäische Patriziatstädte' and 'nordeuropäische Bürgerstädte')[43] to illustrate the temporal classification between beginning and end-point.

But not all has been said with these observations regarding Weber's urban studies. Weber also uses traditional periodization, as we have seen above. I shall deal with this in the next section.

The subordination observed here of continuing entities to higher units, when confronted with problems of periodization, is reminiscent of system–sub-system constructions. This is curious, because these problems of periodization issued from a relatively-closed system construction. This can only signify the complementary nature of both systems constructions. I will return to this problem in the final chapter.

Problems with writing global history: once again Mumford
The periodization in most long-term studies is traditional, that is to say: it is based on the familiar division into an ancient period, a medieval one, an early modern and a modern one, and so on. What is the underlying continuing entity, which according to the beginning of this chapter cannot be absent if periodization is to occur? The answer to this question must be that this entity is formed by European culture. This is actually quite strange: most long-term studies strive towards a global history of cities, and a periodization based on European history would seem not entirely appropriate for this purpose. A global history, after all, demands a global historical periodisation. Troeltsch considers such a periodization impossible. Hence writing a global history is, in his eyes, an unattainable utopia: 'Alles was man als solche vorführt, sind Romane, die von einem gar nicht existierenden Subjekt metaphysische Märchen erzählen.' ['Everything brought forward as such is a fantasy, which tells metaphysical fairy tales concerning a subject which does not even exist']

The world can indeed not be considered a mental unit or a subject or a quasi-personage. It is for this reason that Van der Pot goes one step further and claims that Western development can be considered representative for all of history. In his view, as in that of Troeltsch, *Universalgeschichte* [universal history] coincides with the history of Europäertum.[44] A world history of cities can, in that light, be nothing but a European history of cities.

When we consider the urban historiographies of closed systems, then we indeed see that the long-term studies among them, despite their global presumptions, actually show only a Eurocentric urban historiography. Regions outside Europe such as Egypt, Mesopotamia, and Palestine only figure in them as precursors of or elements contrasting with European history.[45]

The reason for this Eurocentrism should be sought in the fact that traditional periodization is based on the continuing entities of European civilization. Hence it cannot be transferred to regions outside Europe. In Weber's case this non-applicability even leads to a sharp contrast between the static and dependent Asiatic city, which possesses no possibilities for autonomous development, and the European city, which does have these possibilities.

Mumford's *The city in history* is, as we have seen, a long-term study dealing with urban history from ancient times to the present. Hence it offers ample opportunity for examining the model of periodization behind it. In one chapter after another he discusses the genesis of cities in the ancient East, the cities in Greece and the Roman Empire, the medieval city, the 'baroque' city[46] and finally urban developments in the nineteenth and twentieth centuries.[47]

Although this long-term study does aspire to universality – the chapter titles mentioned in the last paragraph attest to his intention of writing a global history – he also admits that the historical developments he presents are closely related to European urban history. Mumford considers the urban developments sketched to be a unique process that does not repeat itself on the same scale in regions outside Europe.[48]

In Van der Pot's footsteps we may claim that traditional periodization occurs in Mumford's 'global' urban history as a result of his seeking the periodization of a familiar quasi-personage. This implies that traditional periodisation can be considered individualizing – in the sense that it leans on changes within a quasi-subject. As such it is less suitable for the writing of 'real' global history.

Objectifying temporality: Systems, sub-systems and phases

In discussing periodization according to subjectifying temporality, we started with the problem of continuity before arriving at problems of periodization. We ended with a discussion of the question of the extent to which Eurocentric periodizations were suitable for the writing of global histories. In this section on periodization according to objectifying temporality, we start with phased temporality. Subsequently the problem of discontinuity will be treated before, here too, arriving at the question of the suitability of a phased temporal division for the writing of global history.

Because it is unfeasible to discuss the phased temporal division of all the works with half-open system constructions mentioned in earlier chapters at length, I shall restrict myself to the temporal classifications of Rozman, Sjoberg and Friedrichs. The choice of Rozman and Sjoberg was determined by the fact that both studies work with passive sub-systems. Rozman bases his periodization on the (macro-)system and Sjoberg on the (passive) sub-system itself. Friedrichs' study of Nördlingen is an example of phases with an active sub-system construction. I have also had to restrict myself with regard to the question concerning the global application of a division into phases. Marx's, de Vries's, Lampard's, Rozman's and Sjoberg's studies all lend themselves well to the writing of global history. Yet, in order to avoid repetition, only those of Marx and Rozman will be examined more closely here.

Phases and discontinuity in macro-systems and sub-systems

The American sociologist Nisbet posits that every social space (i.e. system) consists at any moment of more than that '[. . .] which is simply deducible from some earlier state of the entity under observation'.[49] From there he describes change as that which occurs when one state cannot be explained or derived from a previous state. Between both states there then exists, according to Nisbet, a purely chronological relation.[50] Durkheim had already applied such a conception of change to global history: 'The stages that humanity traverses do not engender one another.'[51] Marx does something similar in his *Grundrisse* of 1857/1859. The phases he observes there in global history are sharply distinguished from one another. The Asiatic mode of production is essentially different from the classical slave economy; the latter from the German mode of production; and this in turn from feudalism and capitalism. Lefebvre writes the following regarding this: 'Dans les Grundrisse, tout est perçu et conçu selon la différence' [In the *Grundrisse*, everything is perceived and conceived according to difference].[52] In this manner a discontinuous time emerges in half-open systems constructions.[53] I would like to call this a 'weak' form of discontinuity. Qualitative differences between phases in a historical process are at issue here.

There is also a strong form of discontinuity. To understand it well, one should consider that phases are often based on theoretical assumptions. Thus we know that Sjoberg's periodization in pre-industrial and industrial cities is based on a functionalistic theory in which technology and social cohesion are crucial parameters for the division into pre-industrial and industrial periods. These parameters are of eminent importance for phased temporality. Phases within the parameters possess weak discontinuity; phases separated by parameters display strong discontinuity.

Alternation of strong and weak discontinuity: Rozman. Rozman concerns himself with phases in the development of urban networks in Japan, China, Russia, England and France. In Chapter 7 the theoretical nature of Rozman's work, or at least its use of models, has already been pointed out. Using an economic and an administrative parameter, the functions of a city as a centre for markets and for administration, respectively, Rozman points out the existence of seven levels in the structure of systems of cities. The earliest evolution of cities is not yet marked by development on all seven levels. As 'civilization' progresses – Rozman does not go further than around 1800 and has therefore only examined pre-industrial urban development – the hierarchy of cities expands to all seven levels. I shall now examine how Rozman envisages that process concretely. He distinguishes between seven stages of pre-modern urban development.

Phase A: This is the pre-modern phase.

Phase B: This phase only possesses a few, fairly isolated, cities. In the case of integration in a larger territorial unit, there is only weak control of the countryside.

Phase C: This stage already has a hierarchy of cities based on a formal administration. There are two levels of cities, as a result of which there is a regular flow of merchandise and people from the lower-level cities and the countryside to a small number of cities of the first or second levels. In this manner large areas are integrated in an administrative system; densely populated cities can therefore be maintained.

Phase D: This phase comes into existence through increasing administrative centralization. As a result of the proximity of a large kingdom, or being contained in one, the need for new administrative centres emerges. The Heijo and Heian empires in Japan, the Kievan state in Russia, the Han dynasty in China and the Roman Empire are counted among these by Rozman. A sub-phase of decentralization also sometimes belongs to this phase, especially when the large empires are in decline. In that case the number of levels remains the same or decreases. In most cases an imperial centre is replaced by various regional rivals. The Roman Empire in early medieval times is an example of this phenomenon.

Phase E: Commercial centralization starts in this stage. Periodical markets emerge in settlements that are widely distant from the administrative centres (level 7 settlements).

Phase F: In addition to local markets, regional markets also emerge. Higher administrative centres now also become commercial centres.

Phase G: This phase can also be described as a (historical) form of society in which all seven levels of cities are developed. In China, Japan, and Russia, the shift of the capital, the national administrative centre, from respectively Nanking to Peking, Kyoto to Edo and Moscow to St Petersburg is a sign that a complete national market has emerged.

It should be noted with regard to the problem of discontinuity that not every phase emerges through external changes. Phases A, B, C, and D are marked by development in which changes occur within the parameter 'administrative centralization'. In the case of phase D the movement towards centralisation abruptly ceases and an opposite movement towards decentralization commences. One cannot yet speak of strong discontinuity here: the administrative parameter is maintained. (Otherwise, in a closed-systems approach this would surely mean the end of a period; see for instance the decline of the Roman empire.)

Strong discontinuity is present at the beginning of phase E. Then a new parameter suddenly emerges, namely commercial centralization, with a new type of central place, the market centre, as a consequence. It is also significant that Rozman stops his analysis of urban networks before the beginning of industrial society. There too a strong discontinuity is very likely to be present.

Rozman's model of pre-modern urban development

PHASE	NUMBER OF LEVELS PRESENT	NAMES OF THE LEVELS PRESENT	CHARACTER OF CITIES
A	0	–	pre-urban
B	1	2	tribute city
C	2	1,5 or 2,5	city state
D	2, 3 or 4	1,4,5; or 2,4,5 or 2,3 or 2,3,5 or 2,3,4,5	imperial cities

Discontinuity

E	4 or 5	1,3,5,6 or 1,3,4,5,7	standard market centre
F	5 or 6	1,3,4,6,7 or 1,3,4,5,6,7	regional market centre

| G | 7 | 1,2,3,4,5,6,7 | national market centre |

Source: G. Rozman, 'Urban networks and historical stages', in *Journal of Interdisciplinary History* IX (1978): 77.

A strong form of discontinuity in sub-systems: Sjoberg. A clear example of temporal classification at a sub-system level is the comparison of the pre-industrial and the industrial city by Sjoberg. On the basis of the parameters 'technology' and 'social structure', which divide a macro-system not defined in terms of cities into a pre-industrial and an industrial phase, the urban sub-system is divided in two. This occurs through the influence of the parameters on certain urban variables. The most notable ones are: the urban function, the family and the administration. In this manner two large static temporal blocks are constructed, which can be depicted as follows:

Parameters	*The pre-industrial city*	*The industrial city*
a. technology and rationalization	Simple technology with little appreciation for commerce and manual labour, inadequate standardization of measures, weights, etc, . . .	Mass production by machine, far-reaching rationalization, perfect standardization of measures, weights, money, etc.
b. social structure variables	Large gap between the elite and the lower classes; elite lives in the centre, lower classes live in the periphery.	More fluidity between classes; elite moves from the centre to the suburbs.
Functions	Primarily religious and administrative functions	Primarily commercial and industrial functions.
Family	'Extended family' is seen as the ideal, primary community in which one lives.	The nuclear family is seen as ideal and is indeed dominant.

Administration	Strongly hierarchical political system, executive power strongly linked to tradition and personal prestige (patronage).	An open political system (democratic pluralism), functioning according to standardized procedures.

Sjoberg's division into phases is completely based on parameters and therefore on a strong form of discontinuity. The phases themselves display an extremely static nature, a characteristic of every division into phases. Every phase in Rozman's work is also static, even in the case of weak forms of discontinuity, as we shall see. No change in continuity, such as we encountered in subjectifying temporality, is present here. This yields the crucial question for phased temporal division: how does the transition from one phase to another occur? We may observe that in Rozman's case there is no analysis of the transition between phases with a weak form of discontinuity. This is usually the case when dealing with weak forms of discontinuity. In the case of strong discontinuity, transitional phases are often distinguished by possessing sub-phases between which there is in turn weak discontinuity.[54]

Transitions in macro-systems and sub-systems: Nisbet

Nisbet distinguishes between four transitional phases for both macro-systems and sub-systems, in which the changes are sometimes generated by the macro-system and sometimes by the sub-system:

- Phase 1 is marked by conventional and atrophied behaviour of the (sub-)system.
- In phase 2 new behaviour emerges from the system. This new behaviour is linked, according to Nisbet, to technical innovations.
- In phase 3 a crisis is in evidence, which either emerges from the sub-system itself (for example traditionalistic resistance to the threat of innovation from outside), or from the innovations initiated by the macro-system (or its environment).
- In phase 4 a new elite that has gained power through the crisis introduces the innovations that originated externally.

In the disruption of traditional behaviour by Western and therefore external colonizers, Nisbet sees an illustration of this process of transition.[55] He makes a sharp distinction between internal and external processes of change, and considers the former more important than the latter. This in contrast to Weber, for example, who, as we know, attributed the historical decline of the Roman Empire to a process of internal change. Nisbet states:

> [. . .] we must remain mindful of the distinction between types of change: those readjustments-nature within a structure and changes of the structure [. . .] even here however I would not claim that great changes can never take place as a consequence of such 'internal' forces within a social system or structure as, say reason and calculated desire. I say only that taking the major changes of human history in the aggregate, very few of them can be understood save in terms of the impact of *external* events [italics: HJ] – events that either create a crisis or are themselves occasioned in part by already existing crisis.[56]

Nisbet is not aware of the constructivist nature of his temporal construction. He thinks that the major changes in history spring from actual crises, while those crises are to a large extent also the product of the arrangement of the past by the historian. He therefore does not explicate his conception of external change in terms of a half-open system construction. Neither does he use the terms 'system' and 'sub-system', but, respectively, 'environment' and 'system'. Because some historians pronounce the environment a system, and thereby make the system into a sub-system, Nisbet's conception of phased transition can serve for both systems and sub-systems.

Transition in the passive sub-system: Sjoberg (Figure 15).   The transitional phase distinguished by Sjoberg between the pre-industrial and the industrial city can be compared to that of Nisbet. Sjoberg distinguishes between the following four – weak discontinuous – phases in the transition from the pre-industrial to the industrial city (needless to say the whole transition is a strong one, because it is a change òf parameters).

Phase 1: The continued existence or even the reinforcement of traditional forms. He mentions as an example the phenomenon of the matchmaker in pre-industrial cities, which becomes more important in the transitional phase.
Phase 2: Change of transitional norms; especially the elite increasingly appreciate economically-useful labour. The second phase resembles not only Nisbet's second phase but also his fourth phase, because of the importance assigned to the elite.
Phase 3: The disappearance of traditional norms and the increase of secularization. The crisis now becomes manifest, which coincides with Nisbet's third phase.

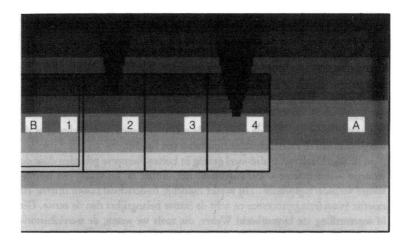

A = system   B = sub-system

1 = first phase: atrophied behaviour in the sub-system
2 = second phase: new behaviour emerges in the system
3 = third phase: crisis in the sub-system, which issues either from the system or the sub-system
4 = fourth phase: the elite introduce innovations in the sub-system

Figure 15. Discontinuity in the pre-industrial city of Sjoberg

Phase 4: The emergence of new structures and values; for example, nationalism as a new integration-ideology.[57] Here an analogy with Nisbet's second and fourth phases can be seen. The resemblance to the manner in which Nisbet analyses the temporal fault line between two static temporal blocks is remarkable. Sjoberg does not apply his transitional scheme to concrete historical situations, as a result of which historiographical problems do not become very prominent in his study. This is not the case in the following author to be discussed, Friedrichs.

Transition in the active sub-system: Friedrichs. Friedrichs's study concerning Nördlingen furnishes an example of discontinuity issuing from an active sub-system. As we know, Friedrichs seeks the transition from feudalism to capitalism for Nördlingen around the end of the seventeenth and the beginning of the eighteenth centuries.

The power of the guilds and artisans in Nördlingen, as present in the late-medieval mode of production, was *abruptly* disrupted from the *outside* at the end of the seventeenth century. This proposition seems disputable at first sight. As early as 1552 Charles V had taken political power in the cities away from the guilds by no longer allowing municipal councils to be elected and having them supplemented by means of co-optation. Furthermore, the artisan guilds came under the supervision of the municipal government. Although artisans could still be members of the town council on their own cognizance during the course of the seventeenth century, at the end of that century this became increasingly rare. This process of internal development apparently does not leave any room for a crisis and hence for a discontinuous conception of change. It seems more likely that we have encountered a gradual change in a continuing entity than a system–sub-system construction in which a sudden novelty has gained ascendancy.

And yet this discontinuity is present. We must look not at the political partial system, but at the ideological one. Even though the late feudal mode of production seems in decline politically, this is certainly not the case ideologically. A communal interest keeps Nördlingen together, a late feudal sub-system, to the end of the seventeenth century. This is clearly expressed when in 1667 the town council forbids the citizens to buy cabinets and drawers outside the city. The argument given is that the citizens: '[. . .] should stand by one another through thick and thin, and must partake of each other's joys and sorrows [and should not] cause any further diminution of each other's livelyhoods, which are already far too difficult to obtain by granting a foreigner their money.'[58] In structuralist-Marxist thought in a feudal formation of society, it is not the economic but the ideological partial system that maintains the feudal-artisan mode of production. Until 1670 the guild economy remained the most important condition for the late feudal formation of society.

After 1670 a crisis developed in the city. The largest textile entre-preneur, Wörner, then increasingly started to make use of the poverty among the wool weavers in order to offer those who could no longer survive independently work in his company. Once they were in his service, he paid a miserly wage for the woven sheets. This led to a revolt of the weavers in 1698. The municipal government decided to intervene on the side of the weavers and founded a co-operative that enabled them to find markets for their products without the intervention of a capitalist entre-preneur. This, however, was the last time that the town council succeeded in maintaining the late medieval economy of the *bürgerliche Nahrung*. In 1712 the co-operative had definitely failed and the town council was forced to recognize the principle of free trade.[59] Friedrichs uses a similar model to that of Stedman Jones. An advanced formation of society, represented here by a mercantile-capitalist and proto-industrial country-side, attacks a feudal-artisan formation of society in the city. The resemblance with Stedman Jones here lies in the opposition between an advanced system and a retarded sub-system. What is different from the case discussed by Stedman Jones is that, the opposition mentioned by Friedrichs clearly issues in a crisis with transitional phases.

The first part of this crisis can best be understood through comparison with the manner in which Nisbet and Sjoberg analyse such weak, discontinuous crises. The first phase of the crisis in Nördlingen occurred in 1667. As the mercantile capitalist mode of production forms a larger threat, traditional values and behaviour are accentuated: the ideology of the *bürgerliche Nahrung* becomes increasingly visible. The second phase is formed by the growing wealth and the stealthy increase in the power of the entrepreneurial families, such as the Troeltschs[60] and the Wörners, in the city. Because the lower layers of the *Bürgerschaft*, in this case the weavers, have the feeling that neither the town council nor the citizenry sufficiently defend their interests and their values, they revolt. The third phase has thereby commenced. The crisis reaches a climax, which leads to the fourth phase. In this phase traditional values and behaviour are strengthened (the co-operative), but finally in 1712 the late-feudal, artisan mode of production definitely disappears. With this the fifth, strongly discontinuous phase – the incorporation of Nördlingen as delayed sub-system in the mercantile capitalist system – has been reached. The result is a new situation in the city itself, in which an extant single class, the *Bürgerschaft*, is divided into an upper- and a lower-middle class. The reinforcement of traditional values and attitudes, as it occurs in Nördlingen, shows similarities to the first phase in Sjoberg's analysis (p. 296); the emergence of a new elite is an element in both Nisbet's fourth phase and Sjoberg's second phase.[61]

From the above it can be deduced that problems with regard to periodization in the systems–sub-systems studies lie largely in the application of transitional phases to concrete historical situations.

Phases and the writing of global history

When discussing the phased models of Rozman and Marx, it was suggested that these have global applications. Further explanation seems necessary.

From a Eurocentric to a global division into temporal phases: Marx. The compounded temporality mentioned in Chapter 8 only becomes completely

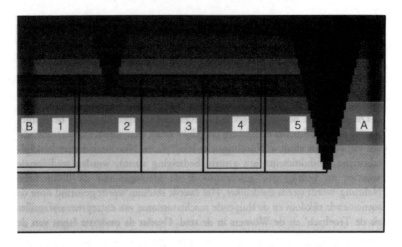

A = system of mercantile capitalist mode of production
B = sub-system of artisan mode of production in Nördlingen
1 = first phase of the crisis: emphasis on the ideology of the *bürgerliche Nahrung*
2 = second phase: increasing wealth and power of the new elite
3 = third phase: revolt of the weavers
4 = fourth phase: reinforcing of traditional values (compare 1)
5 = fifth phase: Nördlingen is incorporated in the mercantile-capitalist system; a new sub-system
    with social differentiation.

Figure 16. Discontinuity in Friedrichs's Nördlingen

clear when we understand Marx's view of the different phases of global history. They have been mentioned earlier: primal communism, the Asiatic mode of production, the ancient slave economy, feudalism, early capitalism, industrial high capitalism, and communism. Yet for the writing of global history, such a periodization is problematic. The Asiatic mode of production does not easily fit in with the other concepts, which are strongly Eurocentric. What is more, Marx distinguishes a German mode of production which accentuates the European bias of his classification.[62] Precisely because global history is so essential to Marxist historical writing, several theoreticians have attempted to globalize Marx's succession of modes of production. To this end, Cohen designed the following universal model of division into phases:[63]

- A pre-class society, without added value production and without classes
- A pre-capitalist class society with small added value production, division of labour and class formation, but still no capitalism. Furthermore, and this is of importance for urban historiography, with cities.

- A capitalist class society with large added value production.
- Finally, a post-capitalist class society with even larger added value production.[64]

Modes of production form the axis on which the formation of societies turns. That is why Marx speaks of *economic* social formations. Another Marxist philosopher, Shaw, elucidates how these modes of production can be fitted into Cohen's scheme. He thereby assumes that Marx wished to design a universal and unilinear development scheme for all world history.[65] Cohen's first phase can be equated to the primal communist mode of production on the basis of Shaw's analysis. The Asiatic and German modes of production form the transition to the second phase, that of the pre-capitalist class society, according to Shaw.[66] By contrast with a multilinear interpretation, the Asiatic mode of production is not positioned as a static non-European economy opposite the dynamic European one, but is placed in one model, hence weakening the dichotomy between European and non-European developments.[67] In the second phase we find two other modes of production, namely: the classical slave economy and medieval feudalism.[68] The third and fourth phases are constituted by capitalism and the classless utopia, respectively.

This globalization of the Marxist classification is possible because all cultural connotations have been left out as criteria. The concept 'mode of production', in the form of an Asiatic and a German mode of production, still had such a connotation. The social-economic criteria of Cohen do not share this connotation. Concepts such as 'class society' and 'capitalism' are, to use the terminology of Marrou and Ricoeur, concepts of the second and third order in which there are no continuing entities with *collective participation* and hence no cultural givens. Continuing entities, *appartenance participative* and the cultures linked to them have, after all, something specific. They therefore obstruct the writing of global history.

Rozman's classification is even more universal than the Marxist one. We shall now see what consequences this has for the writing of global history.

A global temporal arrangement: Rozman.   On the basis of the seven phases of development of urban networks he observed, Rozman displays the recurrent temporal pattern in his temporal classification in the form of a timetable. At issue here is the question of when China, Japan, Russia, England, and France pass through phases B to G. From this we can conclude that some countries go from one phase to another more quickly then others. China starts the B phase as early as in the eighteenth century BC, Japan and Russia in the seventh and ninth centuries AD, respectively, and England and France both in the second century BC. China only reaches phase G in the sixteenth century AD; for Russia and Japan this occurs in respectively the seventeenth and eighteenth centuries, while England and France again achieve this phase simultaneously in the sixteenth to seventeenth centuries.

Rozman's phases of urban development in five countries

Phase	China	Japan	Russia	England	France
B	18th cent. BC	7th cent. AD	9th cent. AD	2nd cent. BC	2nd cent. BC
C	8th cent. BC	–	–	–	–
D	3rd cent. BC	8th cent. AD	11th cent. AD	1st cent. AD	1st cent. AD
E	8th cent. AD	13th cent. AD	15th cent. AD	10th cent. AD	10th cent. AD
F	11th cent. AD	15th cent. AD	16th cent. AD	12th cent. AD	12th cent. AD
G	16th cent. AD	17th cent. AD	18th cent. AD	16/17th cent. AD	16/17th cent. AD

Source: G. Rozman, 'Urban networks and historical stages', *Journal of Interdisciplinary History* 9(1) (Summer 1978): 79.

Four development patterns can be derived from these data:

1. A large number of societies in the world – especially in Africa – have no completed urban networks (stopped before phase G).
2. China, although it started early – at least 1500 years earlier than the others – grows very slowly.
3. Western Europe is less slow than China, but slower than Russia and Japan.
4. Russia and Japan have the quickest urban development, but they still cannot succeed in catching up with Western Europe, which develops very quickly in the E, F and G phases.[69]

Therefore an important conclusion may be that a global model of temporal arrangement does not always lead – as in the case of Sjoberg – to the discovery of similarities. Such a model can also show large differences between various regions.

Not only does Rozman try to apply the phases of his model to several countries, he also tries to explain that the traditional forms of periodization in urban history are inadequate: 'Given the different dates when cities originated in various countries and variations in observed rates of change, no simple chronological classification would be satisfactory.'[70] Because cities and systems of cities emerge at different moments in time, a purely chronological description of urban development is grossly inadequate. It is, after all, incorrect, according to Rozman, to compare two cities at the same moment in time, when one city is the product of a 500-year-old process of urbanization and the other city is the result of a thousand-year-old development of the urban hierarchy. 'For a temporal classification the focus on national urban systems promises to be a truer reflexion of changing patterns than the more haphazard choice of individual cities.'[71] Hence Rozman is explicitly concerned with a culture-transcending, universal, phased model. In its construction he notes that different countries are in different phases at the same moment, and on this basis he concludes that comparison on the basis of 'ordinary' chronological time is inadequate.

The most important conclusion of the last two chapters must be that a subjectifying temporality also yields a subjectifying temporal classification (periodization) and that an objectifying temporality leads to an objectifying temporal classification (phases). The extent of *collective participation* and its formulation, usually in the form of ideal types, play an important role in the subjectifying temporal classification. They give subjectifying temporality an undulating nature, which makes a sharp temporal delimitation more difficult. The coupling of subjectifying temporality to continuing entities also causes subjectifying temporality, to make the writing of global history more difficult. Objectifying time leads to a mostly-static conception of time, in which time can be divided into distinct phases, but in which most of the problems are transferred to the transitional phases. Because objectifying time does not presuppose continuing entities with collective participation, this form of temporal classification is far more suitable for the writing of global history.[72]

It will hopefully have become clear that subjectifying temporality, and the periodization ensuing from it, issues from a method of explanation best clarified in the form of a relatively-closed system construction. For objectifying temporality, something similar holds. This issues from a method of explanation that can be explained as a half-open system construction. The relatively-closed and half-open system constructions emerge from a dichotomous and a complementary method of definition, respectively. The different methods of definition, explanation, conception and classification of time can also be made visible by looking at the comparative methods used by historians. Comparison, however, has been left out of this study.[73]

Notes

1. J. Huizinga, 'Het probleem der Renaissance', in idem, *Verzamelde Werken* 4 (Cultuurgeschiedenis II) (Haarlem 1949), p. 270.
2. A. D. Hall, 'Some fundamental concepts of systems engineering', in S. L. Optner (ed.), *Systems analysis* (Harmondsworth 1973), pp. 110–11.
3. S. M. Blumin, *The urban threshold. Growth and change in a nineteenth-century American community* (Chicago 1976), p. 42.
4. Ibid., pp. 183–8.
5. Ibid., pp. 126 ff.
6. Ibid., p. 218.
7. Ibid., p. 220.
8. P. Ricoeur, *Temps et récit* Tome I (Paris 1983), pp. 275–6.
9. Richard L. Merrit, 'The emergence of American nationalism: a quantitative approach', *American Quarterly* XVII (1965): 319–35 and *Symbols of American community 1735–1775* (New Haven, CT 1966). See also R. F. Berkhofer jr, *A behavioral approach to historical analysis* (New York, London 1969), pp. 232–4.
10. M. Walker, *German home towns. Community, state and general estate 1648–1871* (London 1971), pp. 22–4.
11. Ibid., pp. 68–9.
12. Ibid., p. 69.
13. Ibid., pp. 137 ff., 310–48.
14. M. Weber, *WL*, 191.
15. M. Weber, *WuG*, 736.
16. Ibid., p. 731.
17. Ibid.
18. R. P. Appelbaum, *Theories of social change* (Boston 1970), pp. 101–15.
19. M. Weber, 'Agrarverhältenissen in Altertum', in *SWG*, pp. 35–45.
20. J. H. J. Van der Pot, *De periodisering der geschiedenis. Een overzicht der theorieën* [The periodization of history. An overview of the theories] (The Hague 1951), p. 17.
21. J. Huizinga, *Cultuurhistorische verkenningen* [Explorations in cultural history] (Haarlem 1929), p. 72. See also J. Romein's criticism of it in his 'Het onvoltooide verleden' [The incomplete past], in: *Cultuurhistorische studies* (2nd edition; Amsterdam 1948), p. 75 and onwards. The philosopher of history Van der Dussen agrees with Huizinga. He also does not think too much importance should be given to periodization: 'De nieuwe AGN: een speculatieve totaalvisie

in een eigentijdse verpakking', *Bijdragen en mededelingen voor de geschiedenis der Nederlanden* 97(1) (1982): 15–16.

22. J. Huizinga, *Cultuurhistorische verkenningen*, p. 79.

23. L. Dorsman, 'Periodisering als integrale benadering: Nederlandse historici in het Fin-de-Siècle' [Periodization as an integral approach: Dutch historians in the fin de siécle], *Theoretische geschiedenis* 16(3) (1989): 277–96, esp. 279.

24. It is worth noting that Van der Pot distinguishes two different forms of periodization in a manner analogous to that used here. He signifies these with the terms: ideographic and nomothetic. The temporal classifications used here on the basis of a subjectifying and an objectifying temporality differ from Van der Pot's classification, yet they have their respectively hermeneutic and positivistic origins in common.

25. There are, however, a great number of articles, chapters or contributions to compilations and encyclopedias on this subject. See E. D. Abegg, 'The trait-dominance theory of historical periodization', *Journal of Critical Analysis* 3 (1972): 188–98; W. Bahner (ed.), *Renaissance, Barock, Aufklärung, Epochen und Periodisierungsfragen* (Kronberg 1976); K. H. Blaschke, 'Die periodisierung der Landesgeschichte', *Blätter für deutsche Landesgeschichte* 106 (1970): 76–93; J. Burckhardt, *Die Entstehung der modernen Jahrhundertrechnung* (Göppingen 1972). See also: A. Wirshi-Nernz's review in: *History and Theory* 13 (1974): 181–9; E. Engelberg, 'Zur methodologischen Problemen der Periodisierung', *Zeitschrift für Geschichtwissenschaft* 19 (1971): 1919–50; E. Engelberg (ed.), *Probleme der Geschichtsmethodologie* (Berlin 1972): 121–54; D. Gerhard, 'Periodization in history', in Ch. Perelman (ed.), *Les catégories en histoire* (Brussels 1969), pp. 41–56; A. Momigliano, 'Time in ancient historiography', in: *History and the concept of time, Beiheft 6 of History and Theory* (1966): 1–23; G. W. Wallis, 'Chronopolitics: the impact of time perspectives on the dynamics of change', *Social Forces* 49 (1970): 102–8; J. Topolski, *Methodology of history* (Dordrecht 1976), pp. 593–6. With regard to Dutch history Van der Woude has attempted to rejuvenate the periodization of the early-modern time. See: A. M. van der Woude, 'De "Nieuwe Geschiedenis" in een nieuwe gedaante' ["Modern history" in a new guise] in *De algemene geschiedenis der Nederlanden* (abbr. *AGN*) 5 (Haarlem 1980), pp. 9–36.

26. The complete quotation is as follows: 'ob man bei den Periodisierungen die grossen soziologischen, *dauernden Lebenformen* [italics

HJ] zugrunde legen soll, die wohl selbst geistig bedingt sein mögen, die aber, so lange sie dauern, ihrer seits das geistige Leben formen und bestimmen, Wirkungsmöglichkeiten und Wirkungsrichtungen entscheiden, oder ob man von den letzten und tiefsten geistigen Einstellungen der Perioden ausgehen soll, die auch schon der soziologischen Gestaltung wenigstens mit zugrunde liegen und die treibenden Einheitskräfte darstellen'. See: E. Troeltsch, 'Der Historismus und seine Probleme; erstes Buch: Das logische Problem der Geschischtsphilosophie', in: *Gesammelte Schriften* III (abbr. *GS*) (Tübingen 1922), p. 731.

27. E. Troeltsch, 'Der Historismus und seine Probleme', *GS*, p. 756. The different terms that Troeltsch uses for the *Unterbauten* can also be found at *GS* pp. 747, 755–6.

28. E. Troeltsch, 'Der Historismus und seine Probleme', *GS*, pp. 748–56. See also: J. H. J. van der Pot, *De periodisering der geschiedenis*, pp. 87–8. Note that Troeltsch's *Dauerformen* also have *Wirkungsmöglichkeiten* and *Wirkungsrichtungen*. They can act, and hence coincide with Mandelbaum's continuing entities.

29. See also: J. H. J. Van der Pot, *De periodisering der geschiedenis*, pp. 33–4. Van der Pot even goes so far as to consider a close relationship between an aspect of life or a partial system on the basis of which a historian arranges time, and his attitude to life. A Christian should choose a religious, a historic materialist an economic aspect.

30. E. Troeltsch, 'Der Historismus und seine Probleme', *GS*, pp. 748 and 754.

31. J. H. J. Van der Pot, *De periodisering der geschiedenis*, pp. 94–112 and 181–201.

32. R. F. Berkhofer, *A behavioral approach to historical analysis* (New York, London 1969), p. 227.

33. Ibid., p. 228.

34. L. Dorsman, 'Periodisering als integrale benadering', p. 283. He speaks of a 'common program', which is linked to his more-'stylized' approach, based on the history of art, to the problem of periodization.

35. Ibid., pp. 282–3.

36. Ibid., p. 292.

37. L. Mumford, *The city in history, origins, its transformation and its prospects* (Harmondsworth 1979 [London 1961]), p. 292.

38. Ibid., pp. 469–70. See also: F. Braudel, *Beschaving, economie, en kapitalisme (15de–18de eeuw)* I (Amsterdam 1988), p. 503. Braudel claims a somewhat too-simple relationship between cities and capitalism for Mumford. He interprets Mumford's image of the

cuckoo's egg as too large a product for too small a city. The metaphor of the cuckoo's egg, however, has the stronger connotation of an alien element. See also: L. Mumford, *The city in history*, p. 472.

39. R. F. Berkhofer, *A behavioral approach to historical analysis*, p. 226.

40. In the case of Ankersmit, the names of periods form the main ingredient of his narrative substances. He, too, observes that the same names can be flags for totally different loads. He even couples a complete subjectification of history to this observation. However, he loses sight of the fact that his conception of narrative substances is based on what Marrou and Ricoeur called second- and third-order historical concepts. They are not at all representative for the whole body of historical writing and all concepts it contains. Moreover, it is by no means certain that the interpretation of the historian may not be based on pre-scientific notions such as actually existed in a certain place and time in the past. This is a comprehensible viewpoint that Huizinga, Mandelbaum and others adhere to. Mandelbaum opposes an idealistic conception of historical writing and hence also an idealistic periodization: F. R. Ankersmit, *Narrative logic. A semantic analysis of the historian's language* (Meppel 1981), pp. 174, 185; M. Mandelbaum, *The anatomy of historical knowledge* (Baltimore, MD and London 1977), pp. 115–16, 163–6; and J. Huizinga, 'Het probleem der renaissance', p. 232.

41. M. Weber, 'Die nichtlegitime Herrschaft (Typologie der Städte)', in *WuG*, p. 728.

42. M. Weber, 'Agrarverhältenissen im Altertum', in *SWG*, pp. 35–45.

43. G. Abramowski, *Das Geschichtsbild Max Webers. Universalgeschichte am Leitfaden des Okzidentalen Rationalisierungsprozesses* (Stuttgart 1966), pp. 106–7.

44. E. Troeltsch, 'Der Historismus und seine Probleme', *GS*, pp. 706–7. See also: J. H. J. Van der Pot, *De periodisering der geschiedenis*, pp. 5 and 237.

45. See also: Benevolo's *The history of the city* (Cambridge, MA 1980).

46. Mumford uses the term 'baroque' city in a general historical sense. Benevolo uses it in the more conventional meaning from the history of art. See also G. A. Hoekveld *et al.*, *Geografie van stad en platteland in de westerse landen* (Bussum 1978), Chapter 4: 'De historische stad', pp. 80 ff.

47. In some ways Benevolo's classification is different from Mumford's. In Benevolo's *The history of the city* two chapters (7 and 8), for example, are devoted to the 'renaissance' city, an urban type not present in Mumford. Mumford summarizes the developments of the

nineteenth-century city in the ideal type 'Coketown', while Benevolo still distinguishes two types of city in the nineteenth century, namely the 'liberal' and the 'post-liberal' city.

48. Mumford, *The city in history*, p. 8. Benevolo, who has written a study similar to Mumford's, says unabashedly that cities as 'man-made environment' can primarily be found in Europe, because the idea of the city as 'an integral and self-contained unit' first emerged there, L. Benevolo, *The history of the city*, p. 5.

49. 'The antecedent state does not produce the subsequent one; the relation between them is exclusively chronological': R. Nisbet, 'Introduction: the problem of social change', in R. Nisbet (ed.), *Social change* (New York, Evanston, IL, San Francisco, London 1972), p. 24.

50. Compare this to the quotation from Berkhofer on page 285 (Note 33). The contrast should be evident.

51. Quoted from: R. Nisbet, 'Introduction: the problem of social change', p. 24.

52. H. Lefebvre, *La pensée marxiste et la ville* (Paris 1972), p. 79.

53. The addition of 'in half-open system constructions' is important because a relatively-closed system construction with a continuous undulating temporality can also be read into Marx's texts. In the previous chapter, we have seen how Avineri gave such a temporal interpretation of Marx.

54. The study by De Vries shows a phased temporality on the basis of qualified differences with a weak form of discontinuity; the work of Lampard shows a phased temporality based on parameters and hence displays strong discontinuity.

55. R. Nisbet, 'Introduction: the problem of social change', p. 29. It is curious here that Nisbet uses Weber as example of an author who attaches much importance to external changes, while Marx acts as an adherent of internal processes of change. He argues that Weber attributes economic behaviour (i.e. capitalist behaviour) to a non-economic factor, namely religion, in this case Calvinism. Marx sees the genesis of capitalism in feudalism, which can be considered an economic system. As for Weber, I consider Nisbet's view incorrect; as for Marx, I find his opinion fairly meaningless. Nisbet does not see that there is no opposition of economy and religion as separate systems in Weber. They are only partial systems for him, which form part of one system: the *Entzauberungs* process of European culture. Although Nisbet himself advocates a half-open system approach in which changes come from outside, he considers Marx's temporal

conception an ideal-typical construction (as Avineri advocated in the previous chapter). We know that there is also a completely different notion of how Marx constructs time, namely that of the compounded time (of half-open systems), which I will examine when dealing with Friedrichs's study of Nördlingen. There, too, changes come from outside.

56. R. Nisbet, 'Introduction: the problem of social change', p. 30.

57. G. Sjoberg, 'Cities in developing and industrial societies: a cross cultural analysis', in Ph. M. Hauser and L. F. Schnore (eds), *The study of urbanization* (New York, London 1967 1st edition 1965), pp. 213–63, esp. 224.

58. C. R. Friedrichs, 'Capitalism, mobility, and class formation in the early modern German city', in Ph. Abrams and E. A. Wrigley (eds), *Towns in societies, essays in economic history and historiographical sociology* (Cambridge, MA and London), p. 199.

59. Ibid., pp. 200–1.

60. Not to be confused with the previously-mentioned Ernst Troeltsch.

61. Smelser's *Social change in the industrial revolution. An application of theory to the Lancashire cotton industry 1770–1840*, 4th edn (London 1974) is a clear example of an explanatory transitional study. Because I have restricted myself to urban historiography in this chapter, an analysis of Smelser's work has been left out. With regard to the analysis of Friedrichs's transition it should be noted that the latter was concerned with a transition which started in the macrosystem and was actively opposed by the Nördlingen sub-system. Smelser deals with a transition that started in the sub-system and after several phases was taken over by the system.

62. Nevertheless, in his earlier writings Marx seems a proponent for a move towards a universal world history on realistic grounds. In the 'Deutsche Ideologie' he at first does not consider capitalism as a mode of production, but as a continuing entity supported by the bourgeoisie. This capitalism develops as *ständisches kapital* in medieval cities. Next it evolves into mercantile capital in the Western European nations. Finally it conquers the world as industrial capital. Capitalism as a continuing entity thereby disappears and Eurocentric history becomes world history. 'Die grosse Industrie universalisierte trotz dieser Schutzmittel die Konkurrenz [. . .], stellte die Kommunikationsmittel und den moderne Weltmarkt her, unterwarf sich den Handel, verwandelte alles Kapital in industrielles Kapital und erzeugte damit die rasche Zirkulation und Zentralisation der Kapitalien [. . .]. Sie erzeugte insoweit erst die Weltgeschichte, als sie jede

zivilisierte nation und jedes Individuum darin in der Befriedigung seiner Bedürfnisse von der ganzen Welt abhängig machte und die bisherige naturwüchsige Ausschliesslichkeit einzelner Nationen [continuing entities! HJ] vernichtete [. . .]. Sie erzeugte im Allgemeinen überall dieselben Verhältnisse zwischen den Klassen der Gesellschaft und vernichtete dadurch der besonderheit der einzelnen Nationalitäten': K. Marx, 'Deutsche Ideologie I. Feuerbach', in *MEW* 3, pp. 50–61 (see especially 52 and 60).

63. G. McLennan, *Marxism and the methodologies of history* (London 1981), p. 57; H. Van den Belt, 'De reconstructie van het historisch materialisme', in *Ter elfder ure* 27(2) (series number 34 Geschiedtheorie 2, 1983): 508.

64. G. A. Cohen, *Karl Marx's theory of history: a defence* (Oxford 1978), p. 198.

65. W. H. Shaw, *Marx's theory of history* (London 1978), pp. 118–19.

66. Ibid., pp. 118–29, especially 125.

67. This diverges from Marx's intentions because he – like most nineteenth-century scholars – considered the Asiatic mode of production typically static.

68. Ibid., pp. 128–38.

69. G. Rozman, *Urban networks in Russia 1750–1800 and premodern periodization* (Princeton, NJ 1976), pp. 238–62, and idem, 'Urban networks and historical stages', *Journal of Interdisciplinary History* 9(1) (Summer 1978): 65–91.

70. Ibid., p. 74.

71. Ibid.

72. It should be noted here that system–sub-system studies are perhaps more suited for the writing of global history, but that they are also less synthesizing than studies based on a continuing entity.

73. See for this: H. S. J. Jansen, 'De voorwerpen van vergelijking. Op zoek naar een nieuwe vergelijkingstypologie', *Tijdschrift voor Geschiedenis* 110 (1997): 329–56 and idem, 'Het vergelijken vergeleken. Skocpol and Goldstone', *Theoretische Geschiedenis* 24(3) (1997): 289–304.

-11-

Conclusion

Relatively-closed and half-open systems

Two traditions catch the eye in the historian's conception of urban phenomena. In the first one urban phenomena are conceived of in *opposition* to other phenomena, especially the countryside; the other tradition is marked by complementary definition.[1] In the latter case urban phenomena are studied in their relation to other, sometimes non-urban, forms of society.

Contrasting or dichotomizing definitions entail that some phenomena are and others are not absorbed in the configuration to be studied. Ideal types are the clearest examples of such dichotomizing concepts. Weber's classical polis is an ideal type for cities in antiquity, the cohesion of which is constituted on the basis of locality and military-civilian citizenship, a cohesion that the Asian city lacks. By placing dichotomizing concepts or ideal types at the beginning- and end-points of the history of a first-order entity, in this case a city or a city type, possible lines of development in the process become visible. Through comparison of the ancient polis with the medieval cities, in which the latter are characterized by the formation of local communities primarily on the basis of economic citizenship, a development from classical to medieval life can be sketched.

Complementary definitions, in addition to a description of the phenomenon to be examined, also give the context in which the phenomenon occurs. Just as polders exist by grace of dikes, a belt canal and a drainage system, the context of a historical phenomenon yields the conditions for its existence.

Methods of definition are not only instruments available to historians for synthesizing the past. Explanation, comparison,[2] time conception and temporal arrangement are also at their disposal.

I have appealed to systems theory in order to make the tools of synthesis visible. Systems theory, after all, explicitly occupies itself with relationships between the part and the whole and the mutual relationships of parts. Synthesis, of course, has everything to do with such relationships.

The results of specialized historical research must be placed in larger wholes or mutually related. Systems theory also has the great advantage that it can transcend the gap between the physical sciences and the humanities. As such it is an even more universal *tertium* (the whole of the cognitive rules with which knowledge of reality can be gained, or in any case by which knowledge about reality can be communicated) than concepts from the philosophy of language such as metaphor, intrigue or representation.[3]

Two types of systems prove to correspond quite strongly to the paradigms of synthesis, as can be expected on the basis of the two traditions of conception mentioned earlier. The dichotomous conception of cities and urban phenomena fits a relatively-closed systems construction, and a complementary conception fits the half-open system. These two systems do not concern, as will be clear to the reader, urban phenomena in reality, but the manner in which urban historians conceive the objects of their study. The closed and half-open systems serve as meta-theoretical models with which the theories and argumentations used by urban historians in their treatment of reality can be run to ground and tested as to their synthesizing value.

Closed systems achieve this by treating developments in the past as long as long tubes consisting of several layers and possessing an entrance and an exit. As was noted above, the entrance and exit consist of dichotomizing concepts, often in the form of ideal types. The tube itself constitutes the possible developments of cities or aggregations of cities. The layers in the tube form the different aspects – demographic, economic, social, political and so on – that are important in urban development and that must be brought together in one composition by synthesis. The tube is not a static affair, but is marked by a continuous stream of, shall we say, 'light impulses', which move from the entrance to the exit. Depending on how the entrance of the closed system is programmed, these impulses in the tube will cause some events, – heterogeneous affairs such as actors, goals of actions and instruments of action, circumstances and unintended consequences of actions – to be illuminated.[4] The programming of the input also determines to a great extent in which layers most of the events will appear. If the substructure is heavily emphasized in the programming, many events in the domains of economy, ecology and demographics will be illuminated. If input is programmed by historians who attach much value to phenomena in the superstructure, then mainly political or cultural–mental phenomena will be drawn out.

The entrance of the tube is not the only important factor for the question of which events the light will fall upon; the exit also plays an important role. The end of the tube actually functions with regard to certain events as the kind of antenna that catches light signals and amplifies them. Leaving these technological metaphors behind, this means that the entrance shapes certain ideologies and values of the historian in his illumination of the past, and that the exit, in addition to the values mentioned, also embodies a finalistic element. This finalism warrants some explanation. The historian knows more about the ending of events than the actors did in the past itself. The end-point of the historical process he describes will also determine which events in that process deserve more or less attention. Such a finalism is inevitable, and is an underlying presence in many forms of historical writing. It should be noted that input and output do not completely determine the historian's account of the past. Rather they give several possibilities, several hypotheses regarding the course of events. For the representation of the 'actual' course of events, a precise analysis of the facts and their intentional and causal links is necessary.

Closedness and internalization do not imply that every external influence on urban development is absent, but that one tries in principle to explain the phenomenon through the construction of an internal intentional–causal series. Weber's singular causal imputation is one of the most obvious examples of this methodology. Internal explanations form the normal pattern of explanation, and external ones the extraordinary patterns of explanation. External explanations are usually only called in when the internal causal chain is no longer capable of explaining certain events. The aid of external factors must in any case be called in at the entrance of a closed system. Sometimes internal causes underlie external influences. A clear example of this is Jan Romein's thesis concerning the dialectics of progress. At the end of the eighteenth century, the Dutch Republic was unable to change its constitution. The help of revolutionary France was needed, according to Romein, to revive the Dutch nation. In those cases where an internal development does not succeed in passing certain limits, the breakthrough to more modern situations must be created through external influences.[5] Finally, the philosopher of history Mandelbaum has observed that in those constructions that I have called closed systems and that are comparable to what he calls 'continuing entities' changes can indeed originate outside the system, but that there must always be an internalization of such externally-generated changes.[6] By this he means that this form of synthesis concerns itself with the meaning of external events for the internal course of development of a historical entity.

Historians working with a relatively-closed system construction must take some precautions against making excessively clear-cut representations of affairs. The initial model and the final model of an entity should therefore on the one hand show similarities and on the other show clear differences. The similarities make it clear that the identity is the same; the differences enforce the explication of a process. The separate events between both ideal types thus receive their meaning in the light of the ideal type at the beginning or the end of that process. Thus the closed-system construction becomes the methodological *instrumentarium* of what Ricoeur has called the *mise en intrigue* (emplotment).[7] This also yields the possibility that, for example, economic facts at a certain moment may converge with the final model, while social and political events that take place at the same time fit better with the composition of the initial model. This implies a great deal of heterogeneity of events, which is homogenized by the overall development, the intrigue.[8] Because the whole process issues in an end model, the old finally will make way for the new in all domains. Events are in this way given a unique non-linear course. That is why Ricoeur calls these unique continuing entities 'quasi-personages'.

Because compositions are used that can disintegrate and reintegrate or vice versa – in particular *appartenance participative* can increase and decrease – the finality also loses its linear directness, and historical processes take the form of tidal movement. This implies that time often manifests itself as a movement of growth, flowering and decay and that no sharp breaks can be distinguished. Drawing the boundaries of periods is hence always subject to a certain whimsy. In order to prevent the mist of periodization from growing too large, urban historians often orient themselves on commonly-used and hence more-familiar periodizations, such as those of countries and cultural regions. The traditional periodization into ancient times, the Middle Ages, early-modern and modern times is also often used in close-system constructions.

The half-open system model can be considered the counterpart of the relatively-closed system model. Half-open systems can, as I have noted above, be compared to polders, which are connected to their environment by means of canals. Just as polders can be distinguished from their environment by their dikes, the dikes ensure that the polders are not completely isolated from the environment. Various external influences can affect life in the polder. By systematically letting water in one can determine which vegetation will and which will not flourish in the polder. An irrigation system in this manner determines a number of things that can occur in a polder. Half-open systems owe their name to the fact on the one hand they have a clear boundary with their environment, but on the other they are continually subject to its influence. The effect of the environment on the (half-open) system hence occurs so systematically

Conclusion

that in systems theory the system is often 'demoted' to sub-system and the environment is 'promoted' to system.

Half-open systems concern themselves with a form of synthesis in which various urban phenomena of the sub-system are confronted with more or less familiar correlations in the system. Thus Sjoberg seeks the correlated characteristics of the pre-industrial city by placing it in the context of the more or less familiar patterns of pre-industrial societies. The pre-industrial city forms the sub-system; the pre-industrial society forms the system. The urban phenomena being examined are then explained by placing them in a general pattern, a system. The explanation emerges by answering the question of how they are possible. If we express our surprise regarding the fact that, in old cities, the stately manors of the elite can be found in the vicinity of the church and the town hall, while the very poorest often took up residence in the arches of the city walls, then we can answer that the relationship between techniques of transportation and power in pre-industrial societies leads to such a use of space. The elite, after all, want to be close to the centres of power because of limited transportation.

This implies that changes in the sub-system are usually effected in one or the other way from outside, that is to say: through the operation of the system on the sub-system. The use of space in pre-industrial cities (the sub-system) mentioned above changes because technological changes occur in society as a whole (the system). As a result of improvement in transportation techniques, the rich no longer need to live in the city centre, and they therefore move to the more pleasant environment of suburbia. Usually such explanations are made by correlating phenomena in the sub-system with general social phenomena that are familiar from other studies. This 'normal' system – sub-system construction is marked by a static and anti-finalistic nature. The explanations are retrodictive in nature, reasoning backwards from the sub-system to the system.

This does not mean that sub-systems should merely reflect those correlations found in the system. This is only the case in a 'normal' course of affairs. The sub-systems can also diverge from the system, although they do remain closely linked to it. In the case of such internal changes, the author will give more attention to the divergent pattern. London as a nineteenth-century sub-system shows, in the representation of Stedman Jones, clear divergences from the English capitalist system, because its production sector was still marked by artisanship and small-scale industry. Precisely, this divergent behaviour of London – a divergence that can predominantly be explained in terms of internal factors, such as a traditionalistic attitude amongst artisan entrepreneurs – plays a central

Conclusion

role in Jones's study. Despite this internal divergence London remains closely linked to the English industrial-capitalist system, because it is its political and commercial centre. The same can be said of the social, political and ideological aspects of the London sub-system *vis-à-vis* the English system. The possibility of divergent behaviour of the sub-system makes it clear that, in addition to passive sub-systems, active ones are also possible.

The static and retrodictive nature of half-open system constructions lead to a discontinuous conception of temporality. Different compositions alternate with one another. If there is a strong divergence of the sub-system from the general pattern, compound time emerges. Simultaneous non-simultaneity here, in contrast to what happens in closed-system constructions, is not homogenized. The phase in which the sub-system is runs either ahead of or behind that of the system in such a conception of temporality. Thus London in Jones's opinion (partly) forms a socio-economically retarded sub-system *vis-à-vis* an advanced capitalist system.

This implies for temporal classification that blocks of almost immobile temporality are alternated with moments of crisis. These blocks of time form phases with sharp breaks. The phases drive their characteristics from globally-applicable theories (such as those of certain forms of Marxism), through which traditionalism and Eurocentrism in periodization can be avoided.

Theoreticians and philosophers such as Weber, Berkhofer, Mandelbaum, Von Wright, Topolski and Ricoeur have all made important contributions to the construction of the *instrumentarium* for synthesis mentioned above. The use of concepts such as 'continuing entities', 'appartenance participative' and 'quasi-personage' would have been inconceivable without the work of Mandelbaum and Ricoeur. I am indebted to Berkhofer and Talcott Parsons for the terms 'closed' and 'open systems'. Other systems theoreticians have expanded the arsenal of systems significantly. Concepts such as 'black boxes', 'structural systems' and 'performance systems' spring to mind. I am pre-eminently indebted to Weber. Far earlier than Mandelbaum and Ricoeur he used terms such as 'ideal types', 'continuing entities', 'participatory belonging' and 'first-order entities' or their equivalents for his practical research and the theoretical contemplation of it. With his explanation of the singular causal imputation, he has anticipated Dray's explanatory model of a continuous series.[9]

What is new about the closed system is not the concepts of which it is composed, but their concentration in one construction. Because of this construction, a coherent and pragmatic instrument for synthesis has been created, with which the extant somewhat chaotic instruments of synthesis can be improved.

The half-open system construction is not mentioned anywhere in critical analytic philosophy of history. Notions from systems theory are used now and again, but not moulded in the form of a consistent *instrumentarium* for synthesis. In urban historiography itself, however, the half-open system is a common tool. Usually it is only applied to yield explanations. Other possibilities for synthesis, such as temporality and temporal classification, are barely used. In the above I have attempted to clarify their longer reach.

By the systems-theoretical analysis of urban historiography I hope to have constructed clear (ideal) types of historical thinking. In doing this I hope also to have awakened the slumbering forces of synthesis.

Complementarities

In Chapter 9 I observed two possible readings of Braudel and Marx. This seems to indicate that, despite differences, there are no great contradictions between the relatively-closed and half-open systems approaches in urban historiography.

In the preceding chapter I noted that closed systems pass through stages of additivity. During such a stage of incoherence, a relatively-closed system can easily be seen as a half-open system.

In the same chapter I also observed that relatively-closed systems received their temporal arrangement from superordinate continuing entities. The German home towns derived their periodization from the temporal arrangement of German history. Weber's Asiatic, classical, and medieval cities already indicated in their names the importance of a European non-urban periodization. This phenomenon indicates that relatively-closed system constructions with their diachronous nature need to be complemented with synchronous constructions similar to half-open systems. After all, reference to higher entities for temporal classification creates a construction similar to the system–sub-system relationship.

The reverse is also the case: the use of phases of weak discontinuity, such as can be seen in the work of Nisbet and Sjoberg, to distinguish transitional phases; or maybe, to go even further, the need for phases in general, points to the necessity of discerning diachronous phenomena in synchronous half-open system constructions.[10] This all illustrates the complementary nature of both systems constructions.[11]

Ankersmit also seems to discover a kind of complementarity between synchronous and diachronous historical practice. He considers synchronicity to be constituted by Ranke's adage that 'Every epoch is immediate to God' [jede Epoche ist unmitelbar zu Gott] and diachronicity by the notion that history always pertains to a 'a whole in a process of becoming' [*werdendes Ganze*]. Ankersmit's complementarity and mine can be compared because both cases concern supplementary phenomena between diachronous and synchronous forms of history. They can also be compared in another sense. Ankersmit seeks complementarity in the conception of historistic individuality. He thereby regrets that historists associate objects in the past with individualities and not with historical interpretations.[12] I agree with Ankersmit that there we are concerned with a complementarity of methods of interpretation; after all, my systems are almost nothing more than conceptual constructs. I do suppose, in contrast to Ankersmit, that these conceptual constructs can have many relationships with systems existing in reality.

There is, however, a more significant difference between my notion of complementarity and that of Ankersmit. Referring to conceptions of historistic individuality, as is done by Ankersmit, does not explain the complementarity nature of diachronous and synchronous forms of historical writing. The fact that both synchronous and diachronous forms of historical practice show an identical conception of individuality indicates narrative kinship, but not the adstruction of complementarity. Only the examination of the *infrastructural* logic of diachronous and synchronous historical writing in the form of relatively-closed and half-open system constructions, such as has been essayed in this study, gives insight into this complementarity.

What is the meaning of such a more structural complementarity? First, the observation that diachronous and synchronous historical writing are not identical, but essentially different. This does not become as clear if we only examine the narrative superstructure. Ankersmit therefore does not recognize any positivistic elements in synchronous historical writing, while I consider these elements rather strongly present. Ankersmit's bestowal of historic individualism on both the diachronous and the synchronous writing of history merely leads to the equivalence of both historiographical forms. However, if we devote attention to the logical infrastructure, the differences between a great number of synchronous and diachronous forms of historical writing become much clearer. In Ankersmit's case, identity occurs by grace of the datum that they belong to the same theoretical scientific pattern of thought. This is much less so in my case. I admit that some forms of historical writing are more positivistic and others more hermeneutic, or rather more interpretative, than others. However, these do not, in my opinion, exclude each other, as many philosophers of history claim, but are complementary to one another.

Conclusion

For historical writing, both participation and distance are necessary. Even though relatively-closed historical writing, with its dominant action component, shows strong subjectifying[13] participatory tendencies, its finalism indicates the distance of the historian. *Per contra*, it is true that the distance of the system–sub-system construction founders if the sub-system is characterized as being completely dependent on the system. The sub-system has its own identity, in which, in the case of abnormalistic explanations, even individualizing and therefore subjectifying aspects are involved. Consider what was said earlier regarding the traditionalistic mentality of artisan entrepreneurs in Stedman Jones's London.

The complementary nature of both forms of historical writing accentuates the value of holding the theoretical debate (on the nature of historical writing) not only on the basis of the context of justification or the context of persuasion, but also and especially on the basis of the context of discovery. In particular, the exclusive application of the context of justification has a tendency to deny the complementary nature of positivistic and hermeneutic historical writing. To state this even more strongly: a sharp contrast between positivism and hermeneutics has always been put forward from that context.

All this means that, in addition to a debate in the philosophy of history concerning the nature of the historical sciences, positivist, hermeneutic, narrativist or whatever, research should be conducted on the logic of positivism, hermeneutics and so on as they manifest themselves in historiography itself. Research in domains other than urban historiography will be needed for that. Attention to comparative history and the logic behind it is also important in this context.

On the one side, complementarity does not mean that every historical study should use a closed-system as well as a half-open system approach in order to be an optimal historical work. On the other side, complementarity makes it possible for one historical narrative to contain both more actionist-diachronous approaches and, alternating with more theoretically-oriented synchronous approaches. Thus completing the history of Nördlingen, as it is described by Friedrichs, with Mack Walker's home-town approach does not seem very difficult to me. The explanation of the emergence of the *petite bourgeoisie* then takes on a multi-causal guise, in which in addition to the formation of the patricate, bureaucratism, and nineteenth-century liberalism, a larger role would be given to mercantile capitalism than it is now given in Walker's book.

The importance of such thinking in terms of complementarity does not even have to remain restricted to the historical sciences. I would like to make some basically speculative remarks concerning this – speculative because I do not make them with any specific presumptions. In many sciences one scientific model is chosen. For example, in the medical sciences the positivist scientific model is so dominant that in most cases the patient is not considered to be a sick person, but a case of illness. Without wishing to advance a plea for various 'alternative' quackish panaceas, more attention and empathy for the patient and his or her total psychological-biological well-being in the regular medical sciences would be commendable. Because she is open towards various models of the sciences, the muse Clio could serve as a paradigm for other, rather more one-sided sciences.

The problem of the complementarity of relatively-closed and half-open systems brings another problem of complementarity to light. In saying this I have the argumentative infrastructure and the narrative superstructure of a historical narrative in mind. For the relatively-closed system approach, this complementarity of the two structures does not constitute a problem. These fit, as should be clear from the above, seamlessly on to Ricoeur's plea for an 'intriguing' narrative history.

	Diachronous historical writing	*Synchronous historical writing*
Narrative superstructure	intrigue	metaphor
Argumentative infrastructure	relatively closed system conception	half-open system conception

As to historical writing with an infrastructure marked by a half-open system pattern, the narrative superstructure is also defended by Ricoeur. He distinguishes between 'trivial' and 'novel' metaphors. Referring to M. Black's *Models and metaphors*, Ricoeur states that trivial metaphors 'are supported by specially constructed systems of implication as well as by accepted commonplaces'. From any point of view this statement refers to a narrative superstructure behind which an argumentative infrastructure is hidden, characterized by an approach consisting of systems with passive subsystems. Novel metaphors can in the same way adequately be linked to systems with active subsystems. It would be going too far to discuss here all the implications of this supposition, but it seems to me worthwhile to investigate these problems elsewhere in more detail.[14]

Ankersmit's preference for the metaphor of painting as a representation of the character of historical writing can actually only be applied to synchronous historical writing. Moreover, the metaphor itself as a representation of the historical narrative indicates the great importance that synchronous historical writing has for Ankersmit. A constitutive element of Ankersmit's philosophy of history is what he calls, following

Auerbach, *figura*, or as Mink does, *configurational understanding*. Both these categories concern 'seeing together' that which is chronologically, in the course of time, separated.[15] This is an excellent analysis of the narrative component of synchronous historical writing.

Ankersmit rejects the idea of a methodologically-grounded, argumentative infrastructure of narrative historical writing in general and a more or less positivistic infrastructure of synchronous historical writing in particular. It is indeed the case that positivism seems absent in many culture-historical synchronous studies; but in political, and especially in socio-economic studies, it is certainly not. Analysis of such studies is completely absent in Ankersmit's considerations of history. This, by the way, is also the case in most studies by other narrativists in the critical postmodern philosophy of history. They thereby take away the possibility of developing their own view on the past from historians interested in politics and socio-economics. This runs contrary to the anti-reductionism and distaste for modernist-exclusionary thought that postmodern philosophers (of history) consider so important.

On the other hand, in the social sciences researchers seem to have some interest in the narrative superstructure of the reports they write and the insights they bring forward in it. The economist D. McCloskey differentiates between two ways of understanding: 'either by way of a metaphor or by way of a story'! It is not difficult to see an analogy between McCloskey's categories of understanding and, respectively, the synchronous and the diachronous narratives of historiography.[16]

Finally: In Shakespeare's *Anthony and Cleopatra* a passage occurs comparable to the dialogue between Hamlet and Polonius mentioned in the Introduction. I used the last-mentioned passage to adstruct a certain attitude towards research amongst historians and theoreticians of history; an attitude that suits philosophers of history less well. I wish to use the passage from *Anthony and Cleopatra*, taken from Ankersmit, to illustrate the importance of the personal viewpoint, which not only the philosopher of history must develop, but also the historian:

> Sometimes we see a cloud that is dragonish;
> A vapour sometimes like a bear or lion,
> A tower'd citadel, a pendant rock,
> A forked mountain, or blue promontery
> With trees upon't, that nod unto the world,
> And mock our eyes with air.[17]

In Clio's cloud garden the historian in a certain sense has a more difficult task than the philosopher of history and the theoretician of history.

The historian must even-handedly combine a personal view of the past with the use of methodological rules for research. This is somewhat less the case for philosophers of history, because they can let their visionary thought regarding both the past (as do the speculative philosophers of history) and historical writing (as do the critical philosophers of history) prevail over the research rules. They work primarily in a context of persuasion (even though the context of justification should actually not be absent in their work); and metaphors can be refuted by metaphors. The theoretician of history must make his viewpoint subordinate to the research rules, as I have argued in the Introduction. In his case the context of discovery (but also to some extent the context of justification) will prevail over the context of persuasion. The theoretician must, after all, beware of the trap of the *declarative question*. The historian must be familiar with all three contexts and lend equal importance to all three.

How can the historian do this? The systems-theoretical models for synthesis presented here serve to give historians the opportunity to execute their studies as carefully as possible, to justify their studies, to simplify communication concerning them, and to make criticism by other historians possible. They leave unimpeded the idea that in the end every historian develops his own view of the past he is examining. What he or she accentuates or leaves out in his or her view of reality must occur according to the research rules, but remains a personal choice. A historian is therefore allowed to see a historical phenomenon in various forms and guises, but s/he will also have to explain and justify – which will in the end only make his work more persuasive – why he now sees dragons, then lions, and finally rocks.

Notes

1. De Groot and Medendorp in this context speak, following Robinson, of the analysing and the synthesizing methods of definition, respectively: A. D. de Groot and F. L. Medendorp, *Term, begrip, theorie. Inleiding tot de signifische begripsanalyse* (Meppel, Amsterdam 1986), p. 169. Henrik Von Wright in a similar situation also discusses an Aristotelian and a Galilean tradition: H. Von Wright, *Explanation and understanding*, (New York 1971), p. 2. The American sociologist Edel restricts himself to an Aristotelian and a modern tradition: A. Edel,

Analyzing concepts in social science. Science, ideology and value I, (New Brunswick, NJ 1979), pp. 32–6.

2. Not treated in this book.

3. See for remarks concerning the relationship between the truthfulness of knowledge and the inter-subjectivity of knowledge: Chr. Lorenz, *De constructie van het verleden*, 5th revised edition (Amsterdam, Meppel 1998), pp. 46 and 53.

4. The closed-system construction shows the same properties as Ricoeur's *mise en intrigue*. See P. Ricoeur, *Time and narrative I* (Chicago, London 1984), pp. 65–6.

5. J. Romein, 'De dialectiek van de vooruitgang' [The dialectics of progress], in *Historische lijnen en patronen* (Amsterdam 1971), pp. 40–89, especially 81.

6. M. Mandelbaum, *The anatomy of historical knowledge* (Baltimore, MD and London 1977), p. 133.

7. 'The two reciprocal relations expressed by *from* and *into* characterize the plot as mediating between events and narrated story'. See P. Ricoeur, *Time and narrative I*, pp. 65–70, esp. 65.

8. Ibid.

9. W. Dray, *Law and explanation in history* (Oxford 1970 [1st edition 1957]), pp. 10–73 and 98–104.

10. Illustrative for diachronous transitional phases in a synchronous, half-open study is N. Smelser's *Social change in the industrial revolution. An application of theory to the Lancashire cotton industry 1977–1840*, 4th edn (London 1974).

11. This complementary nature should not be confused with the complementary method of definition, which was discussed in Chapter 2. In the case of complementary definition, we were concerned only with placing the historical phenomenon in a context which, as systemization proceeded, led to system–sub-system constructions. The complementarity intended here concerns the relationship between relatively-closed systems and half-open systems.

12. The terms 'subjectifying and 'objectifying' here are basically used with their traditional connotation.

13. F. R. Ankersmit, 'Een moderne verdediging van het historisme. Geschiedenis en identiteit', in idem, *De navel van de geschiedenis, over interpretative en historische realiteit* (Groningen 1990), pp. 142–3.

14. See P. Ricoeur, 'Metaphor and the main problems of hermeneutics', in M. J. Valdès, *A Ricoeur reader: reflection and imagination* (Toronto, Buffalo 1991) pp. 303–19, esp. 310 and 318.

15. F. R. Ankersmit, *De macht van de representatie Exploraties II: Kulturfilosofie en esthetica* (Kampen 1996), pp. 67–8. See also P. Ricoeur, 'Writing as a problem for literary criticism and philosophical hermeneutics', in: M. J. Valdès, *A Ricoeur reader*, pp. 334–6.
16. D. N. McCloskey, 'The storied character of economics', *Tijdschrift voor Geschiedenis* 101 (1988): 643–54, esp. 646.
17. Quoted from: F. R. Ankersmit, *De macht van de representatie*, p. 15. Ankersmit derived this passage from E. H. Gombrich, *Art and illusion* (London 1960), p. 154.

Bibliography

Abegg, E. D., 'The trait-dominance theory of historical periodization', *Journal of Critical Analysis* 3 (1972): 188–98.

Abramowski, G., *Das Geschichtsbild Max Webers. Universalgeschichte am Leitfaden des okzidentalen Rationalisierungsprozesses* (Stuttgart 1966).

Abrams, Ph., 'Towns and economic growth: some theories and problems', in Ph. Abrams and E. A. Wrigley (eds), *Towns in societies. Essays in economic history and historical sociology* (Cambridge 1978), pp. 9–33.

Abrams, Ph. and E. A. Wrigley (eds), *Towns in societies. Essays in economic history and historical sociology* (Cambridge, London, New York 1978).

Adams, R. M., 'The origins of cities,' *Scientific American* (1960): 153–72.

Adams, R. M., *The evolution of urban society* (Chicago, IL 1966).

Akker, C. van den 'De idee van de mens in het verleden. Een geschied-theoretische analyse van de mogelijkheid handelingen van actoren te verklaren' Unpublished Master's thesis, Nijmegen 1996.

Althusser, L., 'Schets van het begrip historische tijd', *Ter elfder ure (TEU)* 26 (2) (1982) no. 31, Geschiedenistheorie 1: 380–415.

Althusser, L. and E. Balibar, *Das Kapital lesen* I (Reinbek bei Hamburg 1972).

Anderson, M., 'Family and class in nineteenth-century cities', *Journal of Family History* 4 (1979): 130–48.

Ankersmit, F. R., *Narrative logic. A semantic analysis of the historian's language* (Groningen 1981).

Ankersmit, F. R., *Denken over geschiedenis. Een overzicht van de moderne geschiedfilosofische opvattingen* (Groningen 1984).

Ankersmit, F. R., 'Tegen de verwetenschappelijking der geschiedwetenschap', in F. van Besouw *et al.*, *Balans en perspectief. Visies op de geschiedwetenschap in Nederland* (Groningen 1987), pp. 55–72.

Ankersmit, F. R., 'Historical representation', *History and Theory* 27 (1988): 205–28.

Bibliography

Ankersmit, F. R. *et al.*, *Over nut en nadeel van geschiedtheorie voor de historicus* (Leiden 1988).

Ankersmit, F. R., 'Historiography and postmodernism', *History and Theory* 28 (1989): 137–53.

Ankersmit, F. R., 'Over de geschiedenis en tijd', in idem, *De navel van de geschiedenis, over interpretatie en historische realiteit* (Groningen 1990).

Ankersmit, F. R., 'Een rehabilitatie van Romeins conceptie van de theoretische geschiedenis', in idem, *De navel van de geschidenis, over interpretatie en historische realiteit* (Groningen 1990).

Ankersmit, F. R. 'En moderne verdediging van het historisme. Geschiedenis en identiteit', in idem, *De navel van de geschiedenis, over interpretatie en historische realiteit* (Groningen 1990).

Ankersmit, F. R., *De spiegel van het verleden. Exploraties I. De geschiedtheorie* [The mirror of the past. Explorations I. The theory of history] (Kampen 1996).

Ankersmit, F. R., *De macht van de representatie. Exploraties II: Cultuurfilosofie en esthetica.* [The power of representation. Explorations II: Philosophy of culture and aesthetics] (Kampen 1996).

Ankersmit, F. R., 'Hayden White's appeal to historians'. *History and Theory* 37 (1998): 182–93.

Ankersmit, F. R. and J. A. Mooij (eds), *Knowledge and language 3. Metaphor and knowledge* (Dordrecht, Boston, London 1993).

Ankersmit, F.R. and A. A. van den Braembussche, 'De huidige geschiedfilosofie onderschat de rol van de taal bij de vormgeving van ons inzicht in het verleden', *Groniek* 89/90 (1984) *Taal en geschiedenis:* 10–31.

Ankersmit, F. R. *et al.* (eds), *Op verhaal komen: over narrativiteit in de mens en cultuurwetenschappen.* (Kampen 1990).

Appelbaum, R. P., *Theories of social change* (Boston, Dallas, London 1970).

Avineri, S., *The social and political thought of Karl Marx* (Cambridge 1970).

Avineri, S., *Hegel's theory of the modern state* (Cambridge 1974).

Bahner, W., (ed.), *Renaissance, Barock, Aufklärung, Epochen und Periodisierungsfragen* (Kronberg 1976).

Bahrdt, H. P., *Die moderne Grossstadt, Soziologische Überlegungenzum Städtebau* (Munich 1974).

Banks, J. A., 'The contagion of numbers', in H. J. Dyos and M. Wolff, *The Victorian city. Images and realities* I (London, Boston 1973), pp. 105–22.

Bibliography

Bann, S., *The clothing of Clio: a study of representation in nineteenth-century Britain and France* (Cambridge 1984).

Bédarida, F., 'The growth of urban history in France, some methodological trends', in H. J. Dyos (ed.), *The study of urban history* (London 1968).

Belt, H. van den, 'De rekonstruktie van het histories materialisme', *Ter elfder ure* 27(2) (1983) no.34 *Geschiedenistheorie* 2: 504–12.

Benevolo, L., *The history of the city* (Cambridge, MA 1980).

Benjamin, W., 'Paris – Capital of the 19th century', *New Left Review* 48 (1968).

Benson, M., *et al.*, *Politieke economie van de huishoudelijke arbeid* (Nijmegen 1977).

Berg, C. van den, 'Chaostheorie als regressietherapie. Een natuurwetenschappelijke reflectie op de geschiedtheorie' (Master's thesis, Nijmegen 1998).

Berkhofer jr, R. F., *A behavioral approach to historical analysis* (New York, London 1969).

Berry, B. J. L., 'Cities as systems within systems of cities', *Papers of the Regional Science Association* 13 (1964).

Bertels, K., *Geschiedenis tussen struktuur en evenement* (Amsterdam 1973).

Besouw, F. van, *et al.*, *Balans en perspectief. Visies op de geschiedwetenschap in Nederland* (Groningen 1987).

Blaschke, K.-H., 'Qualität, Quantität und Raumfunktion als Wesensmerkmale der Stadt vom Mittelater bis zur Gegenwart', *Regionalgeschichte Bd.III* (1968): 34–50.

Blaschke, K.-H. 'Die periodisierung der Landesgeschichte', *Blätter für deutsche Landesgeschichte* 106 (1970): 76–93.

Bloch, E., 'Ungleichzeitigkeit, nicht nur Rückständigheit', in idem, *Philosophische Aufsätze zur objektiven Phantasie* (Frankfurt am Main 1969), pp. 41–8.

Blockmans, W. P., *Veranderende samenlevingen. De Europese expansie in historisch perspectief* (Kapellen 1978).

Blok, A., *Wittgenstein en Elias, Een methodische richtlijn voor de antropologie* (Amsterdam 1976).

Blom, T. and T. Nighuis, 'Ontology and methodology in sociology and history', in Chr. Lorenz *et al.*, *Het historisch atelier. Controversen over causaliteit en contingentie in de geschiedenis* (Meppel, Amsterdam 1990), pp. 90–141.

Blumin, S., 'Mobility and change in ante bellum Philadelphia', in S. Thernstrom and R. Sennett, *Nineteenth-century cities. Essays in the new urban history* (New Haven, CT and London 1976), pp. 165–208.

Blumin, S. M., *The urban threshold. Growth and change in a nineteenth-century American community* (Chicago 1976).

Blumin, S. M., 'In pursuit of the American city', in Th. K. Rabb and R. I. Rotberg (eds), *Industrialization and urbanization,* (Princeton, NJ 1981), pp. 245 ff.

Böhme, H., *Frankfurt und Hamburg. Des deutschen Reiches Silber- und Goldloch und die allerenglischte Stadt des Kontinents* (Frankfurt am Main 1968).

Böhme, H., 'Stadtregiment, Representativverfassung und Wirtschaftskonjunktur in Frankfurt a. Main und Hamburg im 19.Jahrhundert', *Jahrbuch für Geschichte der oberdeutschen Reichsstädte,* Esslinger Studien Bd.15 (1969): 435–47.

Botter, C. H., *Produktiemanagement* (Deventer 1993).

Boulding, K. E., 'General systems theory – the skeleton of science', *Management Science* 2(3) (1956): 197–208.

Braembussche, A. A. van den, 'De logica van de narratio', *Theoretische Geschiedenis (TG)* 10 (1983).

Braembussche, A. A. van den, 'Historische verklaring en komparatieve methode: bouwstenen voor een theorie van de maatschappijgeschiedenis', *Groniek* 89/90 (1984) 47–75.

Braembussche, A. A. van den, *Theorie van de maatschappijgeschiedenis* (Baarn 1985).

Braembussche, A.A. van den, 'Historical explanation and comparative method: towards a theory of the history of society', *History and Theory* 28 (Feb. 1989): 1–24.

Braembussche, A. A. van den, 'De funderingscrisis van de historische kennis. Lorenz' revindicatie van een historische sociale wetenschap', in Chr. Lorenz *et al.*, *Het historische atelier. Controversen over causaliteit en contingentie in de geschiedenis* (Meppel, Amsterdam 1990), pp. 49–50.

Braembussche, A. A. van den, *Voorbij het postmodernisme. Bedenkingen aan gene zijde van het fin de siècle* (Best 1996).

Braidwood, G. and R. Willey (eds), *Courses toward urban life: archeological considerations of some cultural alternates* (Chicago 1962).

Braudel, F., *L'Ecriture sur l'histoire* (Paris 1969).

Braudel, F., *Civilisation matérielle, économie et capitalisme. XVe–XVIIIe siècle* (Paris 1979); 1: *Les structures du quotidien: le possible et l'impossible;* 2: *Les jeux de l'échange;* 3: *Le temps du monde.*

Bibliography

Braudel, F., *Afterthoughts on material civilization and capitalism* (Baltimore, MD and London 1977).

Braudel, F., *Geschiedschrijving* (Baarn 1979).

Braudel, F., *Civilization and capitalism 15th–18th century,* trans. Siân Reynolds 1: *The structure of everyday life. The limits of the possible* (London 1981); 2: *The wheels of commerce* (London 1982); 3: *The perspective of the world* (London 1984).

Braudel, F., *Beschaving, economie en kapitalisme (15de–18de eeuw) I De structuur van het dagelijkse leven* (Amsterdam 1988).

Braudel, F., *La Méditerranée et le monde méditerranéen à l'époque de Philippe II* (Paris 1989).

Briggs, A., 'The study of cities', *Australian Journal of Adult Education* II (1962): 15–20.

Briggs, A., *Victorian cities* 2nd edn, (Harmondsworth 1968).

Brunner, O., 'Stadt und Bürgertum in der europäischen Geschichte', in idem, *Neue Wege der Sozialgeschichte* (Göttingen 1956), pp. 80 ff.

Burckhardt, J., *Die Entstehung der modernen Jahrhundertrechnung* (Göppingen 1972).

Burke, P., *Venice and Amsterdam. A study of seventeenth-century elites* (London 1974).

Burke, P., 'Some reflections on the pre-industrial city', *Urban History Yearbook (UHY)* (1975): 13–21.

Burrell, G. and G. Morgan, *Sociological paradigms and organisational analysis. Elements of the sociology of corporate life* (London 1979).

Cameron, R., 'Comparative economic history', *Research in Economic History*, Suppl.1 (1977): 287 ff.

Cannadine, D., 'Victorian cities, how different?', *Social History* 4 (1977): 1–6.

Cannadine, D., *Lords and landlords. The aristocracy and the towns 1774– 1967* (Leicester 1980).

Cannadine, D., 'British history, past, present and future', *Past and Present (P&P)* 116 (1987): 169–91.

Cannadine, D., and D. Reeder (eds), *Exploring the urban past. Essays in urban history H. J. Dyos* (Cambridge 1982).

Capra, D., *History and criticism* (Ithaca, NY 1985).

Carr, D., 'Narrative and the real world: an argument for continuity', *History and Theory* 25 (1986): 117–31.

Carrard, Ph., *Poetics of the new history: French historical discourses from Braudel to Chartier* (Baltimore, MD 1992).

Cartwright, W. H. and R. L. Watson jr. (eds), *The reinterpretation of American history and culture* (Washington DC 1973).

Castell, Manuel., *The urban question* (London 1977).

Chandler, T. and G. Fox, *3000 Years of urban growth* (London 1974).

Checkland, S. G., 'Toward a definition of urban history', in H. J. Dyos (ed.), *The study of urban history* (London 1968), pp. 343–61.

Chevalier, L., 'A reactionary view of urban history', *Times Literary Supplement (TLS)* 8 (Sept. 1966).

Chevalier, L., *Working classes and dangerous classes in Paris during the first part of the nineteenth century* (New York 1971).

Childe, G., 'The urban revolution', *Town Planning Review* 21 (1950): 3–17.

Childe, G., *What happened in history* (Harmondsworth 1978).

Chudacoff, H. P., *Mobile Americans: residential and social mobility in Omaha 1880–1920* (New York 1972).

Clark, P. and P. Slack (eds), *Crisis and order in English towns 1500–1700* (London 1972).

Clark, P. and P. Slack (eds), *English towns in transition 1500–1700* (London, Oxford 1976).

Clark, P., P. Burke and P. Slack (eds), *The urban setting* (Milton Keynes 1977).

Cohen, G. A. *Karl Marx's theory of history: a defence.* (Oxford 1978).

Cohen, P. S., *Modern social theory* (London 1968).

Commons, J. R., 'American shoemakers 1649–1895', *Quarterly Journal of Economics* 24 (1909): 39–84.

Crew, D. F., *Town in the Ruhr. A social history of Bochum 1860–1914* (New York 1979).

Cuzcort, R. P. and E. W. King, *20th century social thought* (New York, Montreal, London, Sydney 1980).

Czok, K., *Die Stadt, Ihre Stellung in der deutschen Geschichte* (Leipzig, Jena, Berlin 1969).

Czok, K., 'Forschungen aus Regionalgeschichte', *Historischen Forschungen in der DDR 1960–1970* (East Berlin 1970).

Danto, A. C., *Analytical philosophy of history* (Cambridge, London 1965).

Daunton, M. J., 'Towns and economic growth in eighteenth-century England', in Ph. Abrams and E. Wrigley (eds), *Towns in societies. Essays in economic history and historical sociology* (Cambridge, London, New York 1978).

Davidson, D., 'Actions, reasons and causes', *The Journal of Philosophy* 23 (1963): 685–200.

Davidson, D., 'Actions, reasons and causes', in idem (ed.) *Essays on actions and events* (Oxford 1980).

Bibliography

Debrock, G. (ed.), *Rationaliteit kan ook redelijk zijn. Bijdragen over het probleem van de teleologie* (Assen, Maastricht 1991).

Derrida, J., *Margins of philosophy* (Chicago 1982).

Diamond, W., 'On the dangers of an urban interpretation of history', in F. Goldman (ed.), *Historiography and urbanization. Essays in American history in honor of W. Stult Holt* (Port Washington NY 1968 [1st edn 1941]) pp. 67–108.

Diederiks, H. A. and Verkerk, C. L., 'Stad en achterland in de geschiedenis van Westeuropa', *Sociologische gids* 19(2) (1972): 103–15.

Dijk, H. van, *Rotterdam 1810–1880. Aspecten van een stedelijke samenleving.* Serie: Historische werken over Rotterdam in heden en verleden 17 (Schiedam 1976).

Dijkum, C., and D. de Tombe (eds), *Gamma, chaos, onzekerheid en orde in de menswetenschappen* (Bloemendaal 1992).

Disraëli, B., *Coningsby*, ed. A. Briggs (New York 1962 [1844]).

Dorsman, L., 'Periodisering als integrale benadering: Nederlandse historici in het Fin-de-Siècle', *Theoretische Geschiedenis* 16 (3) (1989): 277–96.

Doyle, D. H., 'Nineteenth-century cities. Evolutionary and instantaneous', *Journal of Urban History (JUH)* V(1) (1978): 109–17.

Dray, W. H., *Philosophical analysis and history* (Toronto, New York, London 1966).

Dray, W. H., *Laws and explanation in history*, (Oxford 1970 [1957]).

Dray, W. H., *Perspectives on history* (London 1980).

Dudley, J., 'Substance, nature and time: a criticism of Aristotle', in P. A. Kroes (ed.), *Nature, time and history. Nijmegen studies in the philosophy of nature and its sciences II* (Nijmegen 1985), pp. 69–84.

Dunk, H. von der, 'Een onwetenschappelijke wetenschap', in *Kleio heeft duizend ogen* (Assen 1974), pp. 1–21.

Dunk, H. von der, *De organisatie van het verleden. Over grenzen en mogelijkheden van historische kennis* (Bussum 1982).

Dussen, W. J., van der, *History as a science. Collingwood's philosophy of history* (Nijmegen, Meppel 1980).

Dussen, W. J. van der 'De nieuwe AGN: een speculatieve totaalvisie in een eigentijdse verpakking', *Bijdragen en mededelingen betreffende de geschiedenis der Nederlanden (BMGN)* 97 (1) (1982).

Dussen, W. J. van der, 'Het belang van geschiedenis als schoolvak' *Kleio* 8 (1983): 18–22.

Dussen, W. J., van der, 'Geschiedenis en filosofie', *Groniek* 89/90 (1984): 103–15.

Bibliography

Dussen, W. J. van der, 'Geschiedfolosofie, theorie en historiografie', *Groniek* 89/90 (1984): 118–28.

Dussen, W. J., van der, 'Geschiedfilosofie als geschiedtheorie', *Groniek* 93 (1985).

Dussen, W. J. van der, *Filosofie van de geschiedenis. Een inleiding* (Muiderberg 1986).

Dussen, W. J. van der and C. Offringa, 'De historiografie is van onmisbare waarde voor de geschiedfilosofie', *Groniek* 89/90 (1984).

Dyos, H. J. (ed.), *The study of urban history* (London, New York 1968).

Dyos, H. J., 'Agenda for urban historians', in H. J. Dyos (ed.), *The study of urban history* (London 1968), pp. 11 ff.

Dyos, H. J., 'Editorial', *Urban History Yearbook* (1974).

Dyos, H. J. and M. Wolff (eds), *The Victorian city. Images and realities* I (London, Boston 1973).

Edel, A., *Analyzing concepts in social science. Part 1: Science, ideology and value* (New Brunswick, NJ 1979).

Eldridge, J. E. T. (ed.), *Max Weber: the interpretation of social reality* (New York 1970).

Emery, F. E., *Systems thinking*, 2nd edn, (Harmondsworth 1978).

Engelberg, E., 'Zur methodologischen Problemen der Periodisierung', *Zeitschrift für Geschichtswissenschaft* 19 (1971): 1919–50.

Engelberg E. (ed.), *Probleme der Geschichtsmethodologie* (Berlin 1972).

Engels, F., 'Die Lage der arbeitenden Klasse in England. Nach eigner Anschauung und authentischen Quellen', in *Marx-Engels Werke* (Berlin 1969), Vol. 2, pp. 225–650.

Engels, F., *The condition of the working class in England*, trans. Florence Kelley-Wischnewetsky [1887], ed. David McClennan (Oxford 1993).

Ennen, E., *Frühgeschichte der europäischen Stadt* (Bonn 1953).

Ennen, E., 'Die Stadt zwischen Mittelalter und Gegenwart', *Rheinische Vierteljahrsblätter* 30 (1968): 118–31.

Ennen, E., *Die europäische Stadt des Mittelalters* (Göttingen 1972).

Everitt, A. (ed.), *Perspectives in English urban history* (London 1973).

Fain, H., *Between philosophy and history. The resurrection of speculative philosophy of history within analytic tradition* (Princeton, NJ 1970).

Feibleman J. and J. W. Friend, 'The structure and function of organization', in F. E. Emery (ed.), *Systems thinking*, 2nd edn (Harmondsworth 1978), pp. 30–55.

Fennema, J., 'Time a concept of growth', in P. A. Kroes (ed.), *Nature, time and history. Nijmegen studies in the philosophy of nature and its sciences II* (1985), pp. 105–19.

Feyerabend, P. K., *Against method* (London 1975).

Fischer, D. H., *Historians' fallacies. Toward a logic of historical thought* (New York, Evanston Illinois, 1970).

Flinn, M. and T. Stout (eds), *Essays in social history* (Oxford 1974).

Foster, J., 'Nineteenth-century towns. A class dimension', in H. J. Dyos (ed.), *The study of urban history* (London 1968).

Foster, J., *Class struggle and the industrial revolution. Early industrial capitalism in three English towns* (London 1974).

Foucault, M., *Histoire de la folie à l'âge classique* (Paris 1972 [1st edn 1961]).

Foucault, M., *Naissance de clinique. Une archéologie du regard médical* (Paris 1963)

Foucault, M., *Surveiller et punir. Naissance de la prison* (Paris 1975).

Fraser, D., *Power and authority in the Victorian city* (Oxford 1979).

Fraser, D., *Urban politics in Victorian England. The structure of politics in Victorian cities*, 2nd edn (London 1979).

Fraser, A. and A. Sutcliffe, *The pursuit of urban history* (London 1983).

Friedrichs, C. R., 'Capitalism, mobility and class formation in the early modern German city', in Ph. Abrams and E. A. Wrigley (eds), *Towns in societies. Essays in economic history and historiological sociology* (Cambridge, MA and London 1975).

Friedrichs, C. R., *Urban society in an age of war. Nördlingen 1580–1720* (Princeton, NJ 1979).

Frisch, M. H., *Town into city. Springfield Massachussetts and the meaning of community 1840–1880* (Cambridge, MA 1972).

Frisch, M. H., 'The community elite and the emergence of urban politics', in: S. Thernstrom and R. Sennett (eds), *Nineteenth-century cities: essays in the new urban history* (New Haven, CT 1976 [1st edn 1969]), pp. 277–96.

Frisch, M. H., 'American urban history as an example of recent historiography', *History Today* 18 (1979): 350–77.

Gerhard, D., 'Periodization in history', in Ch. Perelman (ed.), *Les catégoriès en histoire* (Brussels 1969), pp. 41–56.

Gerschenkron, A., 'Economic backwardness in historical perspective', in D. S. Landes, *The rise of capitalism*, 3rd edn (New York, London 1971), pp. 111–30.

Geurts P. A. M. and F. A. M. Messing, *Theoretische en methodologische aspecten van de economische en sociale geschiedenis* (The Hague 1979).

Giddens, A., *Capitalism and modern social theory. An analysis of the writings of Marx, Durkheim and Max Weber*, 3rd edn (Cambridge, London, New York, Melbourne 1975).

Gillis, J. R., 'German home towns', *Journal of Social History (JSH)* VI(3) (1973): 367–70.

Ginzburg, C., 'Sporen. Wortels van een indicie-paradigma' in idem, *Omweg als methode. Essays over verborgen geschiedenis, kunst en maatschappelijke herinnering* (Nijmegen 1986), pp. 206–61.

Glaab, C. N., 'Summary of the discussion among members of the urban history group', *Urban History Newsletter* 15 (April 1962).

Glaab, C. N., 'The historian and the American urban tradition' *Wisconsin Magazine* 1 (Autumn 1963): 12–25.

Glaab, C. N., 'The historian and the American city: a bibliographic survey', in Ph. M. Hauser and L. F. Schnore (eds), *The study of urbanization* (New York 1965).

Glaab, C. N., 'Historical perspective on urban development schemes', in L. F. Schnore (ed.), *Social science and the city* (New York 1968).

H. P. H. Goddijn (ed.), *Max Weber. Zijn leven, werk en betekenis* (Baarn 1980).

Goff, J. Le, 'The town as an agent of civilization c.1200–c.1500', in C. M. Cipolla (ed.), *The Fontana economic history of Europe*. The Middle Ages (London, Glasgow 1973), pp. 71–106.

Goldstein, L. J., *Historical knowing* (Austin, TX 1976).

Goldstone, J. A., *Revolution and rebellion in the early modern world* (Berkeley, CA, Los Angeles, London 1991).

Gombrich, E. H., *Art and illusion* (London 1960).

Gotesky, R. and E. Laszlo, *Evolution – revolution. Patterns of development in nature, society and knowledge* (New York, London, Paris 1971).

Gras, N. S. B., 'The development of metropolitan economy in Europe and America', *American Historical Review* XXVII (1922): 695–708.

Griffiths, T., 'Economische ontwikkeling in industrieel Europa', in F. van Besouw *et al.* (eds), *Balans en perspectief. Vissies op de geschiedwetenshop in Nederland* (Groningen 1987).

Groot, A. D. de, and F. L. Medendorp, *Term, begrip, theorie. Inleiding tot de significhse begripsanalyse* (Meppel, Amsterdam 1986).

Haase, C., *Die Entstehung der Westfälischen Städte*, 3rd edn (Münster 1976).

Haase, C., *Die Stadt des Mittelalters. Begriff, Entstehung und Ausbreitung*, Vol. 1 (Darmstadt 1978).

Hagan, E. E., *On the theory of social change: how economic growth begins* (Cambridge, MA 1962).

Hall, A. D., 'Some fundamental concepts of systems engineering', in S. L. Optner (ed.), *Systems analysis* (Harmondsworth 1973), pp. 103–20.

Hall, A. D. and R. E. Fagen, 'Definitions of systems', in W. Buckley (ed.), *Modern systems research for the behavioral scientist: a sourcebook* (Chicago 1968).

Handlin, O., 'The modern city as a field of historical study', in O. Handlin and J. Burchard (eds), *The historian and the city* (Cambridge, MA 1963).

Harbers, E., 'Het gewest uitgetest II. Het gebruik van modellen en statistische technieken in de regionale geschiedenis', *Groniek* 16 (no.76): 21–9.

Hare, V. C., *Systems analysis: a diagnostic approach* (New York 1967).

Hart, H. L. A. and A. M. Honoré, 'Causal judgement in history and in the law', in W. H. Dray (ed.), *Philosophical analysis and history* (New York, London 1966).

Harvey, D., *Social justice and the city* (London 1973).

Hasebroek, J., *Griechische Wirtschafts- und Gesellschaftsgeschichte* (Tübingen 1931).

Hauser, P. M. and L. F. Schnore (eds), *The study of urbanization* (New York 1965).

Hegel, G. W. F., *Grundlinien der Philosophie des Rechts oder Naturrecht und Staatwissenschaft in Grundrisse*, ed. H. Reichelt (Suhrkamp edn, Frankfurt a.M. 1972).

Heidegger, H., *Zijn en tijd*, trans. M. Wildschut (1998).

Hershberg, Th., *et al.*, 'Occupation and ethnicity in five nineteenth–century cities, a collaborative inquiry', *Historical Methods Newsletter* (June 1974): 174–216.

Hershberg, Th., 'The new urban history. Toward an interdisciplinary history of the city', *Journal of Urban History* 5 (1) (1978): 3–40.

Hesse, M., 'Models, metaphors and truth', in F. Ankersmit and J. A. Mooij (eds), *Knowledge and language 3. Metaphor and knowledge* (Dordrecht, Boston, London 1993).

Heuss, A., 'Max Webers Bedeutung für die Geschichte des griechisch–römischen Altertums', *HZ* 201 (1965): 529 ff.

Hilbert, A. B., 'The origins of the medieval town patriciate', in P. Abrams and E. Wrigley (eds), *Towns in societies, Essays in economic history and historical sociology* (Cambridge, London, New York 1978), pp. 91–104.

Hobart, M. E., 'The paradox of historical constructionism', *History and Theory* 28 (1989): 43–58.

Hoekveld, G. A., 'Theoretische aanzetten ten behoeve van het samenstellen van maatschappijhistorische modellen van de verhouding van stad en platteland in de nieuwe geschiedenis van Noordwest-Europa', *Economisch en Sociaal-historisch Jaarboek* 38 (1975): 1–47.

Hoekveld G. A., *et al.*, *Geografie van stad en platteland in de westerse landen* (Bussum 1978).

Hoekveld G. A. and B. de Pater, 'A house with many windows'. Unpublished paper (1990).

Hölscher, L., 'The new annalistic: a sketch of a theory of history', *History and Theory* 36 (1997): 317–35.

Holthoon, F. L. van (ed.), *De Nederlandse samenleving sinds 1815* (Assen 1985).

Holthoon, F. L. van, 'Zuil, verzuiling, verzuildheid', *Tijdschrift voor Sociale Geschiedenis* (*TvSG*) 13 (1987): 340–3.

Hoselitz, B. F., 'The role of cities in the economic growth of underdeveloped countries', *Journal of Political Economy* LXI (1953): 195–209.

Howard, E., *Tomorrow: a peaceful path to real reform* (London 1898).

Howe, F. C., *The city, the hope of democracy* (New York 1905).

Hoyningen-Huene, P., 'Autonome historische Prozesse – kybernetisch betrachtet', *Geschichte und Gesellschaft* 9 (1983): 119–23.

Hoyningen-Huene, P., *Reconstructing scientific revolutions. Thomas S. Kuhn's philosophy of science* (Chicago 1993).

Huizinga, J., *Cultuurhistorische verkenningen* (Haarlem 1929).

Huizinga, J., 'Het probleem der Renaissance', in idem, *Verzamelde Werken* 4 (Cultuurgeschiedenis II) (Haarlem 1949).

Huussen jr., A. H., E. H. Kossmann, and H. Renner (eds), *Historici van de twintigste eeuw* (Utrecht, Antwerp, Amsterdam 1981).

Iggers, G. G., 'Die Tradition der Annales in Frankreich, Geschichte als integrale Humanwissenschaft', in *Theoretische en methodologische aspecten van de economische en sociale geschiedenis* II ('s-Gravenhage 1979).

Jacobs, J., *The economy of cities*, 3rd edn (Harmondsworth 1972).

Jansen, H. S. J., 'Geschiedfilosofie en geschiedtheorie', *Groniek* 93 (1985): 180–90.

Jansen, H. S. J., 'Boek van de maand', *Kleio* 27, (10) (1986): 27–32.

Jansen, H. S. J., 'De historische synthese, twee wegen één doel', *Ex Tempore* 9, (2) (1990) no. 26: 119–48.

Jansen, H. S. J., 'Sterk, maar ook flexibel? Politiek-institutionele industrialisatievoorwaarden in Duitsland', in H. Righart (ed.), *De trage revolutie. Over de wording van industriële samenlevingen* (Amsterdam, Meppel, Heerlen 1991), pp. 149–79.

Bibliography

Jansen, H. S. J., 'De worsteling met de engel. De problemen van stadshistorici met hun onderzoeksobject', *Tijdschrift voor Geschiedenis* 104 (2) (1991): 1–23.

Jansen, H. S. J., *De constructie van het stadsverleden. Een systeemtheoretische analyse van het stadshistorisch onderzoek ter bevordering van de synthetiserende geschiedschrijving* (Groningen 1991).

Jansen, H. S. J., 'De beperkte ruimte in Lorenz' geschiedtheoretische atelier', *Theoretische Geschiedenis* 20 (2) (1993): 139–57.

Jansen, H. S. J., 'De Nederlandse stadsgeschiedenis in internationaal perspectief. Een geschiedtheoretische analyse', *Bijdragen en mededelingen betreffende de geschiedenis der Nederlanden* 111 (1) (1996): 47–75.

Jansen, H. S. J., 'Wrestling with the angel: on problems of definition in urban history', *Urban History* 23 (3) (1996): 277–99.

Jansen, H. S. J., 'De voorwerpen van vergelijking. Op zoek naar een nieuwe vergelijkingstypologie. *Tijdschrift voor Geschiedenis* 110 (1997): 329–56.

Jansen, H. S. J., 'Het vergelijken vergeleken. Skocpol and Goldstone', *Theoretische Geschiedenis* 24 (3) (1997): 289–304.

Jansen, H. S. J., 'Waarheid en schoonheid in de wetenschapsgeschiedenis'. *Theoretische Geschiedenis* 26 (1) (1999).

Janssens, A., *Family and social change. The household as a process in an industrializing community* (Cambridge 1993).

Jones, G. S., *Outcast London. A study of the relationships between classes in Victorian society* (Oxford 1971).

Jordan, N., 'Some thinking about "system"', in S. L. Optner (ed.), *Systems analysis* (Harmondsworth 1973).

Karskens, M., *Waarheid als macht. Een onderzoek naar de filosofische ontwikkeling van Michel Foucault.* (Nijmegen 1986).

Katz, M. *et al.*, *The people of Hamilton, Canada West. Family and class in a mid-nineteenth-century city* (Cambridge, MA and London 1975).

Kellet, J., *Railways and Victorian cities*, 2nd edn (Henley-on-Thames 1980).

Kellner, H., *Language and historical representation* (Madison, WI 1989).

Kieft, C. van de, 'La périodisation de l'histoire du moyen age', in Ch. Perelman (ed.), *Les catégories en histoire* (Brussels 1969), pp. 41–56.

Klein, P. W., 'Jonathan Israel's boek over de Gouden Eeuw. Meesterlijk, boeiend, stimulerend en irritant', *NRC/Handelsblad* 26 Aug. 1989 (Saturday supplement).

Klein, P. W., 'De oogverblindende pretenties van Fernand Braudel', *NRC/Handelsblad* 6 April 1991 (Saturday supplement).

Bibliography

Klep, P. P. M. *Bevolking en arbeid in transformatie. Een onderzoek in Brabant 1700–1900.* (Nijmegen 1978).

Klep, P. M. M., 'Urban decline in Brabant: the traditionalization of investments and labour (1374–1806)' in H. van der Wee, *The rise and decline of urban industries in Italy and in the Low Countries (Late Middle Ages – early modern times)* (Louvain 1988).

Kneale, W., *Probability and induction* (Oxford 1949).

Kocka, J., *Sozialgeschichte* (Göttingen 1977).

Kocka, J., 'Stadtgeschichte, Mobilität und Schichtung', *Archiv für Sozialgeschichte* 18 (1978).

Kocka, J., *Sozialgeschichte*, 2nd edn (Göttingen 1986).

Koditschek, T., *Class formation and urban-industrial society. Bradford 1750–1850* (Cambridge 1990).

Kooij, P., 'Stadsgeschiedenis en de verhouding stad-platteland', *Economisch en Sociaal-historisch Jaarboek* 38 (1975): 124–40.

Kooij, P., 'Stadsgeschiedenis', in H. Baudet and H. van der Meulen (eds), *Kernproblemen der economische geschiedenis* (Groningen 1978), pp. 142–50.

Kooij, P., 'Urbanization. What's in a name', in H. Schmal (ed.), *Patterns of European urbanization since 1500* (London 1981), pp. 33–47.

Kooij, P., 'Het gewest uitgetest I. Theorieën en modellen voor de regionale geschiedenis', *Groniek* 16 (no.76).

Kooij, P., *Stadsgeschiedenis* (Zutphen 1989).

Kopitzsch, F. and K. J. Lorenzen-Schmidt, 'Stadtpolitik zwischen Integration und Repression', *Sozialwissenschaftliche Informationen für Unterricht und Studium* 9 (1) (1980): 6–11.

Koselleck, R., *Vergangene Zukunft. Zur Semantik geschichtlichter Zeiten* (Frankfurt am Main 1979).

Kraft, Joseph, 'China diary', *The New Yorker* (11 March 1972), pp. 100–13.

Krings, H., H. M. Baumgartner and Ch. Wild (eds), *Handbuch philosophischer Grundbegriffe Studienausgabe*, Vol. 2: *Dialektik – Gesellschaft* (Munich 1973).

Kuhn, T., *De structuur van wetenschappelijke revoluties* (Meppel, Amsterdam 1972) [*The structure of scientific revolutions* (Chicago 1962)].

Lampard, E. E., 'The history of cities in the economic advanced areas', *Economic Development and Cultural Change III* (1955): 81–136.

Lampard, E. E., 'American historians and the study of urbanization', *American Historical Review* LXVII (Oct. 1961): 49–91.

Bibliography

Lampard, E. E., 'Urbanization and social change; on broadening the scope and relevance of urban history', in O. Handlin and J. Burchard (eds), *The historians and the city* (Cambridge, MA 1963).

Lampard, E. E., 'Historical aspects of urbanization' in P. M. Hauser and L. F. Schnore (eds), *The study of urbanization* (New York 1965), pp. 519–54.

Lampard, E. E., 'The evolving system of cities in the United States, urbanization and economic development', in H. S. Perloff and L. Wingo jr. (eds), *Issues in urban economics* (Baltimore, MD 1968), pp. 81–140.

Lampard, E. E., 'The dimensions of urban history, a footnote to the "urban crisis"', *Pacific Historical Review* (1970): 261–78.

Lampard, E. E., 'The urbanizing world', in H. J. Dyos and M. Wolff (eds), *The Victorian city. Images and realities* (London, Boston 1973).

Lampard, E. E., 'The nature of urbanization,' in D. Fraser and A. Sutcliffe (eds), *The pursuit of urban history* (London 1983), pp. 3–53.

Laslett, P., *The world we have lost* (London 1965).

Latour, B., *Science in action. How to follow scientists and engineers through society* (Stony Stratford 1987).

Lees, A., 'Critics of urban society in Germany, 1854–1914', *Journal of the History of Ideas* XL (1979): 61–83.

Lees, A., *Cities perceived. Urban society in European and American thought 1820–1940* (Manchester 1985).

Lefebvre, H., *La pensée marxiste et la ville* (Paris 1972).

Lepetit, B., 'Event and structure: the revolution and the French urban system, 1700–1840', *Journal of Historical Geography* 16(1) (1990): 17–37.

Lesger, C., 'Hiërarchie en spreiding van regionale verzorgingscentra. Het centrale plaatsensysteem in Holland benoorden het Y omstreeks 1800', *Tijdschrift voor Sociale Geschiedenis* 16(2) (1990): 128–53.

Lindstrom, D. and J. Sharpless, 'Urban growth and economic structure in Antebellum America', in *Research in Economic History* (1978): 161–217.

Lloyd, Chr., 'Realism and structurism in historical theory: a discussion of the thought of Maurice Mandelbaum', *History and Theory* 28 (1989): 296–325.

Lopez, R. S., 'The crossroads within the wall', in O. Handlin and J. Burchard (eds), *The historian and the city* (Cambridge, MA 1963), pp. 27–43.

Lorenz, Chr., 'Kritische geschiedwetenschap; een andere gechiedenis', in L. Brug *et al.* (eds), *Geschiedenis en bevrijding* (Nijmegen 1980).

Bibliography

Lorenz, Chr., *De constructie van het verleden. Een inleiding in de theorie van de geschiedenis* (Meppel, Amsterdam 1987).

Lorenz, Chr., 'Can histories be true? Narrativism, positivism and the "metaphorical turn"', *History and Theory* 37 (1998): 309–330.

Lorenz, Chr., *De constructie van het verleden. Een inleiding in de theorie van de geschiedenis*, 5th revised edn (Amsterdam, Meppel 1998).

Lorenz, Chr., *et al.*, *Het historisch atelier. Controversen over causaliteit en contingentie in de geschiedenis* (Meppel, Amsterdam 1990).

Love, J., 'Max Weber and the theory of ancient capitalism', *History and Theory* 25 (1986): 152–72.

Lubove, R., *Progressives and slums. Tenement housing reform in New York City 1890–1917* (Pittsburgh 1962).

Lubove, R., 'The urbanization process. An approach to historical research', *American Institute of Planners Journal* XXXIII (1967): 33.

Macfarlane, A., 'History, anthropology and the study of communities', *Social History* (May 1977): 631 ff.

Mach, E., *Die Mechanik in ihrer Entwicklung historisch-kritisch dargestellt* (Berlin 1883).

Mackie, J. L., *The cement of the universe. A study in causation* (Oxford 1974).

Mandelbaum, M., 'Societal laws', in W. H. Dray (ed.), *Philosophical analysis and history* (New York 1960), pp. 330–46.

Mandelbaum, M., *The anatomy of historical knowledge* (Baltimore, MD and London 1977).

Manschot, H., *Althusser over het marxisme* (Nijmegen 1980).

Marcus, S., 'Reading the illegible', in H. J. Dyos and M. Wolff (eds), *The Victorian city. Images and realities I* (London, Boston 1973), pp. 257–76.

Marrou, H. I., *De la connaissance historique* (Paris 1954).

Martin, R., *Historical explanation. Re-enactment and practical inference* (Ithaca, NY and London 1977).

Martin, R., 'G. H. von Wright on explanation and understanding: an appraisal', *History and Theory* 19(2) (1990) 205–33.

Martin, R., 'Progress in historical studies', *History and Theory* 37 (1998): 14–39.

Martindale, D., *Community, character and civilization* (London 1963).

Marx, K., *Grundrisse der Kritik der politischen Ökonomie 1857–1859,* (Berlin 1953).

Marx, K., *Zur Kritik der politischen Oekonomie* (Berlin 1972 [1857/1858]).

Marx, K., *Grundrisse der Kritik der politische Ökonomie* (Berlin (Dietz) 1974 [1857/1859]).

Bibliography

Marx, K. and F.Engels, 'Die deutsche Ideologie. Kritik der neuesten deutschen Philosophie in ihren Repräsentanten Feuerbach, B. Bauer und Stirner, und des deutschen Sozialismus in seinen verschiedenen Propheten', in *Marx-Engels Werke* 3, ed. Institut für Marxismus-Leninismus beim ZK der SED (Berlin 1969) (*MEW*).

Maschke, E., 'Deutsche Stadtgeschichtsforschung auf der Grundlage des historischen Materialismus', in: *Esslinger Studien* 12/13 (1966/1967): 124–41.

McAllister, J. W. *Beauty and revolution in science* (Ithaca, NY, London 1996).

McCloskey, D., 'The storied character of economics', *Tijdschrift voor Geschiedenis* 101 (1988): 643–54.

McCloskey, D., 'History, differential equations, narratio', *History and Theory* (1991): 21–36.

McGrath, J. E., P. G. Nordlie and W. S. Vaughan jr., 'A descriptive framework for comparison of system research methods', in S. L. Optner (ed.), *Systems analysis* (Harmondsworth 1973), pp. 73–86.

McLennan, G., *Marxism and the methodologies of history* (London 1981).

Medick, H., 'The proto-industrial family economy', *Social History* (1976): 291–315.

Megill, A. and D. McCloskey, 'The rhetoric of history', in J. Nelson, A. Megill and D. McCloskey (eds), *The rhetoric of the human sciences. Language and argument in scholarship and public affairs* (Madison, WI 1987).

Merrit, R. L. 'The emergence of American nationalism: a quantitative approach', *American Quarterly* XVII (1965): 319–35.

Merrit, R. L., *Symbols of American community 1735–1775* (New Haven, CT 1966).

Miller, Z. L., C. Griffen and G. Stelter, 'Urban history in North America', *Urban History Yearbook* (1977), pp. 6–29.

Mink, L. O., 'Philosophical analysis and historical understanding', *Review of Metaphysics* 20 (1968): 667–98.

Mink, L. O., 'History and fiction as modes of comprehension,' *New Literary History* (1970): 557 ff.

Mitchel, W. H., 'Relevant neoscientific management notions', in S. Optner (ed.), *Systems analysis* (Harmondsworth 1973), pp. 305–24.

Mohl, R. A. 'The history of the American city', in W. H. Cartwright and R. L. Watson jr. (eds), *The reinterpretation of American history and culture* (Washington, DC 1973).

Momigliano, A., 'Time in ancient historiography', in *History and the concept of time, Beiheft 6 of History and Theory* (1966): 1–23.

Morris, R. J. and R. Rodger, *The Victorian city. A reader in British urban history* (London, New York 1993).

Mumford, L., *The culture of cities* (New York 1938).

Mumford, L., 'Rousseau, insurgent Romanticism', in L. Mumford (ed.), *Interpretations and forecasts 1922–1972* (London 1973), pp. 187–93.

Mumford, L., *The city in history. Origins, its tranformation and its prospects* (Harmondsworth 1979 [London 1961]).

Nadel, G. H., 'Periodization', in *International encyclopedia of the social sciences* II (1968): 581–4.

Nagel, E., 'Determinism in history' in W. H. Dray (ed.), *Philosophical analysis and history* (Toronto, New York, London 1966), pp. 347–82.

Nelissen, N., *De stad. Een inleiding tot de urbane sociologie* (Deventer 1974).

Nelson, J., A. Megill and D. McCloskey (eds), *The rhetoric of the human sciences. Language and argument in scholarship and public affairs* (Madison, WI 1987).

Nijhuis, T., *Structuur en contingentie. Over de grenzen van het sociaalwetenschappelijk verklaringsideaal in de Duitse geschiedschrijving* (Assen 1996).

Nisbet, R., *The social bond* (New York 1970).

Nisbet, R., *Social change* (New York, Evanston, Illinois, San Francisco, London 1972).

Nisbet, R., 'Introduction: the problem of social change', in R. Nisbet (ed.), *Social change* (New York, Evanston, Illinois, San Francisco, London 1972), pp. 1–45.

Oakeshott, M., *On history and other essays* (Oxford 1983).

Optner, S., *Systems analysis* (Harmondsworth, Middlesex 1973).

Orr, L., *Jules Michelet: nature, history and language* (Ithaca, NY 1976).

Oud, J. H. L., *Systeemmethodologie in sociaal-wetenschappelijk onderzoek* (Nijmegen 1978).

Pahl, R., *Whose city?* (London 1970).

Park, R. E., E. W. Burgess and R. D. McKenzie, *The city*, New edn by M. Janowitz (Chicago 1967 [1926]).

Perelman Ch. (ed.), *Les catégories en histoire* (Brussels 1969).

Porter, D. H., *The emergence of the past, A theory of historical explanation* (Chicago 1981).

Pot, J. H. J. van der, *De periodisering der geschiedenis. Een overzicht der theorieën* ('s-Gravenhage 1951).

Prigogine, I., and I. Stengers, *Order out of chaos. Men's new dialogues with nature* (Toronto 1984).

Rabb, Th. K. and R. I. Rotberg, *Industrialization and urbanization* (Princeton, N. J. 1981).

Reader, of the Ninth international economic history congress, *Debates and controversies 2. The dynamics of urban decline in the late Middle Ages and early modern times: economic response and social effects* (Berne 24–29 August 1986).

Reisch, G. A., 'Chaos, history and narrative', *History and Theory* 30 (1991): 1–20.

Reulecke, J. (ed.), *Die deutsche Stadt im Industriezeitalter* (Wuppertal 1978).

Richter, M. (ed.), *Essays in theory and history. An approach to the social sciences* (Cambridge 1970).

Ricoeur, P., *Temps et récit. Tome I* (Paris 1983).

Ricoeur, P., *Time and narrative I* (Chicago, London 1984).

Ricoeur, P., *Time and narrative III* (Chicago, London 1988).

Ricoeur, P., 'Metaphor and the main problem of hermeneutics', in M. J. Valdès (ed.), *A Ricoeur reader. Reflection and imagination* (Toronto, Buffalo 1991), pp. 303–19.

Ricoeur, P., 'Narrated time', in M. J. Valdès (ed.), *A Ricoeur reader. Reflection and imagination* (Toronto, Buffalo 1991), pp. 338–54.

Ricoeur, P., 'Time traversed: rememberance of things past', in M. J. Valdès, *A Ricoeur reader. Reflection and imagination* (Toronto, Buffalo 1991), pp. 355–89.

Ridgeway, W., 'Measuring wealth and power in ante bellum America, a new review essay', *Historical Methods Newsletter* II (1975): 74–8.

Righart, H., *De katholieke zuil in Europa. Het ontstaan van verzuiling onder katholieken in Oostenrijk, Zwitserland, België en Nederland* (Meppel 1986).

Righart, H. (ed.), *De trage revolutie. Over de wording van industriële samenlevingen* (Amsterdam, Meppel and Heerlen 1991).

Rigney, A., *The rhetoric of historical representation: three narrative theories of the French revolution* (Cambridge 1990).

Ringer, F. K., 'Causal analysis in historical reasoning', *History and Theory* 28 (1989): 154–72.

Robson, B. T., 'The impact of functional differentiation within systems of industrialized cities', in H. Schmal (ed.), *Patterns of European urbanization since 1500* (London 1981), pp. 113–30.

Rodger, R. (ed.), *European urban history. Prospect and retrospect* (Leicester, London 1993).

Romein J., 'Het onvoltooid verleden', in idem, *Cultuurhistorische studies*, 2nd edn (Amsterdam 1948), pp. 75 ff.

Bibliography

Romein, J., 'De dialectiek van de vooruitgang', in idem, *Historische lijnen en patronen* (Amsterdam 1976 [1952]), pp. 40–89.

Romein, J., 'Het vergruisde beeld', in idem, *Historische lijnen en patronen* (Amsterdam 1976 [1952]), pp. 147–62.

Romein, J., 'De europese geschiedenis als afwijking van het Algemeen Menselijk Patroon', in: idem, *Historische lijnen en patronen* (Amsterdam 1976 [1952]), pp. 417–45.

Romein, J., 'Integrale geschiedschrijving', in: idem, *Historische lijnen en patronen* (Amsterdam 1976 [1952]), pp. 536–85.

Romein, J., 'Theoretische geschiedenis', in idem, *Historische lijnen en patronen* (Amsterdam 1976 [1952]).

Roth, G. and W. Schluchter, *Max Weber's vision of history. Ethics and methods* (Berkeley, CA, Los Angeles, London 1979).

Roth, G., 'Duration and rationalization: Fernand Braudel and Max Weber', in: G. Roth and W. Schluchter, *Max Weber's vision of history. Ethics and methods* (Berkeley, CA, Los Angeles, London 1979), pp. 166–94.

Rottier, H. C. E. M., *Stedelijke strukturen, Een inleiding tot de ontwikkeling van de europese stad* (Muiderberg 1978).

Rowney, K., 'What is urban history?' *Journal of Interdisciplinary History* (JIH) VIII (2) (1977): 319–27.

Rozman, G., *Urban networks in Ch'ing China and Tokugawa Japan* (Princeton, NJ 1973).

Rozman, G., 'Comparative approaches to urbanization, Russia 1750–1800', in M. F. Hamm (ed.), *The city in Russian history* (Lexington, KY 1976).

Rozman, G., *Urban networks in Russia 1750–1800 and premodern periodization* (Princeton, NJ 1976).

Rozman, G., 'Urban networks and historical stages', *Journal of Interdisciplinary History* 9 (1) (Summer 1978): 65–91.

Rozov, N. S., 'An apologia for theoretical history', *History and Theory* 36 (1997): 336–52.

Rubin, D.-H., *The metaphysics of the social world* (London 1985).

Rüsen, J., 'Rhetoric and aesthetics of history: Leopold von Ranke', *History and Theory* 29 (1990): 190–204.

Schaeffer, K. H. and E. Sclar, *Access for all: Transportation and urban growth* (Harmondsworth 1975).

Schilling, H., 'Die Geschichte der nördlichen Niederlande und die Modernisierungstheorie', *Geschichte und Gesellschaft* (GuG) 8 (1982): 475–517.

Schiwy, G., *Der französische Strukturalismus* (Reinbek bei Hamburg 1969/1970).

Schlesinger, A. M., *The rise of the city 1878–1898* (New York 1933).

Schlesinger, A. M., 'The city in American history', *Mississippi Valley Historical Review* XXVII (1940).

Schmal, H. (ed.), *Patterns of European urbanization since 1500* (London 1981).

Schmal, H., 'Epilogue: one subject, many views', in H. Schmal (ed.), *Patterns of European urbanization since 1500* (London 1981), pp. 287–307.

Schmal, H., 'Patterns of de-urbanization in the Netherlands between 1650–1850', in H. van der Wee (ed.), *The rise and decline of urban industries in Italy and in the Low Countries (Late Middle Ages – early modern times)* (Louvain 1989): 287–306.

Schnore, L. F., 'On the spatial structure of cities in the two Americas', in P. M. Hauser and L. F. Schnore (eds), *The study of urbanization* (New York, London 1965).

Schnore, L. F. and P. R. Knights, 'Residence and social structure. Boston in tne ante bellum period', in S. Thernstrom and R. Sennett (eds), *Nineteenth-century cities: essays in the new urban history* (New Haven, CT 1976 [1st edn 1969]).

Schnore, L. F. and E. E. Lampard, 'Social science and the city', in L. F. Schnore and B. M. Fagin (eds), *Urban research and policy planning* (Beverly Hills, CA 1967).

Schnore L. F. and E. E. Lampard, *The new urban history. Quantitative explorations by American historians* (Princeton, NJ 1975).

Schröder, W. H. (ed.), *Moderne Stadtgeschichte* (Stuttgart 1979).

Sennett, R., 'An urban anarchist', *New York Review of Books* (1 Jan. 1970): 22–4.

Sennett, R., *The uses of disorder: Personal identity and city life* (New York 1970).

Sennett, R., 'Middle-class families and urban violence: the experience of a Chicago community in the nineteenth century', in T. K. Hareven (ed.), *Anonymous Americans. Explorations in nineteenth-century social history* (Englewood Cliffs, NJ 1971).

Sennett, R., *Families against the city. Middle class homes of industrial Chicago 1872–1890* (New York 1974).

Sennett, R., 'The coldness of private warmth', *New York Times* (January 1977).

Sennett, R., *The fall of public man* (New York 1977).

Sennett, R. and J. Cobb, *The hidden injuries of class* (New York 1973).

Sewell, W. H. jr., 'Marc Bloch and the logic of comparative history', *History and Theory* VI (1968): 208–18.

Sharpless, J. B., *City growth in the United States, England and Wales 1820–1861* (New York 1977).

Sharpless, J. B., 'Intercity development and dependency: Liverpool and Manchester', in J. D. Wirth and R. L. Jones (eds), *Manchester and São Paolo* (Stanford, CA 1978), pp. 131–56.

Shaw, W. H., *Marx' Theory of History* (London 1978).

Shermer, M., 'Exorcising Laplace's demon: chaos and anti-chaos, history and metahistory', *History and Theory* 34 (1995): 59–63.

Shermer, M., 'The crooked timber of history', *Complexity* 2 (1997): 23–30.

Sjoberg, G., *The pre-industrial city: past and present* (Glencoe, IL 1960).

Sjoberg, G., 'The rise and fall of cities', *International Journal of Comparative Sociology*, IV (1963): 107–20.

Sjoberg, G., 'Cities in developing and industrial societies: a cross-cultural analysis', in Ph. M. Hauser and L. F. Schnore (eds), *The study of urbanization* (New York, London, Sydney 1967 [1st edn 1965]), pp. 213–64.

Sjoberg, G., 'The origin and evolution of cities', in K. Davies (ed.), *Cities, their origin, growth and human impact* (San Francisco 1973 [1st edn 1954]).

Skocpol, T., *States and social revolutions* (Cambridge 1979).

Skocpol, T. and M. Somers, 'The uses of comparative history in macro-social inquiry', *Comparative Studies in Society and History* 22 (1978): 174–97.

Smelser, N. J., *Social change in the industrial revolution. An application of theory to the Lancashire cotton industry 1770–1840,* 4th edn (London 1974).

Smelser, N. J., *Methods in the social sciences* (Englewood Cliffs, NJ 1976).

Smith, M. P., *The city and social theory* (Oxford 1980).

Social Science Research Council (SSRC), *Research in economic and social history* (London 1971).

Soly, H., 'Proletarisering in West-Europa 1450–1850', in F. van Besouw *et al.* (eds), *Balans en perspectief. Visies op de geschiedwetenschap in Nederland* (Groningen 1987), pp. 101–18.

Sorokin, P., Social and cultural dynamics I, in R. P. Cuzzort and E. W. King (edn), *20th century social thought,* 2nd edn, (New York 1976), pp. 131–50.

Spilt, P., 'De annalesschool', *Ter elfder ure* 26, 31 (Geschiedtheorie I, 1982): 348.

Bibliography

Stave, B. M., 'A conversation with M. J. Dyos: urban history in Great Britain', *Journal of Urban History 5* (August 1979).

Stave, B. M., 'A view from the United States', in D. Fraser and A. Sutcliffe (eds), *The pursuit of urban history* (London 1983), p. 421.

Stedman Jones, G., *Outcast London. A study of the relationships between classes in Victorian society* (Oxford 1971).

Stegmüller, W., *Wissenschaftliche Erklärung und Begründung. Probleme und Resultate der Wissenschaftstheorie und analytischen Philosophie I* (Berlin, Heidelberg, New York 1969).

Steinbach, F., 'Stadtgemeinde und Landgemeinde. Studien zur Geschichte des Bürgertums I', *Rheinische Vierteljahresblätter* 13 (1948).

Stelter, G. A. 'Editorial', *Urban History Yearbook* (1980), p. 188.

Stokvis, P. R. D., 'Moderne stadsgeschiedenis, een nieuwe subdiscipline', *Spiegel Historiael* (1986): 333–38.

Stoob, H., *Die mittelalterliche Städtebildung im Südöstlichen Europa* (Cologne, Vienna 1977).

Stoob, H. (ed.), *Die Stadt. Gestalt und Wandel bis zum industriellen Zeitalter* (Cologne, Vienna 1979).

Stoutland, F., 'The causal theory of action', in J. Manninen and R. Tuomela (eds), *Essays on explanation and understanding. Foundations of humanities and social sciences* (Dordrecht 1976), pp. 271–304.

Strebbing, S., *Modern introduction to logic* (London 1933).

Taylor, A. M., 'Evolution – revolution. General systems theory and society', in R. Gotesky and E. Laszlo (eds), *Evolution – revolution. Patterns of development in nature, society and knowledge* (New York, London, Paris 1971), pp. 99–139.

Terpstra, M., 'Het geschiedenisbegrip bij Althusser', *Ter elfder ure* 26(31) (1982): 416–50.

Thernstrom, S., 'Reflections on the new urban history', *Daedalus* 100 (1971): 359–75. Reprinted in P. A. M. Gearts and F. A. M. Messing (eds), *Theoretische en methodologische aspecten van de economische en sociale geschiedenis II* (The Hague 1979), pp. 75–90.

Thernstrom, S., *The other Bostonians* (Boston 1976).

Thernstrom, S. and P. R. Knights, 'Men in motion, some data and speculations about urban population mobility in nineteenth-century America', *Journal of Interdisciplinary History* 1 (Autumn 1970): 7–35.

Thernstrom, S. and R. Sennett (eds), *Nineteenth-century cities: essays in the new urban history* (New Haven, CT 1976 [1st edn 1969]).

Thom, R., *Structural stability and morphogenesis* (London 1975).

Thompson, E. P., 'Responses to reality', *New Society*, 4 October 1973.

Thrupp, S. L., 'The creativity of cities', *Comparative Studies in Society and History* IV (1961/1962): 53–64.

Tisdale, H. E., 'The process of urbanization', *Social Forces* 10 (1942): 311–16.

Tönnies, F., *Gemeinschaft und Gesellschaft* (Darmstadt 1979).

Topolski, J., *The methodology of history* (Dordrecht 1976).

Topolski, J., 'The role of logic and aesthetics in constructing narrative wholes in historiography', *History and Theory* 38 (1999): 198–210.

Trienekens, G., 'Theoretische en methodologische aspecten van de lokale en regionale geschiedenis', in F. van Besouw *et al.* (eds), *Balans en perspectief. Visies op de geschiedwetenschap in Nederland* (Groningen 1987), pp. 167–88.

Troeltsch, E., 'Der Historismus und seine Probleme; erstes Buch: Das logische Problem der Geschichtsphilosophie', in *Gesammelte Schriften* III (Aalen 1961 [1st edn Tübingen 1922]).

Tromp, B., 'De sociologie van de stad bij Max Weber', in H. P. H. Goddijn (ed.), *Max Weber. Zijn leven, werk en betekenis* (Baarn 1980), pp. 113–33.

Tsuru, S., 'The economic significance of cities', in O. Handlin and J. Burchard (eds), *The historian and the city* (Cambridge, MA 1963), pp. 44–55.

Turner, R. E., 'The industrial city, center of cultural change', in P. K. Hatt and A. J. Reiss, jr (eds), *Cities and society* (Glencoe, IL 1957).

Turner, R. E., 'The industrial city and cultural change', in A. M. Wakstein (eds), *The urbanization of America* (Boston 1970), pp. 223–32.

Urban History Yearbook, 'Editorial' (1974).

Valdès, M. J., *A Ricoeur reader. Reflection and imagination* (Toronto, Buffalo 1991).

Vaughan, R., *The age of great cities . . . or modern society viewed in its relation to intelligence, moral sand religion* (London 1843).

Verhoogt, J. P. 'De wetenschapsopvatting en methodologie van Max Weber', in H. P. H. Goddijn (ed.), *Max Weber. Zijn leven, werk en betekenis* (Baarn 1980), pp. 56–81.

Verschaffel, B. 'Geschiedschrijving – een waar verhaal of de waarheid over verhalen?', in F. R. Ankersmit *et al.* (eds), *Op verhaal komen: over narrativiteit in de mens- en cultuurwetenschappen* (Kampen 1990), pp. 83–107.

Vigier, F., *Change and apathy. Liverpool and Manchester during the industrial revolution* (Cambridge 1970).

Bibliography

Vries, J. de, 'Patterns of urbanization in pre-industrial Europe 1500–1800', in H. Schmal (ed.), *Patterns of European urbanization since 1500* (London 1981), pp. 79–109.

Vries, J. de, *European urbanization 1500–1800* (London 1984).

Vries, P. H. H., 'Geschiedbeoefening, historisme en positivisme', *Theoretische Geschiedenis* 12 (2) (1985): 141–78.

Vries, P. H. H., 'De historicus als spoorzoeker. Een analyse naar aanleiding van Carlo Ginzburg, Sporen. Wortels van een indicatieparadigma', *Theoretische geschiedenis* 15 (2) (1988): 163–84.

Vries, P. H. H., *Verhaal en betoog: geschiedsbeoefening tussen postmoderne vertelling en sociaalwetenschappelijke analyse* (Leiden 1995).

Walker, M., *German home towns. Community, state and general estate 1648–1871* (London 1971).

Wallis, G. W., 'Chronopolitics: the impact of time perspectives on the dynamics of change', *Social Forces* 49 (1970): 102–8.

Walsh, W. H., *An introduction to philosophy of history* (London 1977).

Warner, S. B., *Streetcar suburbs. The process of growth in Boston 1870–1900* (Cambridge, MA 1962).

Warner, S. B., 'If all the world were Philadelphia: a scaffolding for urban history 1774–1930', *American Historical Review* LXXIV (1) (1968): 26–43.

Warner, S. B. jr., *The private city. Philadelphia in three periods of its growth* (Philadelphia 1968).

Warner, S. B. jr., *The urban wilderness* (New York 1972).

Weber, M., 'Das Bürgertum', in: *Wirtschaftsgeschichte. Abriss der universalen sozial– und Wirtschaftsgeschichte*. S. Hellmann and M. Palyi. (Munich, Leipzig 1923), pp. 270–89.

Weber, M., *Wirtschaftsgeschichte Abriss der universalen Sozial- und Wirtschaftsgeschichte*, ed. S. Hellmann and M. Palyi (Munich, Leipzig 1923). (Abbr. *WG.*)

Weber, M., *Gesammelte Aufsätze zur Sozial- und Wirtschaftsgeschichte*, ed. Marianne Weber (Tübingen 1924). (Abbr. *SWG.*)

Weber, M., *The city*, ed. Don Martindale and G. Neuwirth (New York 1958).

Weber, M., *Gesammelte politischer Schriften*, 2nd edn (Tübingen 1958).

Weber, M., *Wirtschaft und Gesellschaft. Grundriss der verstehenden Soziologie* (Tübingen 1972). (Abbr. *WuG.*)

Weber, M., 'Die nichtlegitime Herrschaft. (Typologie der Städte)', in: *Wirtschaft und Gesellschaft. Grundriss der verstehenden Soziologie* (Tübingen 1972), pp. 727–814.

Bibliography

Weber, M., 'Ueber einige Kategorien der verstehenden Soziologie', in idem, *Gesammelte Aufsätze zur Wissenschaftslehre*, 4th edn (Tübingen 1973).

Weber, M., 'Die "Objektivität" sozialwissenschaftlicher und sozialpolitischer Erkenntnis', in idem, *Gesammelte Aufsätze zur Wissenschaftslehre*, 4th edn (Tübingen 1973), pp. 146–214.

Weber, M., *Gesammelte Aufsätze zur Wissenschaftslehre*, 4th edn (Tübingen 1973). (Abbr. *WL*.)

Wee, H. van der, 'De methodologie van de nieuwe stadsgeschiedenis', *Studies over de sociaal-economische geschiedenis van Limburg* XXI (1976): 1–14.

Wee, H. van der, *The rise and decline of urban industries in Italy and in the Low Countries (Late Middle Ages – early modern times)* (Louvain 1989).

Weiler, A. G., 'Geschiedenis en hermeneutiek', *Annalen Thijmgenootschap* 57 (1969).

Weiler, A. G., 'Waardebetrokkenheid en waardeoordelen in de geschiedwetenschap. Een theoretische standpuntbepaling tussen analytisch positivisme, marxisme en kritisch neomarxisme', *Bijdragen en mededelingen betreffende de geschiedenis der Nederlanden (BMGN)* 90 (1975): 189–225.

Weiler, A. G., 'The fractured time of history', in Schearer and Debrock (eds), *Nature, time and history. Nijmegen Studies in the Philosophy of Nature and its Sciences* 4(1) (1985): 55–66.

Wesseling, H. L., 'Fernand Braudel', in A. H. Huussen jr., E. H. Kossmann, and H. Renner (eds), *Historici van de twintigste eeuw* (Utrecht, Antwerp, Amsterdam 1981).

West Churchman, C., 'Systems', in S. Optner (ed.), *Systems analysis* (Harmondsworth 1973), pp. 283–93.

White, H., *Metahistory. The historical imagination in nineteenth-century Europe* (Baltimore, MD 1973).

White, H., 'The value of narrativity in the representation of reality', in W. Mitchel (ed.), *On narrative* (Chicago 1981).

White, H., *The content of the form. Narrative discourse and historical representation* (Baltimore, MD and London 1987).

White, H. and D. Capra, *History and criticism* (Ithaca, NY 1985).

Wirth, L., 'Urbanism as a way of life', *American Journal of Sociology* 44 (1938): 1–24.

Woude, A. M. van der, 'De "Nieuwe Geschiedenis" in een nieuwe gedaante', in Van den Woude *et al.* (eds), *De algemene geschiedenis der Nederlanden* 5 (Haarlem 1980), pp. 9–36.

Bibliography

Wright, G. H. von, *Explanation and understanding* (New York 1971).

Wright, G. H. von, 'Determinism and the study of man', in I. Manninen and R. Tuomela (eds), *Essays on explanation and understanding. Studies in the foundation of humanities and social sciences* (Dordrecht 1976).

Wright, G. H. von, *Causality and determinism* (London 1994).

Wrigley, E., 'The town in a pre-industrial economy', in Ph. Abrams and E. Wrigley, *Towns in societies. Essays in economic history and historical sociology* (Cambridge, London, New York 1978).

Zagorin, P., 'History, the referent and narrative: reflections on postmodermism now' *History and Theory* 38 (1999): 1–24.

Zammito, J. H. 'Ankersmit's postmodernist historiography: the hyperbole of "opacity"', *History and Theory* 37 (1998): 330–46.

Zanden, J. L., van, *Arbeid tijdens het handelskapitalisme. Opkomst en neergang van de Hollandse economie 1350–1850* (Bergen 1991).

Zanden, J. L. van, 'Is het handelskapitalisme een aparte theorie waard?', *Tijdschrift voor Sociale Geschiedenis* 22(1) (1996).

Zunz, O. (ed.), *Reliving the past. The worlds of social history* (Chapel Hill, NC and London 1985).

Subject Index

Subject Index

Birmingham, 260
black box, 63, 66–70, 72–77, 81, 82, 85,
    86, 62, 103, 107, 108, 111, 117, 118,
    131–123, 126, 131, 132, 141, 142,
    161
    cultural mechanical, 73
    intentional, 68–70, 72–75, 85, 86, 118,
        121, 122, 132, 141, 147, 156, 157,
        159, 164
    mechanical, 68–70, 72–75, 118, 122,
        131, 132, 141, 147, 156, 157, 162,
        164
    natural mechanical, 73
Boston, 46
boundary maintenance, 65, 66
bound to time and place, 183
bourgeoisie, 222, 224, 227, 229
    see also entrepreneurial
Bradford, 260
Brazil, 157
breakdown of the state,
    see state breakdown
Bristol, 260
Bruges, 33, 250
bürgerliche Nahrung, 225, 298–300
    see also urban-artisan economy
Bürgerschaft, 148, 224, 299
butterfly effect, 103, 106, 107
butterfly's wing, 157
Byzantium, 130

Camberwell, 45
capitalism, 126, 131, 133, 138, 144, 239,
    247–251, 262, 263, 270, 271
    see also mercantile,
capitalist centre,
    see stepping stones
capitalist mode of production,
    see mode of production
causal,
    analysis, 122, 132, 313
    explanation,
        see explanation
    finalistic operation, 194
    functionalistic operation, 194, 201
    operation, 177
    relations,
        see relations
Central Business District (CBD), 207, 209

central,
    places, 173, 183, 184, 187–189,
        191–193
    place theory, 173
    see also hierarchy, seven levels
system,
    see system
centralised sub-system,
    see sub-system
centre of the city,
    see residential function
chaos theory, 92, 98, 101–108, 111–113
Chicago, 257, 265–267, 272, 273
    school, 39–41, 56, 214, 215
chronological,
time,
    see time
citizenry, 224
cities as subsystems of more
    comprehensive systems, 32
city,
    as a caretaker of tradition, 193
    as a central place, 31, 43, 44, 48, 57,
        220
    as a concentration point, 42, 48, 191
    as a creator of new values, 193
    as a dependent variable, 32, 37, 43–45,
        47–79, 53–55
    as agens, 36
    as a concentration point of people and
        activities, 42, 48, 191
    as a geographical bite, 221, 223
    as a locus, 36, 184
    as a multi-functional central place, 31
    as a nodal point, 44, 47
    as a person, 193
    as a site, 98, 110, 184
    as an agent, 48, 49
    as an archive, 98, 100, 153, 184
    as an autonomous entity, 32–42, 45, 47,
        48, 52, 53, 59
    as an entity of its own, 45, 52
    as an entity sui generis, 35, 36, 39, 41,
        49, 253
    as an independent variable, 33, 36, 37,
        39, 42, 46–49
    as an integrated community, 134,
        153–155
    as an organism, 39, 45, 47, 193

Subject Index

Subject Index

Name Index

Abramowski, 49
Abrams, 48, 49, 53, 59
Althusser, 251, 271
Ankersmit, 63, 90, 106, 109, 176, 177, 179, 180, 196, 240, 241, 263, 265–267, 269, 318, 320, 321
Appelbaum, 166, 282
Ariès, 257
Aristotle, 237–239, 265, 269
Ashby, 102
Augustine, 237, 238, 265
Avineri, 248, 270

Bahrdt, 125, 128, 142, 143
Bateson, 102
Benevolo, 142
Berkhofer, 63–65, 284, 285, 287, 304, 306–308, 316
Berry, 173, 195
Bertalanffy, 102
Bismarck, 151
Blaschke, 142, 305
Bloch, E., 239, 263, 266, 272
Blumin, 46, 47, 58, 147, 153–156, 164–166, 210–213, 217, 220, 226, 230, 231, 277–279, 304
Bohr, 102
Bois, 13
Boulding, 2, 63,102
Bowden, 208
Braudel, 33, 34, 37, 47, 48, 53, 241, 245–251, 269, 270, 271, 317
Briggs, 45–47,57, 92, 98–100, 110, 111, 125, 156, 164, 165, 260, 273
Bücher, 37,38
Burchardt, 5
Burgess, 40, 213

Cannadine, 45, 46
Carr, 79, 88, 240, 242–244, 267–269

Castell, 54
Checkland, 19
Childe, 134
Christaller, 43, 44, 57, 66, 173, 192
Chudakoff, 46
Cleisthenes, 131
Cohen, 300, 301, 310
Collingwood, 71, 72
Commons, 212, 231

Danto, 76, 79, 87
Davey, 208, 210, 212, 217, 220
Derrida, 3–7
De Vries, 172, 173, 179, 185–189, 194, 195, 200, 203–205, 208, 291
Descartes, 4
De Tocqueville, 4
Diamond, 42
Dickens, 163
Dilthey, 10
Diocletian, 159
Disraeli, 38
Dobb, 224
Dorsman, 282, 285, 305, 306
Doucet, 208, 210, 212, 217, 220
Doyle, 155, 156
Dray, 1, 122, 137, 141, 146, 316
Droysen, 10
Durkheim, 39, 41, 95, 129, 206, 291
Dyos, 31, 45, 46, 51, 53, 58

Edel, 49, 50, 59
Einstein, 73, 102
Engels, 36, 37, 40, 41, 43, 54, 263
Ennen, 48

Feibleman, 97, 98, 110
Feuerbach, 34, 54
Fielden, 223

Name Index

Name Index

Name Index